The New
Public Personnel
Administration

5th EDITION

The New Public Personnel Administration

Felix A. Nigro
Emeritus, University of Georgia

Lloyd G. Nigro
Georgia State University

F.E. Peacock Publishers, Inc.
Itasca, Illinois

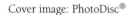

Cover image: PhotoDisc®

Advisory Editor in Public Administration
Bernard H. Ross
School of Public Affairs
American University

This edition is dedicated to Megan Saile, Carolyn and Sarah Gardella, and their parents.

Contents

Chapter ELEVEN   RESPONDING TO THE NEW AMERICAN WORKFORCE   311

Chapter TWELVE   THE FUTURE OF PUBLIC PERSONNEL   347

Preface

This edition of *The New Public Personnel Administration* addresses a field of study and practice that experienced a transformation during the last quarter of the twentieth century. The pace of that transformation, driven by technological innovations such as the Internet, social and demographic changes in the U.S. labor force, and strong political pressures for a variety of reforms designed to create smaller, more responsive and efficient government, accelerated as the twenty-first century grew closer. For better or worse, the political consensus that underpinned public sector merit systems for most of the century just ended no longer exists. Once the object of regulation, public management is now "the customer," and flexibility has replaced standardization and consistency as the centerpiece of efforts to satisfy customers' requirements. Responsiveness to executive leadership has supplanted neutral competence as the hallmark of the *really modern* personnel system. Indeed, even the idea that a civil service is needed to carry out many public functions has been substantially revised, some might say turned on its head.

For many, privatization in one form or another is the option of choice, unless a conclusive "case for bureaucracy" can be made. Public employers are no longer urged to become "model employers" or role models for their profit-driven private counterparts. Quite the reverse; it is demanded that they become more like modern "business," which, it is said, embodies the correct values (efficiency, productivity, rationality, and so forth) and best human resources practices (those centered on supporting high levels of organizational performance and mission accomplishment). There can be little doubt that the initial years of the twenty-first century will be exceptionally challenging for personnel specialists trying to navigate the uncharted waters of yet another new public personnel administration. For public employees, they promise to be difficult years as the employment relationship is restructured and, in many cases, made temporary or contingent. All we can do is hope that when Alexis de Tocqueville wrote the following, he was not describing the consequences of the latest round of civil service reform in America:

> The Americans, who almost always seem poised and cold, are nonetheless
> often carried away, far beyond the bounds of common sense, by some sudden
> passion or hasty opinion. They will in all seriousness do strangely absurd
> things.*

In light of all the changes that have taken place since the fourth
prior edition, preparing the fifth edition of this book has been an ex-
citing, at times exhausting, experience for the authors. Hopefully, the
result is a work that provides its readers with a useful introduction to an
increasingly dynamic public personnel administration, a field of study
and practice that will offer many new challenges and opportunities at
the onset of a new millennium.

The fifth edition is designed to be an advanced undergraduate or
graduate-level introduction to the general field of *public personnel administration*. Clearly, the general outlines of the personnel or human resources management and development processes of public agencies and
large private businesses are similar in many regards. Organizations in
both sectors recruit, select, train, evaluate, and compensate their employees. Often they face the same challenges, such as preventing workplace violence, dealing with substance abuse, responding to the
changing demography of the American workforce, and building effective working relationships with labor organizations. There are, nonetheless, very real and powerful sectorial differences in context, purpose,
and orienting values. Private employers operate in economic markets
that are significantly affected by politics and public policies. Public
agencies function in political settings that are strongly influenced by
economic markets and processes. The personnel function offers many
examples of the practical effects of these differences on the policy as
well as procedural levels. While this book should be of interest to business majors who want to learn about how sector personnel systems operate, it is not a so-called "generic" human resources management text.
It is about personnel policies and practices in U.S. *governments*.

This edition is substantially updated with regard to public policies
dealing with issues such as political activity of public employees, law
and key court rulings in such areas as sexual harassment and affirmative
action, and thinking about how the personnel function in government
might be more effectively and efficiently organized. Special attention
has been paid to the ongoing reforms of public personnel systems on all
levels of government, reforms that seek to bring the personnel function
into a productive partnership with public management and to assure
that civil service's responsiveness to executive leadership and public
opinion. The fifth edition differs from the fourth in several ways:

---

*Alexis de Tocqueville, *Democracy in America* (Garden City, NY: Anchor Books,
1969), p. 610.

- The coverage of all continuing topics has been carefully updated, with new areas covered as appropriate—such as smoking in the workplace.

- There is a new chapter on workplace violence that includes information on what state and local governments are doing to prevent and deal with violence that takes place in the workplace.

- The previous chapters on Pay in the Public Service, Issues in Pay Administration, Job Evaluation and Classification, and Performance Appraisal have been replaced by Chapters 5 and 6, providing streamlined, policy-oriented descriptions and analyses of these topics.

- The concluding chapter has been substantially expanded and focused on several serious challenges to the field and its practitioners that will have to be confronted during the early years of the twenty-first century: the future of civil service reform, integrating human resources management and human resources development, and the legal, economic, and social-psychological relationships between public employers and employees.

In addition to providing an overview of the history of civil service in the United States, this edition includes a statistical "snapshot" of the contemporary public service on the local, state, and federal areas. The statistics set forth in Chapter 1 are intended not only to be informative in their own right, but also to establish useful backgrounds for many of the chapters that follow, such as the ones on responding to the new American workforce, collective bargaining, and sexual harassment. While data such as those presented may be expected to change regularly, the categories of information they represent (e.g., minority and general composition of the civilian labor force and government employment) are relatively stable and relevant to long-term policy issues and concerns. Instructors and students seeking more up-to-date "numbers" in the future can find them in a variety of sources, including the Department of Labor, Bureau of the Census, and U.S. Office of Personnel Management. Many of these sources are easily accessed via the Internet.

This edition also uses text box "Bulletins" to supplement and illustrate points made throughout the book. These Bulletins are derived from a wide variety of sources, such as court rulings, public agencies' web home pages, and government documents. Many of them may also serve as starting points for class discussion. The questions at the end of each chapter have several functions: (1) to encourage reviews of chapter content and related course materials by students, (2) to provoke informed discussions of current events and policy issues, and (3) to spark debates over the purposes and underlying value orientations of personnel policies and practices in government. The suggested readings, for the most part, are restricted to recently published books, but this should not obscure the fact that there are many high-quality journal articles and informative government documents available to students seeking to build on chapter content.

Finally, a comment in response to questions we have been asked about the differences we see, if any, between *personnel administration* and *human resources management* in the public sector. To the degree that the former term is associated with the regulatory policies and practices of traditional merit systems while the latter is understood to communicate a management-centered, results-oriented approach, there clearly is a difference. In government, as well as the private sector, personnel offices are being replaced by departments of human resources, and in many cases, but not all, this is more than an exercise in putting new labels on old bottles. The content of this book reflects contemporary developments and trends in concepts, policies, and practices, and a comparison of the content of the original and current editions shows how much the field has shifted toward a human resources approach or frame of reference. Enhancing organizational capacity and supporting managerial effectiveness are now central themes and explicitly stated purposes of the enterprise. Although we have tried to make sure that this strategic vision of the personnel function is reflected throughout the fifth edition, it is most explicitly set forth in Chapter 3. Moreover, it is important to acknowledge the continuing relevance of values such as social equity, individual rights, and nonpartisanship. While definitions of what these values mean in practice have always been fluid, their impact on public personnel administration in the United States has been and will continue to be profound. Their importance continues to be reflected in this latest edition of *The New Public Personnel Administration*.

It is important that we express our thanks to those who have provided the support and encouragement needed to complete this project. As always, our friends and colleagues at Georgia State University and the University of Georgia have been very helpful. Needless to say, our families have been loyal and patient allies, especially during those difficult times when it seemed that nothing was working quite right. Edna and Carol deserve special recognition and thanks. Finally, we want to thank John Beasley for his excellent editing services. Thanks also to Kim Vander Steen for her invaluable help with several rounds of page proofs.

Lloyd G. Nigro
Felix A. Nigro

Chapter**ONE**

The American Public Service

For many Americans, the terms "human resources department" and "personnel administration" bring to mind legions of "bureaucrats" in green eyeshades minding files and rigidly enforcing arcane rules designed to frustrate all efforts to get work done efficiently, if at all. In some places, this stereotype of the personnel function may be to some degree accurate, as some of us can testify to on the basis of personal experiences. It is true that public personnel does involve the routine enforcement of public laws and policies, as well as making sure that unexciting day-to-day operations such as payroll and benefits administration are carried out in an efficient and timely manner. It would be a mistake to underestimate the importance of these traditional personnel functions, of course, since they are important contributors to agencies' performances. The public personnel administration of the year 2000, however, is far more than an organizational maintenance and rules-enforcement activity. It is rapidly coming to be seen as a necessary aspect of successful public management. As such, it is an organizational role or function that focuses on meeting the challenges of attracting, retaining, managing, and developing the large and diverse pool of highly qualified and motivated people needed by today's government agencies.

Today's United States citizens rely on elected representatives and public administrators to directly provide or to arrange for the delivery of a wide variety of services. To mention just a few, they expect that their children will be educated in safe schools, that their roads and highways will be maintained, that their food and water will not be contaminated, that the streets of their cities will be free of violent criminals, and that their mail will reach its intended destination within two or three days. The quality of American life, in other words, depends heavily on the dedication and performance of those who work for government—on the quality of the public service.

Public personnel policies and practices on the federal, state, and local levels can have major effects on the performances of public agencies and their employees. On the negative side, an Internal Revenue Service (IRS) that is unable to recruit and retain highly qualified personnel is unlikely to administer a complex tax code effectively and fairly. Likewise, as recent events demonstrate, IRS managers who appear to use performance appraisals and compensation policies to encourage, even reward, abusive treatment of taxpayers are inviting public hostility and distrust. Inadequately trained city workers who respond slowly or not at all to overflowing sewers endanger the public health, as do corrupt inspectors who fail to enforce the building code. Overworked police officers and air traffic controllers are more likely to make mistakes that may have disastrous consequences. Partisan and discriminatory hiring practices undermine public confidence in the objectivity and fairness of all public servants, including public managers, police, and tax collectors. On the positive side, demonstrably fair and effective personnel policies and practices can do much to support the efforts of public agencies to carry out their mandates and to build public confidence in government. Public personnel policies and practices clearly are important factors in governments' capacities to function successfully in technical, political, and ethical terms. As the authors of a recent book on civil service reform put it, "the civil service system touches everything in government. If it does not work well, neither can anything else in government" (Kettl et al., 1996, p. 7).

One measure of the importance of the public service in American society is statistical. Accordingly, the balance of this chapter sets forth some of the "facts and figures" that describe the U.S. public service. In addition to providing a general orientation, these data are relevant to many of the topics discussed in the chapters that follow, such as those on equal employment opportunity, recruitment and selection, and collective bargaining.

THE SIZE AND DISTRIBUTION OF THE AMERICAN PUBLIC SERVICE

The public service upon which we all depend for so many services is large, although probably not as large as many Americans assume it is. There are over 19 million public employees in the United States, which is over 14 percent of the civilian labor force or CLF. The CLF, which is composed of all civilians in the noninstitutionalized population aged 16 and over who are employed, or unemployed and seek-

Table 1.1 Government Employment in Other Countries

Country	Total Civilian Employment	Government Employment as a Percentage of Total Employment*
Australia	7,943,000	16.6
Canada	13,292,000	19.6
France	21,744,000	24.8
Germany	35,894,000	15.9
Italy	20,022,000	16.1
Japan	64,530,000	6.0
Spain	11,760,000	15.2
Sweden	3,926,000	32.0
United Kingdom	25,579,000	14.4

*Producers of Government Services, except Australia, Canada, France, and Spain, which are general government.

Sources: Labour Force Statistics 1974–1994, OECD, Paris, 1996, 8–9; National Accounts, OECD, Paris, 1997, pp. 44–45.

ing work, in 1996 stood at about 134 million people. Of those in the public sector, close to 5 million work for the states. Almost 12 million are on the payrolls of local governments (over half work for public school districts). The federal government currently employs around 2.8 million civilians. Is the United States overrun by public employees in comparison to other industrialized democracies? Table 1.1 shows that the United States, even with its federal system of government, does not have an overly large public service in relative terms.

Despite a general tendency on the part of the public to view the federal government as constantly expanding, it has not been the major source of overall growth in the numbers of public employees since the end of the Second World War (1945). Whereas the size of the federal workforce has remained fairly stable, public employment in the states and localities has expanded. In 1970, state workers numbered about 2.8 million (up from 2.2 million in 1966) and there were about 7.4 million in local governments (about one million more than there were in 1966). The rate of *growth* slowed considerably during the 1980s. From 1979 to 1989, state employment grew by 14.5 percent. There was some expansion on the federal and local levels; in both cases, it was under 10 percent. Overall, the

BULLETIN

In 1995, the October payroll for states and local governments was $37.7 billion. The states' paychecks totaled $10.9 billion, while those of the localities added up to $26.8 billion.

Source: U.S. Bureau of the Census.

Table 1.2 Government Employment by Level and Selected Functions

Number of Employees (Thousands)

Function	Federal Civilian	State	Local
National defense	831	—	—
Postal Service	849	—	—
Education	12	1382	5619
Streets and highways	4	253	290
Police protection	86	91	689
FIre protection	—	—	274
Parks and recreation	26	39	207
Judicial and legal	53	128	204
Transit	—	20	188

Sources: Federal—U.S. Office of Personnel Management, Office Workforce Information, Monthly Report of Federal Civilian Employment (SF113-A) (November 20,1997); State and Local—U.S. Bureau of the Census, Public Employment Data (http://www.census.gov/govs/apes/95txt), October, 1995.

creation of jobs in the public sector lagged behind that of the private sector (the CLF grew by approximately 20 percent). Thus, in people terms, government became relatively smaller during the 1980s, and that trend continues. During the first six years of the Clinton administration, the federal workforce dropped by roughly 250,000 or 8.4 percent.

The 19 million public employees are distributed across many jurisdictions. In addition to the national and fifty state governments, there are over 3,000 counties, more than 19,000 municipalities, and over 31,000 special-purpose districts. Add in townships and school districts, and the grand total exceeds 85,000 governmental units. Primary education and law enforcement are largely local responsibilities. States administer welfare programs, construct and run prison systems, and build freeways. The federal government has exclusive control over national defense, currency, and first-class mail services. These differences show up in the relative sizes of governments and the occupational profiles of their workforces. Table 1.2 provides a comparative overview.

In addition to raw differences in population size, functional differences contribute to wide variations in the sizes and compositions of workforces. New York City, which operates a university system as well as its own elementary and secondary schools, and delivers services typically handled by counties, has almost 400,000 full-time employees on its payroll. The cities of Los Angeles and Chicago, on the other hand, have fewer than 50,000 workers. Large populations, combined with a large inventory of services, produce large workforces, so of 5 million

Table 1.3 State Employment by Function (1995)

Function	Full-Time Equivalent Employees	Per 10,000 Population
Total All States	3,971,208	151.4
Financial administration	163,995	6.3
Central administration	47,954	1.8
Judicial and legal	127,637	4.9
Police protection–officers	54,704	2.1
Police protection–other	34,860	1.3
Corrections	409,208	15.1
Highways	243,256	9.7
Air transportation	2,752	0.1
Water transport and terminals	4,696	0.2
Public welfare	226,755	8.6
Health	160,061	6.1
Hospitals	496,191	18.9
Social Insurance Administration	93,783	3.6
Solid waste management	1,552	0.1
Sewage	1,378	0.1
Parks and recreation	38,575	1.5
Natural resources	152,141	5.8
Water supply	935	0.0
Electric power	5,739	0.2
Transit	19,949	0.8
Elementary and secondary school–instructional	26,680	1.0
Elementary and secondary school–other	14,769	0.6
Higher education–instructional	446,982	17.0
Higher education–other	883,835	33.7
Libraries	579	0.0
State liquor stores	7,963	0.3
Other	197,829	7.5

Source: U.S. Bureau of the Census, *Public Employment Data* (http://www.census.gov/govs/apes/95/stall.txt.), October, 1995.

or so inhabitants of Cook County, Illinois, about 200,000 are county employees. Of the approximately 1.33 million full-time positions in the 50 states' systems of higher education, close to 112,000 are in California. New York has about the same number, but fewer than 4,000 are to be found in South Dakota or Alaska. Table 1.3 shows the totals by functional areas for all states in 1995.

Table 1.4 Comparison of Selected State Employment by Function (1995)

| Function | Full-Time Equivalent Employees per 10,000 Population | | | |
	Alaska	California	Georgia	Hawaii
Overall	366.1	107.2	159.2	435.6
Financial administration	16.1	5.5	4.0	8.2
Central administration	7.1	1.1	1.3	4.3
Judicial and legal	18.9	0.9	1.6	18.1
Police protection–officers	4.4	2.0	1.6	0.0
Police protection–other	2.5	1.5	1.6	0.0
Corrections	20.8	13.6	26.5	18.1
Highways	46.8	5.5	8.4	6.7
Air transportation	0.0	0.0	0.0	8.4
Water transport and terminals	0.0	0.0	0.9	1.6
Public welfare	29.7	1.2	10.7	9.1
Health	9.0	3.2	6.1	24.0
Hospitals	5.3	10.9	20.0	27.0
Social Insurance Administration	6.8	6.2	2.6	2.5
Solid waste management	0.0	0.1	0.0	0.0
Sewage	0.0	0.0	0.0	0.0
Parks and recreation	1.6	1.2	4.0	2.1
Natural resources	38.6	5.6	7.4	12.3
Water supply	0.0	0.0	0.0	0.0
Electric power	0.0	0.0	0.0	0.0
Transit	8.7	0.0	0.0	0.0
Elementary and secondary school–instructional	33.9	0.0	0.0	135.5
Elementary and secondary school–other	15.0	0.0	0.0	61.5
Higher education–instructional	19.1	9.5	16.9	23.4
Higher education–other	45.0	26.2	31.6	36.5
Libraries	0.0	0.0	0.0	4.9
State liquor stores	0.0	0.0	0.0	0.0
Other	29.1	11.6	6.1	30.2

Source: U.S. Bureau of the Census, *Public Employment Data* (http://www.census.gov/govs/apes/95/stall.txt.), October, 1995.

These data reveal the states' relatively heavy investments in corrections, highways, hospitals, and higher education, all of which are traditionally state responsibilities. Over the past decade, the rapid expansion of state prison facilities has been a national trend, and many states also have been making heavy investments in higher education. There

Table 1.5 Local Government Employment by Function (1995)

Function	Full-Time Equivalent Employees	Per 10,000 Population
Total All Localities	10,119,314	384.9
Financial Administration	189,927	7.2
Other government administration	192,638	7.3
Judicial and legal	203,559	7.7
Police protection–officers	530,452	20.2
Police protection–other	158,740	6.0
Firefighters	256,001	9.7
Fire–other	18,325	0.7
Corrections	205,767	7.8
Streets and highways	289,887	11.0
Air transportation	33, 362	1.3
Water transport terminals	7,013	0.3
Public welfare	265,058	10.1
Health	208,558	7.9
Hospitals	551,364	21.0
Solid waste management	107,218	4.1
Sewage	123,361	4.7
Parks and recreation	207,300	7.9
Housing and community development	124,279	4.7
Natural resources	36,124	1.4
Water supply	151,998	5.8
Gas supply	10,476	0.4
Transit	187,471	7.1
Elementary and secondary school–instructional	3,736,632	142.1
Elementary and secondary school–other	1,604,563	61.0
Higher education–instructional	121,075	4.6
Higher education–other	156,893	6.0
Libraries	102,791	3.9
Other	263,677	10.0

Source: U.S. Bureau of the Census, *Public Employment Data* (http://www.census.gov/govs/apes/95/locall.txt.), October, 1995.

is, however, considerable variability: Table 1.4 provides a comparison of four different states.

Local governments—cities and counties—have employment profiles that are different from those of the states, since they usually provide different services. Table 1.5 is an overview of local government

Table 1.6 Local Government Employment in Three Large States (1995)

Function	Full-Time Equivalent Employees Per 10,000 Population		
	California	Texas	New York
Overall	361.5	456.4	470.6
Financial administration	6.7	6.6	6.8
Other government administration	6.8	5.9	9.0
Judicial and legal	11.3	8.5	6.1
Police protection–officers	18.2	21.5	34.3
Police protection–other	7.0	6.9	4.9
Firefighters	8.7	9.2	9.8
Fire–other	0.8	0.6	1.0
Corrections	8.8	11.1	13.3
Streets and highways	6.8	10.0	16.6
Air transportation	1.4	2.2	1.0
Water transport/terminals	0.6	0.5	0.3
Public welfare	16.5	2.0	28.5
Health	10.5	8.6	9.4
Hospitals	23.9	23.3	33.8
Solid waste management	2.3	3.5	7.6
Sewerage	3.9	5.1	3.6
Parks and recreation	10.2	7.1	5.9
Housing and community development	4.3	2.7	13.9
Natural resources	2.3	1.5	0.1
Water supply	6.9	7.1	3.1
Electric power	4.6	3.7	0.4
Gas supply	0.1	0.8	0.0
Transit	9.3	5.0	24.8
Elementary and secondary school–instruction	111.5	194.9	139.6
Elementary and secondary school–other	44.0	80.2	66.7
Higher education–instruction	9.0	6.8	6.9
Higher education–other	10.7	9.5	7.1
Libraries	3.5	2.6	3.5
Other	10.9	8.8	13.0

Source: U.S. Bureau of the Census *Public Employment Data* (http://www.census.gov/govs/apes/95loc.txt), October, 1995.

employment throughout the country. State policies in areas such as student–teacher ratios, welfare program administration, and transportation, as well as historical and environmental factors, will cause local government employment profiles to vary from state to state.

Table 1.7 Trends in Federal Civilian Employment: 1980 and 1997

Agency	1980	1997	% Change
State Department	23,497	24,108	2.6
Treasury	124,663	140,369	12.6
Defense	960,116	749,461	-21.9
Justice	56,327	117,261	108.2
Interior	77,357	67,865	-12.3
Agriculture	129,139	106,539	-17.5
Commerce	48,563	34,792	-28.4
Labor	23,400	15,787	-32.5
HHS	155,662	126,523	-18.7
HUD	16,964	10,908	-35.7
Transportation	72,361	64,179	-11.3
Energy	21,557	17,078	-17.9
Education	7,364	4,640	-37.0
Veterans Administration/ Veterans Affairs	228,285	243,311	6.6
EPA	14,715	18,045	22.6
EEOC	3,515	2,631	-25.2
FDIC	3,520	8,265*	135.0
FEMA	3,427	4,888	42.6
NASA	23,714	19,844	-16.3
OPM	8,280	3,603	-56.5
TVA	51,714	14,510	-72.9
U.S. Postal Service	660,014	853,350	29.3

*The Federal Deposit Insurance Corporation grew to over 9,000 (1987) during the savings and loan crisis of the late 1980s.

Source: U.S. Office of Personnel Management, Office of Workforce Information, Monthly Report of Federal Civilian Employment (SF 113-A) (Washington, DC, November 20, 1997); U.S. Bureau of the Census, *Statistical Abstract of the United States: 1991* (Washington, DC, 1991), Table 529.

Table 1.6 compares California, Texas, and New York as an example.

The size and composition of the public service reflects the policy priorities of governments. Much of the recent growth in state bureaucracies is the result of federal policies designed to shift administrative responsibility for public welfare and regulatory services to the state governments. They, in turn, have sought to pass certain program mandates and costs on to local governments. The federal government is itself a good example of how political change affects the public workforce. Although his public image was that of a "bureaucrat cutter," President Reagan actually did not preside over a shrinking federal executive

Table 1.8 Federal Civilian Employment: 1993 and 1997

Agency	September 1993	September 1997	% Change
Total	3,038,041	2,783,704	-8.4
Legislative Branch	38,030	31,355	-18.1
Judicial Branch	28,111	30,641	9.0
U.S. Postal Service and Postal Rate Commission	782,980	853,350	9.0
Executive Branch	2,188,647	1,868,358	-14.6
Selected Executive Branch Agencies			
State Department	25,982	24,108	-7.2
Treasury	165,904	140,369	-15.4
Defense	966,087	749,461	-22.4
Justice	97,652	117,261	20.1
Interior	77,313	67,865	-12.2
Agriculture	113,687	106,539	-6.3
Commerce	37,608	34,792	-7.5
Labor	17,719	15,787	-10.9
HHS	131,066	126,523	-3.5
HUD	13,292	10,908	-17.9
Transportation	70,086	64,179	-8.4
Energy	20,706	17,078	-17.5
Education	4,995	4,640	-7.5
Veterans Affairs	260,349	243,311	-6.5
EPA	18,351	18,045	-1.7
EEOC	2,927	2,631	-10.1
FDIC	22,360	8,265	-63.0
FEMA	4,554	4,888	7.3
GSA	20,690	14,309	-30.8
NASA	25,191	19,844	-21.2
NLRB	2,132	1,992	-6.6
OPM	6,861	3,603	-47.5
TVA	19,129	14,510	-24.1
USIA	8,283	6,534	-21.1
AID	4,218	2,783	-34.0

Source: U.S. Office of Personnel Management, Office of Workforce Information, *Monthly Report of Federal Civilian Employment* (SF 113-A) (Washington, DC), November 20, 1997.

Table 1.9 The 20 Largest Federal White-Collar Occupations
September 1992 and June 1997

Occupation	1992	1997	Percent Change
Secretary	93,401	62,561	-33.0
Computer specialist	53,739	53,334	-0.8
Miscellaneous clerk and assistant	56,144	53,183	-5.3
Miscellaneous administration and program	39,588	42,927	8.4
Management and program analyst	38,150	38,359	0.5
Nurse	38,719	38,296	-1.1
Criminal investigating	32,431	33,699	3.9
Contracting	31,360	27,858	-11.9
Social insurance administration	21,702	25,100	15.7
Electronics engineering	29,706	23,669	-20.3
General attorney	23,057	23,651	2.6
Air traffic control	25,839	23,496	-9.2
General business and industry	16,574	19,612	18.3
General engineering	21,393	18,468	-13.7
Tax examining	16,378	17,566	7.3
Engineering technician	23,579	17,410	-26.2
Accounting technician	20,803	17,020	-15.3
Supply clerical and technician	22,896	16,244	-29.1
Internal Revenue agent	16,156	14,771	-8.6
Contract representative	14,959	14,073	-5.9

Source: U.S. Office of Personnel Management, Office of Workforce Information, *Central Personnel Data File,* September, 1997.

branch. Between 1980 and 1987, the executive departments grew by some 5 percent, and the independent agencies expanded by over 11 percent. Defense did well, expanding from 960,000 to 1,090,000, about 13.5 percent. This growth was anything but uniform across organizations. A few experienced substantial increases, but most lost positions as the Reagan-Bush policy priorities took hold. While there was nondefense growth during the Bush presidency, the Clinton administration's "downsizing" efforts produced an overall decline that included civilian defense employment. The Department of Defense "accounted for almost 64 percent of all downsizing, [but] virtually every Federal

Table 1.10 The 20 Largest Federal Blue-Collar Occupations
            September 1992 and June 1997

Occupation	1992	1997	Percent Change
Material handler	19,687	14,849	-24.6
Aircraft mechanic	13,975	11,146	-20.2
Custodial working	12,876	10,302	-20.0
Maintenance mechanic	11,093	10,064	-9.3
Heavy mobile equipment mechanic	11,168	9,584	-14.2
Electronics mechanic	12,647	7,799	-38.3
Sheet metal mechanic	10,160	6,801	-33.1
Food service worker	8,350	6,478	-22.8
Motor vehicle operating	8,700	6,397	-26.5
Electrician	8,596	5,603	-34.8
Automotive mechanic	6,637	5,456	-17.8
Electronic integrated systems mechanic	5,066	4,113	-18.8
Machining	7,238	4,053	-44.0
Pipefitting	7,129	3,965	-44.4
Aircraft engine mechanic	4,710	3,937	-16.4
Cook	3,548	3,638	2.5
Painting	5,688	3,546	-37.7
Welding	4,787	2,948	-38.5
Air conditioning equipment mechanic	3,694	2,883	-22.0
Engineering equipment operating	2,974	2,602	-12.5

Source: U.S. Office of Personnel Management, Office of Workforce Information, *Central Personnel Data File*, October, 1997.

agency reduced its workforce during this 4-year period" (U.S. Office of Personnel Management, 1997a, p. 4). Table 1.7 tracks the shifting fortunes of federal agencies from 1980 to 1997.

Many of those agencies that show a net increase between 1980 and 1997 actually were "downsized" during the first Clinton term, as Table 1.8 reveals. The Departments of State, Treasury, and Veterans Affairs are good examples. The end of the savings and loan crisis, of course, had produced an impressive reduction of the Federal Deposit Insurance Corporation (FDIC) staff by 1997.

Another way of tracking the evolution of the federal service is to take a look at employment trends in the white- and blue-collar job categories, as seen in Tables 1.9 and 1.10. Taken against the general pattern of downsizing, the long-term prospects of federal employment for blue-collar workers would seem to be dim at best, since all of the occupational categories shown in Table 1.10 have experienced declines well in excess of 8 percent, except cooks. These numbers reflect a vigorous policy of contracting-out for the kinds of work done by these occupations, rather than maintaining in-house capacities. Contracting-out is intended to improve efficiency and flexibility, but it also offers political advantages, most notably "fewer bureaucrats." This work is being done, but not by federal employees. White-collar occupations have not done as badly overall, but a number have experienced cuts well above the average. Particularly noteworthy are a sharp drop in the number of secretaries and steep declines in several engineering categories. Supply, clerical, and technician workers also have not fared well in the federal scheme of things. While technological innovations, such as advanced computer hardware, new data management and analysis systems, automation, and integrated electronic communications media, often increase efficiency and may be expected to produce shifts in employment patterns, declines in the contracting, air traffic control, and Internal Revenue agent occupations may signal long-term threats to some agencies' ability to carry out their mandates and, therefore, to meet public expectations.

THE DEMOGRAPHICS OF THE PUBLIC SERVICE AND THE CIVILIAN LABOR FORCE

The demography of the public service is changing at an accelerating pace. In certain respects, it is becoming more representative of the increasingly diverse and pluralistic society it serves. By 1996, for example, 42.9 percent of federal jobs were held by women, and 28.7 percent were occupied by minorities (U.S. Office of Personnel Management, 1997b). For the U.S. civilian labor force in 1996, 46.3 percent of the jobs were held by women and 25.5 percent by minorities. From 1984 to 1996, federal employment of minorities increased slowly but steadily, as Table 1.11 shows.

There have been corresponding increases in the proportions of women and minorities working for state and local governments over roughly the same period. In 1984, state and local workforces were 41 percent female and 24.5 percent minority. They were up to 44.3 percent female and 28.9 percent minority by 1995 (U.S. Bureau of the Census, 1997a).

Public-sector recruitment, hiring, training, and career development programs are by necessity adjusting to a labor market that has experienced profound demographic changes since the 1950s. A quick scan of the American workplace shows, among other things, a growing

Table 1.11 Federal Executive Branch Employment of Minorities and Women: 1984, 1990, and 1996 (percentages*)

Year	Total	All**	Black	Hispanic	Asian/Pacific Islander	American Indian/ Alaska Native	White Non-Hispanic
1984							
Men	1,212,238	12.6	6.9	3.1	1.8	0.8	47.4
Women	809,095	12.3	8.8	1.7	1.0	0.8	27.7
1990							
Men	1,223,255	12.7	6.5	3.2	2.1	0.9	44.2
Women	927,104	14.6	10.1	2.2	1.4	0.9	28.5
1996							
Men	1,058,566	13.5	6.4	3.6	2.5	1.0	42.5
Women	831,840	15.6	10.2	2.5	1.8	1.0	28.4

*Percentages are based on total employment (men and women combined).

**All minorities.

Source: U.S. Office of Personnel Management, "Executive Branch Employment by Gender & Race/National Origin, 1984–1996," *The Fact Book: Federal Civilian Workforce Statistics 1997 Edition* (1997).

Table 1.12 The Marital Status of Women in the CLF: 1960–1996

	Female Labor Force*			Female Participation Rate (%)			
	Total	Single	Married	Other**	Total	Single	Married	Other
1960	23,240	5,410	12,893	4,937	37.7	58.6	31.9	41.6
1980	45,487	11,865	24,980	8,643	51.5	64.4	49.9	43.6
1996	61,857	15,842	33,618	12,397	59.3	67.1	61.2	48.1

*Thousands.

**Widowed, Divorced, Separated.

Source: U.S. Bureau of the Census, *Statistical Abstract of the United States 1997,* Table 630.

diversity of ethnic and cultural groups, more working mothers, and a steady erosion of the traditional family background and lifestyles assumed by traditional public personnel policies and practices.

Managing diverse workforces has become a staple of many management training programs, and alternative and "family-friendly" work arrangements have become important factors in recruitment and retention strategies, as well as being significant considerations in efforts to increase productivity. The labor force participation of mar-

Table 1.13 The U.S. Civilian Labor Force and Participation Rates* with Projections: 1980 to 2005

Race and Sex	Civilian Labor Force* (millions)			Participation Rate (percent)		
	1980	1996	2005	1980	1996	2005
Total	106.9	133.9	147.1	63.8	66.8	67.1
Race and Sex						
White	93.6	113.1	122.9	64.1	67.2	68.1
Male	54.5	61.8	64.9	78.2	75.8	73.9
Female	39.1	51.3	58.0	51.2	59.1	62.6
Black	10.9	15.1	16.6	61.0	64.1	61.9
Male	5.6	7.3	7.9	70.3	68.7	65.8
Female	5.3	7.9	8.7	53.1	60.4	58.8
Hispanic	6.1	12.8	16.3	64.0	66.5	64.7
Male	3.8	7.6	9.5	81.4	79.6	76.1
Female	2.3	5.1	6.8	47.4	53.4	53.6

*The participation rate represents the proportion of each group in the civilian labor force.
Source: U.S. Bureau of the Census, *Statistical Abstract of the United States 1997*, Table 620.

ried women with children under the age of six rose from 18.6 percent in 1960 to 62.7 percent in 1996 (U.S. Bureau of the Census, 1997a, p. 393). The labor force also is getting older, and this trend (Table 1.14), of course, poses issues related to health and retirement benefits, as well as presenting public management with new challenges in areas such as motivation and employee development.

In 1993, the U.S. General Accounting Office noted that the growing numbers of working women and minorities "had transformed the workplace in the latter half of the 20th century. . . ." It then went on to observe that:

> [T]he aging of the U.S. workforce is a trend that may have an equally profound impact on the world of work in the first half of the 21st century. The median age of the

BULLETIN

The Fastest Growing Occupations in the U.S.: 1996–2006

Database administrators, computer support specialists, and all other computer scientists	+118%
Computer engineers	+109%
Systems analysts	+103%
Personal and home care aides	+85%
Home health aides	+76%

Source: U.S. Bureau of Labor Statistics (1998), "Employment Projections," Table 4b (http://stats.bls.gov/ecopro.table 6.htm).

Table 1.14 An Aging Civilian Labor Force: 1960–1996

	CLF Total*	Age (%)						
		16–19	20–24	25–34	34–44	45–54	55–64	65+
1960	69,628	7.0	9.6	20.7	23.4	21.3	13.5	4.6
1980	106,940	8.8	14.9	27.3	19.1	15.8	11.2	2.9
1996	133,943	5.8	10.0	25.3	27.3	19.7	9.1	2.9

*Thousands.
Source: U.S. Bureau of the Census, *Statistical Abstract of the United States 1997,* Table 624.

civilian workforce rose from 34.3 years in 1980 to 36.6 in 1990 and is expected to reach 40.6 years by 2005. The federal government's workforce is older than the civilian labor force in general—on average, about five years older in 1990. (U.S. General Accounting Office, 1993, pp. 2–3)

The public sector workforce is rapidly aging, and personnel systems on all levels of government will have to respond to this demographic reality (Elliott, 1995).

Although the U.S. labor force has steadily become better educated, the pace of technological innovation and change, along with an explosive growth of information and knowledge in the social and physical sciences, has forced many public employers into a highly competitive marketplace where education, specialized knowledge, and technical expertise are at a premium.

By necessity, the public service has steadily become increasingly professionalized, better educated, and more highly trained. The "professional state," a system of government in which experts working in a wide variety of specialized fields are key actors in the process of making as well as implementing public policies, is a reflection of the central role government plays in American society (Mosher, 1968). On all levels of government, social welfare and insurance, regulatory, economic, research and development, public works, and other functions require people with highly developed technical skills and training. The federal government alone employs close to 200,000 engineers and scientists. The U.S. Department of Agriculture houses almost 25,000 biologists and physical scientists, and another 40,000 work for other agencies. The list of occupational specialties and professional skills needed by the public sector is very long and it is growing. In 1997, for example, 39.8 percent of federal employees held a bachelor's or a higher degree (U.S. Office of Personnel Management, 1997c). The Bureau of Labor Statistics

---

Table 1.15 A Better Educated Civilian Labor Force: 1970–1990

		Educational Achievement as a Percentage of the CLF			
	CLF Total*	Less Than High School	High School	1–3 Years of College	4+ Years of College
1970	61,765	36.1	38.1	11.8	14.1
1980	78,010	20.6	39.8	17.6	22.0
1990	99,175	13.4	39.5	20.7	26.4**

*Thousands.

Source: U.S. Bureau of the Census, *Statistical Abstract of the United States 1997*, Table 622.

**It is also noteworthy that the percentage of women with 4+ years of college went from 11.2 in 1970 to 24.5 in 1990. Likewise, for African-Americans, those percentages were from 8.3 in 1970 to 15.5 in 1990. These trends were expected to continue through the 1990s.

---

projects that the overall employment of persons with professional specialties in the United States will increase by over 25 percent between 1996 and 2006. Executive, administrative, and managerial employment is projected to grow by 17 percent over the same period (U.S. Bureau of Labor Statistics, 1998b). If they are to compete successfully with the private sector for the highly qualified professionals and specialists they need, public employers will have to develop effective recruitment strategies, design efficient and flexible selection processes, and be able to offer attractive pay and benefits. It is also clear that heavy investments in employee development and training will be needed if the public sector workforce is to maintain the currency of its knowledge, skills, and abilities.

The last set of numbers related to the American public service we will review here deal with the growth of unions in public employment. As Table 1.16 shows, public employees are much more likely to belong to unions and to be represented by unions than their private-sector counterparts. The federal government and many states and localities bargain collectively with their nonmanagement employees, and labor relations has become an important specialty within the general field of personnel administration or human resources management.

According to the Bureau of Labor Statistics, overall union membership in the United States has declined steadily since the early 1980s. In 1983, about 20 percent of U.S. workers belonged to unions; by 1997, that percentage had fallen to just over 14 percent. In government, however, over 37 percent (6.7 million) were union members in 1997 (U.S. Bureau of Labor Statistics, 1998b).

Table 1.16 Union Membership and Representation in 1997:
         Private and Public Sectors

Sector	% Union Members	% Represented by Unions*
Private		
Agricultural	2.1	2.4
Nonagricultural	9.8	10.8
Government		
Federal	32.0	39.4
State	29.5	33.4
Local	42.7	47.7

*For purposes of collective bargaining/covered by negotiated contracts.

Source: U.S. Bureau of Labor Statistics, *Developments in Labor-Management Relations*, Table 3 (http://stats.bls.gov/news.release/union2.t03.htm), January 28, 1998.

CONCLUSION

In this chapter, we have taken a very brief look at some facts and fig-ures that should help orient you to the American public service. One very important fact to remember is that demographic, technological, and other trends in the environment of government have powerful effects on the size, composition, and administrative organization of the public service. Contemporary public personnel policies, practices, issues, and problems are reflections of these trends, some of which have deep roots in the political, economic, and social history of the United States. It is therefore difficult to understand the public service of today without at least a general familiarity with its historical back-ground, and Chapter 2 is intended to provide an overview, starting with the founding of the United States.

DISCUSSION QUESTIONS

1. Is a figure of 14 percent of the CLF working for government too high, too low, about right?
    How can we answer this question?
2. What demographic trends should public employers pay particu-lar attention to, and why?
3. What is it about the Japanese economy and system of govern-ment that allows it to have only 6 percent of its civilian employ-ment in government agencies?

REFERENCES

Elliott, Robert H. (1995). "Human Resource Management's Role in the Future Aging of the Workforce." *Review of Public Personnel Administration,* Vol. 15, No. 2 (Spring), pp. 5–17.

Kettl, Donald F., Ingraham, Patricia W., Sanders, Ronald P., and Horner, Constance (1996). *Civil Service Reform: Building a Government That Works* (Washington, DC: Brookings Institution Press).

Mosher, Frederick C. (1968). *Democracy and the Public Service* (New York: Oxford University Press).

U.S. Bureau of the Census (1997). *Statistical Abstract of the United States: 1997* (Washington, DC), Table 508.

U.S. Bureau of Labor Statistics (1998a). "Employment by Major Occupational Group, 1986, 1996, and Projected 2006." *Employment Projections* (http://bls.gov/news.release/ecopro. table 3.htm). Data source: *Monthly Labor Review* (November 1997).

U.S. Bureau of Labor Statistics (1998b). "Union Members Summary." *Developments in Labor-Management Relations* (http://stats.bls.gov/news.release/union2.nws.htm), January 30.

U.S. General Accounting Office (1993). *Federal Personnel: Employment Policy Challenges Created by an Aging Workforce* (Washington, DC: GAO, GAO/GDD-93-138), September.

U.S. Office of Personnel Management (1997a). "The Statistical Story of Federal Downsizing" (Washington, DC: Office of Personnel Management, Employment Service, WRO 97-102), August.

U.S. Office of Personnel Management (1997b). "Race/National Origin: Federal and U.S. Civilian Labor Force." *The Fact Book: Federal Civilian Workforce Statistics 1997 Edition,* pp. 1–3.

U.S. Office of Personnel Management (1997c). "Profile of Federal Civilian Non-Postal Employees," *The Fact Book: Federal Civilian Workforce Statistics 1997 Edition* (Washington, DC: OPM).

Chapter TWO

Public Personnel Administration: A Historical Overview

Although public personnel administration did not emerge as a specialized field of study or practice in the United States until the early twentieth century, governments have been recruiting, hiring, training, paying, managing, and firing public employees since the founding of the Republic. In these terms, of course, the organizational functions now associated with public personnel administration have been around as long as governments have existed, which is many thousands of years. This chapter traces the development of public personnel policies and practices in the United States. Like Chapter 1, it is intended to provide a background and context for the more detailed discussions of current issues and problems found in Sections II and III.

THE ERA OF POLITICAL RESPONSIVENESS: PATRONAGE AND SPOILS

For roughly the first 100 years of its existence (1790–1890), the public service on all levels of government was universally political or partisan in the sense that public employees were expected to actively work for and financially support candidates for elective office on all levels of government. There was no separation between politics and administration. Government jobs traditionally were awarded to those who faithfully served the winning party, its candidates, and its policy agenda. Hence the saying, "to the victor belongs the spoils."

Arguments for patronage or spoils approaches to public employment rely heavily on the idea that democratic governance requires public employees who are responsive to public priorities and electoral mandates. In addition to providing a strong incentive to work for the party, spoils systems virtually guarantee responsiveness to legislators and elected executives, because those hired are at once loyal and fully aware that they may be dismissed for partisan reasons. In theory, hiring and firing on the basis of political loyalty and active support for the party or candidate allows the personnel system to assure bureaucratic responsiveness to elected officials and, through them, to public opinion.

Presidents, as well as governors and mayors throughout the country, have used patronage to build powerful political coalitions. Some students of American history believe that presidential control of the federal patronage greatly strengthened the office's power in the constitutional system of separated powers (Fish, 1904). Abraham Lincoln freely dispensed federal jobs in an effort to build loyalty to and support for the Union cause during the Civil War. In fact, the White House was often overrun by job seekers during his tenure; he is reported to have remarked that "the spoils system might in the course of time become far more dangerous to the Republic than the rebellion itself" (Van Riper, 1958, p. 44).

The spoils system that Lincoln adeptly used and privately feared bore little resemblance to that used by presidents in earlier days. In general, the policy of the first six presidents (1789–1829) was to make appointments to federal offices on the basis of "fitness." In those days, fitness meant that the person was of good character, was able to do the work involved, *and* was in conformity with the political views and policy objectives of the chief executive and his associates. Normally, *all three standards* had to be satisfied. These early presidents did remove some people on purely partisan grounds when they took office, but they usually replaced them with persons they believed to be both loyal and capable of effectively doing the administrative work of government.

Until the Federalists lost control of the presidency, the national government's workforce was drawn almost exclusively from the upper class. American society was very stratified, and "The government of our early days was a government led by the well-educated, the well-born, the prosperous, and their adherents" (Van Riper, 1958, pp. 17–18). The early presidents were looking for men who had backgrounds like theirs, who shared their commitment to the U.S. Constitution, and who believed that governance was a responsibility of their social class. Thus, during this rather brief period, the federal service was very exclusive. Taking into account the requirement for political loyalty, it can hardly be said that the first six presidents implemented a merit system in the modern sense of that term, but the national government did have a "good reputation for integrity and capacity." However, the situation was very different at the state and local levels. By 1829, the practice of handing out jobs simply on partisan grounds had entrenched itself in such large states as New York and Pennsylvania.

The United States of 1829 was in the midst of a profound social, political, and economic transformation. The old social and political order established during colonial times was being undermined by a modern capitalist or market system in which people believed that wealth, power, and position should be and could be *achieved* rather than *inherited*. All that was needed was equality of opportunity and the ambition, intelligence, and hard work needed to take advantage of it. Democracy and an expanding franchise were giving rise to organized parties and to majoritarian politics. The country was expanding westward, urbanizing, and industrializing (Miller, 1972). Swelled by large numbers of immigrants, the population—especially in the cities—was growing rapidly.

President Andrew Jackson's stated views on public personnel policy reflected this changing scene. He rejected the elitist views of his predecessors in favor of a much more democratized approach to public service. Jackson is often called the father of the spoils system because he argued that the public service should be opened to all segments of society and that there was no need for permanence since the duties of most federal jobs were simple and did not require experience. Accordingly, he reasoned, rotation in office was the best policy. In the new era of democratic politics, Jackson's position was popular, responding as it did to "widespread resentment at the monopolizing of public office by representatives of the upper classes." Indeed, some families "had maintained themselves from father to son in the civil service" (Van Riper, 1958, pp. 27, 33).

In light of what happened during the second half of the nineteenth century, Jackson could hardly be called a practitioner of unmitigated spoils. His appointments to top-level federal positions mirrored earlier attention to ability and competence. The available pool of qualified persons was still relatively small, and most of them came from upper-class backgrounds (Mosher, 1968, p. 62). Nonetheless, his egalitarian rhetoric did much to open the gates for spoils on the national level, and those who followed were far more inclined to sweep out incumbents and to replace them with party loyalists. Their objective was a practical one: to win elections by strengthening the party machinery from the grass roots up. By 1860, when Lincoln assumed the presidency, the spoils system had developed to the point that it "had an adhesive grip upon the political machinery of the United States" (Van Riper, 1958, p. 42). The same could be said of personnel administration in the states and cities, especially the large cities where the "machines" prospered and the "bosses" ruled (Freedman, 1994). For example, the goals of New York City's notorious Tammany machine during the 1880s were "To nominate candidates for public office, get out the vote, and win elections. Once in power, the organization enjoyed a patronage feast" (Riordon, 1963, p. xii).

George Washington Plunkitt was a Tammany district leader, or ward boss, who happily explained his political "philosophy" to William Riordon of the *New York Evening Post* in a series of interviews conducted around the turn of the century. Plunkitt colorfully described the logic underpinning the spoils system:

> What is representative government anyhow? Is it all a fake that this is a government of the people, by the people and for the people? If it isn't a fake, then why isn't the people's voice obeyed and Tammany men put in all the offices?. . .We stood as we have always stood, for rewardin' the men that won the victory. . . .Say, the people's voice is smothered by the cursed civil service law; it is the root of all evil in our government. . . .First, this great and glorious country was built up by political parties; second, parties can't hold together if their workers don't get the offices when they win; third, if the parties go to pieces, the government they built up must go to pieces. . . . (Riordon, 1963, pp. 12–13)

CIVIL SERVICE REFORM I: NEUTRAL COMPETENCE IN GOVERNMENT

In the United States, the civil service reform against which Plunkitt railed was an element of the larger progressive movement of the late nineteenth and early twentieth centuries. This movement had many political objectives; one of them was the destruction of the party machines and bosses who ran the nation's major cities. In the reformers' eyes, these machines fostered rampant corruption, institutionalized administrative inefficiency and waste, and ignored the legitimate interests of electoral minorities while taxing them heavily. Advocates of the reform agenda included members of the banking and commercial sector, middle- and upper-income groups, and the growing numbers of university-trained professionals. They wanted a stable infrastructure for their commercial activities and to "take the reins of power away from the lower classes and the Irish bosses." Economic and political self-interest were major factors in the reform movement, but "the major force propelling civil service reform was moral outrage at the greedy excesses of the spoilsmen" (Freedman, 1994, p. 17).

By advancing "neutral competence" as *the* core value of public service, the civil service reformers sought to undermine a critical element of the machine's base of electoral power and administrative control—the patronage. Plunkitt had reason to be alarmed (Schiesl, 1977). He quite correctly understood that the reformers were trying to alter the political landscape fundamentally. His concerns would be realized as more and more governments enacted legislation designed to limit the scope of patronage in public employment.

Plunkitt certainly would have agreed with Justice Lewis F. Powell's dissenting opinion in *Elrod v Burns* (1976). In this decision, a majority of the Supreme Court ruled that removals of "non-policy-making" employees solely for reasons of their affiliation with a political party violated their First Amendment rights. Powell, however, disagreed, saying that it was naive to think that political activities were motivated by "some academic interest in 'democracy' or other public service impulse." He stated, "For the most part, as every politician knows, the hope of some reward generates a major portion of the local political activity supporting parties." Powell concluded, "History and long prevailing practice across the country support the view that patronage hiring practices make a sufficiently substantial contribution to the practical functioning of our democratic system to support their relatively modest intrusion on First Amendment rights." Plunkitt would have applauded vigorously, but Powell was in the minority, and *Elrod v Burns* was the first of several Court decisions that limited constitutionally acceptable patronage to situations where the hiring authority could "demonstrate that party affiliation is an appropriate requirement for the effective performance of the public office involved" (*Elrod v Burns*, 1976). Through these decisions, most notably *Branti v Finkle* (1980) and *Rutan v Republican Party of Illinois* (1990), the Court provided a constitutional underpinning for the merit principle (Daniel, 1992).

IMPLEMENTING NEUTRAL COMPETENCE WITH MERIT SYSTEMS

American democracy and egalitarianism have historically supported the ideal that people should get and keep government jobs on the

> **BULLETIN**
>
> Justice Brennan delivered the opinion of the Court in *Rutan:* "To the victor belong only those spoils that may be constitutionally obtained. . . the *First Amendment* forbids government officials to discharge or threaten to discharge public employees solely for not being supporters of the political party in power, unless party affiliation is an appropriate requirement for the position involved. Today we are asked to decide the constitutionality of several related political patronage practices [or] whether promotion, transfer, recall, and hiring decisions involving low-level public employees may be constitutionally based on party affiliation and support. We hold that they may not."

basis of their relative ability and performance. Likewise, the belief that rewards such as job status and income should be *achieved* by the individual enjoys widespread popular support. Disinterested, nonpartisan administration of the law is also highly valued. With regard to the personnel function, these norms are the foundation of the *merit principle*. Basing the administration of personnel systems on the merit principle was high on the agenda of the civil service reformers.

In application, the merit principle dictates that appointments, promotions, and other personnel actions should be made exclusively on the basis of relative ability and job performance. Since the turn of the century, for appointments and promotions, this has usually meant the administration of competitive examinations. Scores on "objective" tests have been used to rank applicants. For other personnel actions such as pay raises, reduction-in-force, and dismissals, the assumption has also been that the employee's "merit" could be determined through performance appraisals and that he or she should be treated accordingly. Government personnel systems based on these values and assumptions are called *merit systems*. In O. Glenn Stahl's words: "In its broadest sense a merit system in modern government means *a personnel system in which comparative merit or achievement governs each individual's selection and progress in the service and in which the conditions and rewards of performance contribute to competency and continuity of the service*" (Stahl, 1962, p. 28).

On the federal level, after several unsuccessful initiatives, legislation establishing the foundation for a rudimentary merit system was passed by Congress in 1883. The Pendleton Act was passed over a year after the unfortunate President Garfield was shot down by "a disappointed office seeker." The more immediate and less sentimental reason for its passage was the incumbent Republicans' fear that the next president would be a Democrat who would remove all Republican officeholders. The victory for reformers, while a watershed in the history of the U.S. Civil Service, was not overwhelming in its impact at the time. Initially, it covered only about 10 percent of the positions in the executive branch. By 1952, however, well over 90 percent were covered, and presidents were beginning to complain about their inability to establish policy control over an "unresponsive" (Democrat dominated) bureaucracy.

The administrative machinery set up to carry out the Pendleton Act was a bipartisan Civil Service Commission (CSC) rather than an

BULLETIN

In Section 12, the Pendleton Act requires: "That no person shall, in any room or building occupied in the discharge of official duties by any officer or employee of the United States mentioned in this act. . .solicit in any manner whatever, or receive any contribution of money or any other thing of value for any political purpose whatever."

Source: 22 Stat. 27 (1883).

executive agency. This meant that the CSC would enjoy considerable independence from the president in its policy-making and day-to-day administrative activities. However, the CSC was far from autonomous, since the three commissioners were appointed by the president, subject to Senate confirmation, and he or she could remove them. The president also had to approve civil service rules and regulations recommended by the CSC before they could be implemented. Another key provision was presidential authority to place additional positions under the classified civil service or merit system and to remove positions from such coverage. As state and local governments adopted merit systems, they tended to follow the federal example and also created commissions or boards to administer them.

The first merit systems were poorly funded and struggled to survive (many did not). Besides being limited in coverage, they were narrowly gauged; basically, they gave routine tests to applicants, kept employee records, and did little else. Commissions were staffed largely by clerks, and it was the clerks who took care of the departments' personnel chores.

The first state to adopt civil service legislation applying the merit principle was New York in 1883, followed by Massachusetts in 1884. The limited success of the reform movement on the state level is revealed by the fact that no new state laws were approved during the next twenty years. Albany, New York, was the first municipality to establish a merit system (1884). During the 1890s, Milwaukee, Philadelphia, New Orleans, and Seattle were among the cities approving charter amendments that established civil service regulations. The first county to do so was Cook County, Illinois, in 1895. As the machines and reform parties struggled for control of the nation's cities and counties, it was not unusual for merit systems to come and go, depending on the outcomes of elections. Often, commissions established under reform administrations became fronts for spoils when the machines gained the upper hand (Aronson, 1973, p. 38). In Chicago, for example:

> Jobs have been the lifeblood of the Cook County Democratic Organization since. . .the early 1930s. . . .
> In the heyday of the machine during the Daley years (1955–1976) all patronage jobs were personally controlled by Richard J. Daley [and] . . .were allocated to ward and township committeemen in proportion to the individual committeeman's influence and the number of votes his ward delivered for machine candidates. (Freedman, 1994, p. 39)

Although the number of civil service systems at least nominally based on the merit principle continued to expand between 1900 and 1930, the scope of their activities remained quite limited. At best, "merit" was making sure that public employees were appointed through competitive entrance examinations, prohibited from engaging in partisan politics, and compensated on the basis of "equal pay for equal work." In practice, little if any attention was paid to potential connections between personnel practices and organizational productivity and effectiveness. During this period, the scientific management approach and principles-of-administration movement did influence thinking about efficiency in government (Merrill, 1960). Their influence on personnel administration, however, was minimal. For the most part, administrators of merit systems concentrated on "keeping the rascals out" by severely constraining line management's role in personnel matters.

POSITIVE PERSONNEL ADMINISTRATION

The explosive growth of the federal government during the Depression and World War II quickly outpaced the CSC's capacity to handle day-to-day personnel operations. In 1916, there were about 400,000 federal employees; by 1940, that number had risen to one million, and by 1945 it stood at over 3.5 million. In 1935, *total* state and local employment was less than 3 million. As President Franklin D. Roosevelt dramatically expanded the size of the classified civil service to encompass the New Deal agencies, it became clear that much of the Commission's work would have to be decentralized to the agency level. It had become a serious bottleneck. This practical reality, in combination with a recognition that skilled personnel administration might help agencies function more efficiently, led to FDR's 1938 Executive Order 7916 requiring the various departments to set up professionally staffed personnel offices.

Historically, Roosevelt's order signaled the arrival of "modern" personnel administration (U.S. Library of Congress, 1976, pp. 258–260). In this case, *modern* meant expanding departmental-level personnel units and improving the efficiency of services they provided, such as position classification, applicant testing, and records keeping. It also meant that the CSC's responsibilities would shift to policy formulation, research and development, and program evaluation. Since these mandates required that the CSC and departmental personnel offices develop expertise across a wide variety of topics, college graduates began to replace the clerks. Personnel administration gradually became more professionalized and specialized.

The concept of personnel administration as a tool or arm of management began to take hold, not only in the federal government but also in some states and localities. World War II greatly increased the pressure on departmental personnel shops to be responsive and supportive. By the end of the war, the perception of personnel administration as a routine activity with limited technical content and little relation to managerial needs had been largely abandoned by its leading practitioners, as well as by students of public administration. Thus, by the end of the 1940s, Simon, Smithburg, and Thompson (1950) were prepared to state in their widely read textbook that personnel specialists deal with matters "that are of the greatest long range importance to the organization" (p. 312).

The definition of personnel administration's role continued to evolve as efficiency and productivity assumed greater importance. Between 1945 and 1960, the field became somewhat more people-oriented and less fixated on the enforcement of rules and regulations. Essentially, two related criticisms of the prewar approach to personnel administration were heard. First, increasingly professionalized and formalized personnel operations, while efficient in their own terms, frequently worked to frustrate line officials who were interested in accomplishing departmental or organizational goals. Personnel offices typically acquired reputations with line managers as centers of "bureaucratization" where rules and procedures were all-important. Second, personnel specialists tended to assume a highly legalistic definition of their responsibilities while neglecting the implications of a growing body of information on social-psychological factors related to performance and productivity in organizations.

This kind of criticism was probably inevitable, given the increasingly technical nature of the personnel function and the proliferation of personnel offices staffed by specialists. Those in staff roles normally will exert considerable control because they monopolize the expertise needed to administer often complex policies and procedures. In the public sector, they commonly have the legal as well as organizational authority to enforce and adjudicate the rules that managers must follow. Nevertheless, as part of a trend that would culminate on the federal level in the 1978 Civil Service Reform Act, appeals for "flexibility" and a "management orientation" were often heard during the late 1950s.

As to the second criticism, personnel specialists did not seem at all "people minded." They concentrated on day-to-day tasks, applying technical skills but showing little interest in developing a broad-gauged approach to the development and management of the organization's human resources. The human relations approach was having some limited influence in the private sector prior to World War II, but this was not the case in the public sector (Roethlisberger and Dickson, 1939). This situation began to change after the war as an "accent-on-people" orientation gained followers. Advocates believed that the insights of human relations could be applied to the personnel function in the following specific ways:

■ Attending to social and psychological factors in productivity such as supervisory leadership, incentives, and the design of jobs and work settings.

■ Focusing attention on the behavioral as well as technical skills and conditions people need to develop their potential and to function effectively in the workplace. This includes enhancing job satisfaction and commitment to organizational goals through psychologically rewarding work settings, supportive management styles, and opportunities for career development and training.

■ Recognizing the importance of effective supervision on the social and psychological levels. Since supervisors are usually the first point at which employees relate to the organization, it is essential that supervisors be prepared to deal with a broad range of interpersonal and group processes that may affect morale and productivity. Personnel specialists, therefore, should be able to provide this kind of support through training programs and other programs designed to help supervisors be effective in human as well as technical terms.

■ Increasing the knowledge base of personnel administration. In other words, at least some personnel specialists should be conducting research into the social and psychological effects of personnel policies and practices. Applied research of this kind is vitally necessary if personnel administration is to be firmly grounded in an understanding of the human side of organizations.

■ Requiring personnel workers themselves to have sufficiently broad backgrounds of training and experience to understand human behavior. The value of personnel specialists, therefore, should not be judged only in terms of command over techniques such as position classification and testing; they should also be schooled in human relations theory and its practical applications.

By 1960, on the federal level and in a growing number of state and local jurisdictions, some progress could be reported in making personnel systems more professional, better related to management needs, and more attuned to a "human resources management" point of view. The concept of public personnel, as set forth in textbooks, journals, and the recommendations of professional societies and commissions, firmly supported all of these values in addition to the merit principle. However, just how much progress had been made toward realizing them in practice was a matter of opinion. For many governments, patronage was still the dominant and accepted way of doing business. In 1940, the Congress had amended the 1935 Social Security Act (SSA) to require merit-based personnel systems in state agencies administering SSA funds, and this method of "forcing" merit was extended to the broad array of federal grants-in-aid to states and localities that developed during the 1960s and 1970s. Similarly, in most states, prohibitions against partisan activity covered only agencies administering federal funds (as required by the 1940 Hatch Act). Finally, even the most nonpartisan merit systems tended to be inward looking and unresponsive to many of management's concerns.

COLLECTIVE BARGAINING IN GOVERNMENT

The "state of the art" set forth in the personnel texts of the 1950s would be rendered obsolete (or at least very incomplete) by the changes that took place during the next 10 years. One such change was the rapid spread of collective bargaining in the public sector. Prior to 1960, most merit system administrators thought of collective bargaining as something peculiar to the private sector that had no place in government. By experience, they had little or no familiarity with collective bargaining or appreciation of its institutional significance as a system of internal governance in private businesses. They saw it to be a real menace to the merit principle and believed that the unstated goal of most union leaders was to wipe out civil service laws and regulations and to replace them with agreements negotiated under the threat of strikes and other disruptions of public services.

For many personnel administrators, public employee unionization and collective bargaining was in the same category as spoils: something to be vigorously resisted on the legal, legislative, and organizational levels. By 1968, however, the federal courts had firmly established that the First Amendment protected the right of public employees to form and join unions. The courts had also ruled that public workers have no constitutional right to collective bargaining or to strike against their employers. But, more importantly, they identified no constitutional reason why public employers could *not* bargain collectively. Thus, the decision was essentially political, and state legislatures could enact laws requiring localities to engage in collective bargaining, proscribing collective bargaining, or anything in between. It was also possible for the state to say nothing and, in so doing, make collective bargaining a local option. State legislatures, in addition, could decide if the state should bargain collectively with all or some of its workers. In many states, organized employees were politically effective (and unions were warmly received by workers who saw their pay and benefits falling behind those of the private sector), and collective bargaining was to change dramatically the landscape of personnel administration over the next 20 years.

In 1959, Wisconsin was the only state to have passed legislation requiring municipal employers to bargain collectively with unionized workers, and none of the states bargained with its employees. In the federal service, there was no law or executive order providing for collective bargaining or any government-wide labor relations policy. In stark contrast, most nonagricultural workers in the private sector had been guaranteed the right to bargain collectively by the 1935 National Labor Relations Act (NLRA). President Roosevelt had supported the NLRA while expressing strong opposition to any form of collective bargaining in the federal government.

The present situation is very different. By 1985, 40 states and the District of Columbia had statutes or executive orders setting up frameworks for collective bargaining with some or all of their employees. In the federal government, collective bargaining began in 1962 and is now a statutory requirement of the CSRA (postal workers have been bargaining collectively since 1970). In fact, whereas the percentage of private-sector workers belonging to unions and covered by negotiated contracts had declined to around 10 percent in 1997, in the public sector it had grown to over 40 percent.

Currently, about half of all state and local government full-time workers are members of employee organizations of one kind or another. The percentage of organized employees is even higher in such functions as education, highways, public welfare, hospitals, police, fire, and sanitation services. Collective bargaining is no longer a novelty in the public sector. In many jurisdictions, it has become a normal and accepted aspect of personnel administration. One highly visible result has been the emergence of a new specialty within the field: labor relations and collective bargaining. It has also become commonplace to find offices of labor relations either within personnel departments or as separate units.

FROM EXCLUSIVE TO INCLUSIVE PERSONNEL POLICIES AND PRACTICES

Today, the term equal employment opportunity (EEO) means that a personnel system does not discriminate in any aspect of employment for reasons of race, sex, religion, national or ethnic origin, or physical handicap. Stahl's (1962) definition of merit certainly leaves no room for hiring and other personnel actions based on anything other than the individual's qualifications and job performance. There is, however, no doubt that numerous public employers on all levels of government were systematically discriminating against minorities and women in 1962 when Stahl's book appeared. Patronage systems did much to *exclude* minorities, and in practice the merit principle often applied only to white males.

Discrimination of this kind has deep roots in the American public service. President Woodrow Wilson, a strong advocate of civil service reform as a part of the progressive agenda, ordered African-Americans removed from all but menial jobs in the federal service in an effort to build the southern base of the Democratic party. Like ethnic and racial minorities, women have historically been confined to lower-grade jobs in the public as well as private sector. Traditionally, their job opportunities have been restricted largely to clerical, secretarial, and service positions (so-called women's work, according to the then-dominant stereotype).

Until the civil rights movement of the 1960s, the failure of public personnel systems to assure genuine equality of opportunity or EEO went virtually unchallenged. Clearly, social norms, unequal educational opportunities, the exclusion of minorities from the political process, and intentional discrimination by personnel administrators played major roles in the exclusion of minorities and women from all but the lowest levels of the public service. A passive approach to the administration of merit systems also reinforced the pattern. Typically, those running merit systems argued that the very low representation of minority groups in the public service and their concentration in the lowest-ranking jobs was not a violation of the merit principle. They reasoned that so long as there was no *overt* discrimination to be found, the absence of minorities was unfortunate but no fault of the merit system.

While noting that many cases of overt discrimination could be documented, the U.S. Commission on Civil Rights concluded in a 1969 report that "static" and arbitrary civil service procedures did much to exclude minority groups. It cited as examples the use of unvalidated tests, rigid educational requirements, and automatic disqualification for an arrest record. The Commission also stressed that most merit system agencies made no positive effort to recruit minorities by regularly visiting black colleges and universities (U.S. Commission on Civil Rights, 1969).

At the time this report was issued, the civil rights movement was having a major impact on public policy. Several lower court decisions, based on the Fourteenth Amendment and the Civil Rights Acts of 1866 and 1871, made it clear that the federal judiciary was inclined to void discriminatory practices and to impose affirmative action programs if public employers did not do so voluntarily. The Civil Rights Act of 1964, originally applicable only to the private sector, was amended in 1972 to cover the public sector as well. Presidents

Johnson, Nixon, and Carter authored affirmative action programs, and federal rules and regulations requiring EEO and affirmative action remedies of private contractors and governments receiving federal funds were set forth during this period. In general, the 1960s and 1970s were marked by a growing *inclusiveness* of public personnel policies and practices.

The federal courts have also interpreted the prohibitions in the Civil Rights Act of 1964 to include sex discrimination. They have clearly established that, to be upheld, restricting certain job classifications only to men or to women must have a rational basis, or an occupationally valid reason. Affirmative action programs now typically include women in their recruitment, hiring, and career development initiatives. As a result, women are now being hired to fill many kinds of positions previously argued to be too strenuous or otherwise unsuitable for females (e.g., police and fire services). Intentional as well as "socially traditional" forms of discrimination against women, including sexual harassment, are illegal under Title VII of the Civil Rights Act, and the Equal Employment Opportunity Commission (EEOC) is empowered to investigate complaints by women against their employers.

EEO protections also apply to discrimination based on age or handicap. The Age Discrimination in Employment Act of 1967, as amended in 1978, prohibits public as well as private employers from discriminating against persons on the basis of age. Employers must be able to show that age is a legitimate employment qualification, and the courts now require reasonable evidence that a certain entrance or retirement age is disqualifying. In other words, employers may not favor younger workers simply for reasons of age unrelated to ability to do the job in question.

Handicapped persons are protected by the Rehabilitation Act of 1973 and the Americans With Disabilities Act of 1990 (ADA). The Rehabilitation Act applies to public and private agencies that receive federal funds. It requires that these agencies have written affirmative action programs for the handicapped, and reasonable accommodation must be made by the employer to facilitate the employment of handicapped persons (this now includes people who are HIV-positive or have active AIDS). The ADA expanded coverage to most public and private employers.

AFFIRMATIVE ACTION IN PUBLIC EMPLOYMENT:
From *DUKE POWER* to *HOPWOOD*

In 1971, the U.S. Supreme Court issued a landmark decision in which it established the rule that if an employer uses a selection requirement that has disparate effect on the basis of race, sex, religion, or national origin, the employer must be able to demonstrate that the requirement is job-related (*Griggs v Duke Power Company,* 1971). If this cannot be done, the requirement constitutes illegal discrimination. The Court found that Duke Power was using job standards that were not demonstrably related to successful job performance and that they served to disqualify black workers at a substantially higher rate than whites. As to the company's claim that its intentions had been good, the Court said that "good intent or absence of discriminatory intent does not redeem employment procedures or testing mechanisms that operate as 'built-in headwinds' for minority groups and are unrelated to measuring job capability."

For public as well as private employers, *Griggs* was a shock. For the first time, an employer would have to prove in court that its personnel practices were valid and job-related if "the numbers" showed that minorities were not succeeding in the same proportions as non-minorities. In contrast to the situation before *Griggs,* plaintiffs now were not required to show an intent to discriminate or to prove that a personnel policy or practice was invalid or not job-related. Once disparate impact was shown to exist, the burden shifted to the employer. Finally, under *Griggs* and later decisions, *individuals* were not required to show that they had been harmed by a discriminatory practice; rather, remedies applied to affected *classes* of people, such as African-Americans and women.

In the wake of *Griggs* there were numerous lower court decisions enjoining the use of selection methods not proven to be related to satisfactory job performance. Judges ordered personnel agencies to prepare new tests, issued guidelines for validating tests, required outreach recruitment, and mandated other changes in personnel programs intended to increase the hiring of minorities. In some cases, remedies took the form of consent decrees under which, for example, public employers agreed to use remedial hiring ratios and to alter seniority rules to protect minorities under reduction-in-force conditions. Important decisions by the Supreme Court included awarding back pay to victims of discrimination and, in the highly publicized *Bakke* case, it ruled that college admission criteria that take race into account are constitutional (*Regents of the University of California v Bakke,* 1978). In a widely publicized private-sector case, the Court ruled that voluntary affirmative action plans calling for preferential treatment of African-Americans were not in violation of the Civil Rights Act of 1964 (*United Steel Workers of America v Weber,* 1979). Justice Brennan stated that the legislative history of the Act indicated clearly that it was not the intention of Congress to "prohibit all race conscious affirmative action plans."

During the 1980s, presidential support for affirmative action, especially remedies calling for "preferences" and protection of groups or classes as opposed to individuals, evaporated. Presidents Reagan and Bush declared that remedial hiring ratios were a form of reverse discrimination that violated the Fourteenth Amendment and the Civil Rights Act. Both also stated their commitment to EEO and "color-blind" personnel policies and practices.

In 1983, the U.S. Justice Department urged the Supreme Court to rule unconstitutional an affirmative action plan entered into voluntarily by the Detroit Police Department providing for the hiring and promotion of whites and blacks in equal numbers. In this instance, the Court declined to hear the case, but over the next few years it issued a series of decisions that had the practical effect of making it harder to bring discrimination suits and to obtain consent decrees designed to compensate for past discrimination. Other decisions made it more difficult to recover compensatory damages and attorney's fees.

In one case, the Court ruled that an 1866 statute guaranteeing all persons the same right to make and enforce contracts did not prohibit racial harassment on the job and other kinds of racial discrimination after the formation of a contract (*Patterson v McLean Credit Union*, 1989). In another, it reversed the *Griggs* rule that employers were responsible for showing that practices having disparate impact are job-related and required by "business necessity" (*Wards Cove Packing Co. v Atonio*, 1989). Under *Wards Cove*, employers were simply required to show that the practice in question significantly related to a legitimate business ojective. This was, of course, a far less stringent standard than that imposed by *Griggs*.

The Court also ruled that a discriminatory employment action motivated by prejudice did not violate the Civil Rights Act if the employer can demonstrate that the same decision would have been made for reasons unrelated to prejudice (*Price Waterhouse v Hopkins*, 1989). In yet another important decision, it permitted persons unhappy with a consent decree settling a job discrimination suit to challenge the decree in a separate lawsuit (*Martin v Wilks*, 1989) Under *Wilks*, for example, it was possible for a white male to "sit on the sidelines" until a decree protecting minority and female employees from reductions-in-force based strictly on seniority was implemented. This individual could then initiate a lawsuit against the employer seeking to overturn the court order and, in so doing, prevent anything resembling finality or closure. In fact, after *Wilks*, suits challenging long-standing and widely accepted decrees were filed in over a dozen cities, including Birmingham, Boston, and Cincinnati. All in all, 1989 was a very bad year for supporters of affirmative action.

In 1990, the Congress responded to the Court by passing an amendment to the 1964 Civil Rights Act. Known as the Civil Rights Act of 1990, this legislation was designed to overturn key aspects of the rulings outlined above and to strengthen existing protections and remedies. President Bush vetoed the bill, arguing that it would force employers to impose racial and gender quotas in order to avoid expensive lawsuits. The veto was upheld by a narrow margin, but in the following year a compromise was reached under which practices having disparate impact on women and minorities must be "job-related for the position in question and consistent with business necessity" in order to be legal. The president signed the Civil Rights Act of 1991, arguing that it was no longer "a quota bill."

The 1991 Civil Rights Act, in addition to overturning several Supreme Court decisions on EEO and affirmative action, included the following provisions:

- Authorized compensatory and punitive damages for victims of intentional discrimination based on sex, religion, or disability. Damages were limited to a maximum of $300,000 for the largest employers, and this provision does not apply to the public sector.

- Banned the use of so-called "race-norming" of selection tests through adjustments of scores or other changes on the basis of race, national origin, sex, or religion of applicants.

- Created the Glass Ceiling Commission to study barriers to the advancement of women and minorities in the workplace.

Political and judicial efforts to narrow the legitimate scope of affirmative action programs continued, however. During 1995 and 1996, against a backdrop of growing public antipathy toward affirmative action and political rhetoric directed against "preferences," the Supreme Court issued a series of decisions that made the future of affirmative action problematic at best. In *Adarand Constructors v Peña, U.S. Secretary of Transportation,* the Court required minority contractor "set-asides" to meet a "strict scrutiny" standard that applies two tests: (1) is the program required to redress past discrimination? and (2) is the program "narrowly tailored," that is, does it meet its goals with the minimum necessary damage to "innocent victims" while avoiding classifications of people by race, sex, and so forth, if at all possible? Thus, by extension, although affirmative action programs in employment were not determined to be unconstitutional, successfully defending them in the federal courts was made much more difficult than had been the case under earlier decisions (Riccucci, 1997, pp. 67–69).

Another major action by the Court was its refusal to hear on appeal the Fifth Circuit Court of Appeals's decision in *State of Texas v Hopwood* (1996), which declared unconstitutional an affirmative action program of the University of Texas Law School. This program was designed to increase the number of African-American and Hispanic students. The previous year, the governor of California had ordered an end to all state affirmative action programs not required by law and, shortly thereafter, the University of California's Board of Regents ended affirmative action in the system's admissions, hiring, and contracting processes. Finally, Proposition 209, an amendment to the state constitution by initiative, was approved by the California electorate in 1996. If fully implemented, this measure "would eliminate state and local government affirmative action programs in the areas of public employment, public education, and public contracting to the extent these programs involve 'preferential treatment' based on race, sex, color, ethnicity, or national origin" (California Legislative Analyst Office, 1996).

One observer of the current scene has concluded that:

> It appears that as we move into the next millennium the system of law developed on affirmative action will continue to break down. We may no longer see affirmative action programs supported or mandated by the courts, or, as we saw in California, by some state governments. Moreover, given popular sentiment, it is unlikely that the U.S. Congress or the White House can be relied upon to defend [affirmative action's] use. (Riccucci, 1997, p. 34)

THE CONSTITUTIONAL RIGHTS OF PUBLIC EMPLOYEES

Since the 1950s, the federal courts have significantly strengthened the individual's constitutional position in the employment relationship. As late as the mid-1950s, this relationship was dominated by the employer, who was free to impose many conditions on workers that they had to accept to keep their jobs. Historically, the courts had ruled that employees did not have *any* rights in the job that were based on the Constitution. Thus, in fixing the terms of employment, the public employer could and often did deny workers civil and political rights universally enjoyed by those in the private sector.

The due process clause of the Fifth and Fourteenth Amendments

BULLETIN

From an argument in support of Proposition 209, endorsed by Governor Pete Wilson and others: "Government cannot work against discrimination if government itself discriminates. Proposition 209 will stop the terrible programs which are dividing our people and tearing us apart. People naturally feel resentment when the less qualified are preferred. We are all Americans. It's time to bring us together under a single standard of equal treatment under the law."

were held not to apply to public employees because, as the Court reasoned in *Bailey v Richardson,* government employment could not be considered property, it could be "perceived" to be liberty, and it "certainly" was not life. "Due process of law is not applicable unless one is being deprived of something to which he has a right" (*Bailey v Richardson,* 1951). Accordingly, public employees were not entitled to substantive or procedural due process; they could, for example, be barred from political activity (substantive) and denied the right to a hearing in loyalty cases (procedural). In 1892, Justice Holmes had stated for the majority that "The petitioner may have a constitutional right to talk politics, but he has no constitutional right to be a policeman" (*McAuliffe v Mayor of New Bedford,* 1892). This point of view held sway for the next 60 years, and the scope of judicial review of personnel actions taken by managers was very limited. As one observer wrote in 1955, "from the assertion that there exists no constitutional right *to* public employment, it is also inferred that there can be no constitutional right *in* public employment. The progression is that, since there are no fundamental claims in employment, employment is maintained by the state as a privilege" (Dotson, 1955, p. 87).

Beginning in the 1950s, under the leadership of the Warren Court, the federal judiciary issued a series of decisions that effectively demolished what was called the "doctrine of privilege." In its place, the federal courts applied the following standard: "whenever there is a substantial interest, other than employment by the state, involved in the discharge of a public employee, he can be removed neither on arbitrary grounds nor without a procedure calculated to determine whether legitimate grounds exist" (Rosenbloom, 1971, p. 421). The courts, therefore, have narrowed management's discretion by extending certain constitutional protections and guarantees to public employees on all levels of government.

For public employees, one of the most important changes was brought about by a series of Supreme Court decisions in the 1970s establishing that they may have property and liberty interests in their jobs that warrant protection under the due process clause of the Fifth and Fourteenth Amendments to the Constitution. As defined by the Court, property interests include whatever affects the livelihood of an individual (e.g., welfare benefits, eligibility for occupational licenses). Liberty interests may come into play in situations where a personnel action affects the person's reputation, career prospects, or ability to

BULLETIN

From *Board of Regents v Roth:* "The Fourteenth Amendment does not require opportunity for a hearing prior to the nonrenewal of a nontenured state teacher's contract unless he can show that the nonrenewal deprived him of an interest in 'liberty' or that he had a 'property' interest in continued employment, despite the lack of tenure or a formal contract."

find employment elsewhere. In *Board of Regents v Roth* (1972), *Perry v Sinderman* (1972), *Arnett v Kennedy* (1974), and *Bishop v Wood* (1976), the Court defined the conditions under which property and liberty interests could exist and what standards of due process applied under specific conditions.

In the area of freedom of expression, the Court set forth a balancing test under which it rejected the proposition that public employment could be subjected to any conditions no matter how unreasonable. In *Pickering v Board of Education* (1968), the Court ruled that Pickering's First Amendment rights had been violated. However, while teachers could not constitutionally be compelled to give up a right "they would otherwise enjoy as citizens to comment on matters of public interest," the state did have interests as an "employer in regulating the speech of its employees that differ significantly from those it possesses in connection with regulation of the speech of the citizenry in general." In other words, what should be balanced in each case was the interests of the teachers as citizens in regard to their ability to comment on matters of public concern against the interests of the public employer in providing services to the public.

Since *Pickering,* the Court has applied this balancing test to a number of cases, often with the minority expressing the opinion that the majority had "tilted" in the wrong direction. Overall, the Burger and Rehnquist Courts have tended to uphold the employer's position more often than the employee's, and they have been reluctant to entertain anything but cases involving what they see to be fundamental (sweeping) constitutional issues. In practice, this has meant that the present Court is far less likely than the Warren Court to consider cases originating in the employment relationship. This is, nonetheless, a far cry from the earlier conditions under which the courts simply refused to recognize *any* First Amendment protections for public employees (O'Brian, 1997).

Over the past 30 years, the Supreme Court has voided or meaningfully limited public employers' power and discretion in several areas of the employment relationship. Public employees may no longer be required to take vague and overly broad loyalty oaths, and their freedom of political association cannot arbitrarily be limited by blanket prohibitions against membership in the Communist Party, or any other organization for that matter. Likewise,

BULLETIN

From *Perry v Sinderman:* "Lack of a contractual or tenure right to employment does not, taken alone, defeat respondent's claim that the nonrenewal of his contract violated his free speech right. . . .Though a subjective 'expectancy' of tenure is not protected by procedural due process, respondent's allegation that the college had a *de facto* tenure policy. . . entitled him to an opportunity of proving the legitimacy of his claim to job tenure. Such proof would obligate the college to afford him a requested hearing. . . ."

unless the employer can show a rational connection or "nexus" between the personal behavior and his or her job performance, dismissals and other serious actions taken against the employee stand a good chance of being reversed in the courts (Rosenbloom and Carroll, 1990).

POLITICAL ACTIVITIES OF PUBLIC EMPLOYEES

It has been a long-standing practice in the United States to restrict such political activities of public employees as running for elective office and actively campaigning for candidates. Historically, the intention of federal and state legislation imposing such limitations was to prevent partisan coercion of public employees, to assure the political neutrality of the civil service, and to protect the merit principle. Restrictions on political activity have been regularly challenged in court on grounds that they are unconstitutional, but they have survived judicial scrutiny relatively intact. In effect, the federal courts have ruled that restraints on the political behavior of public employees are matters best left to legislative discretion.

The best-known legislative enactments in this area are the Hatch Acts of 1939 and 1940. The first was passed at least in part because of congressional fears that President Roosevelt was building an overwhelming political base in the federal bureaucracy by first hiring large numbers of people noncompetitively into the unclassified service and then later extending merit system coverage to their positions and agencies. The 1939 Hatch Act applies to most workers in the federal executive branch, but it does exclude the president and vice president, heads and assistant heads of executive departments, members of the White House staff, and officials who determine national policy and are appointed by the president with Senate confirmation. Principal responsibility for developing and enforcing the rules and regulations needed to implement the Act was assigned to the U.S. Civil Service Commission. The Office of Personnel Management (OPM) now has that responsibility.

The Act's coverage was extended in 1940 to state or local employees "whose principal employment is in connection with any activity which is financed in whole or in part by loans or grants made by the United States." Later, in an amendment to the 1974 Federal Campaign Act, state and local workers were permitted to engage in certain partisan political activities (e.g., solicit votes in partisan elections and be delegates to party conventions) if state laws did not prohibit them from doing so.

The Hatch Act prohibited the "use of official authority or influence for the purpose of interfering with an election or affecting the result thereof" and, in the case of federal employees, taking "any active part in political management or in political campaigns." For federal employees the most severe penalty for violation was removal, and the minimum penalty was suspension without pay for 30 days. In the case of state and local workers, if the Civil Service Commission (and after 1978, OPM) found that a violation had taken place, it decided whether removal was warranted. If it recommended removal but the state or local government employer did not comply, the federal funding agency was required to withhold from the grant or loan an amount equal to two years' pay of the employee concerned.

In *United Public Workers v Mitchell* (1947) and a companion case, *Oklahoma v United States Civil Service Commission*, the Supreme Court upheld the constitutionality of the Hatch Act and its 1940 amendments covering state and local employees. In 1973, the Court reaffirmed its position in overturning a federal district court ruling that the Act was unconstitutional because it was vague and "capable of sweeping and uneven application." In its six-to-three decision on *United States Civil Service Commission v National Association of Letter Carriers, AFL-CIO*, the Court found there was nothing "fatally overbroad about the statute." The majority went on to say that the CSC's regulations were "set out in terms that the ordinary person exercising ordinary common sense can sufficiently understand and observe, without sacrifice to the public interest," and were not unconstitutionally vague.

Opponents of the Hatch Act then turned to the Congress in search of a legislative remedy. In 1976, Congress passed a bill to permit federal employees to take part in political campaigns and to seek nomination or election to any office. President Ford vetoed the measure, and subsequent efforts in Congress to pass a similar bill were frustrated until 1993.

In late 1993, President Clinton signed the Hatch Act Reform Amendments of 1993. These amendments, effective in 1994, authorized OPM to issue regulations on political activities intended to implement Congress's policy that federal "[E]mployees should be encouraged to exercise fully, freely, and without fear of penalty or reprisal, and the extent not expressly prohibited by law, their right to participate or refrain from participating in the political processes of the Nation" (U.S. Office of Personnel Management, 1998). Final rules issued by OPM in early 1998 address two broad categories of federal employees: (1) those residing in certain designated communities or political subdivisions located in Maryland and Virginia and in the immediate vicinity of the District of Columbia, or in other communities where a majority of the registered voters are federal workers; and (2) those living in the District and elsewhere.

For those in the latter category, with certain exceptions, the Reform Amendments allow federal employees to participate in political campaigns and to run for election to *nonpartisan offices,* such as school boards. They are, however, prohibited from becoming candidates for *partisan political office* and from "soliciting, accepting, or receiving political contributions." For those in the former, if OPM determines that "it is in the domestic interest of the employees" to permit them to participate in local elections for *partisan political office,* they may do so by running as *independent candidates.* They are also allowed to "solicit, accept, or receive a political contribution as, or on behalf of, an independent candidate for partisan office. . . ." Other exemptions from the law covering other federal workers include being permitted to solicit and receive uncompensated volunteer services for themselves as, or on behalf of, independent candidates for partisan political offices, and, more generally:

> To take an active part in other political activities associated with elections for local partisan office and in managing the campaigns of candidates for election to local political office. . .but only as an independent candidate or on behalf of, or in opposition to, an independent candidate. (U.S. Office of Personnel Management, 1998, p. 4560)

Federal employees in all categories are not allowed to (1) run as the representative of a political party for partisan office, (2) solicit contributions for partisan candidates, (3) receive political contributions or volunteer services from subordinates, or (4) participate in political activities while on duty, while "wearing a uniform, badge, or insignia that identifies the employing agency," or if "he or she is in any room or building occupied in the discharge of official duties by an individual employed or holding office in the Government of the United States. . ." (U.S. Office of Personnel Management, 1998, p. 4559).

To varying degrees, most state and local governments restrict their employees' political activities. A few have laws more restrictive than the Hatch Act as amended; for example, they may prohibit voluntary contributions and not allow workers to express their partisan opinions publicly. The pattern on the state level is for most to permit general campaign activities while off duty. About two-thirds allow their employees to be candidates in partisan elections, but there is no uniformity across the states (Thurber, 1993, pp. 45–46). The same variability may be found on the local level.

CIVIL SERVICE REFORM II: EFFECTIVE AND RESPONSIVE GOVERNMENT ADMINISTRATION

By the time Jimmy Carter assumed the presidency in 1976, pressure was building for another round of civil service reform. The first civil service reform movement sought to replace spoils with merit systems and to limit line management's control over many aspects of personnel administration. However, this is not what the term *civil service reform* meant in 1976. It referred instead to efforts to align personnel practices with the day-to-day needs of public managers, to improve the performance of public employees, and to make the "bureaucracy" more responsive to executive leadership.

An important feature of Civil Service Reform II was its emphasis on improving the control chief executives and public managers had over the personnel function. Proponents of reform argued that merit systems have functioned far too independently since their creation and have seemed intent on imposing restrictive and cumbersome controls over line management's discretion in personnel matters. They disagreed with the assumption that elected chief executives and line managers must be kept at arm's length because they cannot be relied upon to protect the merit principle.

According to this line of reasoning, the old reform movement created a separation between general management and personnel administration despite the fact that personnel, like budgeting and finance, is an integral part of the management function in any public agency. Although it may have "kept the rascals out," critics argued that this approach seriously compromised management's capacity to effectively use human resources. If governments were to satisfy public demands and overcome the difficulties created by the "fiscal stress" of the 1970s and 1980s, the split between executive management and the personnel function had to be eliminated. There was, reformers argued, no necessary contradiction between the merit *principle* and a management-oriented personnel system. Accordingly, the following changes were proposed.

The traditional independent civil service commission should be abolished and replaced by an office of personnel management or a department of human resources headed by a director appointed by and directly accountable to the chief executive. This structural change allows the chief executive to establish direct policy control over the personnel function and, through the department of human resources, to use it in support of *organizational* efforts. Advocates of reform reasoned that this arrangement does not necessarily threaten the merit principle if the executive is made legally responsible for protecting that principle and, equally important, is held strictly accountable for violations. In addition, independent boards or commissions established to hear employee appeals and empowered to conduct investigations of personnel practices would assure fairness and prevent political abuses. Critics pointed out that this executive-oriented model, in practice, might easily lead to partisan manipulations of personnel systems if no effective independent regulatory agency existed.

The U.S. Civil Service Reform Act of 1978 (CSRA) followed

this model by abolishing the Civil Service Commission and establishing in its place the Office of Personnel Management whose director reports directly to the president, and the Merit Systems Protection Board (MSPB), which is responsible for the "watchdog" function. In state and local governments, civil service commissions with personnel policy-making, appellate, and administrative responsibilities continued to operate in many jurisdictions. In a growing number, however, the commissions were either abolished or limited to advisory, appellate, and investigatory roles. The personnel director reports directly to the governor in over half of the states.

Another feature of the reform initiatives of the 1970s was an effort to require central personnel agencies and the personnel offices in line departments to eliminate the numerous "unnecessary" rules and regulations they used to closely control managers' discretion in personnel matters. In order to make the personnel function a partner in building the effectiveness of public agencies, procedures had to be streamlined and simplified. Along these lines, in testimony before the Congress in 1978, then CSC Chairman Alan Campbell argued that the CSRA was needed to reduce "the accumulation of laws, regulations, and policies which have grown up over the last 95 years." He included the following in a long list of problems then confronting the federal civil service:

- Supervisors, employees, political leaders, and others were confused about what they could and could not do without violating essential merit principles.

- Excessive centralization of personnel authorities took many types of day-to-day personnel decisions out of the hands of line managers who nonetheless were held responsible for accomplishment in major program areas. Managers had to go through extensive paperwork justifications to obtain Civil Service Commission approval of relatively minor decisions.

- Overcentralized and restrictive systems for examining and selecting employees made it hard for managers to hire expeditiously the best qualified people and to meet their equal employment opportunity goals and timetables.

- Managers faced a confusing array of regulations and procedures standing in their way when they sought to reward good work performance, to discipline employees, or to remove employees whose performance was clearly inadequate and could not be improved.

- A jumble of laws, regulations, and special provisions affecting executive positions made it very difficult for department and bureau heads to utilize their staff effectively. (Campbell, 1978)

According to Campbell and other supporters of the CSRA, problems such as these could be solved only if the personnel system shifted from a *regulatory* to a *service* orientation. In these terms, the proper role of the central personnel agency was to provide general policy guidance and technical assistance to line departments in such areas as EEO, selection, performance appraisal, and training. Within the limits set by law and negotiated contracts, control over the details of the personnel function and authority to tailor practices to specific conditions were to be left to the departments. Finally, a central agency such as the OPM should conduct research and development programs, exercise quality control through periodic evaluations of departmental policies and practices, and provide leadership across the spectrum of human resources challenges facing the government.

Campbell suggested that separate personnel systems were needed for high-level executives and senior career administrators. The success of specific programs, as well as the entire federal establishment, depended heavily on the loyalty, expertise, and energy of this group. Traditional civil service systems, however, did not make any special provisions to assure strong executive leadership and effective use of administrative talent. Procedural flexibility, appropriate incentives, and well-planned career development systems for executives were needed.

This was the rationale for senior executive services (SES), such as that established in the federal government by the CSRA and now found in some twenty states. In an SES, rank is in the person, not in the job or position; this arrangement is supposed to facilitate mobility across agency lines and to promote the emergence of a highly professional cadre of experienced senior administrators. In addition to enhanced mobility, SES personnel systems usually allow some discretion in setting the entrance salaries of executives, and they typically use some form of merit pay and bonuses instead of automatic step and inflation increases. Federal SES members are untenured and may be returned to lower-level positions if their performance is less than satisfactory—a further element of flexibility for agency management.

A central item on the reform agenda during this time was giving management the capacity to reward good performers and to discipline and remove poor performers who did not improve the quality of their work. This meant that sound, valid, and credible performance appraisal systems had to be developed and competently administered in conjunction with merit pay plans. Under the previous personnel systems, few incentives to carefully measure performance existed, and complex, drawn-out, appeals procedures often discouraged supervisors' efforts to remove unsatisfactory employees. Merit pay plans were very helpful in getting legislative approval of civil service reform packages on the federal and state levels, but they proved to be very difficult to implement, and evaluations of their effects on performance were at best inconclusive. This reality did not dampen enthusiasm for the concept in many states and localities.

President Carter, of course, had very little time to implement the CSRA along lines he had intended, and, with Ronald Reagan's election, Alan Campbell was replaced as director of OPM in 1980. His successor was Donald Devine, a conservative Republican who believed the federal bureaucracy was dominated by "liberals." On the federal level, and in many of the states and localities struggling to deal with new political and fiscal realities, civil service reform (and even the idea of civil service as an important and valuable part of American government) lost much of its momentum:

> Devine also had definite ideas about the proper role for the federal government's personnel agency. He rejected the new orientation espoused by Campbell, who emphasized OPM's role as a service agency, and as a management agency. This included, first, a renewed emphasis on the policing function. . ., including such "bedrock" personnel management concerns as proper application of classification standards. While budgets for many agency programs were cut, funding for evaluation and compliance activities was increased. . .in order to carry out an aggressive oversight function. (Ban, 1984, pp. 54–55)

By the mid-1980s, reform along lines advocated by the authors of the CSRA was stalled, at least on the federal level. One student of the CSRA concluded that "one can question whether the newly created organizational structures have succeeded in improving either the protection of the rights of individuals or the clarity and efficiency of the personnel function" (Ban, 1984, p. 58). By the end of the decade, serious concerns about the capacity of the civil service to function in an effective and responsive manner on all levels of government were developing.

In its 1989 report, the National Commission on the Public Service (also known as the Volcker Commission) observed that the need for a highly competent and trustworthy public service in the United States was steadily growing, not diminishing. On both counts, however, the Commission saw a serious deterioration taking place. Its recommendations for changes in federal personnel policies and practices were intended to address what some called the "quiet crisis" of the civil service. The Commission's "central message" was clearly stated: the United States needed to build a national consensus on the importance of a truly excellent public service:

> In essence, we call for a renewed sense of commitment by all Americans to the highest traditions of the public service—to a public service responsive to the political will of the people and also pro-

tective of our constitutional values; to a public service able to cope with complexity; to a public service attractive to the young and talented from all parts of our society and also capable of earning the respect of all our citizens. (National Commission on the Public Service, 1989, p. 1)

While the Commission's elevated vision of the values that should be embodied by the American public service were as old as the Republic, translating that vision (or elements of it) into specific policies and administrative means enjoying broad public support had always been difficult. In part, this problem could be attributed to deeply entrenched public suspicions about "big government" and "bureaucrats." Between 1965 and 1989, the fragile base of public support enjoyed by the public service on all levels of government was greatly eroded by a continuous barrage of partisan attacks, unsatisfied expectations, scandals such as Watergate, fiscal stress, and outright neglect by those in positions of political leadership. In 1990, Lane and Wolf were prepared to describe the condition of the federal personnel system in alarming terms:

Today's federal personnel system is the product of years of neglect—the offspring of a condition where political and ideological agendas predominated over professional concerns. As a result, the personnel mechanisms in place are in disarray and ill-prepared to deal with the problems facing the nation. . . .Piecemeal attempts by the executive branch and the Congress to address specific problems in the system have not arrested its decline. (Lane and Wolf, 1990, p. 17)

Although the federal government was by far the most "studied" in these terms, many states, localities, and school districts appeared to have similar problems. By the end of the 1980s, evidence of declining competence—existing or impending shortages of needed human resources and slumping morale in many areas of the nation's public service—was accumulating at a rate that could no longer be ignored. In many instances, the public sector was fighting a losing battle to recruit and retain people with the skills and abilities needed to meet the complex technical and social challenges confronting governments. Civil service reforms calculated to improve productivity, agency effectiveness, and responsiveness to political leadership had produced, at best, mixed results. Public indifference, partisan attacks, and increasingly noncompetitive rates of pay and fringe benefits lowered morale and dampened enthusiasm for careers in the public service (Goodsell, 1994).

In response to these concerns, the National Commission on the Public Service urged the Bush administration to pursue 15 goals related to personnel policies and human resources management. While each of these goals addressed specific issues, the Commission's general purpose was to focus attention on three basic problem areas: the higher civil service, recruitment and retention, and performance and productivity.

THE HIGHER CIVIL SERVICE

Here, the Commission called for a renewed commitment to building and maintaining a high-quality senior federal service. Like the authors of the 1978 CSRA, the Commission recognized that a competent personnel system on this level is essential because these are the people who are responsible for the administration of federal agencies and for the coordinated policy direction of the federal establishment. It is the higher civil service that provides much of the day-to-day expertise and leadership necessary for successful governance. Public confidence and trust in government depends heavily on the extent to which those at the top of the civil service are seen to be competent, responsive, and consistently honest and fair. The Commission's evaluation of the condition of the higher civil service, along with those of other knowledgeable observers, had to be considered alarming.

> Unfortunately, there is growing evidence that the supply of talented managers, political and career, in government is dwindling. Among presidential appointees. . .turnover rates have become a serious problem. . . .Among career senior executives. . .over half say that if a suitable job outside government became available, they would take it. . . .Today, sadly, fewer than half the government's most senior and most successful executives are willing to recommend a career in public life to their children. (National Commission on the Public Service, 1989, p. 12)

RECRUITMENT AND RETENTION OF QUALIFIED PERSONNEL

The Commission added its voice to those warning of serious weaknesses in government's ability to attract "the best and the brightest" to the career public service. Recruiting talented people with needed technical and professional skills had become difficult in an increasingly competitive labor market. Similarly, turnover and early retirements were undermining the foundation of experience and skill federal agencies needed to function effectively.

The national government's ability to offer competitive pay and benefits had steadily deteriorated during the 1980s, and one report on the situation stated: "according to recent studies, federal pay and benefits trail the private sector by an estimated 7 to 24 percent for comparable jobs, with the gap growing larger every year" (Levine and Kleeman, 1986, p. 6). On the executive level, the gaps were even more striking. For responsibilities comparable to those of federal Level II Executives, private executives made about eight times the pay. In specific "shortage" occupations such as accountants and computer specialists, federal pay was as much as 45 percent behind that in the private sector.

PERFORMANCE AND PRODUCTIVITY

The third area of concern addressed by the Commission was the ability of the federal personnel management system to promote and sustain a "culture of performance." It recognized that the American public had every right to expect that civil servants would work hard to deliver programs in an efficient, timely, and responsive manner. However, simply demanding high levels of performance was not enough. The personnel system had to be supportive. As the Commission's report stated:

> The commitment to performance cannot long survive, however, unless the government provides adequate pay, recognition for jobs done well, accessible training, and decent working conditions. Quality service must be recognized, rewarded, and constantly reinforced. It is not enough to exhort the work force to do better— government must provide tangible signals that performance matters. (National Commission on the Public Service, 1989, p. 34)

Although "pay-for-performance" systems in various forms had been a very popular idea on all levels of government in the United States for some time, efforts to implement them had proven to be far more of a challenge than most reformers had anticipated. Funding of merit pay and bonus plans was often so inadequate that the intended connections between performance and compensation often were not achieved, especially in the minds of public employees, many of whom became openly skeptical and suspicious of management's motives. Likewise, efforts to develop performance appraisal systems

---

BULLETIN

From The Report of the National Performance Review:

"Year after year, layer after layer, the rules have piled up. The [MSPB] reports there are now 850 pages of federal personnel law...1,300 pages of OPM regulations on how to implement those laws and another 10,000 pages of guidelines.... Costs to the taxpayer for this personnel quagmire are enormous. In total, 54,000 people work in federal personnel positions. We spend billions of dollars for these staff to classify each employee within a highly complex system of some 459 job series, 15 grades and 10 steps...."

Source: *From Red Tape to Results: Creating a Government That Works Better & Costs Less* (Washington, DC: U.S. Government Printing Office, 1993), pp. 20–21.

that truly discriminated among levels of performance and enjoyed broadly based support in the workforce had been largely unsuccessful (National Research Council, 1991). In 1989, the U.S. General Accounting Office (GAO) reported that its preliminary examination revealed widespread unhappiness with the federal government's Performance Management and Recognition System (PMRS). Since the PMRS had been designed to overcome the weaknesses of the agency merit pay plans initially established under the CSRA, the GAO concluded that its apparent failure to remedy the situation after some four years was reason for concern, and it concluded that "[t]he lack of an effective program for motivating employees at these levels [GS 13–15] could seriously impede creation of what the [Volcker] Commission called 'a culture of performance' in government" (U.S. General Accounting Office, 1989, p. 3).

The Volcker Commission's report set the stage for renewed reform efforts across a broad front of organizational and personnel-related functions. On the federal level, this process began in earnest with the Clinton-Gore "reinvention" and "reengineering" initiatives, which continue to emphasize decentralization, deregulation, simplification, cooperative labor relations, *and* downsizing the federal workforce. These reforms reflect a broader shift away from support for traditional bureaucratic forms of organization in both the public and private sectors. In the words of a recent GAO report:

> The necessity to improve performance in the face of steady or declining resources led some organizations...to make radical changes in the way they manage people...in place of centralized, rule-based systems, they are creating decentralized, flatter, more flexible arrangements. And in place of highly detailed rules to manage their employees, they are relying increasingly on a well-defined mission, a clearly articulated vision, and a coherent organizational culture to form the foundation for the key business systems and processes they use to ensure the successful outcome of their operations. Recognizing that people are central to any organization's success, these organizations give their managers greater prerogatives to manage and their employees greater opportunities to participate in the decisions that affect them and their work. (U.S. General Accounting Office, 1995a, p. 3)

In the same report, the GAO identified several "interrelated principles common to these organizations," including some that directly apply to the personnel function:

- Holding managers accountable for achieving results, rather than rigidly making them do things "by the book."
- Integrating personnel functions into the organization's

planning and policy-making activities on all levels by decentralizing and deregulating them.

■ Treating employee development and training as an investment required to keep up with changing citizen needs, to meet new skills requirements, and to build overall organizational capacities.

■ Valuing people as assets to be developed and encouraged, as opposed to costs that should be minimized. (U.S. General Accounting Office, 1995a, pp. 5–6)

The National Commission on the State and Local Public Service (1993) issued a widely read report that identified what it considered to be important reform needs on the state and local levels. The Commission was chaired by William F. Winter, so it is usually called the Winter Commission. The report of the National Performance Review (1993) issued by Vice President Al Gore and the Winter Report shared the general orientation described above by the GAO, and both recommended extensive decentralization of the personnel function, delegation of hiring and other authorities to the agency level, and streamlining of personnel processes such as recruitment, hiring, position classification, and appeals (Thompson, 1994). Highlights of the NPR recommendations included the following:

■ That OPM abolish its central registers of applicants and authorize federal agencies to set up their own recruitment and examining programs.

■ That agencies be given greater flexibility in classifying and paying employees.

■ That agencies be allowed to establish their own performance management programs for improvement of performance on the individual and organizational levels.

■ That all agencies establish procedures for resolving disputes that serve as alternatives to established systems in the EEO and labor relations areas, and that OPM eliminate its regulations covering agency grievance systems, so they could tailor their approaches to various situations.

■ That a creative, flexible, and responsive hiring systems be created and that the standard application forms (most notably Standard Form 171) be abolished, which was done in late 1994.

■ That unnecessary red tape be done away with and the entire personnel system be simplified, in part by phasing out the entire Federal Personnel Manual, which was done in late 1993. (U.S. General Accounting Office, 1995b)

Both reports recommended changes that should increase the authority of chief executives over personnel policy through control over top-level appointments and organizational structures. There were some significant differences. In Frank Thompson and Beryl Radin's words: "the most fundamental difference between the Winter and Gore reports involves their orientation toward downsizing. The Gore report sees reinvention as a vehicle for reducing the number of federal employees [see Chapter 1] and saving money, whereas the Winter report offers no such prescription for state and local governments" (Thompson and Radin, 1997, p. 15).

On one level, Civil Service Reform II focuses on improving the competence and productivity of civil servants. At the beginning of the twenty-first century, however, reform means far more than that. It has also come to mean making changes in personnel policies, forms of administrative organization, and day-to-day practices that will meaningfully improve the likelihood that public employees will be highly responsive to the policy goals and directives of elected officials and, through them, to the public interest. Once the great engine of accountability and responsiveness, the patronage has steadily declined in scale and importance and, in an era that requires technical competence and increasing professionalization of the public workforce, no widely accepted functional equivalent has emerged. The highly protective and semi-autonomous personnel systems that emerged from Civil Service Reform I are now closely associated in the minds of the nation's political leaders with a less than fully competent and often unresponsive public bureaucracy (Barzelay, 1992). The challenge is now to "invent" public personnel systems that support the merit principle in practice, allow elected executives to establish firm policy control over the bureaucracy, and do both in a manner consistent with achieving a high level of agency performance and productivity. Most importantly, these new systems must enjoy broad public support and confidence (Hays, 1996).

OTHER NEW AND CONTINUING CHALLENGES

Hopefully, it is clear that American public personnel administration has always confronted a dynamic and changing social, political, economic, and technological environment. If anything, the pace of change in all of these areas will accelerate during the first decade of the new century. The potential for challenging intersections between trends will likely increase, as will the demands on personnel specialists to contribute to solving the management and policy problems that these intersections generate (Hays, 1997). One such area is the changing demography of the American workforce outlined in Chapter 1 (Johnston et al., 1987). The search for effective responses to growing pressures to improve the "family friendliness" of public agencies will continue. Managing an increasingly diverse workforce will almost certainly become a major human resources training and development concern (Pomerleau, 1994). Increasingly, the labor pool from which public agencies will draw their personnel will be composed of women, ethnic and racial minorities, and immigrants. Currently, these groups make up about half of the workforce; however, over the next 10 years, it is estimated that they will contribute over 80 percent of the net additions. As pointed out in Chapter 1, along with the rest of the U.S. population, the public service will be gradually "aging," and this trend will bring with it a variety of challenges in the areas of health care, retirement programs, age discrimination, and job design (Elliott, 1995). As the skills demanded by jobs in the public sector continue to increase, heavy investments in employee training and education and executive development will be required.

Public as well as private employers also will continue to face a host of social, legal, and organizational challenges flowing from larger social problems such as violence, inadequate education and training, and poverty. Health problems in the workplace, such as drug addiction and alcoholism (substance abuse) and AIDS, will continue to demand sustained attention. Implementing laws and public policies intended to prevent discrimination against minority groups, handicapped persons, and women will be an ongoing responsibility of public personnel specialists, as well as line managers.

Emerging areas of concern include the direction and pace of technological change and the growing popularity of privatization as the answer to public demands for lower taxes, fewer bureaucrats, and better public services. The pace of change and innovation in communications, data processing, and other computer-related technologies, for example, has required and will continue to require large investments in employee training and development programs, since skills become obsolete very quickly. New technologies, such as desktop computers and local area networks built around servers, have the potential to profoundly change skills needs of public agencies. The knowledge (intellectual technology) required by virtually all organizational roles, from those who operate and maintain increasingly complicated machinery to white-collar professionals of all kinds, is constantly expanding as well. Attracting, retaining, and sustaining the high-skill or knowledge-based workforce of the twenty-first century will be a major challenge for public employers (Shareef, 1994).

Likewise, the need to determine how best to operate public personnel systems in an environment where many services traditionally

provided by public employees have been shifted to private-sector contractors will need to be confronted. Using market mechanisms—particularly competition for contracts to provide services such as garbage collection, public transportation, security, prisons, water and sewer
systems, and social programs—has become a very popular option. In
addition to current federal support for privatization under the National
Performance Review, the states and localities have been very active:

> The 1993 Council of State Governments' survey found that state
> agencies responsible for social services, transportation, mental health
> care, corrections, health, and education had all increased privatiza-
> tion activities since 1988. The Council reported. . .a trend toward
> expanded privatization across major state agencies. According to the
> International City/County Management Association, city govern-
> ments have also increased the number of and types of services con-
> tracted, such as child welfare programs, health services, street main-
> tenance, and data processing. (U.S. General Accounting Office,
> 1997, p. 2)

The GAO (1997) has observed that public employers "need to
develop strategies to help their workforces make the transition to a
private-sector environment" and it noted that a number of governments are taking steps along these lines, such as allowing public
employee groups to submit competitive bids along with private-
sector corporations, training to prepare workers for new jobs, and
"safety nets" for displaced workers (pp. 5–6). While privatization
may reduce or eliminate a governments' need for certain categories
of worker, it is likely to increase the demand for personnel skilled in
contract negotiations, contract administration, and monitoring of
contractors' performance.

CONCLUSION

In this chapter, we have provided a very general overview of the history of public personnel policies and practices in the United States
since its founding. While this history is certainly intrinsically interesting, it is most important here as the background or context needed to
understand the conditions, issues, and challenges *now* confronting
students and practitioners of public personnel administration. As
Steven Hays (1997) points out:

> Like other functions of public management, PPA's world has been
> rocked repeatedly in recent years. Fiscal crises, a brooding and hyper-
> critical public, and stunningly rapid changes in the personnel system's
> environment, highlighted by technological advances and momentous
> shifts in the labor force, have shaken the discipline's faith in many tra-

ditional practices. Among the numerous, interrelated forces that are reshaping the human resources landscape, volatile economic and political conditions clearly exert the most powerful influence. (p. 2)

DISCUSSION QUESTIONS

1. Can we really trust public managers to conduct agency personnel matters according to the merit principle without close supervision and enforcement by an outside agency, such as a civil service commission?
2. Is affirmative action necessary to protect the advances made by minorities and women in public employment, or have we reached the point at which equal employment opportunity is enough?
3. Is patronage necessary to assure that the bureaucracy will be responsive to the elected leadership and, if some is needed, how much?
4. Should public employees be required to take a leave of absence if they want to run for elective office, and, if elected, should they be required to resign or retire?
5. Can the merit principle be protected if public employee unions are allowed to negotiate personnel policies and procedures with management?
6. Given the evidence that it did not enhance agency performance, what political reasons might Director Donald Devine have had for favoring a centralized, regulatory role for OPM in its dealings with the departments of the federal government?

REFERENCES

Adarand Constructors v Peña, U.S. Secretary of Transportation (1995). WL347345.

Arnett v Kennedy (1974). 416 U.S. 134.

Aronson, Albert H. (1973). "Personnel Administration: The State and Local Picture." *Civil Service Journal,* Vol. 13, No. 3 (January–March), pp. 37–42.

Bailey v Richardson (1951). 341 U.S. 918.

Ban, Carolyn (1984). "Implementing Civil Service Reform: Structure and Strategy," in Patricia W. Ingraham and Carolyn Ban (eds.), *Legislating Bureaucratic Change: The Civil Service Reform Act of 1978* (Albany: State University of New York Press), pp. 42–62.

Barzelay, Michael (1992). *Breaking Through Bureaucracy: A New Vision for Managing in Government* (Berkeley: University of California Press).

Bishop v Wood (1976). 426 U.S. 341.

Board of Regents v Roth (1972). 408 U.S. 564, 92 S. Ct. 2701, 33 L. Ed. 548.

Branti v Finkel (1980). 445 U.S. 507.

California Legislative Analyst Office (1996). *Proposition 209: Prohibition Against Discrimination or Preferential Treatment By State and Other Public Entities* (Initiative Constitutional Amendment), Argument in Favor of Proposition 209 (http://www.ss.ca.gov/Vote96/html/BP/209yesarg.htm).

Campbell, Alan K. (1978). "Testimony on Civil Service Reform and Organization." *Civil Service Reform*, Hearings of the U.S. House Committee on Post Office and Civil Service (Washington, DC: U.S. Government Printing Office).

Daniel, Christopher (1992). "Constitutionalizing Merit? Practical Implications of Elrod, Branti, and Rutan." *Review of Public Personnel Administration*, Vol. 12, No. 2 (January–April), pp. 26–34.

Dotson, Arch (1955). "The Emerging Doctrine of Privilege in Public Employment." *Public Administration Review*, Vol. 15, No. 2 (Spring), pp. 77–88.

Elliott, Robert H., ed. (1995). "Symposium on Human Resource Management and the Aging of the Workforce." *Review of Public Personnel Administration*, Vol 15, No. 2 (Spring), pp. 5–83.

Elrod v Burns (1976). 427 U.S. 96 S. Ct., 2673.

Fish, Carl R. (1904). *The Civil Service and the Patronage* (Cambridge, MA: Harvard University Press).

Freedman, Anne (1994). *Patronage: An American Tradition* (Chicago: Nelson-Hall Publishers).

Goodsell, Charles T. (1994). *The Case for Bureaucracy*, 3rd ed. (Chatham, NJ: Chatham House Publishers, Inc.).

Gore, Al (1993). *Report of the National Performance Review: Creating a Government That Works Better & Costs Less* (Washington, DC: U.S. Government Printing Office), September.

Griggs v Duke Power (1971). 401 U.S. 424.

Hays, Steven (1996). "The 'State of the Discipline' in Public Personnel Administration." *Public Administration Quarterly*, Vol. 20, No. 3 (Fall), pp. 285–304.

———— (1997). "Reinventing the Personnel Function: Lessons Learned From a Hope-Filled Beginning in One State." *American Review of Public Administration*, Vol. 27, No. 4 (December), pp. 324–342.

Johnston, W.B., et al. (1987). *Workforce 2000: Work and Workers for the Twenty-first Century* (Indianapolis, IN: Hudson Institute).

Lane, Larry M., and Wolf, James F. (1990). *The Human Resource Crisis in the Public Sector: Rebuilding the Capacity to Govern* (New York: Quorum Books).

Levine, Charles H., and Kleeman, Rosslyn S. (1986). *The Quiet Crisis of the Civil Service: The Federal Personnel System at the Crossroads* (Washington, DC: National Academy of Public Administration).

Martin v Wilks (1989). 109 S. Ct. 2180.

McAuliffe v Mayor of New Bedford (1892). 155 Mass. 216, 29 N. E. 517.

Merrill, Harwood F. (1960). *Classics in Management* (New York: American Management Association).

Miller, Douglas T., ed. (1972). *The Nature of Jacksonian Democracy* (New York: John Wiley & Sons).

Mosher, Frederick C. (1968). *Democracy and the Public Service* (New York: Oxford University Press).

National Commission on the Public Service (1989). *Leadership for America: Rebuilding the Public Service* (Washington, DC: National Commission on the Public Service).

National Research Council (1991). *Pay for Performance: Evaluating Performance Appraisal and Merit Pay* (Washington, DC: National Academy Press).

O'Brian, David M. (1997). "The First Amendment and the Public Sector," in Phillip J. Cooper and Chester A. Newland (eds.), *Handbook of Public Law and Administration* (San Francisco: Jossey-Bass Publishers), pp. 259–273.

Oklahoma v United States Civil Service Commission (1947). 330 U.S. 127.

Patterson v McLean Credit Union (1989). 109 S. Ct. 2363.

Perry v Sinderman (1972). 408 U.S. 593, S. Ct. 2694, 33 L. Ed. 2d 570.

Pickering v Board of Education (1968). 391 U.S. 563, 88 S. Ct. 1731, 20 L. Ed. 3d 811.

Pomerleau, Raymond (1994). "A Desideratum for Managing the Diverse Workforce" *Review of Public Personnel Administration*, Vol. 14, No. 1 (Winter), pp. 85–100.

Price Waterhouse v Hopkins (1989). 109 S. Ct. 1775.

Regents of the University of California v Bakke (1978). 98 S. Ct. 2733.

Riccucci, Norma A. (1997). "Will Affirmative Action Survive into the Twenty-first Century," in Carolyn Ban and Norma Riccucci (eds.), *Public Personnel Management: Current Concerns, Future Challenges* (White Plains, NY: Longman), pp. 57–72.

Riordon, William L. (1963). *Plunkitt of Tammany Hall* (New York: E. P. Dutton).

Roethlisberger, F. J., and Dickson, William J. (1939). *Management and the Worker* (Cambridge, MA: Harvard University Press).

Rosenbloom, David H. (1971). "Some Political Implications of the Drift Toward a Liberation of Federal Employees." *Public Administration Review*, Vol. 31, No. 4 (July–August), pp. 420–426.

———— and Carroll, James D. (1990). *Toward Constitutional Competence: A Casebook for Public Administrators* (Englewood Cliffs, NJ: Prentice Hall).

Rutan v Republican Party of Illinois (1990). 110 S. Ct. 2734.

Schiesl, Martin J. (1977). *The Politics of Efficiency* (Berkeley: University of California Press).

Shareef, Reginald (1994). "Skill-Based Pay in the Public Sector: An Innovative Idea." *Review of Public Personnel Administration*, Vol. 14, No. 3 (Summer), pp. 60–74.

Simon, Herbert A., Smithburg, Donald W., and Thompson, Victor A. (1950). *Public Administration* (New York: Alfred A. Knopf).

Stahl, O. Glenn (1962). *Public Personnel Administration*, 5th ed. (New York: Harper and Row).

State of Texas v Hopwood (1996). WL 227009.

Thompson, Frank J., ed. (1994). "The Winter Commission Report: Is Deregulation the Answer for Public Personnel Management?" *Review of Public Personnel Administration*, Vol. 14, No. 2 (Spring), pp. 5–76.

Thompson, Frank J., and Radin, Beryl A. (1997). "Reinventing Public Personnel Management: The Winter and Gore Initiatives," in Carolyn Ban and Norma M. Riccucci (eds.), *Public Personnel Management: Current Concerns, Future Challenges* (White Plains, NY: Longman), pp. 3–20.

Thurber, Karl T, Jr. (1993). "Big, Little, Littler: Synthesizing Hatch Act-Based Political Activity Legislation Research." *Review of Public Personnel Administration*, Vol. 13, No. 1 (Winter), pp. 38–51.

United Public Workers v Mitchell (1947). 330 U.S. 75, 67 S. Ct. 556, 91 L. Ed. 754.

United States Civil Service Commission v National Association of Letter Carriers, AFL-CIO (1973). 98 S. Ct. 2880, 27 L. Ed. 2d 796.

United Steel Workers of America v Weber (1979). 443 U.S. 193.

U.S. Commission on Civil Rights (1969). *For All the People. . .By All the People: A Report on Equal Opportunity in State and Local Government Employment* (Washington, DC: U.S. Government Printing Office).

U.S. General Accounting Office (1989). *Pay for Performance: Interim Report on the Performance Management and Recognition System* (Washington DC: GAO), May.

—— (1995a). *Transforming the Civil Service: Building the Workforce of the Future* (Washington, DC: GAO/GGD-96-35), December.

—— (1995b). *Federal Personnel Management: Views on Selected NPR Human Resource Recommendations* (Washington, DC: GAO/GGD-95-221BR), September.

—— (1997). *Privatization: Lessons Learned by State and Local Governments* (Washington, DC: GAO/GGD-97-48), September.

U.S. Library of Congress (1976). *History of Civil Service Merit Systems of the United States and Selected Foreign Countries* (Washington, DC: U.S. Government Printing Office), December 31.

U.S. Office of Personnel Management (1998). "Political Activity: Federal Employees Residing in Designated Localities." *Federal Register,* Vol. 63, No. 20 (January 30), pp. 4555–4560.

Van Riper, Paul P. (1958). *History of the United States Civil Service* (New York: Harper and Row).

Wards Cove Packing Co. v Atonio (1989). 109 S. Ct. 2115.

SUGGESTED READINGS

Bekke, Hans, Perry, James, and Toonen, Theo, eds. (1995). *Comparative Civil Service Reform* (Bloomington: Indiana University Press).

Caldwell, Lynton K. (1944). *The Administrative Theories of Hamilton and Jefferson* (Chicago: University of Chicago Press).

Downs, George W., and Larkey, Patrick D. (1986). *The Search for Government Efficiency* (New York: Random House).

Ingraham, Patricia W. (1995). *The Foundation of Merit: Public Service in the American Democracy* (Baltimore, MD: The Johns Hopkins University Press).

—— and Kettl, Donald F., eds. (1992). *Agenda for Excellence: Public Service in America* (Chatham, NJ: Chatham House).

Osborne, David, and Gaebler, Ted (1992). *Reinventing Government: How the Entrepreneurial Spirit Is Transforming the Public Sector* (Reading, MA: Addison-Wesley).

U.S. Civil Service Commission (1973). *Biography of an Ideal: A History of the Federal Civil Service* (Washington, DC: CSC).

White, Leonard D. (1948). *The Federalists* (New York: Macmillan).

—— (1951). *The Jeffersonians* (New York: Macmillan).

—— (1954). *The Jacksonians* (New York: Macmillan).

Chapter THREE

Personnel and Organizational Effectiveness

Public personnel administration in the United States has undergone a pronounced shift in emphasis over the past 20 years (Hays, 1989, pp. 113–114). While *compliance* or enforcement of merit system laws and regulations is still an important function, positive support of public managers' efforts to improve *organizational* performance has become a high priority (Jorgensen, Fairless, and Patton, 1996).

The contemporary emphasis on the managerial side of public personnel's responsibilities does not mean that other values have been set aside. Establishing personnel policies and practices that promote, as opposed to undermine, organizational performance is certainly a major concern, but it is not the *only* objective. Other values are important. As Buchanan and Millstone (1979) observe, "numerous structural embodiments of democratic morality" may be found in any personnel system, and any of "these structural instruments for the protection of individual rights is capable of disrupting or slowing program operations, in the interest of securing *priority* attention for the 'equal protection' or 'procedural due process' rights of individual citizens" (pp. 273–274). In other words, the values underpinning the operations of public personnel systems encompass far more than using people as instruments of organizational efficiency and goal accomplishment. Protecting the dignity of individuals, assuring their legal and constitutional rights, and creating a fair and equitable employment relationship also are important values to be realized.

In this chapter, we will set forth a *framework* for thinking about the ways public personnel might make positive contributions to managerial and organizational performance. Two broad areas of organizational activity will be examined: (1) attracting human resources from outside the organization that are needed to achieve required levels of performance; and (2) utilizing, motivating, and developing the organizational workforce. Organizational success in both areas is necessary: "Because human resource management focuses largely on the acquisition and utilization of human capital [the knowledge, skill and experience possessed by individuals], it. . .has attained new significance. . . .In fact, many management scholars argue that human resource management is now an important, perhaps *the* most important determinant of organizational effectiveness" (Perry, 1993). Three strategies for obtaining reliable access to human resources are *competition, cooperation,* and *incorporation* (Yuchtman and Seashore, 1967).

THE COMPETITIVE STRATEGY

Competitive approaches stress acquiring human resources by doing better than other organizations in the labor market. Several areas of organizational performance are involved. *First,* as an employer, the organization must be able to offer attractive pay and benefits, as well as a psychologically supportive and physically safe working environment. *Second,* it is important to maintain the organization's prestige as a place to work. Positions in high-prestige agencies often attract qualified people who could make the same or more money in less prominent jobs. *Third,* the organization should have the internal flexibility needed to make timely adjustments to conditions in the labor market. The capacity to align recruitment processes, hiring procedures, compensation plans, and job designs with the *available* pool of human resources is a great advantage. For public employers, these are often very difficult objectives to meet.

Competitive strategies do not mesh easily with the dominant values and practices of the traditional merit systems. The current wave of change and innovation (Civil Service Reform II) has increased agency flexibility in areas such as position classification and selection, and it has strengthened line management's hand in pay administration in some states and localities as well as the federal government. Many personnel systems, nevertheless, are still tightly centralized and heavily rules-oriented (Hays, 1989, pp. 115–117). In some jurisdictions, emphasis is placed on compliance to formal procedures, as opposed to managerial "bottom-line" criteria, such as competitive success in the labor market.

In the public sector, important political, legal, and ethical considerations set limits on the degree to which competitive advantage can be the rationale driving personnel policies and practices. Equal employment opportunity policies, position classification systems, and legislatively mandated pay scales, for example, may require recruitment, selection, and hiring procedures that limit management's discretion and, hence, its capacity to act quickly and conclusively in situations where private corporations are competing for the same people.

Public personnel systems are expected to pursue multiple and, at times, conflicting goals. Unlike their private counterparts, public employers routinely are subject to constant scrutiny by an audience made up of many groups who are intensely interested in one or more phases of personnel administration, from recruitment to retirement. These "stakeholders," including, to name just a few, veterans, minorities, private contractors, and public employee unions, may resist policies intended to increase competitiveness because they see them as threatening other values such as pay equity, equal opportunity, political neutrality, and the "free market." For broad public interest and more narrow partisan reasons, legislators and elected executives are seldom eager to relinquish control over key aspects of personnel policy (Wechsler, 1994). It is, therefore, highly unlikely that the competitive strategies used by public employers can ever be as narrowly organization-centered as those of many businesses. This is not to imply that public employers cannot compete effectively with the private sector for human resources under any conditions. It does mean, however, that they are often required to be very persistent, as well as creative.

Pay, benefits, working conditions, and career opportunities are key elements of a public agency's competitive position. In the long term, the attractiveness of the pay and benefits offered by public employers will vary in relation to economic conditions. A slow or recessionary economy usually makes it easier to attract and retain high-quality employees, since jobs are hard to find. During periods of expansion, when profits are high and good jobs are plentiful, public-sector recruitment suffers and highly mobile employees are more likely to leave for better-paying jobs in the private sector.

Historically, pay schedules and benefits that are legislatively set have tended to adjust slowly and often inadequately to changes in the labor market, but accurate generalized statements about governments' competitiveness are difficult to make. On one hand, for some categories of scientists, professionals, and technicians, comparatively low salaries have made the public sector an unattractive place to work. On the other, for many jobs, public employers consistently have been able to offer prevailing rates of pay and relatively good benefits (e.g., health insurance, retirement plans, and job security). During the 1970s and 1980s, for example, government's competitive position eroded across a wide range of jobs as inflation, the "taxpayers' revolt," and "bureaucrat bashing" had their effects on budgetary priorities and fiscal policies across the country (Levine, 1986, pp. 195–206). As the Volcker Commission pointed out, by the late 1980s, the federal government's inability to compete for talented college graduates and highly qualified professionals had reached crisis proportions.

Public employers mainly rely on legislative appropriations and executive support for the money needed to compete, but widespread public opposition to increasing taxes to fund pay raises means that politicians' backing often is not forthcoming. Governments, in other words, have been told to substantially increase the productivity of public employees, rather than asking for larger budgets to cover growing citizen demand for services. In turn, heavy pressure has been put on public personnel systems to use available funds and employees to maximum effect, rather than depending on general increases to keep pace (Matzer, 1988).

Pay increases and enhanced benefit plans traditionally have been implemented "across the board" without much attention paid to whether they were needed to maintain or build an agency's ability to compete effectively for specific categories of employees. At best, in competitive terms, they have been blunt instruments. For example, for some skills, an across-the-board increase will not be sufficient to keep the agency competitive in a particular location or region, but in another place the salary or wage actually will be higher than required. The same situation can apply to fringe benefits (Hudson Institute, 1986, p. 6). Reductions in personnel budgets, wage and salary "freezes," and other cutbacks typically have been insensitive to competitiveness issues. Recently, some public employers have instituted reforms such as "locality pay," pension portability, and pay-for-performance plans in an effort to create the flexibility needed to support a competitive approach to recruitment and retention.

Government's ability to attract and retain qualified personnel has been impaired by "fiscal stress," but an equally important factor may be the low status or prestige of public employment. As the Volcker Commission pointed out, attitudes about government work and beliefs about career opportunities are significant contributors to the competitiveness of the public sector. In one observer's words:

> Inevitably, negative rhetoric about our public servants becomes a self-fulfilling prophesy, making it difficult to recruit and maintain high quality people in government. The cumulative impact of the negative aspects of the lives of government officials at all levels—negative attitudes about government, demanding interest groups, unrelenting

news media, time consuming and rigid decision making procedures, and financial sacrifice—is making government service unnecessarily frustrating and unattractive to many. (Adams, 1984, p. 5)

The problems created by negative attitudes toward the public service are not restricted to the impact on those considering where to work; relations with influential actors in the organization's environment are affected as well. A vicious circle develops. Politicians, civic leaders, corporate executives, clientele groups, and voters may be hostile or at best noncommittal about the talent, commitment, and responsiveness of civil servants. Financial resources and political support are withheld, and the competitiveness of public employers is further reduced. In the long run, the quality of the public service actually declines, attitudes about it become more negative, and levels of support drop even more. One of the central goals of Civil Service Reform II, therefore, has been to improve the public's image of the competence, integrity, and responsiveness of the civil service. Along these lines, Alan Campbell stated that one of the purposes of the CSRA was to improve the reputation of the federal civil service and, more recently, the *Report of the National Performance Review* (1993), asserted that "Today's crisis is [that] people simply feel that government doesn't work" and "the central issue we face is not *what* government does, but *how* it works" (p. 2). In the section on cutting red tape and decentralizing personnel policy, the *Report* (NPR) said:

> To create an effective federal government, we must reform virtually the entire personnel system: recruiting, hiring, classification, promotion, pay, and reward systems. We must make it easier for federal managers to hire the workers they need, to reward those who do good work, and to fire those who do not. (p. 22)

The NPR argued that adaptiveness and flexibility are often keys to competitive success. Accepting the Volcker Commission's conclusion that "the complexity of the hiring process often drives all but the most dedicated away," the NPR recommended that all departments and agencies be given "authority to conduct their own recruiting and examining for all positions, and abolish all central registers and standard application forms" (pp. 22–23). The reasoning was that, to be competitive, federal agencies must be able to respond to the conditions they face in an effective and timely manner, and deregulation and decentralization make it much easier for agencies to do so. They now are able to seek and secure "delegation agreements" with OPM that permit extensive authority related to staffing functions (U.S. Office of Personnel Management, 1998).

Even if they are able to offer competitive pay and benefits, and have a reasonably good public image, public agencies may have difficulty locating and attracting enough candidates having skills and other qualities that are in high demand. Supply may not meet requirements and, although it normally will adjust to demand over time, in the relatively short term, there may be serious shortfalls in specific skills categories. This kind of situation is caused by a number of factors, including limited capacities of sources such as universities and technical schools, long training or apprenticeship periods, policies of regulatory or licensing bodies, demographic trends, and social biases for and against certain kinds of work.

Eventually, the labor market probably will respond, but matching supply to demand may take several years or more and, as school teachers, aerospace engineers, and others working in fields requiring extensive education and experience can testify, maintaining such a balance is not easy. In contrast, the unskilled and semiskilled component of the labor market responds rather quickly because these workers do not need a great deal of education, training, or experience. However, as we have already noted, the public sector is becoming increasingly professionalized, and its skill requirements are constantly rising. Consequently, a passive approach that fails to monitor organizational needs and to anticipate labor market conditions leaves the public employer open to a performance-threatening situation: the chronic inability to recruit and retain persons for certain key high-skill positions.

One way to improve the match between agency needs and available workers is to make adjustments in internal task structures and technologies. Here, personnel specialists are in a position to make major contributions to human resources planning capacities of public agencies (Ospina, 1992). It is often possible to redesign jobs and to restructure relationships among jobs in ways that improve an organization's capacity to utilize those human resources available to it. Sometimes, positions can be simplified or broken down into several less complex sets of tasks, while others can be enlarged or "enriched" to take better advantage of employees' abilities and potential. Paraprofessionals may be used to reduce the numbers of highly trained, expensive, and scarce professionals such as doctors, registered nurses, lawyers, and engineers that an agency might need. With paraprofessional support, professional personnel may be used differently and more

BULLETIN

"Personnel departments spend thousands upon thousands of useless hours deciding whether such-and-such a job is a GS-12 or a GS-13, telling managers they cannot pay the salary they want to because the classification doesn't allow it, and blocking their efforts to reclassify people. Even when classification changes are approved, the process takes forever. In Massachusetts, where local governments have to get approval from the state, it can take two years."

Source: David Osborne and Ted Gaebler, *Reinventing Government* (Reading, MA: Addison-Wesley, 1992), p. 126.

efficiently. Mechanized, automated, or computerized systems can be installed to replace or supplement human resources in ways that reduce labor costs, lower or redistribute skills requirements, and increase overall productivity. Minimum position requirements and job progression may be altered to accommodate postentry upgrading and retraining; similarly, on-the-job training or educational opportunities can be provided in order to make it possible to fill positions through promotions and transfers.

Public personnel systems have long had the reputation of being unimaginative human resources planners, of legalistic rigidity in their approaches to job design and position classification, and of an inclination to assume that the labor market will respond readily to staffing needs. To the extent to which this reputation is deserved, it signals a serious competitive disability, an organizational weakness that is most evident when human resources are limited or a sellers' market exists. There is, of course, no reason why public employers must be internally inflexible or passive in the face of stiff competition and an other than perfect balance between supply and demand in the labor market.

ADMINISTRATIVE DESIGNS AND COMPETITIVENESS

Merit systems on all levels of government have relied on administrative arrangements that stress detailed control of the personnel function by a central authority and standardization of practices across governmental units or departments. Centralization of policy, rule making, and decision-making authority had its roots in two main goals of Civil Service Reform I: limiting management's influence over personnel matters and establishing neutral competence as the normative core of public personnel practices. While these administrative arrangements may have been effective in keeping the "rascals" out and seeing to it that the merit principle was insulated from the threat posed by extensive managerial discretion, they were notoriously slow, rigid, and insensitive to changing environmental conditions and expanding demands on public agencies. Increasingly complex and volatile environments place the stability-oriented administrative designs of traditional merit systems at a competitive disadvantage. Contemporary approaches to relationships between organizations and their environments emphasize the point that successful organizations employ administrative structures and processes that are well adapted to the specific environments they confront. In other words, from a competitive standpoint, an administrative structure is (or should be) a strategic response to a particular set of environmental conditions. Organizations that successfully deal with dynamic, diverse, and highly competitive conditions tend to rely heavily on decentralized decision making within broad policy guidelines, and they stress managerial flexibility and discretion on the operational levels.

When time and material resources are limited, competition is intense, and environmental conditions are rapidly changing, a structurally supported capacity to "read" or monitor the environment and to "tailor-make" organizational responses is needed. In practice, this means that the authority, expertise, and other resources necessary for diagnosing situations, making decisions, and implementing personnel strategies must be decentralized or diffused throughout an organization. One way of accomplishing this objective is to deploy personnel "generalists" as consultants to and resources for line managers who have the authority, for example, to make "on-the-spot" job offers as long as they adhere to general policies. Another structural option is to have a central personnel office for overall policy making, evaluation, and audit purposes, but to delegate day-to-day personnel operations to agency offices having extensive authority to develop policies and methods best suited to handling the competitive challenges presented by local conditions.

THE COOPERATIVE STRATEGY

Like competition, cooperation is a strategy designed to maintain organizational access to essential human resources. Basically, cooperation involves entering into mutually beneficial "agreements" with other organizations and resources-controlling actors in the environment. These arrangements may be bilateral or multilateral, and more or less formal, but in any case they involve commitments intended to reduce levels of uncertainty and risk faced by all of those involved (Thompson, 1967, pp. 25–38). Unlike competition, which usually results in "winners" and "losers," cooperative strategies focus on building or negotiating relationships that benefit *all* of the participants. We will focus here on three common forms of cooperation directly related to public personnel policy and administration—intergovernmental joint ventures, contracts with businesses and not-for-profit suppliers of goods and services, and negotiated labor agreements with public employee unions.

CREATING JOINT VENTURES

Public agencies may be able to address certain human resources problems by agreeing to pool or share their personnel, as well as other organizational capacities, under specified conditions. In addition to increasing organizational effectiveness by allowing these agencies to increase their quantitative and qualitative ability to handle problems, such as natural disasters, these negotiated arrangements may also lower the personnel costs of each participant. Multigovernment cooperative recruitment, testing, and placement services are feasible. Other types of intergovernmental cooperation include joint ventures to provide training for law enforcement personnel and agreements whereby police and fire departments use one another's personnel. In the training field, it has been possible for some state and local workers to attend federal training sessions that deal with problems or policy issues requiring intergovernmental action, such as those offered by the Federal Bureau of Investigation, the U.S. Internal Revenue Service, and the Federal Executive Institute (FEI). User-funded statewide or multistate regional training centers for police and firefighters provide services well beyond the individual capacities of the employers who send their personnel to these centers for basic or advanced training.

Direct sharing of personnel is possible under agreements negotiated between jurisdictions on the same or different levels of government. Cities may agree to share police and fire personnel under emergency, disaster, or other special conditions. Costs are shared and the participating jurisdictions usually retain "recall" rights, but emphasis is placed on recognizing interdependency and dealing with it through mutual support—as opposed to very expensive, perhaps futile, efforts to become self-sufficient. Within governmental units, interagency joint ventures are also feasible, an interesting example being the "cross-training" of workers in two or more organizations (e.g., police and fire departments) so that they are able to back each other up and, if need be, move from one job to another in response to shifting workloads.

Governments also contract with each other for services in functional areas such as law enforcement, fire protection, sanitation, streets and roads, and administration (Sonenblum, Kirlin, and Ries, 1977). Under these intergovernmental contracts, one government undertakes to provide services to another for a fee. For example, counties often "sell" police services to incorporated municipalities. Other services commonly contracted for by municipalities are water supply, sewage treatment, tax collections, and libraries.

Intergovernmental contracting is used by smaller jurisdictions because it is usually less expensive than building an in-house capacity to deliver a full range of services. It gives the user immediate access to established personnel systems, equipment, and skills of the supplier. It also appears that intergovernmental contracting may reduce operating costs to smaller communities, mainly because of the economies of scale enjoyed by large suppliers. From the provider's side, the contract allows it to sell unused or underutilized capacity, and to generate a "profit" that can be used to support and expand operations. Thus, in economic terms, the intergovernmental contract becomes a winning proposition for both parties.

CONTRACTING WITH PRIVATE CORPORATIONS AND NONPROFITS

Privatization is currently a popular option for the public sector, and governments on all levels are scrutinizing their operations to determine which might be more productively handled by outside contractors. While contracting out for goods and services is far from unusual in the United States, as noted in Chapter 2, fiscal stress and changing philosophies of government have generated considerable interest in and agitation for extending its scope to services ordinarily provided by public employees. Thus, parks and recreation, building inspection and maintenance, sanitation, fire and police services, prisons, and even general administration are among the many functions now considered reasonable possibilities for contracting-out.

Although competition among rival profit-oriented contractors is supposed to lower costs to the taxpayer, contracting creates a cooperative relationship between supplier and consumer, since they agree to help each other through an exchange. The same may be said for contractual arrangements with nonprofit organizations to deliver social and health services, such as child care, shelters, and medical clinics. An interesting cooperative approach to developing the large numbers of military officers needed during wartime, as well as "cold war," is the Reserve Officer Training Corps (ROTC) through which the Department of Defense taps into the capacities of civilian universities and colleges while providing funding to these institutions. In organization theorist James D. Thompson's words, contracting involves the negotiation of "an agreement for the exchange of performances in the future" (Thompson, 1967, pp. 34–36). Contracting, of course, is not cost-free in human resources terms; it is an alternative to the direct delivery of services, not a device for eliminating administrative oversight responsibilities, and contracts must be negotiated and administered by people with expertise in these areas.

From a human resources management point of view, contracting-out is potentially attractive for several reasons. First, under certain conditions, primarily the existence of active and genuine competition among alternative suppliers, it can lower the per-unit cost of public services. Second, contracting-out increases administrative flexibility. Rather than build expensive in-house capabilities involving long-term investments or "sunk costs," public agencies can "rent" the human and other resources of the contractor. This advantage is particularly important when public agencies are asked to carry out programs or to assume responsibilities requiring skills and technologies not readily available on an in-house basis, or when an activity is of a temporary nature. State departments of transportation (DOTs) provide a good illustration of this point. DOTs contract out the actual construction of new highways to private businesses that hire the needed personnel and provide the necessary equipment. When the highway is finished, the DOT and contractor part company unless they have negotiated another contract for maintenance services. The DOTs themselves focus on continuing activities such as project design and specifications, contract negotiation and administration, and fiscal management. Another interesting (and controversial) example is the federal government's use of private contractors to operate its nuclear weapons production facilities.

With contracting, programs can be terminated, reoriented, or downsized without the need to go through the demoralizing, costly, and protracted reductions-in-force (RIF) procedures that are typical of merit systems. The contractor takes on these risks and uncertainties. Also, in situations where private enterprises or not-for-profits are able to offer compensation packages superior to those available to public employers, it may be possible to use contracting to tap "expensive" human resources by avoiding personnel ceilings, inadequate wage and salary scales, and cumbersome staffing procedures. Finally, by shifting responsibility for day-to-day management to the contractor, governments may improve their ability to reduce or at least to slow the growth of administrative overhead costs; it may also be possible to escape having to add supervisory personnel as new programs are acquired or existing ones expanded.

The third category of reasons for contracting-out involves political factors. As the U.S. Department of Defense (DOD) amply illustrates, an extensive web of contractual relationships provides the foundation for a powerful political coalition. Private corporations and labor unions often come to rely heavily on the money and jobs they get through government contracts; they develop a vested interest in the political and budgetary "health" of public agencies such as the DOD. From an agency point of view, the active support of concerned (self-interested) contractors and other clientele groups is vitally important when budgets have to be defended

BULLETIN

"The thorniest problem in contracting an existing activity is what to do with the redundant government employees. This issue must be faced and resolved at the onset. The most successful approach minimizes the number who will lose jobs; it involves a hiring freeze, transfers, training, attrition, and jobs with the contractor."

Source: E.S. Savas, *Privatization: The Key to Better Government* (Chatham, NJ: Chatham House, 1987), p. 258.

against proposed cuts and, of course, when efforts are being made to expand or add new programs.

A related symbolic value of contracting is the ability to deflect criticism that governments are overgrown, inefficient, and encroaching on the proper domain of private enterprise. Since public attention is easily drawn to the size of the civil service, significant expansion is more than likely to produce attacks from those fearing tax increases, "creeping socialism," or "big government." In very practical terms, while contracting-out does not necessarily mean smaller budgets or even higher productivity in the long run, it is a way of acquiring the use of facilities and human resources without the political risks associated with having to request more money for more "bureaucrats."

Negotiated Labor Agreements

Although public attention is usually drawn to the adversarial side of labor–management relations, particularly strikes and other job actions in the public sector, collective bargaining is a process intended to provide a framework for long-term cooperation between employers and unions. A negotiated labor contract is a legally binding document detailing the terms and conditions under which management and the employee organization or union will jointly administer key elements of the personnel system. It also specifies how each side will supply the other with some of the "inputs" it needs to operate effectively, and it sets up mechanisms for resolving disputes between the parties that arise in the process of administering the contract.

Management typically agrees to pay clearly stipulated wages and salaries, to provide fringe benefits such as health care and pensions plans, and to maintain safe working conditions. Management may also reduce uncertainty for the union by agreeing to various forms of so-called union security (e.g., dues checkoff and an agency or union shop). The union, on the other hand agrees to "deliver" human resources and to participate in the good faith administration and enforcement of the rules of the workplace as set forth in the contract. Finally, and this is critical from an organizational point of view, the union agrees to follow contractually established appeals procedures for resolving conflicts between management and workers. In effect, the union and the employer become partners in an effort to minimize the possibility that the workplace will be disrupted or productivity reduced by unresolved conflicts.

Collective bargaining is a way of identifying, formulating, and implementing cooperative solutions to problems presented by the interdependence of management and labor organizations (Walton and McKersie, 1965, p. 3). Where employee organizations or unions are forces in their environments, public employers must be equipped to deal with them effectively; in most cases, this means being able to work out mutually beneficial relationships. So-called "win–lose" confrontations resulting in job actions, strikes, court sanctions, firings, and the like are almost inevitably very costly to both sides. Therefore, considerable attention is now paid to the development of effective labor relations programs in government. Labor relations offices have been created by many jurisdictions in order to provide the expertise necessary to organize and carry out negotiations and to assist line management in the administration of contracts.

The Incorporation Strategy

Competition and cooperation are strategies that will work if an organization's environment can reliably generate the needed human resources. If an agency faces an economy or labor market that is unpredictable in these terms or is chronically incapable of supplying appropriately trained and educated people in sufficient numbers, creating an *internal* source may be the more appropriate strategy. What this approach does is reduce or eliminate uncertainty by expanding or restructuring the organization to establish direct administrative control over the supplier.

In a country such as the United States, with its vast system of education and training, public as well as private employers find it possible to obtain many of the skills and other human capabilities they need from sources outside the organization. Most also need to supplement or complement external sources with internal training and development programs that often fall under the personnel or human resources department. Even highly educated and trained recruits are likely to need on-the-job-training (OJT) in specific techniques and organizational practices. On a more basic skills level, it is now commonplace to hear complaints from managers in both sectors about the failure of public education to reliably graduate students who are able to read, write, and compute at levels required by today's increasingly complex organizational processes and technologies.

In some cases, the response has been to establish classes within organizations in which employees receive education and training in the basic skills they need. On a much more advanced level, the employer or government may have to create its own system of higher education because no functional equivalent exists outside the organization. Since, for example, there is little or no capacity to train qualified career military officers outside of government in the United States, the military academies were established to perform that function—starting with

West Point in the early nineteenth century. This is an incorporation, or build-your-own-capacity, strategy. Police and fire training academies are another example of the incorporation strategy in practice.

On the federal level, good illustrations of the incorporation strategy may be found in the field of civilian training and development. The Federal Executive Institute, an OPM facility, offers broadgauged administrative training for high-ranking executives. Established in 1968, the FEI was designed to fill what was viewed as a serious gap in the federal system for developing senior career executives. It caps an extensive training and career development system that gives the federal government a valuable internal complement to external suppliers. Because the system is financed, staffed, and administered by OPM and the federal agencies, the content and methods of training can be closely controlled and designed to meet specific needs. These internal resources reduce uncertainty by improving the probability that federal agencies will have reliable access to a steady stream of qualified managers and executives.

Over the past 50 years, government in the United States has grown in response to public demands for new and expanded services. Where governmental effectiveness is crucial and a capacity to perform services such as police, fire, air traffic control, national defense, and public health is essential, long-term investments in an internal capacity to train and develop the required human resources may be justified. Incorporation initiatives are seldom without controversy because they are, in effect, extensions of government. While the issue of *what* services government will or should provide is always on the political agenda of a democracy, as an organizational function, public personnel administration is more directly concerned with *how* effectively and efficiently to acquire and use the human resources needed to deliver public services. Seen in this context, incorporation is simply one of several approaches available to public policy makers.

ENHANCING WORKFORCE PRODUCTIVITY

At least potentially, personnel specialists are in a position to help create working conditions and to design incentives systems that encourage workers to make the many technical and behavioral contributions that public agencies need to be effective. Personnel policies and practices should promote the following:

- Low absenteeism, or regular attendance and participation in organizational tasks and activities by members, by creating working conditions that lead to high levels of job satisfaction.

▓ Low turnover of highly skilled and other difficult-to-replace employees by establishing material and nonmaterial rewards that induce people with valuable skills, knowledge, and experience to stay with the organization.

▓ Competence by workers in the technical and social requirements of their positions or jobs.

▓ A workforce that is consistently willing to carry out more than formal job or position requirements by actively cooperating with others, by helping to advance the organization's interests, by developing innovative ways to solve problems, and by working to keep skills current and to acquire new abilities. (Katz and Kahn, 1978, p. 403)

Achieving and sustaining these behavioral patterns is difficult, and it is an effort that requires organizations to design and administer mutually beneficial *transactions* or exchanges with their members.

PERSONNEL AND THE INDUCEMENTS-CONTRIBUTIONS TRANSACTION

The inducements-contributions transaction is a mutually profitable exchange of values between organizations and their members (Simon, 1965, pp. 110–122). The terms "inducement" and "incentive" are often used interchangeably in this context. In organization theorist William G. Scott's words, the term "'incentive' is applicable to any inducement, material or nonmaterial, which impels, encourages, or forces a person to perform a task to accomplish a goal" (Scott, 1967, pp. 284–285). A major question facing management, therefore, is which incentives available to the organization will influence employees to make those contributions it needs to perform effectively and efficiently.

Research on the connections between technological, social, and psychological factors in the workplace and such contributions-related variables as morale, job satisfaction, and productivity has generated a very complicated and incomplete picture. Porter and Miles have described the situation in the following terms:

> After all this time and effort. . .we still have at best only a hazy and far from firm grasp of motivation. In our opinion, there is no single theory relating to motivation that can be completely and unqualifiedly accepted as accounting for all the known facts, and there is no definite set of prescriptions that are unequivocally supported by the research data. (Porter and Miles, 1974, p. 545)

Simplistic and overgeneralized assumptions about human nature and how it relates to organizational needs have been largely discredited, but they have not been replaced by any broadly accepted and empirically confirmed alternatives. The near term will not bring anything resembling a set of principles that tells public managers how to design and run a universally effective system of organizational inducements or incentives. This does not mean that progress has not been made. Today's public managers are as a group far more likely to be sensitive to the social and psychological dimensions of motivation than were earlier generations, who concentrated almost exclusively on formal command systems and economic incentives.

Another problem has to do with the assumptions about the personnel management function that are associated with bureaucratic forms of organization. Modern ideas about motivation in organizations stress gearing incentives to specific conditions and to the social-psychological traits of small groups and individuals. However, bureaucracies are designed to handle people in large groups or categories and to deal with them in largely depersonalized and formalized ways. Centralization and standardization, hallmarks of the "Weberian Bureaucracy," have been typical of the approaches taken to managing incentives by public personnel systems which, of course, function largely in bureaucratic settings (Bendix, 1962, pp. 423–431). In practice, line managers and supervisors have had little control over the design and day-to-day administration of incentives plans. Not surprisingly, much of the current argument for management-centered personnel systems hinges on the proposition that meaningful increases in productivity will come only when supervisors have the capacity to *manage* performance by tailoring incentives and their administration to the conditions and people they must deal with.

EXTRINSIC AND INTRINSIC INCENTIVES

It is traditional to divide the list of incentives potentially available to organizations into two general categories: extrinsic and intrinsic. Extrinsic incentives are material and psychological rewards that are external to the job itself. Pay, working conditions, and fringe benefits are examples of *material* extrinsic rewards. Promotions, professional honors, and commendations are *nonmaterial* extrinsic rewards that may function as incentives. The vast majority of organizations rely primarily on material extrinsic inducements.

Intrinsic incentives are the psychological rewards to the individual that flow from doing the work itself. Persons, in other words, are intrinsically motivated if they do something because they derive feelings of competence, personal worth, selfdetermination, solidarity with coworkers, or simple happiness. Here, the available evidence strongly suggests that much of the effort people put into their jobs is related to how interesting, challenging, and personally meaningful the jobs are. Varied activities, influence over how work is done, and autonomy or self-direction are also important needs for many employees (Vasu, Stewart, and Garson, 1990, pp. 47–56). Bearing in mind that people differ in the degree to which they have these needs, the overall pattern is for job satisfaction to be higher for jobs that offer these kinds of intrinsic rewards.

Job content, operating technologies, and working relationships are at least potentially sources of important organizational inducements. Public managers and personnel specialists should pay close attention to the social-psychological implications of how jobs are designed and interrelated, as well as to the impact of supervisory styles and group dynamics on employee attitudes and behavior. In both cases, it may be possible to create conditions under which people are more likely to be more productive and committed than they would be if management limited its attention and efforts to external material and nonmaterial incentives.

MEMBERSHIP-BASED AND INDIVIDUALIZED INCENTIVES

Extrinsic as well as intrinsic incentives may be divided into two types, depending on how they are administered. Under one approach, the organizational choice is to tie incentives to membership in functional units, job classifications, hierarchical levels, or some other grouping of employees. Satisfactory performance means that employees may keep their membership in the group and, in turn, will receive the same rewards as all other members. For purposes of connecting inducements to contributions, or rewards to performance, organizational attention is focused on identifying those who have met a standard of *acceptable* performance. Historically in the public sector, for example, those with "satisfactory" annual performance ratings would receive the same percentage pay raises.

In contrast, another way of structuring inducements-contributions transactions is to tie rewards *directly* to an individual worker's job performance or output. Rewards such as pay increases, bonuses, promotions, and honors are allocated on the basis of differences in productivity among individuals. For example, each person in a work group or job category (e.g., a secretarial pool or nursing staff) is paid according to his or her scores on certain measures of performance. Membership-based systems are still the dominant type in the public sector, but currently there is widespread sentiment to the effect that at best they encourage mediocre performance while offering no positive incentive to do work that is above average or superior in quantity and quality:

> This situation [the widespread use of membership-based induce-
> ments] represents a sharp departure from the traditional American
> value of individualism. A central theme of our cultural heritage sup-
> ports the idea that individuals will fail or succeed through their own
> efforts and hard work. When people receive equal rewards regardless
> of effort or achievement, the implicit message from management is:
> "We don't care about extra effort, so why should you?"(Yankelovich
> and Immerwahr, 1983, p. 26)

Membership-based inducements have not been found to be particularly successful devices for promoting above-average performance
by *individuals*. However, employers may be able to achieve high levels of *overall* productivity by setting high standards for achieving and
maintaining membership in a work group, organization, or job category. There is also evidence to suggest that under certain conditions
"gainsharing" or group-based performance rewards can raise productivity and increase job satisfaction. Since organizations are seldom
merely collections of competing individuals, relying instead on high
quality performance by interdependent groups, membership-based
inducements may be the most appropriate (Gilbert and Nelson, 1989;
Siegel, 1994).

Nonetheless, overlaying membership-based with individualized
incentives now has a great deal of support in the public sector.
Although most of the attention has been focused on "pay-for-performance" or "merit pay" systems, other individualized inducements are
available. They include time off, educational opportunities or sabbaticals, payment for unused sick leave, honors and commendations, and
cash awards for cost-saving suggestions. In the merit pay area, there
has been renewed interest in using within-grade salary increases as
rewards for better-than-average to superior performance instead of
the common practice of giving them to workers who achieve "satisfactory" ratings. The federal government, many localities, and about
half the states are using some form of merit pay, pay-for-performance,
or bonus system.

STRUCTURING THE RELATIONSHIP BETWEEN INDUCEMENTS AND CONTRIBUTIONS

Despite the saying that "a happy employee is a productive employee,"
there is little evidence to suggest that simply meeting the material,
social, and psychological needs of people will somehow make them
work harder or be more productive. Actually, a large body of research
on job satisfaction does not support the idea that job satisfaction
causes greater effort or better performance. There is, in fact, no logical reason why it should. As Scott and Mitchell (1976) put it:

[T]here is no reason to believe that liking the job will prompt one to higher levels of effort. People are attracted to jobs for various reasons (the work conditions, the friendships, the supervision, and so on). They may find that all of these things can be obtained without extra effort, and indeed, this is the case in many organizations. It is true that some rewards may be lost such as a bonus or a promotion, but in many cases these incentives are not of utmost importance. The other incentives are typically not related to effort, and it should not be surprising, therefore, that overall job satisfaction is only slightly related to output. (p. 159)

From an organizational point of view, the problem is to identify and "manage" inducements in a manner explicitly designed to achieve needed contributions.

EXPECTANCY THEORY

One approach to solving the problem of productivity enhancement is offered by the expectancy theory of motivation. According to this theory, the level of *effort* people will put into a behavior or task is related to three factors. The first is *expectancy,* or the extent to which a person believes that a certain behavior or outcome is possible; for example, getting to work on time or finishing a project. The second is *instrumentality,* or the degree to which the behavior in question is seen to be likely to result in a specific outcome for the individual, such as getting a pay raise or promotion. The third is *valence,* which is the relative value or importance attributed to that outcome by a person. Using always coming to work on time as the example, expectancy theory predicts that the level of effort made to get to work on time will depend on (1) whether a person really believes it is possible to do this, given the circumstances he or she faces; (2) the degree to which the person is convinced that the inducement offered by the organization, such as a pay raise, will actually happen if he or she always gets to work on time; and (3) the relative value placed on the inducement itself (Gortner, Mahler, and Nicholson, 1997, pp. 281–285).

Expectancy theory posits that people have needs that they want to satisfy, that they are able rationally to calculate expectancies and instrumentalities, and will behave accordingly. Management, in turn, must know what rewards are valued by workers and be able to set up conditions wherein (1) the worker has a high level of expectancy, and (2) the connections between job performance and rewards established by the organization are clear and highly predictable in their administration. Continuing with the illustration of coming to work on time, if a public employer's productivity is suffering because many of its employees habitually arrive a few minutes after the start of the work day, expectancy theory suggests that the following course of action will work better than punishment-centered responses, which might depress morale and encourage various forms of evasion. Initially, management should have as its goal the implementation of a system of positive incentives that promises to increase workers' efforts to be at work on time. One factor it must consider is the extent to which they believe it is possible to get to work on time routinely (expectancy). There may be reasons why people often are late that the organization may be able to address, such as inadequate public transportation or a lack of affordable child care facilities. Once expectancy is high, management is in a position to take the next step, which is an incentive plan that connects attractive outcomes to the behavior it wants, coming to work on time. In addition to offering rewards that are valued by workers (valence), the plan must be administered in a consistent and highly predictable manner by supervisors (instrumentality).

Expectancy theory does have some practical limitations. It requires management to acquire a great deal of information about individuals, their attitudes and circumstances. It also proceeds on the assumption that everybody engages in rational, quasi-economic calculations before choosing a particular course of action, and "critics suggest that expectancy theory defers too much to the nineteenth century ideal of the economic man. . .[but] employees cannot be as knowledgeable about outcomes as the model assumes" (Stewart and Garson, 1983, p. 33). Nevertheless, expectancy theory does offer guidelines for thinking about structuring and managing relationships between inducements and contributions.

First, it stresses the importance of clearly communicating to employees the linkages between job performance and rewards. Second, it reminds policy makers and supervisors that personnel systems must be administered in a manner that firmly establishes these linkages in the eyes of employees. Third, it tells management that it must make an effort to understand, at least in general terms, the importance that different groups and types of employees place on specific material and nonmaterial rewards. Information of this kind is necessary if an inducements strategy is to be reasonably well-aligned with the values and needs of employees. Fourth, expectancy theory highlights the roles of perceived and objective ability in employee effort and performance. Perceptually, ability is a factor in expectancy; that is, does the person believe he or she has the ability to perform? Objectively, it sets limits, because no amount of effort will yield performance if ability actually does not exist or cannot be developed, as many aspiring professional athletes have discovered. Equally important factors in ability are the technical and other resources the organization makes available to its workforce. No matter how much effort they make, framing carpenters wielding hand saws are not likely to be as productive as those using power saws.

It is possible to improve the ability of an organization's human resource base in addition to increasing the effort it exerts. Personnel-related actions of this kind include investments in recruitment programs, upgrading selection and promotion standards, making available training and other employee development opportunities, and designing jobs and career paths to take better advantage of workers' interests and abilities. Investments in technological aids (e.g., computers, word processors, communications equipment, and automated machinery) and related training often raise productivity on the individual as well as organizational levels.

Fifth, expectancy theory illuminates the significance of perceived as well as actual equity and fairness in the allocation of rewards. If employees believe that rewards are not actually given on the basis of accurate and unbiased measures of performance, this perception may seriously cripple any incentives plan. Supervisors, who are in large measure responsible for its administration, must be trusted to competently and impartially implement the plan. Operationally, perceived equity also depends on clearly defined performance objectives and standards, and on the existence of broadly accepted and trusted performance evaluation procedures and instruments.

Conclusion

The human resource management perspective requires above all that personnel specialists take an organizational point of view. Increasingly, they are being asked to have the analytic skills and information needed to formulate and implement strategies for acquiring human resources that reach well beyond the organization's formal boundaries. With regard to better utilizing human resources, there are at least four areas of activity in which personnel specialists can make important contributions.

- They should be prepared to help in the design, administration, and evaluation of incentives plans that reflect current knowledge about human motivation and behavior in organizations.

BULLETIN

"Despite all the horror stories and years of scorn heaped on federal employees, our government is staffed by people committed to their jobs, qualified to do them better, and hungry for the opportunity to try. The environment and culture of government has discouraged many of these people; the system has undermined itself."

Source: *Report of the National Performance Review* (Washington, DC: U.S. Government Printing Office, 1993), p. 123.

- They have an important role to play in the design of systems to attract, select, and place employees who are most likely to respond favorably to the range of inducements an organization is able to offer. Today's public personnel administration is more advanced in its capacity to screen applicants on the basis of their technical qualifications than it is in defining the behavioral demands of jobs and predicting responses to social and psychological variables in the workplace.

- They can take the lead in developing ways of monitoring employee perceptions and attitudes. Management needs accurate and timely information about how workers feel about their jobs, supervisors, coworkers, working conditions, and personnel policies and practices.

- They should be prepared to play an important analytic or evaluation role by conducting rigorous evaluations of the human resources management programs of the organization, including those related to incentives, employee training and development, and performance evaluation. Well-done evaluations are needed to provide a solid foundation for initiatives designed to improve performance.

Steven Hays (1989) found that "the central theme of much of the relevant literature is that the personnel office must become more closely integrated with line management" (p. 114). In the current environment, personnel specialists need to have the expertise and, equally important, the organizational perspective needed to actively support public managers' efforts to enhance performance and productivity on all levels.

Discussion Questions

1. Why would people want to work for the public sector if they can make more money working for a private business?
2. What could public employers do to make working for government more attractive to college graduates?
3. Would you prefer to work for an employer who offers group-based or gainsharing performance incentives or one who has an individualized incentives plan? Why?
4. What could public employers do to better anticipate and plan for labor market conditions?
5. In what functional and program areas could local governments develop cooperative agreements to share personnel, training facilities, and other resources?

REFERENCES

Adams, Bruce (1984). "The Frustrations of Government Service." *Public Administration Review,* Vol. 44, No. 1 (January–February), pp. 5–13.

Bendix, Rinehard (1962). *Max Weber: An Intellectual Portrait* (New York: Anchor Books).

Buchanan, Bruce, and Millstone, Jeff (1979). "Public Organizations: A Value-Conflict View." *International Journal of Public Administration,* Vol. 1, No. 3, pp. 261–305.

Gilbert, G. Ronald, and Nelson, Ardel E. (1989). "The Pacer Share Demonstration Project: Implications for Organizational Management and Performance Evaluation." *Public Personnel Management,* Vol. 18, No. 2 (Summer), pp. 209–225.

Gortner, Harold F., Mahler, Julianne, and Nicholson, Jeanne Bell (1997). *Organization Theory: A Public Perspective,* 2nd ed. (New York: Harcourt Brace).

Hays, Steven (1989). "Environmental Change and the Personnel Function: A Review of the Research." *Public Personnel Management,* Vol. 18, No. 2 (Summer), pp. 110–126.

Hudson Institute (1986). *Civil Service 2000* (Washington, DC: U.S. Office of Personnel Management).

Jorgensen, Lorna, Fairless, Kelli, and Patton, David W. (1996). "Underground Merit Systems and the Balance Between Service and Compliance." *Review of Public Personnel Administration,* Vol. 16, No. 2 (Spring), pp. 5–20.

Katz, Daniel, and Kahn, Robert (1978). *The Social Psychology of Organizations,* 2nd ed. (New York: John Wiley and Sons).

Levine, Charles H. (1986). "The Federal Government in the Year 2000: Administrative Legacies of the Reagan Years." *Public Administration Review,* Vol. 46, No. 3 (May–June), pp. 195–206.

Matzer, John, Jr., ed. (1988). *Pay and Benefits: New Ideas for Local Government* (Washington, DC: International City Management Association), pp. ix–xxiv.

Ospina, Sonia (1992). "When Managers Don't Plan: Consequences of Nonstrategic Public Personnel Management." *Review of Public Personnel Administration,* Vol. 12, No. 2 (January–April), pp. 52–67.

Perry, James L. (1993). "Strategic Human Resource Management." *Review of Public Personnel Administration,* Vol. 13, No. 4 (Fall), pp. 59–71.

Porter, Lyman W., and Miles, R. P. (1974). "Motivation and Management," in J. W. McGwire (ed.), *Contemporary Management: Issues and Viewpoints* (Englewood Cliffs, NJ: Prentice-Hall).

Report of the National Performance Review (1993). "Creating a Government That Works Better & Costs Less" (Washington, DC: U.S. Government Printing Office).

Scott, William G. (1967). *Organization Theory: A Behavioral Analysis for Management* (Homewood, IL: Richard D. Irwin).

―――― and Mitchell, T. R. (1976). *Organization Theory: A Structural and Behavioral Analysis* (Homewood, IL: Richard D. Irwin).

Siegel, Gilbert B. (1994). "Three Federal Demonstration Projects: Using Monetary Performance Awards." *Public Personnel Management*, Vol. 23, No. 1 (Spring), pp. 153–164.

Simon, Herbert A. (1965). *Administrative Behavior*, 2nd ed. (New York: Free Press).

Sonenblum, Sidney, Kirlin, John J., and Ries, John C. (1977). *How Cities Provide Services: An Evaluation of Alternative Delivery Structures* (Cambridge, MA: Ballinger Publishing).

Stewart, Debra W., and Garson, G. David (1983). *Organizational Behavior and Public Management* (New York: Marcell Dekker).

Thompson, James D. (1967). *Organizations in Action* (New York: McGraw Hill).

U.S. Office of Personnel Management (1998). "Template of Personnel Flexibilities for Use by Agencies Selected for Conversion to Performance-Based Organizations, Parts II and III" (Washington, DC: U.S. Office of Personnel Management) (http://opm.gov/wkfcperf/html).

Vasu, Michael L., Stewart, Debra W., and Garson, G. David (1990). *Organizational Behavior and Public Management*, 2nd ed. (New York: Marcel Dekker).

Walton, Richard E., and McKersie, Robert B. (1965). *A Behavioral Theory of Labor Negotiations* (New York: McGraw-Hill).

Wechsler, Barton (1994). "Reinventing Florida's Civil Service System: The Failure of Reform." *Review of Public Personnel Administration*, Vol. 14, No. 2 (Spring), pp. 64–76.

Yankelovich, Daniel, and Immerwahr, J. (1983). *Putting the Work Ethic to Work* (New York: Public Agenda Foundation).

Yuchtman, Ephraim, and Seashore, Stanley (1967). "A System Resource Approach to Organizational Effectiveness." *American Sociological Review*, Vol. 32, No. 2 (December), pp. 891–903.

Suggested Readings

Barnard, Chester I. (1938). *The Functions of the Executive* (Cambridge, MA: Harvard University Press).

Donahue, John D. (1989). *The Privatization Decision: Public Ends, Private Means* (New York: Basic Books).

Lawler, Edward E., III (1994). *Motivation in Work Organizations* (San Francisco: Jossey-Bass).

Perry, James L. (1996). *Handbook of Public Administration*, 2nd ed. (San Francisco: Jossey-Bass).

Vroom, Victor H. (1964). *Work and Motivation* (New York: John Wiley & Sons).

Walton, Mary (1986). *The Deming Method* (New York: Praeger).

Chapter**FOUR**

Recruitment and Selection

To be effective, an agency's human resources program must be able to identify, recruit, and acquire people who are well qualified at entry, responsive to available incentives, and able to develop new skills and abilities. Success in acquiring and retaining needed human resources depends on many factors, some of which may be beyond the control of public managers. Inadequate pay and benefits, deteriorating working conditions, and public antipathy have done much to make jobs in the public service unattractive to many of today's potential applicants, particularly those with skills that are in high demand. Many of the "best and brightest" products of U.S. higher education look to the private sector for jobs that pay well and offer high-prestige careers, so the public sector starts out with a competitive disadvantage. An expansive economy, where jobs are plentiful in the private sector, makes recruiting more difficult. But these are not the only reasons that public employers may have difficulty attracting qualified personnel.

Historically, traditional merit systems have not invested heavily in aggressive recruitment efforts unless forced to do so by outside agencies, such as the federal courts. They often have settled for a passive (announce-and-wait) approach to filling vacancies and new positions. Rules and processes designed in large measure to prevent patronage hiring and discrimination have been notoriously complicated and cumbersome. Highly qualified job applicants are driven away by these systems' complexity and slowness, or they simply never apply. Public managers, in turn, are frustrated by their inability to acquire the human resources they need in a timely and efficient manner.

A major task now confronting public personnel is to develop recruitment and selection techniques and processes that (1) take a management point of view by actively supporting efforts to acquire, develop, and retain the human resources needed by government; and (2) are in conformance with the merit principle and meet the standards set by existing EEO and antidiscrimination law and policy. On the federal level, for example, the Civil Service Reform Act of 1978 requires that recruitment "should be from qualified individuals from appropriate sources in an endeavor to achieve a work force from all segments of society, and selection and advancement should be determined solely on the basis of relative ability, knowledge, and skills, after fair and open competition which assures that all receive equal opportunity."

As the CSRA's language implies, although recruitment and selection are conceptually discrete steps, they are in practice inseparable. As the Volcker Commission noted, complicated and slow selection procedures undermine recruitment efforts because potential candidates "see getting government jobs as an exercise in frustration." On the other side of the coin, ineffective recruitment may leave the employer in the position of having to select from a list of eligibles that does not have enough qualified applicants on it. Important positions may remain open for a long time. Weak recruitment programs often produce candidate pools that underrepresent women and minorities, an outcome that makes it very difficult to achieve affirmative action goals and, in a larger sense, to convince these groups that EEO is really a serious concern for the employer.

In its guidance to state agencies, the State of Georgia's Merit System identifies the following as important considerations in the formulation of an effective recruitment program:

- The program should permit employers to identify recruitment sources, such as universities and trade schools, that are the most likely to provide enough applicants with the needed skills and abilities.

> **BULLETIN**
>
> 'California's present personnel system was originally designed to eliminate political influence from the hiring and promotion of public employees and ensure, instead, public employment based on merit. This continues to be an essential goal. But, over time, California's civil service system has become rule-laden and inefficient. This stifles initiative and innovation and frustrates supervisors and managers in their efforts to reach common sense personnel decisions.
>
> Source: *California Department of Personnel Administration Civil Service Reform Objectives* (http://www. dpa.ca.gov /statesys/ dpa/ policy/csr4pag3.htm), 1998.

- It should be funded and staffed at the levels required to carry out an active recruitment effort.

- In addition to meeting short-term or immediate needs, the program should be designed to meet long-term needs by acquiring entry-level personnel who will later be able to advance and fill more responsible positions.

- Recruitment must be seen as the initial step in the selection process and, therefore, it must "ensure compliance with existing federal and state laws and guidelines concerning fairness, equal opportunity, and. . .[it must] minimize potential adverse impact on legally-protected groups."

- The program should meet the public's expectation that all phases of the hiring process will be "fair" in the sense that merit and EEO are the core values guiding that process. (Georgia Merit System, 1997, pp. 1–2)

RECRUITMENT: FINDING AND ATTRACTING QUALIFIED APPLICANTS

In many countries, government workers traditionally have been accorded high social status and prestige. Highly qualified candidates are more often than not willing to accept lower pay than they could get in the private sector because of the status and authority that comes with public service careers. Public attitudes and social values thus allow government to pick and choose from candidate pools that offer the most talented and best-educated people the society has to offer. With rare exceptions, this has not been the case in the United States, and public employers on all levels have had to struggle to overcome a general inclination to value careers in the private sector over those in the public service. Recent thinking about recruitment in the U.S. public sector has stressed three approaches to overcoming, or at least compensating for, government's problems in this area. The first involves taking advantage of government's potential to compete successfully for minorities and women. The second concentrates on reducing public employers' dependence on outside sources by continuously upgrading the skills of existing employees to meet changing or new requirements. This approach involves commitments to substantial investments in training and other human resources development (HRD) programs (Hudson Institute, 1988, pp. 38–41). The third consists of several initiatives designed to improve the image of the public service as an employer and to make the public sector an effective economic competitor across certain critical segments of the labor market, particularly college graduates and the technical and professional occupations (National Academy of Public Administration, 1987).

In all cases, a recruitment plan should:

- Clearly define who is responsible for the implementation of its components and set goals and timetables for completion of each of these components.
- Include procedures for ongoing evaluation and revision of the plan in light of the results achieved, including the performance of the workforce.
- Specify the kinds of job and job vacancy information that will be made available internally to existing workers, as well as to the general public.
- Assure that accurate information will be readily accessible to all interested parties through a variety of media, such as publications, postings, radio and television, and the Internet.
- Identify and establish reliable contacts with productive referral sources, including promotions and transfers, current employees, schools and colleges, employment agencies, and executive search companies.
- Target and establish contact with applicants who are the most likely to have needed qualifications and skills.
- Clearly set forth the policies and procedures to be used in recruitment efforts designed to improve diversity. (Georgia Merit System, 1997, p. 4)

MINORITY RECRUITMENT

Although its record is certainly far from perfect, the public sector has been a leader in the process of breaking down barriers to the employ-ment and promotion of women and minorities. To the degree that public employment is associated with equality of opportunity and career mobility for minorities and women, government has the basis for an advantage in the competition with private businesses (Hudson Institute, 1988). An example of minority-oriented recruitment is pro-vided by OPM's Hispanic Employment Initiatives, which include helping to implement Executive Order 12900, the *White House Initiative on Educational Excellence for Hispanic Americans.* In addi-tion to issuing guidance on recruiting strategies for Hispanic students, OPM works with federal agencies to identify job opportunities and institutions that offer training and education opportunities that pre-pare Hispanic students to qualify for those jobs. Other OPM initia-tives in this area are:

- Providing employment information to students, faculty, and the Hispanic community by sponsoring Employment

Information (Touch Screen) Computer Kiosks and placing them in Hispanic-serving institutions.

▪ Expanding the Presidential Management Intern (PMI) recruitment program to include visiting more institutions that are graduating significant numbers of Hispanics.

▪ Providing assistance in coordinating placements with federal agencies of Hispanic students under the National Internship Program of the Hispanic Association of Colleges and Universities (HACU). HACU interns are college students with grade point averages of 3.0 or better who work in federal agencies for 10 weeks over the summer.

▪ Using the flexibilities available under the federal Student Employment Program (this program is described below) to bring Hispanic students into federal occupations where there are shortages of qualified applicants, as well as all other occupations.

▪ Developing mentoring programs to encourage and support young Hispanics' educational development and career progress.

▪ Encourage participation of Hispanics in agency career development programs, including intergovernmental rotational assignments for senior executives, management, and professional/technical occupations. (U.S. Office of Personnel Management, 1997a)

The Hudson Institute also recommended that public employers develop recruitment programs geared to the changing demographics of the labor force and, more broadly, to the growing diversity of U.S. society. The rapidly growing proportion of women in the workforce creates an opportunity *if* innovations such as flexible work schedules, extended leave policies, and child care benefits are "pursued aggressively." The Institute's comments with regard to the federal government are equally relevant to the recruitment programs of the states and localities.

> Few employers have been able to satisfy the desires of two-earner families for more time away from work to care for children and aging family members. Organizations that are able to offer more flexible work schedules. . .are more likely to have their pick of the available candidates for hard-to-fill jobs. . . . [E]very agency should be seeking to find cost-effective ways to assist parents in providing high-quality child care. The Federal government should not allow itself to lag behind other employers. . .if it wishes to hire and keep large numbers of mothers (and fathers) during the 1990s. (Hudson Institute, 1988, p. 39)

INVESTMENTS IN CONTINUOUS TRAINING AND EDUCATION

Rapid social and technological change places great pressure on organizations to maintain workforces that have the skills, knowledge, and abilities needed to handle new responsibilities and job tasks. It is no longer safe to assume that a high school or college education, once completed, will equip workers with the basic knowledge and skills they need to handle their jobs until they retire. Historically, this has been the assumption, and when government needed personnel with new or different skills, it recruited them from outside sources. Retraining or reeducating existing staff to fill positions that may not actually exist for several years has been a seldom exercised option because it has been virtually impossible to generate political support for these kinds of investments.

In the long term, however, one way to reduce the pressure on external recruitment is, in effect, to create conditions under which an *internal recruitment* dimension is added to the mix. This may be done by anticipating human resources needs and by systematically upgrading and changing the skills profiles of those who already work for public agencies. This approach applies particularly to situations where certain skills are already in short supply or are likely to be in the foreseeable future. Skills upgrading programs such as tuition reimbursement for job-related education and training, sabbaticals to pursue advanced degrees, and specialized training opportunities may be used in the fields where they are most needed and by agencies that will benefit most in terms of recruitment and retention. Education and training of this kind also could be designed to help employees work their way up a career ladder from, for example, paraprofessional to professional positions. Another goal might be to improve the basic skills of those who would otherwise not be qualified for lower-level jobs.

Along these lines, OPM developed a series of initiatives designed to strengthen federal human resources development efforts. They covered (1) probationary period training for new employees, (2) basic skills and literacy training, (3) continuing technical/professional education and training, (4) retraining for occupational changes, (5) participation in professional associations, and (6) academic degree training. OPM also supports training and development programs for supervisors and managers, and it helps federal agencies to assess their needs in these areas (U.S. Office of Personnel Management, 1992).

RECRUITING COLLEGE GRADUATES

During the 1990s, the number of public sector jobs requiring college degrees increased, but the number of people graduating with bachelor's and master's degrees actually declined somewhat. Although the shortage is expected to be particularly acute on the federal level, state and local governments may also have problems recruiting the college graduates they need to fill technical and professional positions (Hamman, Desai, and Mitchell, 1993). Even under the best of conditions, the competition for talent will be intense, and public employers commonly face several self-imposed obstacles.

First, in comparison to large corporations and firms, public employers do not have a track record of investing heavily in campus recruitment. In 1989, an OPM study of college recruitment efforts concluded that most federal agencies showed a lack of commitment to campus recruitment and, when the federal government did recruit on campus, its presence was too limited and sporadic to effectively promote federal jobs. When asked about federal recruitment efforts in 1990, college students told the GAO that they were not getting enough information about job opportunities and how to apply for them. They also got the *feeling* that jobs were unavailable and that the agencies did not value students as potential employees. College placement offices, typically well stocked with recruiting literature from businesses, seldom had up-to-date materials on jobs and careers in federal agencies. The image of the public sector did not help, since students were not disposed to approach agencies directly because they believed that contacting the government was a frustrating and lengthy process.

> As one undergraduate public administration student told us [the GAO], "Obtaining information on [federal] employment is very hard. It takes forever to get the forms. You write them a letter saying you want the information, and about four months later you'll get the information, and then you're wondering who it is from. You forget by then." (U.S. General Accounting Office, 1990a, pp. 53–54)

In an effort to solve these kinds of problems, OPM launched several recruitment initiatives intended to help federal agencies. Among the first efforts was *Career America,* a collection of sophisticated brochures describing career opportunities and highlighting attractive features of federal service. The *Career America* publications were made available to federal agencies at relatively low cost. OPM now "sells" federal agencies a service it calls the *Career America Connection,* "a nationwide automated telephone system that provides quick, easy-to-use, current Federal Employment information 24 hours a day, 7 days a week" (U.S. Office of Personnel Management, 1997b, p. 1). Other informational resources include automated "on-line" systems that provide job information, assistance in completing applications, and status reports on applications that have been submitted. OPM also offers federal agencies customized Federal Employment Information Touch Screen Computer

Kiosks, which provide "daily updated Federal employment information at the touch of a finger" (U.S. Office of Personnel Management, 1997c, p. 1).

The GAO found in 1990 that college students favor personal contacts with employer representatives over other recruitment methods, and campus interviews and presentations to classes or student groups are given high marks for effectiveness because they make face-to-face meetings with knowledgeable employees possible. Brochures such as the *Career America* portfolio and electronic media did attract interest, but are not substitutes for personal contacts. Recruiting videos, for example, were not judged to be particularly effective, in part because many students believed they did not provide an accurate description of work and careers in government agencies. Impersonal prerecorded telephone messages and computer information systems did not please college students. Along similar lines, "career fairs" where public employers set up booths on university campuses and collect resumes are not likely to attract top candidates, most of whom don't go to job fairs or wait to be processed through OPM registers. They are "courted by the private sector and skimmed off like cream" (U.S. General Accounting Office, 1990b, p. 19). The GAO suggested that college placement centers have a federal employment contact person so that information could be channeled and questions answered quickly and accurately, and many federal agencies now provide the names, addresses, and numbers of contact persons for positions they are currently seeking to fill.

STUDENT HIRING PROGRAMS

Another way of helping people to become familiar with job and career opportunities in the public service is to hire students on a part-time basis. Here, an example is provided by OPM's Student Educational Employment Program. Established in 1994, this program offers federal employment opportunities to students in accredited high schools, technical and vocational training centers, and two- or four-year colleges and universities. It has two components, the Student Temporary Employment Program (STEP) and the Student Career Experience

BULLETIN

"The Career America Connection Teleservice Center provides callers the option of live operator assistance. In addition the Office of Personnel Management can customize an automated telephone system for individual agencies." Key features include (1) facts about the federal hiring process, (2) information on salaries and benefits, and (3) faxing or mailing of application materials within 24 hours.

Source: U.S. Office of Personnel Management (http://www.opm.gov/employ/ html/CAC.HTM), October 28, 1997.

Program (SCEP). Under STEP, students' work does not have to be directly related to their academic programs and career goals. The SCEP, however, is intended to provide work experience that is directly related to academic and career interests, and students "may be noncompetitively converted to *term, career* or *career-conditional* appointments following completion of their academic and work experience requirements" (U.S. Office of Personnel Management, 1997d, p. 1). According to OPM:

> In Fiscal Year 1996, there were 34,578 participants in the Student Educational Employment Program. The Temporary Employment Component had 26,045 (75 percent) participants; the Career Experience component had 8,533 (25 percent) participants. The number of female participants [was] 19,852 (57 percent of program participants). There were 16,540 minorities. . .[and] Blacks had the largest representation with 10,002 students (29 percent. . .). There were 1,058 *career* or *career-conditional* conversions from the Career Experience component in FY 96. (U.S. Office of Personnel Management, 1997e, p. 1)

Internships such as the Presidential Management Intern Program also may be effective recruiting devises. Established in 1977, the PMI is designed to attract highly qualified graduate students. Students are nominated by their schools and undergo a competitive selection process. Once they graduate, those selected are given the opportunity for challenging assignments including rotational responsibilities, mentoring, and attendance in development seminars. Those who successfully complete the program are eligible for conversion to permanent positions. On the state level, for example, The Illinois Commission on the Future of the Public Service recommended in 1991 that the state expand all of its internship and cooperative education programs because they "provide the greatest potential for increasing the pool of undergraduate and graduate students interested in public service" (Illinois Commission on the Future of the Public Service, 1991, p. 32). Currently, the Illinois Department of Natural Resources offers internships to college and graduate students in natural resources management, conservation law enforcement, environmental education, and other areas. The Department's programs "allow students to obtain practical experience and meet hands-on training requirements necessary to earn their degrees" (Illinois Department of Natural Resources, 1998, p. 1). Another Illinois initiative is the Prescott E. Bloom Internships in Government Program. In one, college juniors, seniors, and graduate students "work in the Governors's Office and in various agencies under the Governor's jurisdiction learning, first hand, the operations of Illinois State Government." In another, college graduates spend a year assigned on a rotational basis to various departments in the

Governor's Office and to an Executive Branch agency (Office of the Governor, State of Illinois, 1997).

CHANGING THE IMAGE OF PUBLIC EMPLOYMENT

The image of what it is like to work in government compounds already negative feelings about pay and benefits in the public sector. Many potential job applicants see government as an environment in which it is next to impossible to get anything done, as offering careers where they are unlikely to be able to fully use their talents, as a place infested with specialists in "red tape," and where dreary working conditions prevail. Fueled by political rhetoric, media depictions, and the long-standing American tendency to ascribe all manner of evils to "the bureaucracy," this image of the public service is a serious liability.

To the degree that these perceptions are factually inaccurate, public employers need to come up with strategies for countering and changing them. Public information and education programs designed to describe the challenges, rewards, and opportunities associated with public service and careers in particular agencies may be productive, particularly if recruiters are prepared to follow up in terms relevant to potential applicants. Systematically building direct contacts with the public service through internship and co-op programs also should be helpful. More broadly, as the Volcker Commission noted, the nation's political leadership must be willing to describe the public service and its functions in positive terms *and* to back its words with supportive policies and needed resources.

ADMINISTRATION OF RECRUITMENT PROGRAMS

On all levels of government, complaints about procedural rigidities, overcentralized and unresponsive personnel offices, and a widespread lack of organizational attention to recruitment are commonplace. Studies of the recruitment process reveal that relatively successful programs share certain characteristics.

BULLETIN

"The State of Illinois maintains a commitment to the continuing improvement of public service for its citizens. The success of this commitment depends upon an available talent pool of bright, highly motivated individuals who are prepared to assume important government positions. Recognizing that college and graduate students represent a significant reservoir of potential government talent, the Governor's Office has, since 1977, sponsored two internship programs. . . ." A third, the 1998 Vito Marzullo Internship Program, has the following purposes:

1. Helping to meet the public sector's future need for competent administrators.
2. Encouraging talented college graduates to consider careers in state government.
3. Helping students complement their academic expertise with vocational training within their fields.
4. Achieving affirmative action goals.

Source: State of Illinois, Office of the Governor, 1998.

First, and probably most important, top-level management actively supports and participates in the planning, implementation, and evaluation phases of agency recruitment programs. Second, recruitment activity is decentralized in the sense that line managers are directly involved and have been delegated considerable authority to plan and carry out recruiting initiatives and, under some conditions, to offer jobs to highly qualified candidates without waiting for the approval of a central personnel agency. Third, line managers work closely with personnel specialists in the design and implementation of recruitment strategies keyed to specific agency needs and labor market conditions. Fourth, those actually doing the recruitment in the field should have the necessary resources and technical support, be well trained and fully informed about agency needs and opportunities, and possess the authority required to make commitments on behalf of the employer. Fifth, appropriate media and technologies should be available to support all phases of the recruitment and selection process.

SELECTION: METHODS, ISSUES, AND PROBLEMS

A hallmark of the first civil service reform movement was its focus on the methods used to select people for public service jobs and to determine who should be promoted. Its intensive concentration of both forms of selection was a direct result of the movement's effort to eliminate patronage or spoils as an organizing principle of public personnel administration. Thus, traditional merit systems emphasize political neutrality and objectivity at every stage of the selection process. In order to achieve this goal, the selection process had to be designed *and* controlled by personnel specialists housed in central personnel agencies or independent commissions.

Conventional civil service selection procedures stress measuring a candidate's ability to perform a specific job. In order to make this determination, one or more "tests" are used. Scores on these tests are used to compare or rank those who apply. Technically, all measurements of capacity are considered tests, and they do not necessarily involve taking a written (pencil-and-paper) examination. The mix of tests used will vary, depending on the skills, knowledge, and abilities required. The tests applied by public employers usually will involve some combination of the following:

- Minimum qualifications requirements.
- Evaluations of training, education, and experience.
- Written tests of knowledge and analytic skills.
- Job performance tests and simulations.

- Oral examinations by individual examiners or boards.
- Background checks or investigations.
- Medical and physical examinations.

In civil service selection, the goal is to determine if an applicant has the knowledge, skills, abilities, and other traits deemed necessary or important to successful performance in a particular job. The content of most selection tests is supposed to be based on the results of careful *job analysis* (U.S. Office of Personnel Management, 1979b). Although most civil service tests in the United States are geared to the requirements of *positions,* some are intended to assess the likelihood that an applicant will have a successful career in a variety of *occupations* or *administrative roles.* These types of tests are most often used for entry-level professional positions, and the questions "do not require applicants to possess knowledge or experience which can only be acquired on the job" (U.S. Merit Systems Protection Board, 1990). They emphasize general traits such as verbal skills and reasoning abilities, which are believed to be closely linked to performance.

TEST VALIDITY

From a technical standpoint, the purpose of selection tests is to provide the employer with a reasonably accurate prediction of how applicants are likely to perform in specific jobs. In other words, the problem is to construct tests that are *valid.* In Norma Riccucci's words, "test validation continues to be relied on to conceptualize and operationalize merit. . ." (Riccucci, 1991, p. 80). A valid test measures only what it is intended to measure (e.g., knowledge of labor law or accounting principles). Tests must also be *reliable* or consistent in their results. All other things being equal (controlling for other potential sources of variation), if a person takes the test twice (or a hundred times), the scores should be roughly the same. If the scores are significantly different, the test is unreliable and unlikely to be valid.

The validation methods generally accepted by specialists in testing are (1) criterion-related validity, (2) content validity, and (3) construct validity. These three validation strategies are described by the American Psychological Association (1966) in its *Standards for Educational and Psychological Tests and Manuals.* The term *test* includes all selection methods used to make employment decisions such as interviews, written tests, and evaluations to training and experience.

In *criterion-related validity,* test scores of those hired are correlated with performance measures. Assuming that these performance ratings are accurate, a valid test should produce scores that are positively correlated with performance. An important limitation of this approach is that those who do not pass the test (or receive a passing score but are not hired) are given no opportunity to perform. A method devised to deal with this limitation known as *concurrent validity* involves administering a proposed new test to incumbent employees and comparing their scores with their performance ratings. Test scores should be positively associated with performance ratings if the test is valid. Critics argue that the concurrent validation technique promotes the creation of selection tests that overemphasize the characteristics of incumbent workers, not the actual requirements of positions.

In *content validity,* the goal is to develop a test that closely matches the content or skills, knowledge, and abilities (SKAs) of a job. Examples are written job knowledge tests and performance tests in which the actual duties are carried out, as in typing, driving, or welding. A content validity approach is attractive to public employers. However, in addition to the problems discussed below in the section on performance tests, questions may be asked about how scores are interpreted in hiring decisions and the extent to which job analysis accurately reflects conditions faced by those holding the positions in question (Riccucci, 1991, pp. 81–83).

In a *construct validity* approach, attempts are made to establish strong theoretical or empirical connections between certain general traits or constructs, such as intelligence or creativity, and satisfactory job performance. A test for a legal position provides an example of the difference between content and construct validity. Such a test would have content validity if it asked questions about specific provisions of the law with which the incumbent must be familiar (e.g., the tax status of municipal bonds). If an ability to read and comprehend statutory language is needed for successful job performance, the test would have construct validity if it accurately measured this capacity. Since construct validity often relies on constructs that are hard to define, such as intelligence, and convincing empirical evidence of associations between scores on measures of constructs and elements of job performance is often hard to find, it is a controversial approach.

VALIDITY AND EQUAL EMPLOYMENT OPPORTUNITY

In principle, selection tests should discriminate among job applicants only on the basis of their relative ability to perform the work in question. In *Griggs v Duke Power Company* (1971), the U.S. Supreme Court ruled that if a selection test had an adverse or disparate impact with regard to race, color, religion, or national origin, *and its validity had not been established,* its use constituted unlawful discrimination under Title VII of the Civil Rights Act of 1964. The Equal Employment Opportunity Act of 1972 then extended coverage to "governments," "governmental agencies," and "political subdivisions." In practical terms, this meant that if a selection test was challenged on EEO grounds and could not be validated, it had to be discarded by the employer and replaced with one that could be validated using an accepted methodology.

During the late 1960s and early 1970s, the Equal Employment Opportunity Commission, U.S. Department of Labor, and Civil Service Commission each issued guidelines on selection procedures. Their guidelines concerning how to demonstrate the job-relatedness of selection methods were not the same, and efforts to get uniform guidelines failed. The principal issue was a disagreement between the EEOC and the Civil Rights Commission on the one hand and the Civil Service Commission, Labor, and Justice on the other. In late 1976, the latter agencies agreed upon and adopted what were called the Federal Executive Agency or FEA Guidelines, but the Civil Rights Commission and the EEOC were opposed, and the EEOC retained the guidelines it had adopted in 1970 (Equal Employment Opportunity Commission, 1970; Federal Register, 1977). The EEOC guidelines were more difficult to satisfy.

The following were the principal points of disagreement:

1. The EEOC guidelines did not offer a concrete definition of *adverse impact* but indicated that its existence would be determined by comparing the rates at which different applicant groups pass a particular selection procedure. The FEA guidelines, on the other hand, did set forth a definition of sorts: a "substantially different selection rate . . . which works to the disadvantage of members of a racial, sex, or ethnic group." A rule of thumb for determining if selection rates were substantially different was provided. This so-called 80 percent rule stated that if the selection rate for a group was within four-fifths of the rate for the group with the highest rate, the enforcement agency will generally not consider adverse impact to exist.

2. The EEOC guidelines required validation of every component of the selection process used to fill a position. In practice, this meant making investigations of adverse impact for all examination components, even when the examination as a whole did not have an adverse impact. In contrast, the FEA guidelines stated that adverse impact was to be determined for the overall selection process for each job category. If no overall adverse impact was found, there was no obligation to validate the various selection components. If adverse impact was found, then each com-

ponent would have to be analyzed, and any having adverse impact would have to be validated if the employer wanted to continue using them.

3. Whereas the EEOC expressed a preference for criterion-related validity, the FEA pointed out that "generally accepted principles of the psychological profession do not recognize such preference, but contemplate the use of criterion-related, content, or construct validity strategies as appropriate." Criterion-related validity studies are often difficult to conduct because small jurisdictions do not test or hire enough people in single job classifications to give a statistical sample large enough for meaningful analysis comparing test scores and performance measures. In large jurisdictions, the sample is usually big enough in only a few classifications.

4. The EEOC required that an employer, while in the process of validating a selection procedure, be able to show that an alternative procedure with less adverse impact does not exist. The main objection to this standard was that it could mean an endless "cosmic" search for alternatives with less adverse impact. The FEA guidelines stated that in the course of a validity study the employer should try to find and use procedures that have as little adverse impact as possible. Once a good faith effort had been made and the chosen procedure had been shown to be valid, the employer did not have to search further for alternatives.

5. Finally, the EEOC guidelines required that tests be validated for each minority group in order to assure that differential validity did not exist. Differential validity describes a situation in which a test has significantly different validity coefficients for different race, sex, or ethnic groups. Clearly, to use a test that routinely overestimates or underestimates job performance for one group or another would be unfair. The FEA guidelines were less demanding, because they simply recommended that data be compiled separately for all groups to determine test fairness.

After extensive negotiations, agreement on Uniform Guidelines for Employee Selection Procedures finally was reached in 1978 (Federal Register, 1979). In general, they followed the FEA guidelines closely. The Uniform Guidelines are not regulations, but they have had a major impact because the Supreme Court has said that as the administrative interpretations of the enforcing agencies they are entitled to "great deference." Nonetheless, when legal disputes arise, the final determinations as to test validity requirements and whether an employer has met them are made by the courts.

Apart from the question of costs to employers, the Uniform Guidelines have been criticized as technically unsound in some respects, unclear in many others, and requiring excessive records keeping. Efforts to change them have met strong political opposition. In any case, the reality is that against a long history of relatively little pressure for test validation, public personnel agencies were suddenly placed in the position of having to validate a wide variety of selection tests for EEO reasons. Obviously, meeting the full requirements of the Uniform Guidelines is now and will continue to be a challenge to public employers. The technical, organizational, and political barriers to fully realizing this aspect of the merit principle are formidable. However distant the ideal, test validation is now fully established as an important objective for public personnel systems, and it applies to all of the tests described below.

MINIMUM QUALIFICATIONS

The reason for imposing minimum qualifications such as extent and type of education, training, physical abilities, and experience is to screen out applicants who are realistically not likely to be able to carry out the tasks and responsibilities associated with a position. Examples would be requiring applicants for legal positions to have a degree from an accredited school of law, requiring firefighters to be able to lift and carry a certain weight, and asking that applicants for senior administrative positions have had prior experience in equivalent or related positions. Residency in the employing state or locality may be required.

The key standard for minimum qualifications is that they are actually *essential* to job performance and do not arbitrarily deny persons who might be able to do the job a chance to compete. Until recently, little attention was paid to establishing the validity of minimum qualifications, and the personnel technicians' best judgment sufficed. With regard to predicting applicants' relative ability to perform, minimum qualifications such as requiring a high school diploma of janitors, truck drivers, and machine operators are at best questionable. As a practical matter, public employers must now be prepared to offer convincing evidence of validity, because the courts are routinely striking down minimum qualifications that cannot be shown to be logically related to the demands of a particular job. Currently, the trend is to remove minimum requirements that cannot be validated and to add flexibility by allowing for substitution of education for experience up to a certain point (and vice versa), and by including the catch-all phrase, "or any equivalent combination of training and experience."

There may be some minimum qualifications imposed as a matter of law and social policy. Residence, age, and citizenship status requirements, while not necessarily related to job performance, may serve wider political, social, or economic purposes. It is not unusual for police departments to require that their officers reside in the city or county where they work in order to build effective community relations. National child labor laws were passed to protect children from exploitation by employers, and even the most talented thirteen-year-old is not eligible for a computer programmer position in a local government. In 1978, the Supreme Court ruled that New York State could make U.S. citizenship a requirement for police positions, on grounds that policy making is the exclusive responsibility of citizens *and* the exercise of discretion by police officers is a form of policy making (*Foley v Connelie*, 1978). Since these types of requirements are fixed by federal, state, or local laws, the personnel agency has no discretion in their application beyond determining whether or not to argue for changes in the law.

EVALUATION OF TRAINING AND EXPERIENCE

Evaluations of training and experience may be used in combination with written or oral examinations in order to generate a more complete evaluation of applicants' skills, knowledge, and abilities (SKAs). In other cases, written and oral examinations may not be practical, and the evaluation of training and experience constitutes the entire examination. This is called an *unassembled examination* because candidates do not gather in one place to sit for a written test.

Suitable written tests may not exist or may be redundant because the applicants have already passed examinations for licenses or degrees needed to practice their profession (e.g., law, medicine, engineering, social work). Experience has shown that many highly qualified persons will not apply for government jobs if they have to take a written test, believing that their academic degrees, professional credentials and licenses, and experience should be enough to demonstrate their competence. Unassembled examinations are often used in the federal service, in some cases for entry-level professional positions, and some use is made of them in state and local governments. Evaluation of training and experience, plus an oral examination, is a combination commonly found on all levels of government.

The evaluation of training and experience is based on a more or less thorough understanding of the SKAs required by a position. Applicants are ranked by trained examiners according to the extent to which they have these SKAs, a process that is inevitably judgmental. Many personnel experts believe that the most effective way of minimizing the subjective content of the evaluation process is to use the job element method. Job elements are SKAs determined through job analysis to be significant requirements for successful performance. Using this method, candidates are ranked using various "evidences" determined to be acceptable for showing relative competence in the different job elements. For example, ratings of the job element "Knowledge of the Theory of Electronics" are based on such evidence as "verified experience in mathematical analysis requiring electronic theory *or* outstanding record in advanced theory courses *or* score of 85–100 on theory test" (Maslow, 1968).

WRITTEN TESTS

Written tests are extensively used in the public sector to measure job knowledge or skills. Personnel agencies may construct tests or purchase them from consulting or other organizations, such as the International Personnel Management Association. Small jurisdictions typically do not have the expertise or financial resources needed to develop and validate their own written tests. Multiple-choice tests are most commonly used. Essay-type examinations are rare, primarily because they are difficult to construct, take a long time to grade, and are open to the interpretations and biases of the readers. Despite problems associated with validity and adverse impact, written tests are likely to continue as the dominant way of rating applicants for a large variety of civil service positions. For personnel departments and agencies, they are administratively convenient and provide a quantitative and seemingly objective basis for ranking candidates. This does not mean that they are equally popular with agency management and job applicants.

Commenting on OPM's then-new written tests for entry-level professional positions (Administrative Careers with America or ACWA), the MSPB concluded in 1990 that they had the potential to be an efficient and inexpensive way of making selections when hiring a large number of employees from among a large number of applicants. By 1994, however, the GAO had concluded that this was not the case, since "agencies said they have generally found alternative hiring methods better meet their needs" (U.S. General Accounting Office, 1994, p. 3). According to the GAO:

> Agency hiring officials said they prefer other hiring methods to ACWA for several reasons. They believe that using ACWA certificates is more time-consuming than using other hiring methods. Agencies

receive ACWA certificates from OPM soon after they are requested, but the agencies may need/take several weeks to (1) contact the candidates; (2) receive and review their resumes; (3) interview them; and (4) verify past employment, education, and experience. Although these steps are required when agencies use other hiring methods, they can often be completed earlier in the process. (pp. 3–4)

The GAO noted other problems with the ACWA as a recruitment-selection device, including:

- Applicants who had lost interest in federal employment failed to respond to agencies' inquiries or to decline consideration for jobs, further slowing the process.
- Under the conditions imposed by the "rule of three" (see pages 110–111 and veterans preference, agencies were having difficulty meeting affirmative action goals for women through ACWA certificates.
- Most of the applicants found their experience with the ACWA frustrating, and the GAO's survey revealed that 85 percent of the respondents were dissatisfied with some aspect of the process.
- Over half of the respondents to the GAO survey thought their chances of getting a federal job were outstanding or good after getting their scores because they had not been given much information about hiring patterns—which should have revealed that a minute percentage of those with passing scores are hired; over a two-year period, 300,000 exams were given, there were over 182,000 passing scores, and 3,228 applicants were hired. (pp. 4–5)

A clear indication of the extent to which federal agencies preferred alternatives to ACWA hiring is provided by Table 4.1. Under the Outstanding Scholar Program, federal agencies may hire candidates with a 3.50 or better grade point average or who have graduated in the top 10 percent of their class. They are not required to take the ACWA test. Under Veterans Readjustment Appointments, agencies are able to hire eligible veterans noncompetitively. Temporary employees may be hired for up to four years without OPM approval, with appointments being renewed annually. The GAO noted that agencies often fill permanent positions with temporary employees in order to speed up the hiring process, escape limits on permanent employment levels, and to "hire a selected employee who could not be reached on an OPM certificate" (p. 6). Additional flexibility is available through excepted appointments under Schedules A, B, and C, which can include positions in the ACWA occupations. Finally, positions may be filled

Table 4.1 Hires into Occupations Covered by ACWA: Fiscal Years 1991 and 1992

Type of Appointment	Number of Appointments
ACWA	2,797
Outstanding scholar and other direct hire	8,905
Veterans readjustment	1,194
Temporary	3,733
Excepted	5,574
Internal placements	15,002

through reassignments, transfers, reinstatements, and promotions into ACWA occupations without taking or passing the ACWA (pp. 6–7). Given the experience with the ACWA process and standing registers of eligibles, OPM decided to make them an optional screening method for agencies, and "candidates now apply for a specific job, either directly through the agency or at OPM" (Ban, 1997, pp. 197–198).

PERFORMANCE TESTS

Simply stated, a performance test asks the applicant to perform essential tasks related to job performance; the test simulates major facets of the job. Theoretically, all kinds of SKAs could be tested using performance tests, but they are most likely to be used to evaluate skills such as typing speed and accuracy, operating vehicles and machinery, and doing computational tasks. Simulating complex jobs and situations is technically difficult and expensive. As computer technologies and software become more sophisticated, it is probable that more complex mixes of SKAs will be evaluated using performance tests, such as those now being used in simula-

BULLETIN

From OPM on the Outstanding Scholar Program:

"[It] is a special hiring authority established for entry-level administrative positions at the GS-5 and GS-7 grade levels. The Outstanding Scholar Program is authorized under terms of a consent decree (Luevano vs. Newman) and can only be used for the specific series and job titles listed [here]. It is not applicable for other entry-level professional jobs such as accountants, engineers, physical science careers, or jobs in the biological sciences or mathematics. [It] is not applicable at grades below GS-5 or above GS-7. If you meet the requirements. . ., you may be offered a direct appointment by a Federal agency without having to go through the normal competitive hiring procedures. The direct appointment process cuts through all of the red tape and can save you weeks of time." Career fields available under the program include: Health, Safety, and Environmental Jobs; Benefits Review, Tax, and Legal Jobs; Business, Finance, and Management Jobs; Personnel, Computer, and Administrative Jobs; and Law Enforcement and Investigative Jobs.

Source: (http://www.usajobs.opm.gov/ b11.htm), 1998.

tors to test pilots' responses to a range of situations they will (or might) face in real life.

In comparison to the other kinds of tests, performance tests yield very direct measures of how candidates perform on a series of job elements. Accordingly, these tests have high "face validity." From the perspective of the test taker, they are concrete and, if clearly job-related, likely to be seen as fair and objective. For these reasons, many jurisdictions are switching to performance tests when this is feasible in technical as well as budgetary terms. A major limitation is cost, since often expensive equipment must be acquired and maintained, and related personnel costs may be high.

ORAL EXAMINATIONS

The terms *oral examination* and *interview* are often used synonymously. Interview may also mean the conversation that a hiring official has with persons whose names are certified from a list of eligibles. These applicants have already passed the battery of tests, and the official is given a choice from among a certain number of names. Our reference here is to an oral that is a *weighted* part of the entire examination. The weight assigned varies with the importance given to the worker traits that the oral is designed to measure. Orals are often used to measure applicant's ability to communicate ideas and to interact effectively with others. Such abilities often carry heavy weight for managerial positions, but they are likely to have relatively less impact on overall examination scores for technical or manual jobs. As a result, oral examinations are used most extensively for managerial and administrative positions, but it is not unusual for them to be a part of test batteries for entry-level professional positions as well.

Oral examinations are used to (1) evaluate candidate's SKAs, or (2) illuminate job-related personality traits not probed by written or performance tests. Many experts on selection believe that the oral should be used primarily for the latter purpose because other, less subjective, measures of SKAs are available. The accuracy of written personality tests, on the other hand, is at best doubtful.

The results of oral examinations are inherently liable to distortions flowing from interviewer bias and poor structuring of the interview's content and process. To deal with these problems, oral examinations must be "well planned in terms of the behaviors and responses to be observed, the evaluation standards to be applied, and the procedures for conducting the process" (U.S. Office of Personnel Management, 1979a). In order to assure comparability and consistency, examiners should record their observations according to a standardized format. Training of interviewers is very important because their expertise is the foundation for confidence in the validity of the ratings, and including women and minority group members on interview panels minimizes the possibility that discrimination will occur. It may also increase the probability that women and minorities will have confidence in the fairness of the process.

THE GROUP ORAL PERFORMANCE TEST

The panel interview is the most common form of oral, but another type is the group oral performance test. In the group oral, candidates are assembled in small groups, and a topic is assigned for discussion. Civil service examiners evaluate how the candidates *perform* during the discussion, particularly how they interact with the other members of the group. Advocates of the group oral argue that it shows how well the candidates "think on their feet" and, since the examiners only listen, they have more time for careful observation.

However, as critics point out, the group oral is staged, and the participants may not behave as they would in a normal administrative situation. Since the attention of examiners may be frequently disrupted, they may really have *less* time to size up each person than they would in a panel interview. Furthermore, the examiners may end up rating each participant in terms of how the group performed rather than the actual requirements of the position in question. In other words, the group oral raises significant validity and reliability concerns. As a way of compensating for these liabilities, some jurisdictions use both a panel-type interview and a group oral, then average the candidates' scores on both.

BACKGROUND INVESTIGATIONS

Background investigations are used for a variety of purposes. For the vast majority of civil service jobs, they are routine reference checks done through mail and telephone inquiries. For some categories of positions, investigators employed by the central personnel agency will visit and interview former employers and others who have direct knowledge of an applicant's educational preparation, work experience, abilities, and personal qualities. On the state and local levels, the most intensive and comprehensive background checks are done for law enforcement positions. For federal jobs where access to sensitive or secret information is involved, detailed and comprehensive loyalty and security checks are conducted by the FBI. Recently, OPM contracted out its background-check function to a private corporation established by former employees. Faced with limited resources and time, public employers do not conduct thorough background investigations for most positions. The relative neglect of this phase of the selection process is regrettable, because those who have worked with or supervised candidates on previous jobs often can supply far more, information about them than can be obtained in an interview.

The Probationary Period

Although technically it is not a test or an examination, the probationary period is the last stage in the screening process; no matter how much effort is put into making preemployment tests valid, they may not screen out some applicants who actually lack the ability, motivation, or work habits needed to perform satisfactorily in particular jobs. The probationary period (usually six months to a year) gives supervisors the chance to evaluate new employees' situations and to approve for permanent status only those who have done satisfactory work. Probationary employees usually do not have appeal rights. If unsatisfactory workers are not separated at this point, it is almost always much more difficult to fire them later, since they may acquire so-called property interests in their jobs.

All too often, management does not act as if the probationary period were an important part of the selection process. In practice, only a tiny percentage of appointees—in many cases less than 1 percent—is removed during or at the end of the probationary period. This has traditionally been the situation, despite such schemes to prod supervisors as requiring the appointing officer to certify in writing that the employee's services have been satisfactory, in the absence of which certification all salary payments are suspended. Needless to say, the practice of routinely moving probationary employees to permanent status without careful performance evaluations undermines the selection process.

Lists of Eligibles and Related Issues

For every position or category of positions, applicants are evaluated and ranked according to their "scores" on one or more tests. Background checks and medical examinations normally are used after an initial offer of employment is made. Each test is weighted in accordance with the civil service agency's determination of the relative importance of the qualifications it is intended to measure. For example, mathematical skills may be very important to an accounting position, but relatively unimportant in the case of a file clerk or secretary. Minimum qualifications are not weighted since the applicant must meet them in order to receive further consideration. The same rule applies to background checks and medical examinations.

Tests are sequenced, with minimum qualifications coming as the first hurdle. If the applicant satisfies the minimum qualifications, he or she then undergoes one or more of the following: an evaluation of training and experience, a written test, or a performance test. If they are used, oral examinations come next, followed by a background investigation. This sequencing is economical in the sense that it places the most expensive and time-consuming tests at the end of the process where the fewest number of candidates need to be considered. It would make little sense, for example, to administer physical agility tests to everybody who applies for a firefighter position before determining if they meet a minimum requirement such as a high school degree.

A distinctive feature of civil service systems in the United States is that candidates who pass entrance or promotional examinations are placed on *lists of eligibles,* where they are ranked in order of composite scores. When hiring officials in agencies have openings to fill, they request the civil service agency to certify names of eligibles from these lists in the order specified in the civil service law and regulations. There are two basic kinds of hiring procedures using lists of eligibles: register hiring and case examining. Register hiring is a process using standing lists of eligibles rank-ordered by scores. These "inventories" of candidates are created to fill openings as they arise. Case examining "involves recruiting, examining applicant submissions, and producing a certificate of eligibles for specific individual vacancies rather than using a register of candidates that has already been established" (U.S. Merit Systems Protection Board, 1995, p. vii). Case examining is currently the most common competitive hiring method used by the federal government.

Until recently, the "rule of three" (the three highest-ranking eligibles) was by far the most common one for certifying names from eligible lists. Historically, this rule emerged as a device for protecting the merit system but at the same time giving some discretion to appointing officers. The assumption was that the examination scores would reflect real differences in ability to do the work and that three was a reasonable number of names to certify for each opening. In prac-

BULLETIN

A Vacancy Announcement from the City of San Jose, California

"Senior Analyst for Research and Development in the Office of the Chief of the Police Department. Open to City of San Jose Employees Only. MINIMUM QUALIFICATIONS: Any combination of training and experience equivalent to completion of a Baccalaureate Degree from an accredited college or university in accounting, business, public administration, or any related field leading to a bachelor's degree, and 4 years of increasingly responsible experience in general management/administrative analytical work in the areas of personnel, budget, fiscal and/or organizational methods analyses, including general staff analytical work. Possession of a valid driver's licence is required."

tice, veterans preference, which results in extra points and serves as a "tie-breaker" when applicants have the same score, tends to bias the system in favor of veterans when the rule of three is used. Advocates of the rule of three argued that certifying more names, or the entire list of those *passing* the examination, would increase the risk that line managers would use the opportunity to make appointments on a partisan basis. Some jurisdictions were so concerned about political "contamination" that they adopted a "rule of one," and a few state and local governments still operate on that basis. As questions about validity have increased, EEO concerns have mounted, and pressures for flexibility have grown, more and more public employers have moved in the opposite direction. Some states, for example, have modified the rule by allowing the three highest test *scores* to be certified, a practice that often results in more than three candidates being certified, since ties are commonplace. In 1995, the U.S. Merit Systems Protection Board (MSPB) issued a report on the rule of three in which it concluded that a growing body of evidence supported the following conclusions:

- The rule of three does not represent the best way to foster merit-based hiring.
- The interaction between the rule of three and current approaches to veterans preference often produces results that are not in the best interests of managers or job candidates, including those with veterans preference. (U.S. Merit Systems Protection Board, 1995, pp. ix–x)

The MSPB recommended that the rule of three be replaced by "a requirement that selecting officials shall select from an adequate number of well qualified candidates who are referred to them by the appropriate OPM or delegated examining office" (p. x). In addition, the report suggested that federal agencies go to a "category rating system" (such as the "quality" and "eligible" categories used in a U.S. Department of Agriculture demonstration project) as opposed to numerical ratings.

THE UNEWASY RELATIONSHIP BETWEEN COMPETITIVENESS, VALIDITY, AND EEO: FROM PACE TO ADMINISTRATIVE CAREERS WITH AMERICA

Presumably, for those who believe in the merit principle, the best of all possible worlds would be one in which public employers have highly competitive recruitment processes using valid selection tests that produce no adverse impact whatsoever. Unfortunately, as the case of the Professional and Administrative Career Examination (PACE) illustrates, such ideal outcomes are difficult to achieve.

A chronic complaint about public-sector recruitment is that it is slow, so slow in fact that many highly qualified applicants become frustrated and accept offers elsewhere. For entry-level administrative positions in the federal service, lengthy delays were often the result of centralized control over the ranking and certification of applicants for positions publicized by agencies. The rationale for this procedure was that it was the most reliable way to assure that quality candidates were referred to the agencies for selection and, thus, to protect merit from potential abuses on the agency level. Until 1982, OPM used a nation-wide written examination to rank applicants for entry-level profes-sional and administrative career (PAC) positions. Thousands of col-lege graduates sat for this exam every year. In 1981, the Professional and Administrative Career Examination, or PACE, was derailed by a class action suit challenging its validity. During 1981, a consent decree was negotiated that required OPM to stop using PACE and to replace it with job-specific written tests that did not have an adverse impact on minorities.

Prior to the consent decree, OPM had gone to great lengths to establish the validity of PACE. The first step had been to identify the abilities or constructs important for successful performance in PACE jobs and to decide how they would be measured. Twenty-seven PACE occupations accounting for about 70 percent of PACE hires during the early 1970s were chosen for intensive analysis. Senior-level super-visors in these occupations prepared lists of the duties of the jobs in these 27 occupations, assessed the relative importance of these duties, and rated the required SKAs according to their importance to suc-cessful job performance. These ratings created one basis for identify-ing the abilities to be measured on the written test. The other basis was a comprehensive review of "hundreds of tests whose construct validity had been explored in diverse settings."

The OPM analysts matched the SKAs and other traits identified in the 27 PACE occupations with those found in earlier tests, and they wrote examination questions similar to those in the earlier tests. After PACE was administered, OPM made criterion-related validity studies that revealed a positive relationship between test scores and job per-formance scores of persons already in PACE positions, such as Social Security claims examiners (an example of concurrent validity research).

The general abilities found necessary for successful job perfor-mance in PACE jobs included:

1. Verbal skills, meaning the ability to understand and inter-pret complex technical reading materials and to communi-cate effectively orally and in writing;

2. Judgment, or the capacity to make decisions or to take actions in the absence of complete information and to solve problems by inferring missing facts or events to arrive at the most logical conclusion;

3. Induction, relating to the ability to discover underlying relations or principles in specific data by formation and testing of hypotheses;

4. Deduction, meaning skill at discovering implications of facts and logically applying general principles to specific situations; and

5. Numbers-related abilities, such as performing arithmetic operations and solving quantitative problems when a specific approach or formula is not specified.

PACE did have a disparate or adverse impact on African-Americans and Hispanics. Data compiled by OPM on the April 1978 administration of PACE showed that 8.5 percent of whites taking the test received "unaugmented scores" (not including veterans preference points) of 90 or higher, but the percentages of African-Americans and Hispanics who took the test and got such scores were 0.3 and 1.5 percent, respectively. In practice, very few appointments were made of persons earning scores of under 90. Other administrations of PACE produced similar results.

Those who brought the class action suit challenging PACE's validity argued that the five constructs upon which the test was based were far too general in nature to measure the ability to succeed in all of the 118 occupations covered. They also questioned the technical soundness of OPM's validity research. For better or worse, the courts did not have the opportunity to rule on PACE's validity. Instead, two weeks before Ronald Reagan assumed office, the Carter administration entered into a consent decree to settle the suit (*Luevano v Campbell*, 1981).

Opponents of "preferential hiring" interpreted Carter's action as a politically motivated response to minority group pressures. The Reagan administration strongly opposed the decree and was able to negotiate modifications, including elimination of a requirement that the government continue affirmative action efforts until African-Americans and Hispanics were at least 20 percent of all employees at the GS-5 and higher grade levels in the job categories covered by PACE. As OPM Director Donald Devine later said, the Reagan administration had wanted to withdraw from the terms of the decree but had regretfully concluded that the matter was in the "hands of the court, beyond the power of the government unilaterally to bar" (Valdes, n.d.).

The main terms of the modified decree (*Luevano v Devine*) were:

1. OPM was to phase out PACE as a selection test by 1985;
2. Applicants for PACE occupations were to be selected using alternative examination procedures based on the requirements of the particular occupation;
3. If the alternative procedures had adverse impact, their validity had to be established;
4. Federal agencies were to make "all practicable efforts" to eliminate adverse impact from the interim use of PACE or from alternative procedures through recruiting and other special programs; and
5. The D.C. District Court was to retain jurisdiction for five years after the implementation of an alternative examining procedure for each occupation.

On May 11, 1982, OPM announced that PACE was being abolished and replaced by a new Schedule B appointment authority. Schedule B applies to positions where it is not practical to hold competitive examinations. Under Schedule B authority, agencies are allowed to hire people for entry-level professional and administrative positions without competitive examinations if they can show there are no qualified internal candidates. Those selected in this manner are placed in the excepted (noncompetitive) service. Until 1987, employees selected in this manner were required to compete for competitive positions to advance to the GS-9 level. If they were selected for a GS-9 position, they were converted to the competitive service. In 1987, however, President Reagan issued Executive Order 12596, which authorized *noncompetitive* conversions of Schedule B appointments based on "proven performance."

The Reagan administration offered several explanations for ending PACE and turning to Schedule B appointments. First, it argued there were no alternative written tests and other merit selection procedures available. Second, reductions in federal hiring rates were expected to result in substantially fewer appointments from outside the service. Third, the cost of developing validated competitive examinations consistent with the decree would be prohibitive. In fact, at the time, OPM showed little interest in a serious effort to develop alternative selection procedures, and its general counsel was quoted as saying that the intention was to allow *Luevano* to "sink of its own weight." By late 1987, OPM had developed 16 tests which, by its own estimate, covered only about 60 percent of the positions involved.

Whatever the motivations of those concerned, the use of Schedule B appointments did much to decentralize hiring for professional and administrative positions in the federal government. Under Schedule B, agencies develop and use their own recruitment and selection procedures. Federal line agencies, long frustrated with centralized and slow-moving hiring processes that undermined their recruitment efforts, were generally pleased with the Schedule B authority for PAC positions.

However, interests concerned about protecting the merit principle, maintaining overall "quality control" over agency hiring practices, and assuring that potential applicants could access the system from outside were less than enthusiastic. OPM's monitoring and evaluation efforts were minimal, and it was very difficult for agencies to get approval to fill entry-level PAC positions from outside the government. College placement offices were given "almost no information" about job opportunities for specific entry-level positions in the excepted service, and the delays and frustrations involved in attempting to locate and be considered for positions caused many well-qualified candidates to pursue other options. The GAO and MSPB were critical, calling for more effective OPM oversight and guidance.

In early 1987, a suit brought by the National Treasury Employees Union (NTEU) signaled the end of OPM's glacial movement toward alternative selection procedures. The D.C. District Court ruled that OPM "had acted improperly in deciding to place in the excepted service all job categories formerly covered by PACE and in deciding to abolish the PACE ahead of schedule when no alternative examinations were available." The judge also ruled that OPM had not made a convincing case about the "prohibitive costs" connected with developing and validating alternative tests. The original order gave OPM only six months to produce a competitive examination, and it ordered OPM to stop using Schedule B authority to fill PACE positions. Although a stay was granted, the need to implement a legally as well as technically viable alternative was obvious.

In 1988, OPM set forth a two-pronged strategy for replacing PACE. First, it proposed expansion of direct-hire programs such as the Outstanding Scholar Program described above. Second, it announced the development of the Administrative Careers with America or ACWA examinations covering six occupational categories: (1) health and environment, (2) writing and information, (3) business and program management, (4) human resources and administration, (5) examining and adjudicating, and (6) investigation and inspection. A seventh category included some 16 occupations having specific educational or experience requirements (e.g., economist, international relations, and museum curator). Applicants for positions in this seventh category were to be rated on the basis of their training and experience. All applicants for ACWA positions were also required to answer a series of questions intended to provide information traditionally sought through interviews: self-discipline, leadership qualities, and problem-solving skills. This component of the ACWA was called the Individual Achievement Record (IAR), which had a multiple-choice format and was machine scored.

Veterans preference points were added to the total ACWA score and the candidate placed on a standing list of eligibles. The new examinations were first given in June 1990 and OPM revoked Schedule B authority, effective July 1, 1990. The less than satisfactory experience with ACWA as a way of improving the competitiveness of federal recruitment and selection processes since that date was previously discussed and, by the late 1990s, it had been effectively supplanted by a variety of recruitment and selection procedures driven largely by agency needs and priorities.

Initially, however, OPM's strategy was to balance agency-level demands for flexible, streamlined, recruitment and selection against pressures for central oversight and control. Although federal agencies applauded the idea that they should be given direct-hire authority for students with high grade point averages, this proposal was controversial because of concerns about validity, EEO, and the potential impact on workforce quality. The new examinations, while generally well received, raised questions about their capacity to improve recruitment success because, as the GAO observed, OPM's application procedure was potentially slow-moving and, as a result, potentially frustrating to agencies as well as applicants. The GAO's most recent evaluation of the ACWA suggests that it has indeed been slow-moving and frustrating (U.S. General Accounting Office, 1994).

The GAO had noted earlier that the ACWA program might "also create difficulties for agencies, especially those with active recruiting programs" because:

> The ACWA program effectively breaks the link between recruiting and hiring. Unless a student interested in an ACWA occupation can be employed through the Outstanding Scholar provision, there is no guarantee that agencies can hire the candidates they meet and interview on college campuses. (U.S. General Accounting Office, 1990a, p. 22)

In 1990, the GAO noted that while the "ACWA is aimed at supporting the goal of merit-based non-discriminatory hiring," its impact on federal agencies' ability to compete in the labor market is uncertain. By 1994, the GAO was prepared to say that "statistics for fiscal years 1991 and 1992 tend to support the belief that ACWA is less effective in helping agencies meet affirmative action goals for females. . . . However, the percentage of minorities hired through ACWA was similar to that of minorities hired through other methods" (U.S. General Accounting Office, 1994, p. 13). After almost 20 years of turbulence and controversy in the area of recruitment and selection, the federal personnel system is still struggling to devise an approach that satisfies demands for flexibility and competitiveness, supports efforts to increase the representation of women and minorities in administrative and professional jobs, and can be shown to be valid in all of its important phases.

CONCLUSION

Over the past 20 years, many public personnel systems have implemented extensive delegations of authority to agencies in the areas of recruitment, testing, and hiring in an effort to remove procedural barriers to effective and efficient management. This move away from the regulatory or compliance-centered personnel systems toward a "deregulated" and management-centered *human resources* approach responds to strong political pressures for reform, public dissatisfaction with government's performance, and a new definition of public management's role that stresses flexibility and accountability for results or outcomes. In this new environment, "we will always have to struggle to find the proper balance between the need for control to prevent abuses and the need to give managers enough discretion to do their jobs well" (Ban, 1997, p. 201). Rather than making the job of the personnel specialist easier, the current reforms require an ongoing effort to simultaneously advance the values of responsiveness, merit, equal employment opportunity, and performance.

DISCUSSION QUESTIONS

1. As a college or university student, what steps would you like to see taken to improve the recruitment efforts of public employers on the local, state, and federal levels?

2. Is using grade point averages (GPA) or class standing to make direct hires under the federal Outstanding Scholar Program a good way of assuring that agencies will be hiring highly qualified applicants?

3. With extensive delegations and deregulation of the recruitment, testing, and hiring processes, will it be possible to protect the merit principle and equal employment opportunity?

4. How can public agencies do a better job of preparing their employees to fill more responsible positions and to be promoted?

5. What could be done to assure that supervisors will carefully evaluate new employees during their probationary periods?
6. What is your image of the public sector as a place to work in comparison to the private and nonprofit sectors?

REFERENCES

American Psychological Association (1966). *Standards for Educational and Psychological Tests and Manuals* (Washington, DC).

Ban, Carolyn (1997). "Hiring in the Public Sector: 'Expediency Management' or Structural Reform?" in Carolyn Ban and Norma M. Riccucci (eds.), *Public Personnel Management: Current Concerns, Future Challenges* (New York: Longman), pp. 189–203.

Equal Employment Opportunity Commission (1970). "Guidelines for Employee Selection Procedures." *Federal Register,* Vol. 35, No. 149, August 1.

Federal Register (1977). "Questions and Answers on the Federal Executive Agency Guidelines on Employee Selection Procedures" (Part VI, Vol. 42, No. 14), January 21.

———— (1979). "Adoption of Questions and Answers to Clarify and Provide a Common Interpretation of the Uniform Guidelines for Employee Selection Procedures" (Vol. 44, No. 43), March 2.

Foley v Connelie (1978). 98 S. Ct. 1067.

Georgia Merit System (1997). *Guidelines for Model Human Resource Procedures and Standards—Recruitment and Job Posting* (wysinyg://581http://www.gms.state.ga.us//modelpro/recruit.htm), June 13.

Griggs v Duke Power (1971). 401 U.S. 424.

Hamman, John A., Desai, Uday, and Mitchell, Thomas (1993). "Competing for Talent and Diversity in Local Government Personnel: Recruitment Practices in Illinois Local Government." *Review of Public Personnel Administration,* Vol. 13, No. 1 (Winter), pp. 22–37.

Hudson Institute (1988). *Civil Service 2000* (Washington, DC), June.

Illinois Commission on the Future of the Public Service (1991). *Excellence in Public Service: Illinois' Challenge for the '90s* (Chicago: Chicago Community Trust/Government Assistance Project), January.

Illinois Department of Natural Resources (1998). *DNR Internship Programs* (http://dnr.il.us/events/intpro.utm), June.

Luevano v Campbell (1981). 93 F.R.D. 68 (D.D.C.).

Maslow, Albert P. (1968). "Evaluating Training and Experience," in J. J. Donovan, *Recruitment and Selection in the Public Service* (Washington, DC: International Personnel Management Association).

National Academy of Public Administration (1987). *Statement Concerning Professional Career Entry into the Federal Service* (Washington, DC), April.

Office of the Governor, State of Illinois (1997). *1998 Michael Curry and Vito Marzullo Internship Programs* (Springfield, IL: Office of the Governor), November 15.

Riccucci, Norma M. (1991). "Merit, Equity, and Test Validity." *Administration and Society*, Vol. 23, No. 1 (May), pp. 74–93.

U.S. General Accounting Office (1990a). *Federal Recruiting and Hiring: Making Government Jobs Attractive to Prospective Employees* (Washington, DC), August.

———— (1990b). *Letter to The Honorable David Pryor, Chairman, Subcommittee on Federal Services, Post Office and Civil Service Committee on Governmental Affairs* (Washington, DC), September 27.

———— (1994). *Federal Hiring: Testing for Entry-Level Administrative Positions Fall Short of Expectations* (Washington, DC), March.

U.S. Merit Systems Protection Board (1990). *Attracting and Selecting Quality Applicants for Federal Employment* (Washington, DC: MSPM), April.

———— (1995). *The Rule of Three in Federal Hiring: Boon or Bane?* (Washington, DC: MSPB), December.

U.S. Office of Personnel Management (1979a). Federal Personnel Manual Letter 335-13, *Guidelines for Evaluation of Employees for Promotion and Internal Placement* (Washington, DC), December 31.

———— (1979). *Job Analysis for Selection: An Overview* (Washington, DC), August.

———— (1992). *OPM HRD Policy Initiatives* (Washington, DC), June.

———— (1997a). *Hispanic Employment Initiative* (http://www.opm.gov/pressrel/html/9point.htm), September.

———— (1997b). *Career America Connection Teleservice Center and Recruiting Messages* (http://opm.gov/employ/html/cac.htm), October.

———— (1997c). *Federal Employment Information Touch Screen Computer Kiosks* (http://www.gov.employ/html/feic.htm), October.

——— (1997d). *Student Educational Employment Program* (http://www.opm.gov/employ/students/intro.htm), December.

——— (1997e). *Student Educational Employment Program: Program Highlights From 1996* (http://www.opm.gov/employ/students/studrpt.htm), December.

Valdes, William C. (n.d.). *The Selection of College Graduates for the Federal Civil Service: The Problem of the "PACE" Examination and the Consent Decree* (Washington, DC: National Academy of Public Administration).

SUGGESTED READINGS

Gatewood, Robert D., and Feild, Hubert S. (1998). *Human Resource Selection*, 4th ed. (Fort Worth, TX: The Dryden Press).

Hays, Steven W. (1998). "Staffing the Bureaucracy: Employee Recruitment and Selection," in Stephen E. Condrey (ed.), *Handbook of Human Resource Management in Government* (San Francisco: Jossey-Bass), pp. 298–321.

Kilpatrick, Franklin P., Cummings, Milton C., and Jennings, M. Kent (1964). *The Image of the Federal Service* (Washington, DC: The Brookings Institution).

Chapter FIVE

Performance Appraisal and Pay for Performance

In this chapter, we will be looking at two very closely connected features of personnel policy in the public sector. The first is a renewed interest in creating performance appraisal systems that actively support the performance management efforts of public agencies. The second is an effort to establish "pay-for-performance" systems that reliably have positive effects on the motivation and productivity of public employees. To be credible, pay for performance requires that supervisors and employees have confidence in the objectivity and fairness of the performance appraisal process. If performance ratings are going to be major factors in pay decisions, it is important that all concerned believe they are accurate and actually discriminate among levels of performance. Likewise, the pay-related outcomes of these appraisals must be seen to be meaningful, as well as equitable. Over the past 20 years, the U.S. public sector has undergone a significant transformation in these areas, a transformation driven by the general shift toward a management-centered approach to personnel administration that is described in Chapter 2.

THE NEW PERFORMANCE APPRAISAL

A striking feature of contemporary thinking about personnel policy is its focus on using employee appraisals as the centerpiece of an organizational *performance management process.* Emphasis is being placed on relating the performance objectives and accomplishments of *individuals* to those of the *organization* and its *programs*. In these terms, the methods used to evaluate and reward employee performance on all levels should be designed to promote the goals and policy objectives of public agencies. In other words, the current emphasis on the *managerial functions* of performance appraisal systems.

The Civil Service Reform Act (CSRA) played a major role in stimulating renewed interest in performance appraisals in the public sector. It was enacted against a backdrop of intense public criticism of government in general and of "bureaucrats" in particular. By the mid-1970s, the American electorate was willing to accept the argument being advanced by candidates for office that its taxes were too high and government programs were not meeting expectations because public employees were overpaid and underworked. Removing unproductive public workers or making them improve their performance became a popular public policy goal (and mandatory campaign promise). To improve productivity, it was widely believed that performance measurement systems that accurately discriminated among levels of job achievement and made it possible to link employee compensation to performance were badly needed (Daley, 1991).

THE RISE AND FALL OF TRADITIONAL APPRAISAL SYSTEMS

Two factors converged during the 1970s and early 1980s to change state-of-the-art approaches to performance appraisal in government. First, the traditional systems were in disrepute on all levels of government. In technical terms, they simply were not doing what they were supposed to, and few managers took them very seriously. Second, in political terms, the pressures for greater bureaucratic productivity, accountability, and responsiveness created a climate that forced meaningful reforms in a number of areas, including performance appraisals and their uses.

Under conventional merit systems where management's discretion in personnel matters is deliberately limited, appraisals or service ratings are supposed to concentrate on how well an employee is carrying out the tasks associated with a job or position. The supervisor's role is largely to provide answers to trait- and task-related questions derived from job analysis done by personnel specialists. The results are supposed to be used to help make objective decisions regarding personnel matters such as retention, training, pay, and promotion. Technical questions focus on identifying and ranking job elements, and on how to accurately measure a worker's performance along each of these dimensions. In practice, the traditional appraisal process operated in virtual isolation from the planning, program design and implementation, and management control functions of public agencies.

The methods used in many merit systems had their origins in the precepts of scientific management and the aims of Civil Service Reform I. From scientific management came the concepts of job design and analysis, empirical observation, and measurement. Management's role was to design and interrelate jobs in a manner that generated the highest possible levels of technical efficiency. This required a careful empirical analysis of what workers were doing, the identification and combination of tasks into efficient packages or jobs, and measurement of worker performance against key job elements. Followers of the scientific management school firmly believed that appraisals keyed to specific jobs were essential if the workforce was to be managed in an efficient and harmonious manner. For the most part, however, they did not extend their thinking on this matter beyond the "shop" level or systematically consider how appraisals done by first-level supervisors might be linked to the broader concerns of upper management. The civil service reformers, on the other hand, had a different agenda in mind. Based on their experience with spoils, they did not trust managers to objectively administer a personnel system, including performance appraisals. Instead, they favored leaving the design and administration of performance appraisals to specialists housed in nonpartisan civil service commissions.

The idea of rigorously objective performance appraisals formulated by disinterested specialists using scientific methods was particularly attractive because, at least superficially, it meshed nicely with American norms of individualism and egalitarianism. "Science" promised accurate job-related measures free from subjective biases of all kinds. Merit systems were supposed to provide the disinterested and professional environment required to create and administer valid and objective evaluations of the individual's work. Such appraisals, in turn, would guarantee fair and equitable treatment of all workers. Performance, and performance alone, would determine pay and status. These values were very much in line with the merit principles advocated by the reformers, and they were enshrined in civil service laws on all levels of government.

As merit systems were established and expanded, the design and operation of performance appraisal systems came to be dominated by technical specialists working for commissions or their functional equivalents. At their best, the methods used to construct appraisal instruments rather closely followed those recommended by the scientific managers. Line management's role was limited to providing job-related information needed by these specialists as they formulated rating schemes, keeping necessary records and filling in rating forms. In its study of the available research on pay for performance, the National Research Council notes that this "measurement tradition" dominated the field until the late 1970s (Milkovich and Wigdor, 1991). This tradition, based in psychometrics and testing, stresses accurate measurement as a precondition for accurate evaluation of performance.

> By and large, researchers in measurement have made the assumption that if the tools and procedures are accurate (e.g., valid and reliable), then the functional goals of organizations using tests or performance appraisals will be met. (Milkovich and Wigdor, 1991, p. 45)

It is difficult to conceive of a genuine merit system without a credible system for appraising individual performance. Nevertheless, while the majority of states and localities have had some kind of rating system on the books for many years, and the federal government has been in the business since the establishment of the old Civil Service Commission, performance appraisals have been a notoriously weak link in the chain of techniques needed to firmly connect merit principles with merit system practices. At least three interrelated kinds of problems plagued efforts to realize the goals of the scientific managers and civil service reformers.

Technical Problems

First, for all but the most routine and simple kinds of work, identifying and clearly defining the performance dimensions of civil service positions were not easy. Professional and administrative jobs are often complex and variable. Static and necessarily general position descriptions seldom provided a meaningful picture of what these people were actually doing. Even if agreement on performance dimensions could be reached, developing administratively feasible methods for accurately measuring performance on the job turned out to be an equally difficult technical problem. The scientific managers had developed their concepts and tested their methods in industrial settings for the most part. Their interest in shop level work had not been extended in any systematic way to supervisory, professional, or administrative jobs. Since few public jobs are industrial in nature, scientific management's measurement techniques were of limited value.

The technical problems were considerable. Furthermore, attempting to solve them was expensive; developing performance measurement plans and formats based on job standards required expertise and time. Administering and maintaining these plans was also costly. Predictably, given pressing claims on limited resources, interest in performance appraisals waned throughout the public sector. Funding was minimal, and relatively little staff time was devoted to appraisals. Training programs for supervisors were nonexistent or superficial. In turn, supervisors did not invest much time in the process, and they typically delayed completing evaluation forms until the last minute. Ratings were skewed toward the high end of the scale as supervisors sought to avoid conflict and accusations of being unfair. It was not unusual for over 95 percent of the ratings to be in the "satisfactory" or higher categories.

Managerial Problems

The second category of problems was managerial. The scant attention paid to performance appraisals by supervisors was not only a reflection of technical problems. It was also a response to the largely peripheral role line management played in their design and use. Investing heavily in these systems did not make much sense. Supervisors were not rewarded for doing so by their bosses, and negative ratings often yielded nothing more than stressful interpersonal conflict and time-consuming appeals by resentful workers to suspicious civil service boards. Public managers are asked to effectively and efficiently accomplish objectives established under law and by the policy initiatives of their superiors. From this perspective, performance appraisals are useful only to the extent that they promote managers' efforts to control, guide, and coordinate the actions of subordinates. Did existing performance appraisal systems help managers manage? Overall, the answer was that they did not. At best, they were not very relevant and, therefore, appropriately treated as required formalities or annual rituals. At worst, they erected barriers to effective management by stimulating cynicism and distrust of supervisors, by stripping managers of any meaningful control over incentives such as pay, and most importantly, by greatly constraining supervisors' role in defining performance goals and standards. Under these conditions, veteran managers should not have been expected to take performance appraisals very seriously.

Organizational Problems

The third set of problems was organizational. Performance appraisals were not connected to mainline administrative functions such as planning and budgeting. Nor were they used as part of higher administration's efforts to control programmatic activities. Appraisal methods and procedures did little to support administrators' efforts to set goals, to monitor organizational performance, and to allocate human as well as material resources effectively. From the standpoint of those trying to achieve goals on the organizational and program levels, employee performance appraisals, for all practical purposes, were *administratively* irrelevant. Accordingly, like supervisors down the line, higher-level public executives were not inclined to expend their limited resources on efforts to enhance performance appraisals. From an organizational point of view, these were done largely to satisfy on paper the demands of civil service statutes and merit system rules.

A VICTORY OF FORMS OVER SUBSTANCE

As might be expected under these conditions, performance appraisals became forms to be filled out, signed off on, complained about, and forgotten. Various kinds of plans were used, the most common being trait rating. Typically, a graphic rating scale was used on which the supervisor marked on a continuum the degree to which a particular factor described the employee. Since a graphic rating scale allows the supervisor to rate subordinates rapidly by making check marks in the spaces indicated on the form, it does have the virtue of being easy to administer. It is largely for this reason that trait rating was widely adopted. Mostly, the factors were personality traits, such as initiative, courtesy, cooperativeness, and enthusiasm. Their connections to actual job performance could only be assumed. It was not unusual for these rating forms to include some very generally stated items about the quantity and quality of work, but this was usually the extent of inquiry into actual job performance. Factors were seldom clearly defined, and those doing the rating normally were given little or no specific guidance as to how to measure the degree to which a factor described the ratee. Figure 5.1 is an example of a generic trait rating format; this one was used by a large city during the early 1980s.

Weaknesses commonly associated with the generic trait-rating approach include:

1. The content of the rating form is not job-related or specifically applicable to many positions;

2. The format allows so much room for interpretation that ratings often vary widely among supervisors and across organizational units, which tends to undermine the credibility of the ratings that workers receive;

3. The lack of objective measures of performance creates conditions under which supervisors can exercise their prejudices or, even if they try to be objective, might be suspected of biasing their evaluations in favor of some and against others; and

4. The format encourages a superficial effort by supervisors, since it involves nothing more than checking off a series of boxes, which can be done in a few minutes.

Figure 5.1 Example of a Trait-Rating Form

Employee's Name	Employee's Payroll Title	Social Security Number
Bureau Office	Department	Position Number
Time in Present Classification ____ Years ____ Months	Period of Job Performance Evaluated From:	To:
Period of Time Evaluator has Supervised Employee: From:		To:
Type of Report: ☐ Annual ☐ First Probationary ☐ Final Probationary ☐ Other _____		

OUTSTANDING – Almost always does far better than the job requires.
HIGHLY SATISFACTORY – Very often performs noticeably more or better work than is required.
SATISFACTORY – Fully competent employee; does what is required in the position.
MARGINAL – Minimally satisfactory; employee could attempt some improvement.
REQUIRES IMPROVEMENT – Performance unsatisfactory but may improve within a reasonable time.
INSUFFICIENT – Consistent inability or unwillingness to perform satisfactorily.

IF ANY ITEM IS NOT APPLICABLE TO THE PERSON RATED, OMIT THAT ITEM AND NOTE "N/A"

INSUFFICIENT	REQUIRES IMPROVEMENT	MARGINAL	SATISFACTORY	HIGHLY SATISFACTORY	OUTSTANDING			N/A
						ATTENDANCE	–To what extent is employee at work regularly?	
						PUNCTUALITY	–To what extent does employee report to work on time?	
						USE OF TIME	–Does employee work steadily, refrain from wasting time?	
						INITIATIVE	–Does employee take needed action without waiting to be told?	
						JUDGEMENT	–Are the decisions the employee makes sound decisions?	
						COOPERATION	–Does employee assist coworkers needing help, avoid quarrels?	
						REPORTING	–Does employee inform you of work progress, problems that arise?	
						RELIABILITY	–Does employee complete assignments without excessive supervision?	
						JOB KNOWLEDGE	–Does employee know what to do and how to do it (without assistance)?	
						WORK QUANTITY	–How much work does the employee accomplish compared to the amount required?	
						WORK QUALITY	–Is employee's work usually accurate and complete?	
						(Evaluate factors below or additional factors IF any apply to the employee's responsibilities)		
						LEADERSHIP	–Does employee obtain satisfactory performance from subordinates?	
						PLANNING	–Does employee set appropriate goals, establish priorities, anticipate future needs?	
						ORGANIZING	–Delegates responsibility and authority effectively; avoids coordination problems?	
						DIRECTING	–Keeps subordinates informed of work plans, procedures and changes?	
						FOLLOW-UP	–Ensures that subordinates complete assignments and accurately on time?	
						FLEXIBILITY	–Does employee change to meet changing requirements of the job?	
						ACCOUNTABILITY	–Does employee accept full responsibility for all aspects of assignments?	
						Equal Employment		
						Opportunity	-Ensures that affirmitive EEO actions are taken in	
							all appropriate aspects of employment?	

By 1981, the Urban Institute had concluded that "evidence currently available indicates that systems utilizing supervisor ratings of personal traits and focusing on nonspecific aspects of performance are not valid or effective enough to be worthwhile" (Greiner et al., 1981, p. 227).

In the federal government, the situation was very similar. In 1978, while the Carter administration was moving the CSRA through the Congress, the GAO recommended fundamental changes in the performance rating systems being used by federal agencies. It reported that many workers simply were not getting useful feedback about their performance (U.S. General Accounting Office, 1978). Often, performance requirements were nonexistent or so vague as to be useless, and many position descriptions were outdated. A Civil Service Commission regional director said, "Supervisors are often unable to furnish statements on what is actually required on the job, beyond performing the duties listed in the position description. This leads us to believe that performance requirements appear only when they are needed to document an outstanding or unsatisfactory rating." Although both the Performance Rating Act of 1950 and agency rules required that they do so, many supervisors had not established performance standards or discussed them with their subordinates. The GAO report also noted that up to half of all supervisors had *never* received training in the major elements of performance evaluation, and some who had did not think it was very useful.

Federal managers who tried to make the existing system work were frustrated by poorly conceived legislation and restrictive court decisions. The Performance Rating Act of 1950 required summary adjective ratings of overall performance: *Outstanding, Satisfactory,* and *Unsatisfactory.* The law provided that outstanding ratings could be given "only when *all* aspects of performance not only exceed normal requirements, but are outstanding and deserve special commendation" (emphasis added). This is a very demanding standard to meet and, from a supervisory point of view, meeting it required a heavy investment in time and effort to document an outstanding rating. Thus the law encouraged supervisors to give satisfactory ratings to the vast majority of employees who were doing acceptable or *better* work.

For marginal and unproductive employees, the 1950 Act provided that a rating of unsatisfactory was grounds for removal from the position in which the performance was unsatisfactory. However, in 1960, a court of claims ruled that the Lloyd-LaFollette Act of 1912 and the Veterans Preference Act of 1944 took precedence. In short, dismissal could not be automatic because the ruling was interpreted to mean that federal workers had *two* statutory appeals rights, the first after receipt of a notice of unsatisfactory performance and the second after initiation of dismissal action by management. Under these conditions, federal managers usually bypassed giving unsatisfactory ratings and went directly to adverse action proceedings. This strategy saved both time and money, but it meant that virtually all federal employees were rated satisfactory. Between 1954 and 1978, the GAO calculated, 99 percent of all ratings had fallen into this category.

To make matters worse, the Federal Salary Reform Act of 1962 contained a provision eliminating an automatic within-grade pay increase for everybody rated satisfactory or better. Instead, the basis for granting the increases should be an independent determination by the agency head that the employee had met an "acceptable level of competence." The rationale was that supervisors were not critically rating performance because they did not want to deprive employees of within-grade increases or otherwise damage their status. Instead of encouraging and supporting genuine efforts by supervisors to discriminate among levels of accomplishment, the 1962 Act simply forced agency heads to routinely give certifications of acceptable performance because they were in no position to do otherwise. In general, federal employees were at best ambivalent about the objectivity and utility of pre-CSRA performance appraisals (Ingraham and Ban, 1984, pp. 70–86).

Until the late 1970s, performance appraisal languished as a backwater of public personnel administration. In theory, its importance to merit systems and management effectiveness was recognized. In practice, efforts to define and accurately measure performance experienced minimal success in the public sector, but the idea became firmly entrenched in the professional and research literature, and debate over the relative virtues of a variety of techniques for measuring performance surfaced on a fairly regular basis. Research focused on alternatives to the trait-rating approach such as critical incident methods, behaviorally anchored rating scales, evaluation by objectives, and narrative models (Milkovich and Wigdor, 1991, pp. 54–76). However, proposals to overhaul performance appraisal policies and practices in the public sector had relatively little impact until pressures for civil service reform forced the issue. The early 1980s were marked by enthusiastic and optimistic efforts to place appraisals at the center of Civil Service Reform II (Downs and Larkey, 1986, pp. 190–200).

In comments made some ten years after the enactment of the CSRA, former OPM Director Alan K. Campbell noted that the federal reforms were intended to respond to a personnel establishment that had developed into a "protective negative system primarily designed to prevent patronage, favoritism, and other personnel abuses." He said:

> Attitude surveys of federal managers at that time indicated that they were as disillusioned about how well the system worked as the general public. They did not believe they could manage the system; they

believed that the oversight agencies imposed restrictions and regulations that made it impossible for them to be effective. (U.S. General Accounting Office, 1988, p. 12)

Campbell's admonition that performance appraisal systems will not work unless they are "based on a carefully drawn plan for the organization's activities over. . .[its] planning cycle" suggests the outlines of the approach taken to performance appraisals by many U.S. governments during the last 20 years. Emphasis has been placed on the development of appraisal instruments and processes that require supervisors to evaluate employees' performance in terms of specific job responsibilities and organizational objectives. In reformed systems, ratings are visibly connected to a variety of key aspects of human resources management, most importantly pay. In many jurisdictions, administrative control over evaluation formats and procedures has been greatly expanded in response to the argument that effective performance management requires a "deregulated" and "decentralized" approach (Thompson and Radin, 1997).

A MANAGEMENT APPROACH TO PERFORMANCE APPRAISAL

Technically, the 1980s were marked by concern "less with questions of validity and reliability than with the workability of the performance appraisal system within the organization, its ability to communicate organizational standards to employees, to reward good performers, and to identify employees who require training and other development activities" (Milkovich and Wigdor, 1991, p. 46). Within the framework of this management orientation, performance appraisals were added to the inventory of resources executives might use to leverage greater bureaucratic responsiveness and accountability. Extensive delegations to departments of authority to design and administer appraisal systems (within broad policy guidelines) came to receive strong support from many personnel specialists as well as line managers. Evaluation methods based on management-by-objectives (MBO) concepts became popular elements of efforts to make agency goals and plans the basis of performance measures used throughout the organization.

With regard to accuracy, attention has shifted from the properties of rating scales to factors affecting the ability of those doing the rating to provide accurate judgments of performance. Employee acceptance and organizational utility are central objectives of the management orientation and, therefore, it stresses the importance of the organizational setting (social, psychological, and technical) within which the appraisal process takes place. Although the influence of the rating technology being used on accuracy is recognized, particular emphasis is placed on "the conditions that encourage raters to use the performance appraisal systems in the way that they were intended to be used" (Milkovich and Wigdor, 1991, p. 47). For example, there is research evidence to support the idea that the perceived effectiveness of performance appraisal systems is strongly related to the employee confidence in their accuracy and fairness (Roberts, 1995, p. 37). Acceptance by supervisors or raters is also critical:

> Rater acceptance is high when raters understand the rationale justifying the system and its goals, are confident in their ability to effectively administer the system, [when] the perceived benefits exceed the costs, the appraisal system does not conflict with other personnel systems. . . , and the manager's employees have favorable attitudes toward the system. (Roberts, 1992, p. 22)

By the mid-1990s, the regulatory concerns of the first civil service reform movement had faded into the background and the executive and managerial uses of performance appraisals had assumed center stage. These uses are now, in one writer's words, "ubiquitous in the public sector" (Fox and Shirkey, 1997, p. 205). One example is the State of Georgia's Performance Management Process (PMP), which is a component of the GeorgiaGain project. A central element of the project is a performance-based compensation system. The PMP is designed to "set expectations for quality performance and productivity that can be measured, and reward employees for meeting those expectations" (Georgia Merit System, 1997, p. 2).

Under the Georgia PMP, managers and employees are supposed to share accountability for job performance. They are expected to collaborate on an annual process that "measures actual performance against expectations and rewards on-the-job achievement." According to *Manager's Guide* to the PMP, this interactive process involves four phases: planning, coaching, evaluation, and development.

- In the *Planning Phase,* the manager "develops an individual Performance Plan, with input from the employee, that clearly defines job responsibilities, performance expectations, and performance measures."
- During the *Coaching Phase,* the manager "documents employee performance and gives regular feedback and encouragement." The manager is expected to help the employee solve performance problems and to provide formal feedback at least once a year.
- The *Evaluation Phase* is the point at which the manager and the employee "review the manager's assessment of the

employee's overall performance as measured against defined expectations." Two areas of performance are rated, these being job performance and compliance with organizational rules of behavior and attendance.

- The last step in the PMP cycle is the *Development Phase,* during which the manager and the employee jointly set performance expectations and development goals for the next cycle "that will help improve or enhance the employee's effectiveness at work. The development plan may set specific training objectives or refine/expand the scope of the employee's job." (Georgia Merit System, 1997, p. 3)

Georgia uses its Performance Management Form (PMF) as the centerpiece of its performance planning and evaluation process. The PMF is used to develop a performance plan and to record and document the annual performance rating, and "it may also contain the employee's Development Plan." All State of Georgia classified employees must have an individual performance plan, and department heads have the discretion to determine if unclassified employees in their agencies should be included. Normally, performance plans are based on official state job descriptions "in order to bring as much consistency as possible to the responsibilities (and expectations) assigned to positions in the same job." However, performance plans should describe the responsibilities of someone in a particular position, not simply a class or group of positions, and they "can be tailored to fit the *employee* in the position. . ." (p. 8). A copy of the Georgia PMF and instructions may be found in Appendix 5.A.

The Georgia PMP is designed to avoid a number of problems that typically combine to seriously undermine the effectiveness of performance appraisal systems. Reviews of appraisals under the CSRA in a number of federal agencies revealed, for example, that:

1. For a variety of reasons, employees were not active participants in the development of the performance standards for their jobs.

BULLETIN

GeorgiaGain

"The GeorgiaGain design concept rewards state employees for putting the public first in their job performance through efficient, effective customer service. Classified employees, regardless of organizational level, are eligible for pay-for-performance increases based on meeting or exceeding clearly defined performance standards for their jobs. Performance standards are set at levels which mandate that employees must be truly committed to productivity and public service to meet them, and must truly excel in job performance to exceed them."

Source: GeorgiaGain Compensation Services: An Overview of Georgia's Performance Management and Compensation System (http://www.gms.state.ga.us//gagain/aboutgg.htm), 1988.

2. Workers were not informed by their supervisors of the performance standards at the beginning of the appraisal period.

3. Performance standards, if they existed, were not clearly stated in measurable terms, failed to distinguish between levels of accomplishment, and did not clearly define unacceptable performance.

4. Agencies' procedures for linking ratings to personnel actions, such as pay increases, were vague, and employees could not see a direct and logical connection between their ratings and these actions. (U.S. General Accounting Office, 1983; U.S. General Accounting Office, 1987)

In its report prepared for OPM, the National Research Council reviewed the available research on performance appraisals in the public and private sectors, and it reached the following conclusions:

▪ First, in the applied setting of day-to-day personnel management, heavy investments in measurement precision are not economically viable because they are unlikely to improve the overall quality or usefulness of performance appraisals.

▪ Second, the Council recommended that performance evaluation policies emphasize "informed managerial judgment and not aspire to the degree of standardization, precision, and empirical support that would be required of, for example, selection tests." (Milkovich and Wigdor, 1991, p. 3)

In the context set by these conclusions, the Council advanced several summary observations concerning the measurement side of appraisals:

▪ Job analysis and specification of performance standards are not substitutes for supervisory judgment, but they are important because they may help focus the appraisal process for both the supervisor and the employee.

▪ Supervisors are able to form "reasonably reliable estimates of their employees' overall performance levels." However, consistency is not a guarantee of accuracy; systematic error and bias are still possible. It is, for example, possible for supervisors consistently to undervalue the performance of women or members of racial and ethnic minorities.

▪ Although there are many rating scale types and formats, they will yield similar results if "the dimensions to be rated are well chosen and the scale anchors are clearly defined."

Anchors are more or less specifically described levels of performance displayed on a continuum from, for example, 1 = unacceptable to 5 = exceptional. There was no convincing evidence found to support the proposition that distinguishing between behaviors and traits has much effect on rating outcomes. It seems that supervisors form generalized evaluations that strongly color "memory for and evaluation of actual work behaviors." Likewise, there is little evidence to suggest that rating systems based on highly job-specific dimensions produce results much different from those using "global" or general dimensions. (p. 144)

All of these points imply that the degree to which an appraisal system actually contributes to the performance management process is largely dependent on the degree to which all concerned are invested in its success through (1) a commitment to supervisory training and employee development, (2) active and informed participation of supervisors and employees in the setting of standards and developmental goals, (3) use of fair and objective measures of performance, and (4) a visible commitment to procedural fairness in all phases of the rating process (Roberts, 1995; Roberts and Reed, 1996). In these terms, the Council's report noted that successful performance appraisal systems in the private sector share certain characteristics:

[They are] firmly imbedded in the context of management and personnel systems that provide incentives for managers to use performance appraisal ratings as the organization intends. These incentives include managerial flexibility or discretion in rewarding top performers and in dismissing those who continually perform below standard. . . .Managers are themselves assessed on the results of their performance appraisal activities. (Milkovich and Wigdor, 1991, p. 164)

TOTAL QUALITY MANAGEMENT AND PERFORMANCE APPRAISAL

Considerable attention has been devoted to improving and refining performance appraisal techniques and systems that focus on the individual employee. This long-standing approach assumes that the key to improving productivity and quality of services in the public sector is accurately measuring and controlling the performance of each worker. A different approach, total quality management (TQM), challenges this assumption. In one writer's words, "most of those using TQM persist in managing performance through individual ratings—a practice antithetical to TQM" (Bowman, 1994, p. 129). Since TQM has been very influential in the public sector over the past 20 years, its point of view on performance appraisal should be understood.

TQM approaches the entire organization as a complex set or system of interdependent *processes* and it asserts that performance problems do not begin with employees, "but from lack of understanding of the work processes" (Bowman, 1994, p. 129). The goals of the TQM approach are to study work processes in order to identify barriers to quality, to satisfy internal and external customers, and to create an organizational culture that values quality and continuous improvement. The objective of TQM, in other words, is to change organizational systems in order to improve quality, as opposed to changing individual workers. Individual performance appraisals, according to their critics, overlook the systemic basis of productivity and quality, and they fuel competition and suspicion, which undermine the cooperation and teamwork needed to sustain a culture of continuous improvement. Supporters of TQM, therefore, recommend that traditional performance appraisals be abandoned and replaced with a concentration on identifying and eliminating systemic sources of variation in the quality of products and services that are *not* under the control of individual employees.

Rather than dropping individual performance appraisals and moving to a group-centered model, the usual response by public employers applying TQM methods has been to try to make traditional performance appraisals work better by increasing employee participation and setting the entire process in a "developmental" frame of reference. This does not move the focus of concern from the individual to the organizational system and its processes. Several reasons have been identified why public managers and employees are reluctant to abandon the traditional systems:

- Managers often use performance appraisals as a way to control their subordinates, and they are reluctant to make changes that would give employees greater discretion and influence over work processes. Organizations using TQM tend to be structurally "flatter" and to have more open communications than traditional bureaucracies, and they give their workers more discretion because "empowerment allows employees to respond to client needs in a timely and customized way." (Berman, 1997, p. 282)

- Managers "may be reluctant not only to embrace radical approaches, but also to abandon those that benefitted them during their career. In fact, many find appraisals to be a useful, if technically problematic, ideological tool. When they sign-off on them, their job is done; the responsibility for quality and productivity is returned to where, in their view, it belongs—the subordinate." (Bowman, 1994, p. 132)

■ Employees often are suspicious of management's purposes when changes are proposed, and they tend to prefer evaluation systems that are familiar over those with which they have no experience, even if the familiar system is less than satisfactory.

■ For managers and workers alike, traditional performance appraisal systems are hard to abolish because they are so closely connected to many other important personnel functions, such as training, compensation, promotion, and termination. Changing the appraisal process to fit the TQM model would necessarily require making significant and potentially threatening changes to the existing personnel system. (Bowman, 1994, pp. 132–133; Berman, 1997, pp. 283–286; Connor, 1997)

Some public employers have made efforts to reform their performance appraisal systems along lines that are more congruent with the central values of TQM by including contributions to team performance and quality of work as evaluation criteria. Overall, however, public employers have not moved away from individual performance appraisals to any significant extent. TQM's reliance on group appraisals and rewards continues to be a widely recognized barrier to its full implementation by government agencies on all levels. As one observer puts it, "Fears that team appraisals will breed free-riding, rating uncertainty, and placing one's financial destiny in the hands of coworkers are real, realistic, and not easily assuaged" (Durant, 1998, p. 465). In practical terms, the American cultural stress on individual effort, achievement, and rewards is unlikely to support anything resembling a complete conversion to TQM's doctrine of evaluating systems, not people. However, appropriate combinations of team and individual evaluations should be possible and, in the American setting, necessary.

MULTISOURCE PERFORMANCE APPRAISALS

In addition to the TQM challenge to traditional performance appraisals, there has been considerable interest in the potential advantages of replacing the hierarchical or "top-down" appraisal process with one that obtains feedback from a variety of sources in addition to the supervisor, including subordinates, peers, and customers or clients.

Multisource performance appraisals are designed to overcome the limited perspective inevitably associated with having only one rater: "Since the behaviors a single rater can observe are limited, the result can be an 'unrepresentative sample' of a given employee's or a given manager's performance" (Coggburn, 1998, p. 68). Frequently proposed alternatives or complements to conventional appraisal systems are: self-appraisal, peer review, upward feedback from subordinates, and assessment centers. Each of these methods offers some benefits in the areas of reliability, validity, and procedural fairness that may be combined to create a new appraisal model. In this model, performance information comes from several individuals who work or interact with the person being evaluated (deLeon and Ewen, 1997, p. 4).

In brief, under the multisource assessment model, evaluation criteria consisting of core competencies and desired supervisory behaviors are developed by a group of trained employees. Feedback on these criteria is obtained from sources throughout the organization in order to assure that they are relevant and fair. Definitions of actual behaviors that would satisfy these standards are then developed. In the next step, the employee being reviewed selects an evaluation team composed of work associates, including his or her supervisor and others in a position to provide accurate feedback on performance. The employee may also provide a self-appraisal. Access to the feedback obtained through this process is limited to the employee and the supervisor, and training is conducted to show employees how to "interpret their performance appraisals and design action plans based upon them" (deLeon and Ewen, 1997, p. 4).

In their study comparing the multisource to the conventional performance appraisal model in a federal agency, deLeon and Ewen found that "employees gave significantly higher approval ratings to the new performance appraisal system on every dimension" (p. 5). These dimensions were fairness, accuracy, usefulness, and understanding. Similarly, Coggburn (1998) reports that subordinate appraisals, if implemented in a manner designed to reassure supervisors about the qualifications and attitudes of subordinates and to provide the training needed by those involved, may be useful in at least two ways. First, they help establish a defensible rationale for personnel actions, since the "law regarding performance appraisals and personnel decisions strongly supports the use of more than one rater whenever performance judgements are made to promote, demote, discharge, or determine merit pay" (p. 70). Second, subordinate appraisals may provide valuable feedback that supervisors can use to identify areas where they need to improve their management skills through training or other developmental activities.

PAY FOR PERFORMANCE IN THE PUBLIC SERVICE

Pay for performance (PFP) is a hallmark of Civil Service Reform II. Virtually all calls for civil service reform and actual reforms have included some form of PFP. An important reason for the popularity

of merit pay has been public demands for more bureaucratic accountability and productivity. In James L. Perry's words:

> It [pay for performance] is a message from politicians and the public
> that the governed are in control and things are as they should be. At
> the same time, it is a way for administrators to communicate that
> they are responsive to important external constituencies and that
> they are doing something about perceptions of lagging performance.
> (Perry, 1991, p. 80)

Using PFP to raise productivity has been a basic element of management thinking in the United States since the late 1800s, and the
early scientific managers are well known for their efforts to rationalize
pay systems for factory workers along so-called "piece-rate" lines.
Their goal was to increase efficiency in the blue-collar workplace. The
current emphasis on merit pay in government emerged in a climate of
fiscal stress, and it concentrates for the most part on motivating and
raising the productivity of white-collar workers.

Although some states and localities were experimenting with
PFP before passage of the CSRA, Title V of the Act was a high-
profile break with traditional pay practices in the public sector, which
tied wages and salaries to positions and seniority, with pay increases
being allocated across the board to all satisfactory performers.

> Borrowing from private-sector practices, Title V. . . .sought to moti-
> vate better performance and to deter poor performance by increas-
> ing grade level 13–15 managers' salaries by amounts determined by
> their rated performance. . . . (Perry, 1991, p. 74)

Since 1978, PFP programs have been adopted by over 20 states and
many local governments (Greiner, 1986; U.S. General Accounting
Office, 1990). By the late 1980s, well over 25 percent of major U.S.
cities reported that a primary use of performance appraisals was to
allocate pay for managerial and nonmanagerial personnel (Ammons
and Rodriguez, 1986; England and Parle, 1987).

Pay for performance plans come in a variety of forms, including
those using one-time bonuses or variable pay, permanent increases to
base salary, and group-based bonuses or "gainsharing." Individual
bonuses and base-pay increases are by far the most common in the
U.S. public sector. In some jurisdictions, only supervisory and managerial personnel are covered, but in others PFP is restricted to nonmanagerial personnel. In some states and localities, both groups are
covered by the same or different systems. In other words, pay for performance is a generic term that applies to a wide variety of monetary
incentives programs. Their one unifying theme is the goal of establishing clear and reliable linkages between performance ratings and

pay and, through the administration of those linkages, to motivate workers and to manage performance.

No matter the form it takes, PFP's widespread popularity is based in large measure on the proposition that it remedies a fundamental flaw in traditional compensation systems by making pay *contingent* on performance, as opposed to the position grade and seniority of the employee. Logically, it accepts the cognitive model of motivation set forth in the expectancy theory discussed in Chapter 3. Expectancy theory suggests that pay should be treated as a management tool because it can be a powerful source of day-to-day control over employee behavior. Traditional systems of pay administration (membership-based inducements), it is argued, do not give supervisors the kind of discretion and flexibility they need to use pay as an effective motivator (Gabris and Mitchell, 1985).

During the period of initial enthusiasm for PFP, other advantages attributed to it included the following:

1. Improved attractiveness to highly qualified and hard-to-recruit college graduates;

2. An increase in the probability that superior performers would feel valued and equitably compensated for their efforts;

3. Focusing management's attention on the importance of accurate performance appraisals using measurable standards and objectives;

4. Providing supervisors with an effective means of pressuring poor performers to improve or leave;

5. Encouraging supervisors and subordinates to communicate clearly about goals and expectations; and

6. Enhancing organizations' overall capacity to allocate limited financial resources in an effective manner.

Despite these expectations, the public sector's experience with pay-for-performance programs has not been entirely encouraging:

> Despite the popularity of pay for performance in the public sector, by the late 1980s and early 1990s the effectiveness of this compensation strategy was called into question. Research on the topic had generated evidence that pay-for-performance systems, particularly merit pay plans, could often be problematic. Numerous scholars documented difficulties associated with merit pay, including problems connected with performance evaluation, the apparent reluctance of government to adequately fund the systems, and the fact that merit pay often led to dysfunctional competition among employees. (Kellough and Selden, 1997, pp. 1–2)

The list of possible problems with PFP as a reliable performance management tool is a long one. An over emphasis on external material rewards such as pay may, for example undermine intrinsic sources of motivation such as self-esteem and contributions to organizational achievements. Employees' attention and effort may be diverted from organizational goals as they seek to meet personal performance objectives. Merit pay for individuals as opposed to groups may also promote competition and conflict in situations where interdependencies among jobs require coordination and collaboration. Overall, the experience with PFP in the public sector provides ample reason for caution and careful evaluation. The National Academy of Sciences' recent study of PFP led its authors to conclude that there is no solid empirical evidence that PFP and merit pay programs are effective (Milkovich and Wigdor, 1991).

In its 1991 Report, the Pay-for-Performance Labor-Management Committee established under terms of the Federal Employees Pay Comparability Act noted the Council's findings. It advised OPM that "Governmentwide implementation of any new pay for performance system for General Schedule employees should be preceded by a period of extensive and comprehensive experimentation involving a variety of programs that are tailored to the contextual conditions of Federal agencies.". . (PFP Labor-Management Committee, 1991, pp. i–ii). In a similar vein, a committee established to evaluate the federal service's Performance Management Recognition System (PMRS) determined "that there is virtually no empirical evidence that the PMRS has increased individual or organizational productivity" (PMRS Review Committee, 1991, p. 14).

A CAUTIONARY TALE: THE FEDERAL EXPERIENCE WITH MERIT PAY

The federal merit pay program is by far the most extensively described and evaluated. The national government's experience with PFP is instructive because it highlights several of the problems outlined above. The hard lessons learned on the federal level are also of potential value to states and localities seeking better outcomes from their PFP initiatives.

BULLETIN

On CSRA Merit Pay

"A merit pay scheme like the CSRA reform that rewards the relative performance, ambiguously measured, of a fixed proportion of an employment population. . .is apt to have all sorts of undesirable motivational effects that may actually lower individual and organizational performance. Individual expectations are a serious problem. If you reward the top one-third in relative performance, employees who are not selected but nonetheless consider themselves among the top third. . .are apt to be angry and take their anger out on the job. Their response may be to become less efficient. . .particularly if they believe they are already there and that it is only poor measurement, politics, discrimination, and the like that says otherwise."

Source: George Downs and Patrick Larkey, *The Search for Government Efficiency* (New York: Random House, 1986), p. 198.

The Merit Pay System (MPS) established under the CSRA is usually seen as the first federal effort to implement PFP but, starting with the recommendations of the First Hoover Commission in 1949, there had been incremental efforts made to strengthen the link between pay and performance. The Commission recommended that employees get within-grade increases only when their supervisors certified that they had earned them with satisfactory or better performance. The Classification Act of 1949 established the 10-step pay ranges for each of the GS grades, and the Performance Rating Act of 1950 required agencies to set up performance appraisal systems with three summary ratings (Outstanding, Satisfactory, and Unsatisfactory), but within-grade step increases were tied to seniority, and an outstanding performance rating had *no* monetary consequences.

The first congressional attempt to reward superior performance was the Incentives Awards Act of 1954 which "authorized recognition and cash payments for superior accomplishments, suggestions, inventions, or other personal efforts." The Federal Salary Reform Act of 1962 required that an "acceptable level of competence" standard be used in granting within-grade increases, and it also stressed rewarding exceptional performances with quality step increases (QSIs) to base pay (PMRS Review Committee, 1991, pp. 1–2). By 1977, however, the staff working on the CSRA legislation for President Carter concluded that the linkage between pay and performance was at best weak, with within-grade increases all but automatic and cash awards and QSIs seldom used. The CSRA required that federal agencies set up *real* merit pay plans.

Under the CSRA, GS 13–15 employees covered by merit pay were placed under a "GM" pay plan designation, and the pay range for GM employees' grades was open, which meant that there were no preset rates for steps within the grade. The other major government-wide feature of the MPS was that half of the GM employees' general comparability adjustment had to be placed in "merit pay pools" that the agencies used to fund merit increases. Funds that agencies would have otherwise used for within-grade increases and QSIs were also diverted to merit pay pools. Based on their performance ratings, GM personnel competed with one another for increases paid out of these pools. General Schedule employees, on the other hand, continued to receive full comparability adjustments as an entitlement. Otherwise, federal agencies were given considerable discretion to develop their own merit pay systems.

The intention of the framers of the CSRA was to make this the first step, to be followed by an extension of merit pay to all federal executive branch personnel if the experience with the GM level proved successful. However, it did not take long for serious problems to develop. In 1981, a decision by the comptroller general resulted in a substantial reduction in the funding for merit pay, and GM employees complained that they were getting smaller pay increases and thus less total pay than their counterparts in the General Schedule. With the funding cuts, unhappiness with the MPS spread rapidly as GM employees received what they saw as "meaningless" merit increases. By the mid-1980s, the GAO was reporting that support for the MPS was very weak, with about half of the GM group wanting to return to the General Schedule. In its studies, the GAO found that over 75 percent of the respondents believed that merit pay had not motivated them to be more productive (U.S. General Accounting Office, 1984).

A study of attitudes toward merit pay in five agencies by Pearce and Perry (1983) found that employees were no more motivated under the MPS than they had been under the previous arrangements. Federal managers reported that increased effort was *less* likely to lead to a good performance rating, and they expressed the belief that merit pay did not encourage them to perform their jobs well or contribute to their agencies' effectiveness. Pearce and Perry concluded that the results of the merit pay experiment did not warrant extending the coverage of the rest of the General Schedule.

Why did a program intended to motivate better performance fail so badly? First, agency appraisal systems had been put into effect under a very short deadline and without pretesting. As a consequence, many GM employees believed that the performance standards for their positions were not correct and that the ratings they received were inaccurate. Second, a requirement that no more money be spent on merit pay than had been under the previous system (an expenditure-neutral policy) set a restrictive upper limit on the pay increases that could be earned with superior performance ratings. Fixed limits on merit pay pools created conditions under which one employee's gain was another's loss, a "win-lose" situation that tended to generate small and trivial differences in rewards. For each agency, as the number of superior performers increased, their pay raises decreased. In other words, outstanding performance came to be seen by many as not being instrumental to meaningful pay raises.

Third, in response to the experiences detailed above, pay pool administrators modified distributions of performance ratings in order to achieve higher pay-outs for those receiving outstanding ratings, but this undermined confidence in the objectivity and fairness of the MPS. The phenomenon of "managed ratings" raised the question, "If the ratings are accurate, why should they be manipulated?" Fourth, the MPS was implemented in an atmosphere of hostility toward public employees, an attitude cultivated by the Reagan administration and shared by many in Congress who opposed fully funding the system.

Budgetary restraints and rigidities further aggravated employee suspicions about how the MPS was being administered.

In 1984, Congress responded to the MPS's failures by passing legislation abolishing it and replacing it with the Performance Management Recognition System (PMRS), previously mentioned. The PMRS represented a return to a more centralized approach to federal pay administration, and many of the MPS's flexibilities were eliminated in order to restore pay equity across agencies and between GS and GM personnel. The PMRS required that GM employees who received performance ratings of "fully successful" be given full annual comparability and merit increases of 1 percent (those rated "outstanding" got 3 percent). Those rated one level below fully successful were guaranteed one-half of the comparability increase, and those rated unsatisfactory received no adjustment. The PMRS also encouraged the use of cash bonuses or performance awards to recognize exceptional performance.

The original legislation contained a five-year sunset provision, and when the Congress evaluated the PMRS in 1989, "they were confronted with major discontent with the current system, but no consensus as to what should replace it." The PMRS was extended for 18 months, with some minor changes, including a requirement that agencies develop a performance improvement plan (PIP) for all employees rated below fully successful. In light of the continuing problems with merit pay for managers, an extension of pay for performance to the entire federal white-collar workforce was removed from the Comparability Act of 1990, and the Pay-for-Performance Labor-Management Committee was established to study the issue. In early 1991, Congress extended the PMRS through September 30, 1993. One 1991 amendment provided for the establishment of a PMRS Review Committee to review the system and make recommendations to the director of OPM on policy for a fair and effective performance management system for federal managers.

The Review Committee's report concluded that the PMRS had failed to meet three basic standards. First, performance ratings were suspect and not perceived as accurate. Second, there were serious doubts about the extent to which real differences in performance were linked to meaningful pay-outs. Third, many GM employees saw the system as unfair in its administration as well as outcomes. In order to address these flaws in the existing system, the Committee made some 38 recommendations for improvements. These proposals covered a wide range of topics, including improved performance appraisal processes, expanded system coverage, increased funding of merit increases, and training for GM employees and their supervisors. Overall, the Committee expressed support for the *concept* of pay for performance, adding that it favored an incremental approach to improving the PMRS, "rather than the creation of an entirely new system." Finally, the Committee urged the Congress to allow federal agencies greater "flexibility to expand and adapt pay for performance for their particular structure, culture, and objectives" (PMRS Review Committee, 1991, pp. 49–52).

The Pay-for-Performance Labor-Management Committee's report was equally cautious about creating a new merit pay program. In light of the existing state of knowledge and research, it concluded that the General Schedule system for measuring and rewarding performance was a "workable pay for performance system." Noting that GS employees had to be rated "satisfactory" to receive within-grade increases and that quality step increases were available, the Committee urged federal agencies to make better use of the resources available to them:

> What is often lacking in managing the General Schedule system is a commitment to use the flexibilities that are authorized under current regulations governing performance and incentive awards to recognize employee accomplishments. Rather than replacing one base pay adjustment system with another, the Federal Government may be well served by a renewed focus on, and dedication to, improved management of the current General Schedule system. (PFP Labor-Management Committee, 1991, p. ii)

Other Committee recommendations included:

1. Full and adequate funding of the program so that employees could see pay-outs as meaningful;
2. Giving federal agencies "authority to design and administer individual pay for performance programs to satisfy their specific needs, objectives, workforce characteristics, and organizational culture;"
3. Taking actions designed to assure fairness and to prevent adverse impact "on any class of employees"; and
4. Creation of mechanisms through which employees would be able to effectively participate "in the design, implementation, and evaluation of pay for performance programs."

In 1993, Congress passed the Performance Management and Recognition System Termination Act. Employees who had been covered by the merit pay program were returned to the General Schedule pay system. For all practical purposes, this was a major setback for merit pay, since "the federal service was required to abandon the concept of individualized wage incentives added to base pay" (Kellough and Selden, 1997, p. 2). Subject to OPM policies, federal agencies may now have their own incentives plans, including cash awards and one-time bonuses.

The federal experience does not appear to have deterred state and local employers from implementing merit pay plans. Between 1987 and 1997, the number of states using some form of pay for performance grew from 22 to at least 30. In 90 percent of these states, individualized increases to base salary or standard merit pay is the approach being used. In over half of these states, bonuses are also available to certain categories of workers (Kellough and Selden, 1997). In 1997, for example, the State of Georgia implemented a PFP system for its civil service employees. For Georgia employees who meet, exceed, or far exceed performance standards, annual pay increases (adjustments to base pay) have two components: (1) a market adjustment to increase competitiveness, and (2) a variable monetary award amount keyed to the performance rating. Those who receive a rating of "does not meet expectations" receive no increase. In all cases, of course, increases are subject to the availability of state funds.

In their study of states' pay for performance systems, Kellough and Selden (1997) found:

- The trend toward PFP has continued despite mounting evidence, such as that provided by the federal experience and research studies, that it has not had the desired or expected results in many cases.

- Individual merit pay is the dominant approach, but bonuses and group incentives are also used in some states.

- Over half of the personnel managers responding to the study expressed confidence that their PFP systems had clarified organizational expectations and performance standards. Likewise, more than half believed that PFP had clarified the relationships between performance and monetary rewards.

- Only about a third of the respondents to Kellough and Selden's survey reported that merit pay had increased employee motivation and productivity, and they note that although these are supposed to be the central benefits of PFP, "the relatively small proportions of respondents seeing these outcomes associated with merit pay suggest that this approach to pay for performance may not always be a reliable mechanism for enhancing employee motivation and satisfaction." (p. 5)

- Political appointees, in comparison to career civil servants, were more favorable toward PFP. This finding is more than likely a reflection of the symbolic value of PFP in the partisan political arena, as Perry has pointed out.

■ Personnel managers with private-sector backgrounds tended to be more skeptical about PFP's benefits than those with only public sector experience. While there is a general assumption that PFP is widely successful in the business world, it has not been without problems. Those with corporate experience also may be more sensitive to the barriers to successful implementation created by the public environment, such as the legal limits on managers' flexibility and discretion in personnel matters. (Kellough and Selden, 1997, p. 4)

■ Pay for performance systems covering managers *only* were more popular than those including nonmanagerial personnel. Apparently, extending PFP beyond the management ranks creates additional administrative complexities, fuels labor–management conflicts, and raises other problems that make it less attractive to many personnel managers in state governments.

With regard to anticipated benefits, discouraging reports about PFP on the state level were that having a merit pay plan (1) did not greatly improve recruitment success or turnover rates, (2) did not significantly reduce labor costs, and (3) did not appear to increase political executives' control over career bureaucrats. Negative features of PFP that might be anticipated from previous research on merit pay plans in the federal government and elsewhere did in fact surface on the state level (Ingraham, 1993). For example, merit pay was associated with "red tape," increased demands on supervisors' time, and more paperwork. There were also serious concerns and suspicions about objectivity, consistency, and procedural fairness (Kellough and Selden, 1977, pp. 5–6).

About one-third of U.S. local governments had some form of PFP in operation by the mid-1990s, with most reporting that it has been at least somewhat useful. As appears to be the case on the state level, the most significant benefits are related to the clarification of goals, expectations, and performance standards, as well as to specifying the relationships between levels of performance and pay outcomes. PFP's effects on motivation, productivity, and job satisfaction, while seen to be somewhat positive by local government personnel managers in one study, were not exceptionally strong (Streib and Nigro, 1993a; Streib and Nigro, 1993b). Problems with PFP in local governments mirror those on the federal and state levels.

CONCLUSION

Clearly, a performance evaluation process that is supported by supervisors and employees is a very important component of any merit system. In

---

Table 5.1 Top 10 Problems with PFP on the Local Level

Lack of adequate funding
Failure to discriminate among levels of performance
Perceived inequities in performance awards
Conflict between raters and those being evaluated
Lack of employee confidence in performance evaluation techniques
Excessive demands on supervisors' time
Employee suspicion and distrust of management's motives
System failure to meet employee expectations
Lack of supervisory compliance with program requirements
Resistance from unions

Source: Gregory Streib and Lloyd Nigro, " Pay for Performance in Local Governments: Use and Effectiveness," in *The Municipal Yearbook: 1993* (Washington, DC: ICCMA), pp. 50–56.

---

practice, the merit principle requires that public employees on all levels be covered by evaluation processes that are valid and have results that may confidently and legitimately be used as the basis for a variety of personnel actions. To the extent that these conditions do not exist, the credibility of the entire system is undermined. Historically, the appraisal systems used by public employers have been technically crude and ineffective as performance management tools. Over the past 20 years, the push to create performance appraisal systems that accurately and reliably discriminate among levels of performance has been driven by the popularity of PFP as the centerpiece of virtually all civil service reform initiatives.

The available evidence strongly suggests that individualized merit pay models, while by far the most used, are not realizing the ambitious goals set for them by civil service reformers. Nonetheless, there continues to be strong support for the concept of pay for performance in government. The continued support for PFP and new ventures, such as Georgia's system, is probably explained by a mix of several factors. First, the traditional approaches to performance evaluation and pay do not conform to the merit principle and they are at odds with the current emphasis on management-centered personnel practices. Second, merit pay has already been adopted by many jurisdictions and "sold" to the public, so giving up on the concept is difficult, in terms of both "sunk costs" and the credibility of elected executives. Third, it does serve as a symbolic response to public criticism of "inefficient bureaucrats" and to executives' calls for greater accountability (Kellough and Selden, 1997, pp. 7–8). In all probability, therefore, the public sector will continue to experiment with a variety of approaches to PFP, including bonuses and gainsharing. If

TQM becomes more widely used in government, more emphasis may be placed on a *mix* of individual and group performance measures and rewards. It is also likely that multiple-source appraisals will grow in popularity as employers seek ways to enhance participation and communication, to establish employee development as an integral goal of appraisals, and to strengthen confidence in the objectivity and fairness of ratings throughout the organization.

DISCUSSION QUESTIONS

1. Does PFP result in the performance management process relying too heavily on money as a motivator?
2. Would you prefer to work for an employer that uses individualized merit pay, or one that relies on group-based rewards?
3. Do U.S. businesses really practice PFP for workers, managers, and executives?
4. Do you believe that supervisors' performance appraisals really can be objective?
5. Do you think multisource appraisals are a good idea?
6. If you were a supervisor, would you have confidence in your subordinates to provide objective evaluations of your performance?
7. Is PFP just another political "gimmick" that will fade away and be replaced by another?
8. Do you think one-time bonuses are better than increases to base pay if more effective performance management is the goal?

REFERENCES

Ammons, David N., and Rodriguez, Arnold (1986). "Performance Appraisal Practices for Upper Management in City Governments." *Public Administration Review*, Vol. 46, No. 5 (September–October), pp. 460–467.

Berman, Evan (1997). "The Challenge of Total Quality Management," in Carolyn Ban and Norma M. Riccucci (eds.), *Public Personnel Management: Current Concerns—Future Challenges* (New York: Longman), pp. 281–294.

Bowman, James S. (1994). "At Last an Alternative to Performance Appraisal: Total Quality Management." *Public Administration Review*, Vol. 54, No. 2 (March–April), pp. 129–136.

Coggburn, Jerrell D. (1998). "Subordinate Appraisals of Managers: Lessons From a State Agency." *Review of Public Personnel Administration*, Vol. 18, No. 1 (Winter), pp. 68–79.

Connor, Patrick E. (1997). "Total Quality Management: A Selective Commentary on Its Human Dimensions." *Public Administration Review,* Vol. 57, No. 6 (November–December), pp. 501–509.

Daley, Dennis (1991). "Performance Appraisal in North Carolina Municipalities." *Review of Public Personnel Administration,* Vol. 11, No. 3 (Summer), pp. 32–50.

deLeon, Linda, and Ewen, Ann J. (1997). "Multi-Source Performance Appraisals." *Review of Public Personnel Administration,* Vol. 17, No. 1 (Winter), pp. 22–36 (page numbers cited are from ABI Inform: Article Text).

Downs, George W., and Larkey, Patrick D. (1986). *The Search for Government Efficiency: From Hubris to Helplessness* (New York: Random House).

Durant, Robert F. (1998). "Total Quality Management," in Stephen E. Condrey (ed.), *Handbook of Human Resource Management in Government* (San Francisco: Jossey-Bass), pp. 453–473.

England, Robert E., and Parle, William M. (1987). "Nonmanagerial Performance Appraisal Practices in Large American Cities." *Public Administration Review,* Vol. 47, No. 6 (November–December), pp. 498–504.

Fox, Charles J., and Shirkey, Kurt A. (1997). "Employee Performance Appraisal: The Keystone Made of Clay," in Ban and Riccucci (eds.), *Public Personnel Management,* pp. 205–220.

Gabris, Gerald T., and Mitchell, Kenneth (1985). "Merit Based Performance Appraisal and Productivity: Do Employees Perceive the Connection?" *Public Productivity Review,* Vol. 9, No. 4 (Winter), pp. 311–327.

Georgia Merit System (1997). *Manager's Guide: Georgia Performance Management Process* (Atlanta: Training & Organization Development Division).

Greiner, John M. (1986). "Motivational Programs and Productivity Improvement in Times of Limited Resources." *Public Productivity Review,* Vol. 10, No. 39 (Fall), pp. 81–102.

—— Hatry, H.P., Koss, M.P., Millar, A.P., and Woodward, J.P. (1981). *Productivity and Motivation: A Review of State and Local Government Initiatives* (Washington, DC: The Urban Institute Press).

Ingraham, Patricia W. (1993). "Pay for Performance in the States." *American Review of Public Administration,* Vol. 23, No. 3, pp. 189–200.

Ingraham, Patricia W., and Ban, Carolyn, eds. (1984). *Legislating Bureaucratic Change: The Civil Service Reform Act of 1978* (Albany: SUNY Press).

Kellough, J. Edward, and Selden, Sally Coleman (1997). "Pay for Performance Systems in State Government." *Review of Public Personnel Administration,* Vol. 17, No. 1 (Winter), pp. 5–21 (page numbers cited are from ABI Inform: Article Text).

Milkovich, George T., and Wigdor, Alexandra (1991). *Pay for Performance: Evaluating Performance Appraisal and Merit Pay* (Washington, DC: National Academy Press).

Pay for Performance Labor-Management Committee (1991). *Strengthening the Link Between Pay and Performance* (Washington, DC), November.

Pearce, Jone L., and Perry, James L. (1983). "Federal Merit Pay: A Longitudinal Analysis. *Public Administration Review,* Vol. 43, No. 4 (July–August), pp. 315–328.

Performance Management and Recognition System Review Committee (1991). *Advancing Managerial Excellence: A Report on Improving the Performance Management and Recognition System* (Washington, DC), November.

Perry, James L. (1991). "Linking Pay to Performance: The Controversy Continues" in Ban and Riccucci (eds.), *Public Personnel Management,* pp. 73–86.

Roberts, Gary E. (1992). "Linkages Between Performance Appraisal System Effectiveness and Rater and Ratee Acceptance." *Review of Public Personnel Administration,* Vol. 12, No. 3 (May–August), pp. 19–41.

——— (1995). "Developmental Performance Appraisal in Municipal Government: An Antidote for a Deadly Disease?" *Review of Public Personnel Administration,* Vol. 15, No. 3 (Summer), pp. 17–43.

——— and Reed, Tammy (1996). "Performance Appraisal Participation, Goal Setting and Feedback." *Review of Public Personnel Administration,* Vol. 16, No. 4 (Fall), pp. 29–60.

Streib, Gregory, and Nigro, Lloyd G. (1993a). "Pay for Performance in Local Governments: Programmatic Differences and Perceived Utility." *Public Productivity & Management Review,* Vol. 17, No. 2 (Winter), pp. 145–159.

——— (1993b). "Pay for Performance in Local Governments: Use and Effectiveness." *The Municipal Yearbook: 1993* (Washington, DC: International City/County Management Association), pp. 50–56.

Thompson, Frank J., and Radin, Beryl A. (1997). "Reinventing Management: The Winter and Gore Initiatives," in Ban and Riccucci (eds.), *Public Personnel Management,* pp. 3–20.

U.S. General Accounting Office (1978). *Report to the Congress by the Comptroller of the United States: Federal Employee Performance Rating Systems Need Fundamental Changes* (Washington, DC), March.

———— (1983). *Report to the Director, Office of Personnel Management: New Performance Appraisals Beneficial But Refinements Needed* (Washington, DC), September 15.

———— (1984). *Report to the Chairwoman, Subcommittee on Compensation and Employee Benefits, Committee on Post Office and Civil Service, House of Representatives: A 2-Year Appraisal of Merit Pay in Three Agencies* (Washington, DC), March 26.

———— (1987). *Blue Collar Workers: Appraisal Systems Are in Place, But Basic Refinements Are Needed* (Washington, DC), June.

———— (1988). *Civil Service Reform: Development of 1978 Civil Service Reform Proposals* (Washington, DC).

———— (1990). *Pay for Performance: State and International Pay for Performance* (Washington, DC), October.

SUGGESTED READINGS

Borins, Sandford (1998). *Innovating with Integrity: How Local Heroes Are Transforming American Government* (Washington, DC: Georgetown University Press).

Cleveland, Jeanette, and Murphy, Kevin R. (1995). *Understanding Performance Appraisal; Social, Organizational, and Goal-Based Perspectives* (Thousand Oaks, CA: Sage Publications).

Gilley, Jerry W. (1998). *Developing Performance Management Systems* (Reading, MA: Addison Wesley Longman).

Goetsch, David L., and Davis, Stanley B. (1996). *Introduction to Total Quality* (Paramus, NJ: Prentice Hall).

Koehler, Jerry W. (1995). *Total Quality Management in Government* (Delray Beach, FL: Saint Lucie Press).

Shand, David, ed. (1996). *Performance Management in Government: Contemporary Illustrations* (Washington, DC: Organization for Economic Cooperation and Development).

Smither, James W. (1998). *Performance Appraisal: The State of the Art in Practice* (San Francisco: Jossey-Bass).

West, Jonathan P. (ed.) (1995). *Quality Management Today: What Local Governments Need to Know* (Washington, DC: International City/County Management Association).

Instructions for Use of the Performance Management Form (PMF)

General

The Performance Management Form (PMF) is used to document employee performance plans and two types of evaluations based on those plans. The evaluations documented on the PMF are:

(1) annual performance evaluations leading to salary increase recommendations, and

(2) evaluations performed at the end of working test periods to support permanent status decisions.

Please note:

(1) To document permanent status decisions, agencies may choose to use the shorter Management Review Form (MRF), rather than using the PMF.

(2) The MRF cannot be used to document a salary increase decision: a full evaluation, documented on the PMF, is required for the annual performance evaluation that determines salary increase recommendations.

(3) The same PMF may be used to document both a salary increase decision and a permanent status decision, so long as:

    (a) the same performance plan is in effect,

    (b) the PMF documenting one type of decision has been completed no more than 90 days prior to the effective date for the other type of decision, and

    (c) the agency policy does not require that a new PMF be completed.

(4) A PMF must be completed and signed not more than 90 days prior to the effective date of a salary increase.

The PMF consists of nine sections:

1: Employee Information	6: Salary Increase Recommendation
2: Performance Plan Signatures	7: Employment Status
3: Job and Individual Responsibilities	8: Evaluation Signatures
4: Terms and Conditions of Employment	9: Employee Development Plan
5: Overall Ratings	

Additional pages may be attached to any section of the form if space is insufficient.

Planning

Prior to the beginning of the new performance period, the supervisor:

- enters in *Section 3* responsibilities and performance expectations for the employee and indicates which responsibilities are critical to the job;

- enters under Performance Expectations in *Section 4* any additional expectations related to terms and conditions of employment that are specific to the job or work unit;

- reviews the preliminary plan with his or her manager to ensure that the proposed responsibilities and expectations are appropriate in light of overall unit plans and work assignments.

In a planning session at the beginning of the performance period, the supervisor and the employee:

- discuss the responsibilities and expectations for the coming year, making changes or additions as necessary in *Section 3*;

- review the pre-printed "statewide" responsibilities in *Section 3* and check the boxes that apply to the employee and the job. (Each agency should have a policy on whether inclusion of any or all of these responsibilities is required on every employee's Plan or is discretionary on the part of the supervisor.);

- review the preprinted Performance Management Responsibility in *Section 3* and, if the employee directly supervises other employees, mark it as "Critical";

- review the expectations relate to terms and conditions outlined in *Section 4*;

- identify any developmental or training goals for the upcoming performance period and enter in *Section 9*;

- enter signatures and dates in *Section 2*. (The PMF, with responsibilities and expectations entered, constitutes the employee's individual Performance Plan. After the Plan is reviewed and signed by the reviewing manager, the supervisor retains a copy, gives a copy to the employee, and processes/files other copies as directed by agency policy.)

- If a significant change is made to the Performance Plan during the year, following discussion of the change, the supervisor should have the employee sign in the indicated space in *Section 2*.

Annual Performance Evaluation

At the end of the performance period, the supervisor uses the Performance Management Form to document the evaluation of the employee's performance. The supervisor rates the employee's performance on the individual items in *Sections 3 and 4*. In *Section 9*, the supervisor notes any progress the employee has made in meeting developmental or training goals. In *Section 5* the supervisor enters an overall rating for Job and Individual Responsibilities and an overall rating for Terms and Conditions of Employment.

In *Section 6*, the supervisor indicates whether the employee is eligible for a performance increase. (Actual awarding of increases is subject to availability of funds and to modification of pay delivery policies.) In order to be eligible, the employee must receive an overall rating of Met Expectations or higher on the Job and Individual Responsibilities component of the evaluation. An employee who receives an overall rating of Did Not Meet Expectations on either Responsibilities or Terms and Conditions is not eligible for an increase. Employees receiving an overall rating of Needs Improvement on the Terms and Conditions may or may not be eligible for a performance increase, depending on individual agency policy.

The completed PMF is reviewed by the supervisor's manager. The supervisor then conducts the performance evaluation meeting with the employee. Both parties sign the document in *Section 8* to indicate that the meeting has taken place. After the PMF is signed by the reviewing manager, it is filed according to agency policy, a copy is given to the employee, and the supervisor retains a copy.

Permanent Status Review

If the PMF is used to document an evaluation leading to the granting of permanent status, the form is completed in the same way as for an annual performance evaluation, but instead of indicating a salary increase recommendation in *Section 6*, the supervisor puts a checkmark in the "Permanent Status Approved" box in *Section 7* (or puts checkmarks in both sections, if the PMF is being used simultaneously for both types of evaluation). Follow agency policy for filing and distribution of copies.

continued page 154

Page 1

Print Date

MS 10-60 (8/95)

State of Georgia
PERFORMANCE MANAGEMENT FORM
(PMF)

Organizational Unit _____

Organization Number _____

Section 1: Employee Information

Last Name, First Name MI	Social Security No.	Position No.	Performance Period
			from: _____ to: _____
Class/Job Title	Class/Job Number	Supv. Position No.	Supervisor's Title and Class/Job Number

Section 2: Performance Plan Signatures

Performance Plan Signatures—Employee

I understand my job and individual responsibilities, the performance expectations, and the terms and conditions under which I am expected to work.
Comments:

_____   _____
Date   Employee Signature

I understand the changes made to my responsibilities and performance expectations or terms and conditions.

_____   _____
Date   Employee Signature

Performance Plan Signatures—Supervisor/Manager

I have discussed the job and individual responsibilities, performance expectations, and terms and conditions with the employee.
Comments:

_____   _____
Date   Evaluating Supervisor Signature

I have reviewed the Performance Plan and find the requirements appropriate.
Comments:

_____   _____
Date   Reviewing Manager Signature

[ ] Annual Performance Evaluation   [ ] Permanent Status Evaluation   [ ] Personnel File   [ ] Employee Copy   [ ] Supervisor Copy

continued page 155

Page 2

Section 3: Job and Individual Responsibilities

Instructions: Describe the employee's key responsibilities. These may be Job Responsibilities (ongoing responsibilities typically performed by incumbents in the job) or Individual Responsibilities (responsibilities assigned to this particular employee, such as time-limited special projects or individual developmental goals). Indicate the responsibilities -- typically no more than three -- that are critically important to successful performance of the job. Describe performance expectations for each responsibility. At the end of the performance period, describe the employee's actual performance and indicate the rating achieved.

Job or Individual Responsibility	Performance Expectations	Actual Performance	Performance Rating
[ ] Critical			Expectations [ ] Did Not Meet [ ] Met [ ] Exceeded [ ] Far Exceeded
[ ] Critical			Expectations [ ] Did Not Meet [ ] Met [ ] Exceeded [ ] Far Exceeded
[ ] Critical			Expectations [ ] Did Not Meet [ ] Met [ ] Exceeded [ ] Far Exceeded
[ ] Critical			Expectations [ ] Did Not Meet [ ] Met [ ] Exceeded [ ] Far Exceeded
[ ] Critical			Expectations [ ] Did Not Meet [ ] Met [ ] Exceeded [ ] Far Exceeded

continued page 156

Page 3

Responsibility	Performance Expectations	Actual Performance	Performance Rating
[ ] Critical			Expectations [ ] Did Not Meet [ ] Met [ ] Exceeded [ ] Far Exceeded
[ ] Critical			Expectations [ ] Did Not Meet [ ] Met [ ] Exceeded [ ] Far Exceeded
[ ] Critical			Expectations [ ] Did Not Meet [ ] Met [ ] Exceeded [ ] Far Exceeded
Instructions: Performance Management is a key responsibility of all supervisors and must be marked as critical on each supervisor's performance plan. Check "Not Applicable" only if employee does not supervise. [ ] Not applicable [ ] Critical **Performance Management Responsibility** Creates and maintains a high performance environment characterized by positive leadership and a strong team orientation.	1. Defines goals and/or required results at beginning of performance period and gains acceptance of ideas by creating a shared vision. 2. Communicates regularly with staff on progress toward defined goals and/or required results, providing specific feedback and initiating corrective action when defined goals and/or required results are not met. 3. Confers regularly with staff to review employee relations climate, specific problem areas, and actions necessary for improvement. 4. Evaluates employees at scheduled intervals, obtains and considers all relevant information in evaluations, and supports staff by giving praise and constructive criticism. 5. Recognizes contributions and celebrates accomplishments. 6. Motivates staff to improve quantity and quality of work performed and provides training and development opportunities as appropriate.		Expectations [ ] Did Not Meet [ ] Met [ ] Exceeded [ ] Far Exceeded

continued page 157

Page 4

Instructions: Listed below are responsibilities which support the State's strategic goals. If any of these "statewide" responsibilities do not apply, they should be marked "not applicable." Check the appropriate box to indicate whether the responsibility is "not applicable," "applicable" or both "applicable and critical."

Responsibility	Performance Expectations	Actual Performance	Performance Rating
[ ] Not Applicable [ ] Applicable [ ] Applicable and Critical **Teamwork** Encourages and facilitates cooperation, pride, trust, and group identity; fosters commitment and team spirit; works cooperatively with others to achieve goals.	1. Communicates accurate information to others in a professional and courteous manner; conveys a willingness to assist. 2. Shows consideration for others, works cooperatively with any co-worker; provides constructive feedback without undue criticism of others; displays appreciation of differences in approaches, personalities, and viewpoints of others. 3. Solicits input of those who are affected by plans or actions; gives credit and recognition to others who have contributed; demonstrates concern for treating people fairly and equitably. 4. Accepts responsibility for own mistakes and takes action to prevent similar occurrences; works to resolve conflicts and to identify solutions in which all parties benefit. 5. Identifies team goals and ways to work with coworkers to accomplish those goals; works to keep group activities productive/focused on results.		Expectations [ ] Did Not Meet [ ] Met [ ] Exceeded [ ] Far Exceeded
[ ] Not Applicable [ ] Applicable [ ] Applicable and Critical **Customer Service** Works and communicates with the general public, internal customers and/or external customers to provide information and quality services and/or products targeted to meet customer expectations.	1. Treats customers with respect, courtesy and tact; listens to customer and interacts with customer as a person while maintaining business relationship. 2. Communicates with customers and obtains all information necessary to determine and address their specific needs; tactfully explains why, if service cannot be provided. 3. Offers options, as appropriate, so that customers can decide what they want to do; demonstrates fairness and good judgement when seeking possible exceptions or in going the extra mile to meet customers' expectations. 4. Responds to customers in manner and timeframe promised or follows up to explain status; demonstrates understanding of, and concern for, the customer's situation and perspective. 5. Provides clear, accurate information; explains procedures or materials or provides supplemental information; anticipates problems and questions; asks for customer feedback on procedures, products or services.		Expectations [ ] Did Not Meet [ ] Met [ ] Exceeded [ ] Far Exceeded
[ ] Not Applicable [ ] Applicable [ ] Applicable and Critical **Organizational Commitment** Displays a high level of effort and commitment to performing work; operates effectively within the organizational structure; demonstrates trustworthiness and respon-sible behavior.	1. Demonstrates eagerness to learn and assume responsibility; seeks out and accepts increased responsibility; displays a "can do" approach to work. 2. Shows persistence and seeks alternatives when obstacles arise; seeks alternative solutions; does things before being asked or forced to by events. 3. Works within the system in a resourceful manner to accomplish reasonable work goals; shows flexibility in response to process changes and adapts to and accommodates new methods and procedures. 4. Accepts direction and feedback from supervisors and follows through appropriately.		Expectations [ ] Did Not Meet [ ] Met [ ] Exceeded [ ] Far Exceeded

continued page 158

Page 5

Section 4: Terms and Conditions of Employment

Instructions: Every employee must be evaluated on each of the five categories of terms and conditions shown below. Specific performance expectations that pertain to the agency, the work unit, or the particular job should be entered under Performance Expectations. At the end of the performance period, describe the employee's actual performance and indicate the appropriate rating for each category.

Terms and Conditions	Performance Expectations	Actual Performance	Performance Rating
Works When Scheduled Works when scheduled; begins and ends work as expected; calls in according to policy when arriving late for work or when absent; observes provisions of Fair Labor Standards Act; observes policies on break and lunch periods; uses work time appropriately.			[ ] Did Not Meet [ ] Needs Improvement [ ] Met
Requests and Uses Leave Appropriately Submits leave requests on a timely basis. Requests and uses the proper type of leave in accordance with established rules and policies. Provides documentation for use of leave when required.			[ ] Did Not Meet [ ] Needs Improvement [ ] Met
Dresses Appropriately Presents a neat, clean appearance; dresses appropriately for job. Practices personal hygiene. Wears clothing suitable to job task and environment based on clientele served. Wears full, regulation uniform, if required.			[ ] Did Not Meet [ ] Needs Improvement [ ] Met
Observes Health, Safety and Sanitation Policies Observes established policies on health, safety, security and sanitation; notifies proper authorities of circumstances or situations that present potential health hazards.			[ ] Did Not Meet [ ] Needs Improvement [ ] Met
Follows All Other Rules and Policies Performs work according to rules, regulations, policies, and guidelines. Ensures required licensures and certifications are current. Does not improperly use or knowingly permit others to use state property improperly. Does not engage in activities other than official business during working hours. Does not engage in prohibited political activity. Does not report for work under the influence of alcohol or drugs.			[ ] Did Not Meet [ ] Needs Improvement [ ] Met

continued page 159

Page 6

Section 5: Overall Ratings

Overall Rating for Job & Individual Responsibilities

[ ] Did Not Meet Expectations*
[ ] Met Expectations
[ ] Exceeded Expectations
[ ] Far Exceeded Expectations

Overall Rating for Terms & Conditions

[ ] Did Not Meet Expectations*
[ ] Needs Improvement
[ ] Met Expectations

Section 6: Increase Recommendation

[ ] NOT Eligible for Performance-Based Increase*
[ ] Eligible for Performance-Based Increase

Section 7: Employment Status

[ ] Working Test/Permanent Status Approved

* Note: Any employee rated in Section 5 as Did Not Meet Expectations is ineligible for a Performance-Based Increase

Section 8: Evaluation Signatures

Employee Signature and Comments

I have reviewed the contents of this form with my supervisor and have been advised of my ratings and employment status or increase eligibility status. I have made any comments I wish in this section. My signature does not necessarily indicate agreement.

Supervisor/Manager Signatures and Comments

This rating reflects my evaluation of the employee's performance. I have discussed this evaluation with the employee.

_____
Date

Reviewing Manager Comments (if any):

_____   _____
Date   Evaluating Supervisor Signature

_____   _____
Date   Reviewing Manager Signature

_____   _____
Date   Employee Signature

_____
Appointing Authority Signature (optional)

continued page 160

Page 7

Section 9: Employee Development Plan

Instructions: List developmental goals or areas for improvement that will be addressed by on-the-job development assignments and/or by formalized training experiences. Indicate actions to be taken by supervisor and/or employee and specify the time frame for their completion. At the end of the performance period, describe any progress the employee has made in meeting development or improvement goals.

Developmental Goals/Areas for Improvement (Employee's and Supervisor's Input)	Planned Development/Training Activities (Agreed Upon by Employee and Supervisor)	Actual Progress

continued page 161

[ ] Working Test Mid-Point Review
[ ] Working Test/Permanent Status Review

MANAGEMENT REVIEW FORM

[ ] Interim Progress Review
[ ] Other Review

MS 10-61 (7/96)

Name	Social Security No.	Hire/Promotion Date
Class/Job Title	Position No.	Review Date
Department Work Unit	Organization No.	Review Period from ___ to ___

Statewide Responsibilities	NI	M	N/A
1. Teamwork	[ ]	[ ]	[ ]
2. Customer Service	[ ]	[ ]	[ ]
3. Organizational Commitment	[ ]	[ ]	[ ]

Terms and Conditions	NI	M	N/A
1. Works When Scheduled	[ ]	[ ]	[ ]
2. Requests and Uses Leave Appropriately	[ ]	[ ]	[ ]
3. Dresses Appropriately	[ ]	[ ]	[ ]
4. Observes Health, Safety and Sanitation Policies	[ ]	[ ]	[ ]
5. Follows All Other Rules and Policies	[ ]	[ ]	[ ]

Job and Individual Responsibilities (Give 4-5 word Identifier)

	NI	M	N/A
1.	[ ]	[ ]	[ ]
2.	[ ]	[ ]	[ ]
3.	[ ]	[ ]	[ ]
4.	[ ]	[ ]	[ ]
5.	[ ]	[ ]	[ ]
6.	[ ]	[ ]	[ ]

Recognition/Comments

Performance/Terms and Conditions Improvements Needed

Developmental Goals

I have discussed the contents of this form with my supervisor and have been advised of my performance status relative to the responsibilities/terms and conditions stated on my performance plan.

I have discussed the progress of this employee relative to the responsibilities/terms and conditions stated in the employee's performance plan.

Permanent Status Approved [ ]

_____   _____
Employee's Signature   Date

_____
Supervisor's Signature

_____   _____
Reviewing Manager's Signature   Date

Chapter SIX

Issues in Classification and Pay

The design and maintenance of job evaluation and pay plans normally is a major responsibility of personnel specialists, especially in merit systems where emphasis is placed on achieving "equal pay for equal work" and on assuring that pay is logically related to job characteristics and skills requirements. Both functions have become specialties within public personnel, and a detailed technical treatment is well beyond the scope of this book. However, in this chapter, we will focus mainly on current issues and trends in position classification and pay policies in the public sector.

JOB EVALUATION AND POSITION CLASSIFICATION

Job evaluation is the process of comparing individual positions and ranking or grading them for pay purposes. Whatever the method used, it results in the assignment of each position to a pay level or grade. Job evaluation is based on *job analysis,* which is considered essential for establishing pay plans that are internally equitable and enable the employer to compete in the labor market by offering "prevailing rates." It also generates much of the detailed information needed for recruitment, selection, training, performance evaluation, and other phases of the modern personnel program.

In the public services of the United States, the usual method of job evaluation is *position classification*. In this approach, all positions considered about equal in duties, responsibilities, and qualification requirements are grouped in the same *class*. In the federal service, the Classification Act of 1949 requires that the criteria used to assign positions to classes (classification standards) take the following into consideration.

- The nature and variety of work performed in carrying out a position's responsibilities.
- The amount and kind of supervision provided to the person occupying the position.
- The nature of guidelines available for performing the work.
- The level of originality or independent decision making required.
- The importance and scope of decisions, commitments, and conclusions reached by the position's incumbent.
- The number and kinds of positions over which the position in question exercises supervisory authority.
- The technical skills, experience and other qualifications required to successfully carry out the position's responsibilities. (National Academy of Public Administration, 1991, p. B4)

Responsibility for the development and application of classification standards is usually assigned to a central personnel agency, such as the federal OPM. Title 5 of the United States Code governs the classification of positions in the General Schedule (GS), and it requires OPM to define federal occupations, establish official position titles, and describe the various levels of work. The GS is composed of 15 grades, each with 10 pay steps (Figure 6.1). To carry out this responsibility, OPM "approves and issues position classification standards that must be used by agencies to determine the title, series, and grade of positions covered by title 5" (U.S. Office of Personnel Management, 1997a, p. 4). In the federal case, classification standards may be used in one of two different ways of classifying positions: the narrative or factor evaluation systems (FES).

Most standards set forth before 1978 are in a narrative format under which a classification specialist "grades" the position by determining the appropriate level for each factor. A narrative position description typically includes four kinds of information:

- An *introduction,* in which the primary purpose of the position and its relationship to the organization are described.
- A *statement of major duties and responsibilities,* which covers the important, regular, and recurring duties and

Figure 6.1 1999 Federal General Schedule

SALARY TABLE 1999-GS

1999 GENERAL SCHEDULE

INCORPORATING A 3.10% GENERAL INCREASE

Effective January 1999

Annual Rates by Grade and Step

	1	2	3	4	5	6	7	8	9	10	Within-Grade Increase Amounts
GS-1	$13,362	$13,807	$14,252	$14,694	$15,140	$15,401	$15,838	$16,281	$16,299	$16,718	Varies
2	15,023	15,380	15,878	16,299	16,482	16,967	17,452	17,937	18,422	18,907	Varies
3	16,392	16,938	17,484	18,030	18,576	19,122	19,668	20,214	20,760	21,306	$546
4	18,401	19,014	19,627	20,240	20,853	21,466	22,079	22,692	23,305	23,918	$613
5	20,588	21,274	21,960	22,646	23,332	24,018	24,704	25,390	26,076	26,762	$686
6	22,948	23,713	24,478	25,243	26,008	26,773	27,538	28,303	29,068	29,833	$765
7	25,501	26,351	27,201	28,051	28,901	29,751	30,601	31,451	32,301	33,151	$850
8	28,242	29,183	30,124	31,065	32,006	32,947	33,888	34,829	35,770	36,711	$941
9	31,195	32,235	33,275	34,315	35,355	36,395	37,435	38,475	39,515	40,555	$1,040
10	34,353	35,498	36,643	37,788	38,933	40,078	41,223	42,368	43,513	44,658	$1,145
11	37,744	39,002	40,260	41,518	42,776	44,034	45,292	46,550	47,808	49,066	$1,258
12	45,236	46,744	48,252	49,760	51,268	52,776	54,284	55,792	57,300	58,808	$1,508
13	53,793	55,586	57,379	59,172	60,965	62,758	64,551	66,344	68,137	69,930	$1,793
14	63,567	65,686	67,805	69,924	72,043	74,162	76,281	78,400	80,519	82,638	$2,119
15	74,773	77,265	79,757	82,249	84,741	87,233	89,725	92,217	94,709	97,201	$2,492

responsibilities of the position. For supervisors, this should include a description of the kind and degree of supervision exercised (authority to plan work, assign and review work, and evaluate performance).

- A *description of the controls over the position,* which is a statement of how the work is assigned, the kind of supervision and guidance received, and the kind of review given to work in progress or upon completion.

- A *statement of special qualification requirements,* which sets forth knowledge, skills, education, and certification or licenses required if they are not apparent from reading the rest of the position description.

Appendix 6.A to this chapter is an example of a narrative position description for a State of Georgia position that includes the additional dimension of performance standards for each responsibility. In this case, the employer has established performance standards for positions in order to provide a foundation for its pay-for-performance system. Employees' performance should be evaluated on all of the relevant standards.

The FES format was adopted by the federal government in 1975, and it is the system most often used to assign *nonsupervisory* positions to grades in the GS. It uses nine factors common to most nonsupervisory positions in GS occupations, and factor points are assigned to each position. The total number of points determines a position's grade. The FES factors are as follows:

- Factor 1 defines the knowledge required by the position. This factor addresses the kind of knowledge and skills required and how they are used in doing the work.

- Factor 2 deals with supervisory controls over the position, including how work is assigned, the employee's responsibility for carrying out the work, and how the work is reviewed or evaluated.

- Factor 3 covers the kinds of guidelines available for doing the work and the judgment needed to apply these guidelines or to develop new guidance.

- Factor 4 addresses the complexity of the work involved, including the difficulty in identifying what needs to be done, the difficulty level of the work, and the level of originality or creativity required.

- Factor 5 deals with the scope and effect of the work, which includes the impact or importance of the work product.

- Factors 6 and 7 relate to personal contacts, including the conditions or settings in which such contacts are made and the reasons for these contacts.
- Factor 8 covers the physical demands of positions, which may vary widely in terms of the nature, frequency, and intensity of activity.
- Factor 9 details the nature of the work environment, job hazards, and the safety precautions required to perform the work safely.

In general terms, FES position descriptions should cover all of the information needed to assign points in all nine factor areas, which may not be the case for a narrative description. FES position descriptions are detailed and will contain the information needed to classify positions using either narrative or FES standards. According to the OPM, "many federal agencies have decided to prepare all position descriptions following the FES factor format" (U.S. Office of Personnel Management, 1997a, p. 17).

PAY GRADES

Many different positions may be assigned to the same class, or a class may contain only one position (e.g., budget director, fire chief, or county coroner). Each class is assigned a pay grade on the basis of the duties, responsibilities, and qualifications considered necessary for the grade level. In the federal GS, jobs are clustered in 22 *occupational groups,* each of which is subdivided into *job series* or subgroups that includes all jobs at various skill levels in a particular kind of work. For example, the Personnel Management and Industrial Relations Group has almost 20 series, including the Personnel Management Series, the Personnel Staffing Series, and the Contractor Industrial Relations Series. All jobs or positions in a series are related to each other in terms of their difficulty, complexity, and skills requirements. Based on this information, they are assigned to a class using existing standards. The intended result is equal pay for work of substantially equal difficulty and responsibility, no matter the occupational group. Appendix 6.B shows how occupational group, job series, GS grade, and position description are combined in a typical job opening notice from the U.S. Department of Agriculture.

THE EXPERIENCE WITH POSITION CLASSIFICATION

The historic contribution of position classification in the public sector often was to bring relative order out of a chaos of misleading job titles, grossly inequitable pay for the same kind and level of work, and recruitment and selection processes largely uninformed by a detailed understanding of job content and its relationships to organizational functions and human resource needs. Adoption of position classification and accompanying compensation plans, beginning in the early 1900s, was an important stage in the development of merit systems because it curbed the widespread practice of manipulating pay rates for partisan reasons. The position classification approach also gained wide professional support as a reform that applied scientific management's emphasis on job analysis and efficiency to the technical problems of public administration. Reform candidates for elective office were supportive because position classification conveyed their commitment to "rational and businesslike" approaches to government. Nevertheless, position classification and its practitioners have a long history of being at the center of ongoing battles between supporters of traditional merit systems and those in favor of a management-centered model. The former argue that position classification is fundamental to achieving and maintaining neutral competence. The latter are fond of describing it as a major example of the "triumph of technique over purpose" (Sayre, 1991).

Objectives of Position Classification

According to the National Academy of Public Administration (NAPA), the design and administration of contemporary position classification systems should promote the accomplishment of two broad objectives. First, they should support efforts to treat job applicants and employees in an equitable and nonpartisan manner. Second, they should be consciously designed to promote effective and efficient agency performance. The first objective reflects the values of the first civil service reform movement and its stress on regulating and policing the personnel-related actions of managers. It was, in turn, assumed that only a politically neutral and technically competent civil service could be efficient and effective. The second of NAPA's objectives for position classification is related to the contemporary focus on human resources management. In NAPA's words, classification systems "must be brought more into the mainstream of essential processes in an organization's management structure." These should be as important as an agency's budget, information or accounting systems; in fact, they should have the ability to interface with these and other administrative systems to enhance the management process" (National Academy of Public Administration, 1991, p. 14).

Criticisms of Classification Systems

Traditional position classification systems in government have come under attack from critics who argue that they are incapable of achieving either of NAPA's objectives. With regard to fairness and equity, the accuracy and objectivity of job analysis and classification actions have always been suspect, since none of the systems in use comes close to completely eliminating professional or managerial judgment and discretion. Actually, position classification often is a subjective process, which is true of all forms of job evaluation including the so-called quantitative formats such as FES. In many lines of work, it is very hard to draw absolutely clear lines between positions with regard to levels of difficulty and responsibility. Classification analysts, in other words, are far more than clerks plugging numbers into formulas; they are often required to exercise considerable discretion and judgment:

> OPM prepares classification standards on the assumption that the people using them are either personnel specialists or managers trained in how to classify positions and knowledgeable about the occupations and organizations concerned. Regardless of the specific format of the standard, you must consider and apply it as a *guide* to grade level decisions. You should not use grade level criteria mechanically to match or "force fit" a position to specific elements, factors, situations, or duties. You must always use sound classification judgment to determine the extent to which an individual job fits the *intent* of the standard. (U.S. Office of Personnel Management, 1997a, p. 34)

Classification audits conducted by central personnel agencies such as OPM almost always reveal that a certain percentage of classification decisions on the agency level are simply wrong because of factual inaccuracies and misinterpretations of classification standards (U.S. Office of Personnel Management, 1981). Classification errors of this type are inevitable and may be minimized by regular "desk audits" of positions and better training of those doing the classification.

The more significant challenge to the fairness of the classification process and the equity of its outcomes comes from the possibility that its discretionary nature will allow personal and organizational biases to play significant roles. Most importantly, those with a stake in a classification action are in a position to try to influence the analyst's decision. Many so-called overgrading "errors" may be traced to self-interested pressures from line managers who for one reason or another wanted higher salaries for *their* subordinates. More broadly, however, elected executives, line managers, and personnel specialists may become involved in a struggle for control over the classification process, and analysts are in a position to act as "organizational politicians" who are more responsive to powerful organizational actors than they are to merit principles or the formal rules of position classification (Shafritz, 1973).

Another reason to question the objectivity of position classification in government is the well-documented phenomenon called "grade creep," which refers to an unplanned rise in the average grade of all employees in a jurisdiction or agency. Periodically, legislative oversight committees or executive budget offices will "discover" that average grades have risen and, with them, personnel budgets. In short order, there will be calls for adjustments and downgrades, politicians will complain about "overpaid and underworked bureaucrats," taxpayers will become irate over the increase in the government's expenditures for wages and salaries, and employee organizations will mobilize to oppose downgrading of positions.

Some of the inflation in average grade level is the result of intentional overgrading. Motives include keeping a valuable employee who has received an outside offer, compensating for inflation that has eroded purchasing power, or rewarding exceptional performance. Over time, the cumulative effect may be a breakdown of internal pay equities, the emergence of highly visible biases in the grade structures of agencies, and a widespread perception among workers that the administration of the system is neither objective nor fair.

Inflated job descriptions do occur, classifications are sometimes manipulated, and some public employees do receive salaries that are out of line with their job responsibilities and qualifications. If enough of this goes on long enough, it can lead to significantly higher average grades throughout the government or in certain agencies. However, the reasons for grade creep are usually far more complicated than simple greed and favoritism. Much of it is associated with the changing nature of the public workforce. Governments on all levels are hiring growing numbers of professional, administrative, and technical employees needed to carry out new and often complex programs. There is no reason to assume, therefore, that the largest numbers of public employees will be in the lowest grades. To the contrary, the largest numbers frequently are toward the middle of the grade structure. Often, however, public employers fail to acknowledge this reality in their formal classification plans and workforce projections. Figure 6.2 shows the distribution of federal GS employees for 1996 and 1997. It is worth noting that the average federal GS grade had risen from 6.73 in 1960 to 9.49 in 1996 (U.S. Office of Personnel Management, 1997a, p. 9).

Another rather predictable cause of grade creep is the direct connection between classes and pay ranges. A great deal of overgrading happens because jobs are in relatively narrow classes with pay grades that cannot be changed without legislation. Legislative bodies and chief executives are notoriously reluctant to raise pay scales, and pressure builds over time to place positions in higher grades in order to prevent turnover of valuable employees and to reward superior performance. From an organizational performance

Figure 6.2 Distribution of General Schedule Employment (1996 and 1997)

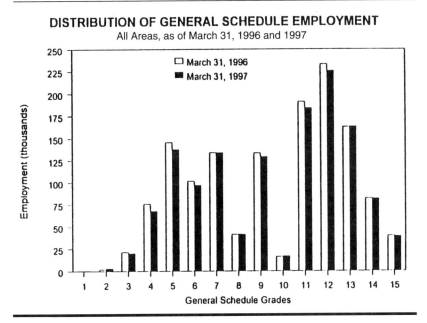

point of view, grade creep, while informal and extralegal, may be a functional response to the rigidity of the formal system. Over time, however, the classification plan and related procedures are likely to become a facade behind which operates an opportunistic and highly inequitable approach to position classification having little if any connection to organizational performance. In the long run, therefore, grade creep undermines both fairness and effective management of human resources.

Impact of Collective Bargaining

Another source of inconsistencies and distortions in classification plans may be agreements negotiated with employee organizations. In most governments, setting job evaluation standards and the classification of individual positions are management prerogatives and are not negotiable. Traditionally, unions have concentrated on improving pay and fringe benefits, but this does not mean that they have always been content to leave job evaluation completely to management. In some places, they have succeeded in making classification standards subject to negotiation, and disputes over their interpretation may be subject to binding arbitration.

Most public managers are strongly opposed to making position classification a negotiable matter. They argue that management's effectiveness will be undermined if it cannot unilaterally determine the job evaluation plan and the classifications of individual positions. To classification analysts, bargaining in these areas is anathema, because they consider the process of evaluating and ranking jobs a technical matter requiring substantial training, experience, and professional judgment, one not to be decided through negotiations and compromise. For the most part, this point of view has held sway on all levels of government, but there are exceptions. One of these is the U.S. Postal Service, where job evaluation is subject to negotiation under terms of the Postal Reorganization Act of 1970.

When public employers bargain collectively with unions representing several bargaining units, they often find it hard to maintain a unified job evaluation and pay plan. This problem develops when there are several bargaining units; no single union is likely to win the representation in all the units, thus the employer must bargain with a number of different unions. In each unit, the union will concentrate on doing all it can to improve pay and benefits for its members. Improvements negotiated for one unit may create inequities for employees doing the same kind and level of work in other units. As a result of unit-by-unit bargaining, separate job evaluation and pay plans eventually are created for each unit; the grading and pay are equitable *within* each unit, but not *between* units.

Performance-Related Issues

With varying degrees of success, public-sector classification systems have concentrated on achieving fairness and equity and, in so doing, have tended to neglect the organizational performance concerns of managers. Over the past half-century, U.S. public administrators have rather consistently complained that existing classification structures and processes impose barriers to effectiveness and efficiency. In its review of studies and articles published between 1941 and 1991, NAPA found that the following problems were most often cited:

1. Classification standards are complex and hard for nonspecialists to understand, much less use on day-to-day basis. In practical terms, this means that managers and supervisors play little, if any role, in the classification process, which is the province of analysts who have little interest in management's human resource problems.

2. Central personnel agencies do not provide needed leadership and they are notoriously resistant to change, especially to changes that reduce their control over classification standards and procedures.

3. Public managers experience the process as burdensome and unintelligible, and they see little reward in supporting an effort to accurately describe and classify positions.

4. Supervisors learn to pressure analysts to overgrade positions, and they do not use the system as a human resources management tool.

5. The rank-in-position approach is rigid and inflexible. It does not accommodate specific agency needs, and classification standards often neglect employees' impact on the job and important differences in levels of performance.

6. Classification plans and position descriptions are typically at least several years out of date (it is not unusual to find systems that have not been revised for decades), which makes it difficult to recruit for new occupations, to clearly define and anticipate human resource needs, and to meet staffing requirements in rapidly changing technical fields. (National Academy of Public Administration, 1991, pp. 17–18)

Overall, NAPA's study revealed that federal personnel directors, classifiers, administrative officials, and managers favored several important reforms. These included (1) authorizing significant delegations of classification authority to line managers, (2) broadbanding, or consolidation of existing grades into three or four grades with wide pay ranges, and (3) allowing skills-based pay differentials. In fact, these kinds of changes are found in the systems used by federal agencies excluded from the statute covering classification (Title 5) and in several OPM-sponsored demonstration projects that tested alternative approaches to one or more aspects of personnel administration. High levels of satisfaction with these innovative or different classification systems was found to be linked to these agencies' ability "to pay salaries more in keeping with the marketplace than is possible for agencies covered by Title 5" (p. 33).

In addition to their inability to offer competitive pay, the agencies conducting demonstration projects cited at least three human resources management problems as reasons for reforming the classification system. First, overly complex classification standards with too many narrow occupations and grades undermined management's efforts to recruit highly qualified personnel, to effectively assign work, and to sustain high levels of *organizational* performance. Second, it was taking far too long to have positions classified; it often took months to complete the staffing process and to fill a vacant position. Third, inflexible classification structures tended to force outstanding performers out of their primary areas of expertise and into higher-graded supervisory jobs where they could make higher salaries (pp. 33–34).

REFORMING CLASSIFICATION SYSTEMS

The current emphasis on flexibility and responsiveness to specific agency needs has focused attention on three reform models potentially available to governments. First, the rank-in-position model could be replaced by a rank-in-the-person system for part or all of the civil service. Second, authority over the design of grading systems could be delegated to the agency level where they can be tailored to specific needs and conditions. Third, existing government-wide systems could be modified by allowing more agency-level discretion under general policies set forth by central personnel agencies.

RANK IN THE PERSON

In many countries, personnel systems are structured around "rank in the person," and civil servants' educational backgrounds, technical and administrative qualifications, special abilities, and relevant experiences (not a particular position) determine their pay and organizational status. The rank-in-position concept dominates the public service on all levels of government in the United States, and rank-based systems have been generally restricted to the foreign service, military services, and agencies such as the Department of Veterans Affairs, Federal Bureau of Investigation, and the Central Intelligence Agency. On the local level, police departments typically use a rank-in-the person system or some variant that combines it with the position-based model.

The U.S. Department of State's Foreign Service offers a good example of a U.S. version of the rank-in-person approach (U.S. Department of State, 1998). Currently, the Foreign Services numbers about 12,000, which includes the Senior Foreign Service, Foreign Service Officers and staff, and ambassadors. *The Foreign Service is career-oriented and everybody starts at the same stage.* Foreign Service careers may have up to three stages: junior officer, career officer, and senior foreign service officer. Upon entry, foreign service officers are referred to as junior officers and they are in a probationary status. In contrast to a position-based approach, functional or technical specializations are not expected on the first step of the career ladder. Junior officers, therefore, enter into the career line without a specific functional designation or specialty. On entering, they receive basic orientation at the National Foreign Affairs Training Center and up to seven months in training (mostly language skills) before their first overseas assignment, which can run from two to four years.

Emphasis is placed on general skills and potential to continuously develop and to make successful progress through the various stages of the career line. All junior officers are reviewed for tenure and commissioning as career foreign service officers (FSOs) by a Commissioning and Tenure Board about 36 months after entry. The only standard used for tenuring and commissioning is "a candidate's demonstrated potential to serve effectively as an FSO over a normal career span." The Board evaluates candidates in five areas: intellectual skills, interpersonal skills, leadership, managerial skills, and substantive knowledge. *FSO careers stress broadly gauged functional expertise and flexibility.* They are assigned a functional specialty or "cone" at the time they are offered tenure, and they are expected to spend most of their career working in that specialty area. Presently, there are four cones:

- Officers in the *Administrative Cone* coordinate the support operations of U.S. embassies and consulates around the world. Their duties are diverse, including hiring foreign nationals, managing financial operations, and purchasing equipment and material.

- Those in the *Consular Cone* have two primary functions. They issue visas to foreign country nationals who wish to enter the United States, and they provide special services to American citizens overseas.

- If they are assigned to the *Economic Cone,* FSOs develop assessments of commercial and economic issues ranging from fishing rights to environmental impacts of economic development. They also establish professional contacts to obtain information on local economic conditions and their implications for American trade and investment policies.

- FSOs in the *Political Cone* assess foreign support for U.S. policies and establish contacts with a wide range of local groups and organizations in order to determine their positions on domestic and foreign policies in certain countries.

After they receive tenure, FSOs acquire functional, specialized expertise during their first several assignments. As their careers develop, they will serve in out-of-cone positions, and the Department of State encourages them to acquire skills in more than one functional area so that they can achieve the knowledge and experience needed to serve effectively in a variety of roles. *Continuous development and regular promotion are required to stay in the service; simply having performed adequately at one level is not enough.* Having broad policy and management skills as well as specialized expertise is important, because promotions are competitive and, for each grade, there is a time limit before which candidates must be promoted to the next grade. Those who are not promoted must leave the Service (selection out). Recommendations for promotion are determined by a Selection Board, which reviews the files and performance evaluations of all FSOs in each grade who are eligible for promotion. After this review, the Board issues a list of officers whom it recommends for promotion, based on merit. The top of the FSOs' career line is the Senior Foreign Service, a relatively small group of officers (there are about 1000) who formulate, organize, coordinate, and implement U.S. foreign policy. These are the most responsible and sensitive positions in the Service, and entry into this level of responsibility and authority is highly competitive.

Arguments in favor of replacing position-based with rank-based systems stress their flexibility, adaptability, and "fit" with decentralized personnel management structures. In 1991, for example, the U.S. Merit Systems Protection Board favorably evaluated the modified rank-in-the-person system used by the Department of Veterans Affairs (VA). The statute under which the VA operates (Title 38) establishes "a methodology in which the qualifications of each *person* are evaluated against agency-established qualification standards, and a grade (rank) is assigned to the person based on his or her individual qualifications regardless of the position held." Another difference from the Title 5 model is the use of groups of VA employees (standards boards) in the same or related occupations to recommend the grade to which a person should be assigned. The VA's approach is not a pure rank-in-the-person system because the position held often determines an incumbent's ability to qualify for a higher grade, and "the highest three registered nurse grades and the highest two grades for physicians are assigned exclusively on the basis of the position held" (U.S. Merit Systems Protection Board, 1991, pp. 17–18).

In light of its study of the VA's personnel system, the MSPB concluded that it offered a potential alternative for some agencies and occupations operating under Title 5. Specifically, its report noted that the VA's managers believed the method used to set employee grades was easier and more equitable. In its recommendations, the MSPB suggested that those concerned with reforming the Title 5 system consider the use of peer panels as a part of the grade- and pay-setting process because they increase flexibility and are more likely to reflect an understanding of the actual work environment. The MSPB also cited the VA's extensive delegations of personnel authority to line managers as providing a model that the rest of the federal service should consider (pp. 45–48).

In recent years, there has been strong support for applying the rank concept to high-level professional and executive employees. In the federal government, the Senior Executive Service is a limited example, and several states have established versions of the SES under which top managers are assigned a rank and pay grade. In the United States, however, possibilities of adopting the rank principle for middle- and lower-level jobs appear small. A primary objection to such reforms is that they would lead to a revisitation of the chaos and pay inequities that prevailed before position classification plans were adopted.

Also, rank-based classification schemes based on those of other countries have been rejected by U.S. lawmakers as an antidemocratic way of staffing civil services that could lead to the creation of powerful administrative elites. In U.S. merit systems, relative ability to perform the work assigned to a specific position is supposed to be the main standard, and it is argued that this is a democratic approach to staffing that can only work in the context of a well-designed and administered position-based system. Rank-based systems, on the other hand, tend to emphasize the general educational backgrounds and social skills of those seeking to pursue careers that lead to high-level posts in the civil service, and this almost always restricts access to members of social and economic elites, particularly those who have attended certain universities. These career lines, in practice, are "closed" to others with different social and educational backgrounds. Under such conditions, the hierarchies of civil service bureaucracies mirror the larger class structures of societies, with representatives of the upper class at the top. Although there may be ways of "democratizing" access to and progress through rank-in-the-person career systems, Americans have traditionally been suspicious of them in most areas of civilian bureaucracy.

FRAGMENTATION

The fragmentation option is advanced by those who believe that a single classification system or concept simply cannot effectively address the human resources management needs and problems of all agencies under all conditions. In the federal service, numerous complete and partial agency exclusions from Title 5, demonstration projects, and ongoing modifications of traditional classification practices reflect the need to adapt these systems to fit specific agency circumstances. In its 1991 report, NAPA identified a trend that has continued to this day:

> Each excluded agency, in accordance with its own priorities, needs and culture, established or is in the process of establishing its own position classification system. These programs run the gamut from continued use of the GS grades and OPM position classification

standards to not classifying positions at all, but rather adopting a rank-in-person classification system. (National Academy of Public Administration, 1991, p. D-3)

REFORMING EXISTING SYSTEMS

In practice, efforts to deal with the problems posed by conventional job evaluation and position classification systems on all levels of government in the United States have concentrated on (1) increasing their flexibility, (2) making it easier for supervisors to understand and use them, and (3) connecting them in supportive ways to the human resources management efforts of agencies. With the exception of senior executive services and a limited number of agencies, rank-in-the-person models have not taken hold, and fragmentation has not been adopted as a comprehensive reform strategy.

Probably the most significant reform trends have been decentralization of classification authorities to the agency and subagency levels within policy guidelines and standards set by central personnel offices such as OPM, and the restructuring of classification plans through broadbanding. A central theme of almost all reform proposals has been the need to make position classification systems flexible and responsive to managerial and organizational conditions and needs. One element of flexibility widely supported by public managers is the elimination of numerous narrow classes in favor of a relatively small number of occupational categories and grade levels. Narrowly defined and numerous classes often work to greatly limit management's discretion to adjust job tasks and rates of pay without having positions reclassified by personnel specialists. Broadbanded classification and pay grade structures make it much easier for managers to design and interrelate positions around work processes. They also facilitate recruitment on the basis of occupations and career planning, make moving people from job to job in the organization much less complicated, and support efforts to administer pay in ways intended to meaningfully reward performance and recognize differences in skills and abilities.

The popularity of broadbanding with public managers is illustrated by the frequency with which it appears as a central theme in demonstration projects designed to test new and innovative approaches to personnel management in the federal government. These demonstration projects, authorized by Title VI of the CSRA and approved by OPM, have more often than not included a broadbanding component. The first experiment of this kind was the Navy's China Lake Demonstration Project, which was approved for implementation by OPM in 1980 and extended indefinitely (made permanent) through legislation in 1994. A key feature of this project was a simplified classification system that consolidated GS grades into broader pay bands. Under the China Lake reforms, managers were allowed increased control over classification, pay, and other personnel matters (Nigro and Clayton, 1984). OPM conducted a series of evaluations of this project over a decade, and it concluded that it was successful in improving personnel management in the covered research and development laboratories. Specifically, simplified and delegated classification procedures dramatically reduced the time needed to complete classification actions, and conflicts between personnel specialists and managers were reduced. According to the OPM evaluation:

> Recruitment, retention and reduced turnover of high performers and increased turnover of low performers have all improved. Perceived supervisory authority over classification, pay, and hiring increased, as did employee satisfaction with pay and performance management . . . . (U.S. Office of Personnel Management, 1998, p. 2)

As the OPM commentary on the China Lake demonstration suggests, broadbanding often is associated with extensive delegation of classification authority to line managers. Under these arrangements, general, understandable, classification standards or criteria are used by managers to place specific positions in classes. The role of classification analysts working in personnel departments becomes helping to formulate these general standards and assisting management in their application, but not making case-by-case classification decisions. Formal appeals processes and periodic audits are used to assure conformance with systemwide merit policies, and to make sure that managers are not violating the norms of fairness and equity. In addition to empowering managers and allowing them to use the classification process as a human resources management tool, decentralizations of this kind are supposed to lower the overall cost of administering the classification plan by simplifying and speeding up the process. They may also relieve central personnel departments of large inventories of routine classification actions that must be handled before personnel specialists can respond to the organization's human resources development and management needs. Most of the currently active federal demonstration projects include broadbanding (U.S. Office of Personnel Management, 1998, pp. 1–4). An example is the approach to classification and career paths set forth in the Naval Warfare Centers' project design:

> A fundamental element of the system is a simplified white collar classification and pay component. The proposed broad banding scheme reduces the fifteen GS grade levels and the Senior Level (SL) and Scientific and Technical (ST) pay levels, into five to six broad pay

bands. GS occupations are further broken down into three separate career paths: Scientific and Engineering (ND), Administrative and Technical (NT), and General Support (NG). The OPM-developed classification standards are replaced by a small number of one-page, generic benchmark standards developed within the Demonstration Project. These standards also serve as the core of the position description and replace lengthy individually tailored position descriptions. These generic level descriptors encompass multiple series and provide maximum flexibility for the organization to assign individuals consistent with the needs of the organization, established level or rank that the individual has achieved, and the individual's qualifications. Career progression between levels will occur by promotion. . . . (Federal Register, 1997, p. 8589)

In addition, within each band, there are several levels: (1) student/trainee or entry-level; (2) developmental; (3) full performance; and (4) expert and/or supervisor/manager.

PAY IN THE PUBLIC SERVICE

In contrast to the seemingly dry and technical subjects of job evaluation and classification, issues and problems related to the public employees' pay spark great public interest and may be counted on to generate many political controversies. Needless to say, many aspects of pay administration are highly technical and require the skills of trained specialists in fields such as economics and accounting. Here, we will concentrate on broad policy issues, managerial concerns, and efforts to improve the effectiveness of *pay systems* in the public sector. However, pay is only one part of the compensation "packages" available to public employers. These packages include benefits that may add up to 25 percent of an employee's compensation, so the discussion of pay that follows should be understood in this context.

Policy issues and political debates related to civil servants' wages and salaries may attract intense public interest. Many taxpayers are prone to outrage when they learn about what appear to be excessive pay rates and overly gen-

BULLETIN

1997 Average Pay of Municipal Chief Financial Officers

Geographic Region	Mean Salary
Northeast	$52,253
North Central	52,376
South	51,429
West	66,309
City Type	
Central	71,556
Suburban	56,723
Independent	44,308
Form of Government	
Mayor-council	50,352
Council-manager	57,614

Source: International City/County Management Association, The Municipal Yearbook–1998 (Washington, DC: ICMA), p. 81.

erous benefits, especially if they are less than happy about government's performance. Local media, of course, are ever alert to "scandals" involving "overpaid" and "underworked" public servants. The public's overall impression is that public employees, at worst, are well paid, and that they have very secure jobs. Public employees, in turn, see themselves as relatively underpaid, as well as unappreciated.

Public sector pay is in very important respects a *political outcome*. Most public employees are paid with legislatively appropriated funds that come from tax revenues; at least a large proportion of their total compensation will come from these sources. Even during times when revenues are growing, there are many competing claims on these financial resources, including personnel budgets. Legislators and elected executives with limited options must focus on personnel-related costs when expenditures have to be cut or growth curtailed. Pay rates and compensation policies often become issues as politicians and interest groups maneuver for public support and votes. Pay is almost always a major issue in collective bargaining. Union negotiators demand "more" and management counters that fiscal conditions and demands on existing resources require smaller increases or, perhaps, reductions. Public employees vote and join organizations that support candidates for elective office and lobby legislative bodies for better benefits and higher pay. Legislatively mandated improvements in pension plans (which may be "pay as you go") and other long-term financial commitments that are part of employee compensation packages worry experts in public finance and others who ask where the money needed to meet these future obligations will come from.

Workforce diversity has generated pay-related conflicts and policy debates. Women and minority groups see ample reason to conclude that they have been and continue to be victims of inequitable pay policies and practices. They demand reforms such as "comparable worth," which critics argue are political efforts to overturn the "economically rational" outcomes of the interactions of supply and demand in labor markets. Political, technical, and legal battles over these issues are ongoing.

As noted in Chapter 3, public employers may be confronted by serious recruitment, retention, and motivation problems stemming at least in part from a chronic inability to offer truly competitive pay. In some cases, the response has been to create several pay plans within the same government in order to address special problems on a case-by-case basis. Often, this approach is resisted by those who believe in preserving the standardization and internal equity that are hallmarks of traditional merit systems' classification and pay plans. In a 1986 report on the status of the federal civil service done for NAPA, Charles Levine and Rosslyn Kleeman noted "increasing support for proposals that would have the effect of 'splintering' the civil service into several separate pay schedules and formulas" (Levine and Kleeman, 1986, p. 30). Much of this pressure to "break up" the General Schedule had its roots in an effort to make pay more competitive for certain occupations and to allow agency management greater overall flexibility in personnel matters. Although such changes may be necessary, Levine and Kleeman worried that a continued pattern of incremental adjustments (as opposed to comprehensive reform) might lead to a situation where certain occupations and politically powerful agencies could escape the limitations of the General Schedule while others were unable to do so:

> Under such a process, the civil service system seems likely to break into two parts, "the haves" and the "have-nots," gradually fraying first the edges and then the core of the present system. . . .The outcome, therefore, is likely to be a mixture of some up and a few down; i.e., a dual system that is fully competitive in some places and not competitive for top quality employees in others. (p. 31)

Continued fragmentation, in other words, posed the threat of a system so complex that it could not be managed in "an accountable fashion," and pay disparities between occupations and agencies might frustrate all efforts to maintain fairness and equity. Finally, in Levine and Kleeman's judgment, it could threaten the very idea of *one* federal civil service and, in effect, replace it with *several* services (pp. 30–31). Hopefully, by now it is clear that controversies over the design and administration of pay and compensation systems in the public sector seldom concern merely technical issues. More often than not, they are driven by the competing interests and values of a variety of stakeholders, and by clashing points of view about how the civil service should be organized and administered.

Pay Policies in U.S. Government

In the United States, the prevailing norm is that government should have pay rates that are comparable with those in the private sector for similar jobs; that is, it should offer the "prevailing rate." This is a change from earlier times, when it was generally assumed that public servants, particularly white-collar workers, should expect to make less than their private-sector counterparts. The convention at the time was that since public employees enjoyed far greater job security and superior benefits, they should expect smaller paychecks. The payment of prevailing wages (in specific labor markets) for blue-collar workers, however, does have a long history, going back to 1862 in the federal service. During the early part of the Civil War (1861–1865), when the

Federal side was struggling to build a navy capable of cutting off the Confederacy's maritime commerce with Europe, Congress passed a law directing the Navy Department to offer prevailing rates of pay in the shipyards. Today, many state and local governments also use the prevailing rate standard for setting blue-collar pay.

In applying the principle of prevailing or comparable rates, public employers are trying to make use of information generated by the interplay of supply and demand in a labor market. Prevailing rate surveys are done to establish pay rates for *benchmark jobs,* or jobs that are comparable across organizations and employment sectors. These jobs are then placed into a salary grade structure based on the average competitive rates of pay. After reviewing this structure, management places all remaining jobs in it on the basis of their value in relation to the benchmark jobs.

In theory, a prevailing rate or market pricing evaluation approach allows public employers to construct pay scales that allow them to acquire and retain needed human resources without paying more than they need to. Although the methods used to conduct and interpret prevailing rate surveys may be complex, the logic underpinning them is straightforward: identify and pay the going market price for a particular combination of skills, knowledge, and abilities (SKAs).

Although the desirability of offering prevailing rates as a matter of public policy enjoys widespread support, there are issues to be confronted. Prevailing rates are not sensitive to social-psychological and political distortions of the "ideal" or theoretical market. Consequently, they may perpetuate long-standing inequities and patterns of economic discrimination in society, such as those that have resulted in lower prevailing rates of pay for women. Later in this chapter, we will discuss "comparable worth," which is designed to establish pay equity for women. Another highly relevant set of issues is centered on the degree to which the methods used to conduct prevailing rate surveys are influenced by the efforts of stakeholders to skew their outcomes. For example, should the survey be restricted to a metropolitan area, a state, a region, or the nation? Should other governments and charitable organizations be included? Nurses in public hospitals have historically suffered because these institutions routinely surveyed each other, thereby keeping pay at "Florence Nightingale" levels for years. Should fringe benefits and "intangibles" be factored into the equation? If so, relatively generous pension plans (deferred compensation) may be used to justify keeping wages down. What criteria should be used to establish comparability between organizations? Is working in a small police department the same as working for a large metropolitan department? How should positions with no functional equivalents in the private sector be handled? Public managers, executives, legislators, employee organizations, and taxpayer's associations are among the groups actively seeking to have these crucial decisions made in their favor. The "politics of prevailing rates" is quite intense and very relevant to the seemingly objective "numbers" produced by surveys of prevailing rates.

Establishing what the prevailing rate for a job is does not assure that the rate will be offered in the labor market or actually paid. For public employers, the political climate inevitably has a major impact on how information about prevailing rates is used (or not used) by legislative bodies and chief executives. This reality often has translated into a general reluctance to spend the money necessary to achieve and sustain prevailing rates for many public-sector jobs, especially those on the higher levels of the civil service. States and localities may be forced to choose between achieving comparability and adequately funding a variety of important programs with strong, aggressive, constituencies. When authorizing changes in base pay, legislators tend to be more generous with those in the lower ranks. These lower-paid workers are more numerous, and they are more likely to be able to exert strong political pressure. Managerial and executive personnel, on the other hand, usually do not have much "clout" in the electoral process. In the face of relatively high pay on the top levels of the nonelected bureaucracy, legislators and the voting public are more likely to be responsive to the plight of the "underdog." Finally, the wages of non-managerial personnel may be set through collective bargaining, whereas managers do not have unions representing their interests.

In the federal government, congressional pay historically has placed a ceiling on executive branch pay because legislators have resisted paying civil servants more than they make. In general, legislators' paychecks increase slowly (incrementally) because of the political firestorms ignited by large adjustments; the federal government is no exception to this rule. This slowly rising "cap" on federal pay, in combination with regular presidential refusals to recommend systemwide increases that could achieve comparability, has at times led to a debilitating gap between federal and private sector pay for certain hard-to-recruit occupational categories and higher grades (U.S. General Accounting Office, 1990a, 1990b).

BULLETIN

1997 Average Salaries of Municipal Police Officers

Entrance Salary	**Maximum Salary**
$28,238	$38,477

1997 Average Salaries of Municipal Firefighters

Entrance Salary	**Maximum Salary**
$26,899	$35,206

Source: International City/County Management Association, *The Municipal Yearbook–1998* (Washington, DC: ICMA), p. 120.

Governments on all levels have experienced *salary compression* problems. Salary compression is the result of caps on top salaries, grade creep, and annual across-the-board inflation adjustments to existing pay scales. The net effect of compression is to flatten the organization's pay structure, gradually closing the gap between the highest- and lowest-paying positions. Over time, therefore, salary compression frustrates efforts to establish meaningful differences in pay on the basis of job responsibilities and qualifications. It is impossible to offer prevailing rates, and this situation makes it very difficult to recruit and retain highly qualified administrative and technical personnel who can command higher pay for the work they are doing from other governments or private enterprises.

RECENT DEVELOPMENTS IN T HE FEDERAL SERVICE

Controversies and difficulties in setting wages and salaries are well illustrated by the experience of the federal government over the past thirty-five years. The comparability or prevailing rate principle was first established by Congress for white-collar workers in the Federal Salary Reform Act of 1962. This legislation provided that "federal salary rates shall be comparable with private enterprise salary rates for the same levels of work." Nonetheless, white-collar pay was so far behind by 1967 that Congress passed another law authorizing the president without requirement of congressional approval to bring federal pay up to private rates, "as nearly as practicable," in two big pay adjustments.

In the Federal Pay Comparability Act of 1970, Congress delegated to the president the salary-fixing authority for General Schedule and Foreign Service employees. The president is assisted by an "agent" he or she designates, presently the director of OPM, the director of the Office of Management and Budget (OMB), and the secretary of labor, acting jointly. The 1970 law also established a Federal Employees Pay Council and an Advisory Committee on Federal Pay. The Council consists of five members from three employee organizations representing substantial numbers of GS employees. The Advisory Committee has three members from outside the government who are noted for their impartiality and expertise in labor relations and pay policy. The president appoints them after reviewing recommendations from the director of the Federal Mediation and Conciliation Service and "other interested parties."

As instructed by the Pay Comparability Act of 1970, the Bureau of Labor Statistics (BLS) conducted a national survey of private-sector professional, administrative, and technical pay (PATC Survey). The president's agent instructed the BLS concerning which jobs to include in the survey and the establishments to be surveyed, and OPM and the BLS jointly maintained job descriptions for each of the various work levels in the occupations surveyed. Each work level was to be defined in a manner that allowed it to be compared with grade levels in the General Schedule. BLS data collectors visited the establishments included in the survey, identified the jobs that matched the BLS-OPM job descriptions, and collected the salary information. The Act stated that comparability was to be with private-sector jobs, so jobs in state and local governments were not included in the PATC survey.

After reviewing the survey's findings, the agent prepared a report for the president with recommendations as to the size and form of pay adjustments needed to maintain comparability. The views and recommendations of the Federal Employees Pay Council and other unions not represented on the council were included in the report. In turn, the Advisory Committee on Federal Pay reviewed the agent's report and submitted a second, independent, report to the president. The president then adjusted federal pay rates, the changes to be effective on or after October 1 of the applicable year. However, if the president believed it inappropriate to make the adjustments suggested by the agent because of "national emergency or economic conditions affecting the general welfare," an alternative plan could be sent to Congress. This plan would go into effect within 30 days of transmittal unless either house passed a resolution of disapproval.

Presidents have routinely exercised their authority under the law to submit alternative plans providing for substantially less than full comparability. Predictably, the gap between federal white-collar and private-sector pay reached crisis proportions by the late 1980s. In addition to the general erosion of comparability, federal competitiveness in specific locations was further crippled by Washington's reliance on national averages to determine comparability. Private-sector pay rates varied considerably across localities, regions, and labor markets. In San Francisco, for example, the 1988 BLS survey showed that a secretary was paid 60 percent more than one doing the same kind of work in Scranton, Pennsylvania, but federal pay was the same in both cities. In some places, the federal government paid more than the private sector, but the private sector paid more than the federal government in about 90 percent of the cases. In many metropolitan statistical areas (MSAs), the private sector enjoyed competitive pay advantages running well over 20 percent (U.S. General Accounting Office, 1990a, pp. 5–17).

Prior to 1990, the only way the federal government could vary GS pay by locality for certain occupations was by offering "special rates." OPM had to approve agency requests for special rates based on recruitment or retention problems "caused by higher private-sector pay or other reasons." The agencies making these requests had to certify that they had the funds needed to pay the higher rates within their existing budgets. By 1990, about 13 percent of the GS (190,000 employees) was on special rates, and severe problems in a number of agencies such as the FBI and IRS (agents resisted transfers to places like New York City, where they could not afford a reasonable standard of living) were highlighting the need for a general reform of the system (Shoop, 1990).

THE FEDERAL EMPLOYEES PAY COMPARABILITY ACT OF 1990

In general terms, federal white-collar pay policies have become more management-centered and flexible. In large measure, the logic driving the system has shifted from equity and consistency to enhanced competitiveness and responsiveness to management's human resources needs. After considering several alternatives, the Congress passed and President Bush signed the Federal Employees Pay Comparability Act (FEPCA) in late 1990. Like most such reforms, this legislation represented a compromise between those who favored comprehensive reform and actions designed to quickly reach comparability and those preferring incremental adjustments and close attention to budgetary consequences. The president retained across-the-board authority to alter pay recommendations, and the executive branch was given greater discretion in matters of pay administration. A nine-member (three neutral experts and six representatives of employee organizations) Federal Salary Council was created to advise the president on locality pay matters. The Act set forth four guiding principles for setting pay under the General Schedule: (1) there should be equal pay for substantially equal work within each local pay area; (2) within local pay areas, pay distinctions were to be maintained on the basis of work *and* performance distinctions; (3) federal pay should be comparable with *non-federal*, as opposed to only private-sector, rates for the same levels of work; and (4) "any existing pay disparities between federal and non-federal employees should be completely eliminated."

The FEPCA's main provisions were expressly designed to allow greater flexibility by:

- Setting up criteria and procedures under which pay disparities could be reduced by adding locality-based comparability adjustments to systemwide increases in the GS's base pay schedule;
- Providing for special-pay authorities in order to help agencies fill critical positions that had remained vacant because of an inability to compete successfully in the labor market;

- Authorizing establishment of special occupational pay systems needed to achieve comparability; and
- Approving delegations of a wide variety of case-by-case (nonbase) pay decisions to the agency management level, thereby providing legislative support for one-time bonuses or variable pay for performance arrangements geared to agency needs and conditions.

Another significant feature was the elimination of the old PATC and its replacement with a new BLS survey including "nonfederal" jobs in state, local, and nonprofit agencies. A principal criticism of the methods used by OPM and the BLS for determining white-collar comparability rates had been their failure to include jobs in state and local governments and in nonprofit organizations. The FEPCA responded to these concerns by specifying that the president shall direct the pay agent to prepare a report that compares pay under the General Schedule with that of nonfederal workers for the same levels of work within each pay locality.

In the Federal Salary Reform Act of 1962, the Congress had excluded comparisons with jobs in state and local governments because it was convinced at the time that salary data from this segment of the workforce (then about six million) would be outweighed by private-enterprise data. Since state and local employment has more than doubled by 1990, this logic was no longer valid, particularly since certain kinds of jobs not included in the PATC survey are numerous on these levels of government (e.g., nurses, police officers, firefighters, and social workers). In an example of the politics of prevailing rate surveys, since pay is often lower in small state and local governments, unions representing federal employees have strongly objected to including them in prevailing rate surveys. The management point of view, of course, is that they should be included.

The impact of the 1990 legislation on federal pay has been significant. There is now considerable diversity in pay plans, although roughly 75 percent of full-time workers are still covered by the GS. Figure 6.3 shows that by 1998 about 10 percent of all full-time federal employees were not under either the white-collar GS or the blue-collar Wage System. In addition, the locality pay provisions of the Act have meaningfully improved the federal government's capacity to compete in high-cost-of-living areas. It has also allowed far greater flexibility with regard to occupational groups and senior-level positions. The FEPCA "requires not only an annual GS pay adjustment, but a second adjustment that varies by geographic locality." In 1997, the national adjustment was 2.3 percent, while locality adjustments were given in 29 locality pay areas. For 1997, locality rates ranged

Figure 6.3 Distributionof Non-GS Federal Workers by Selected Pay Plans and Agencies as of March 31, 1998

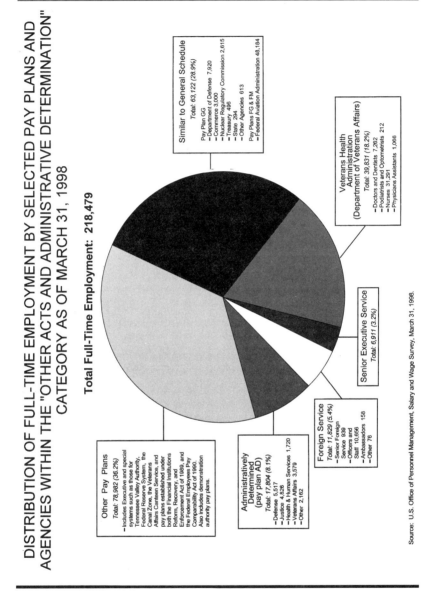

DISTRIBUTION OF FULL-TIME EMPLOYMENT BY SELECTED PAY PLANS AND AGENCIES WITHIN THE "OTHER ACTS AND ADMINISTRATIVE DETERMINATION" CATEGORY AS OF MARCH 31, 1998

Total Full-Time Employment: 218,479

Similar to General Schedule
Total: 63,122 (28.9%)

Pay Plan GG
– Department of Defense 7,920
– Commerce 3,000
– Nuclear Regulatory Commission 2,615
– Treasury 496
– State 294
– Other Agencies 613
Pay Plans FG & FM
– Federal Aviation Administration 48,184

Veterans Health Administration (Department of Veterans Affairs)
Total: 39,831 (18.2%)

– Doctors and Dentists 7,262
– Podiatrists and Optometrists 212
– Nurses 31,291
– Physicians Assistants 1,066

Senior Executive Service
Total: 6,911 (3.2%)

Foreign Service
Total: 11,829 (5.4%)
– Senior Foreign
   Service 939
– Officers and
   Staff 10,656
– Ambassadors 158
– Other 76

Administratively Determined (pay plan AD)
Total: 17,804 (8.1%)
– **Defense 5,517**
– Justice 4,826
– Health & Human Services 1,720
– Veterans Affairs 3,579
– Other 2,162

Other Pay Plans
Total: 78,982 (36.2%)
– Includes Executive and special
   systems such as those for
   Tennessee Valley Authority,
   Federal Reserve System, the
   Canal Zone, the Veterans
   Affairs Canteen Service, and
   pay plans established under
   both the Financial Institutions
   Reform, Recovery, and
   Enforcement Act of 1989, and
   the Federal Employees Pay
   Comparability Act of 1990.
   Also includes demonstration
   authority pay plans.

Source: U.S. Office of Personnel Management, Salary and Wage Survey, March 31, 1998.

from 4.8 to 11.5 percent. In addition to the GS, locality pay adjustments were extended to several other pay plans, including Scientific and Professional, Senior Level, Senior Foreign Service, and the SES. Special geographic pay adjustments were also authorized for law enforcement officers in five different metropolitan areas (U.S. Office of Personnel Management, 1997a, p. 49). Figure 6.4 shows the locality rates of pay effective January 1999 for SES positions. A comparison between Figures 6.1 and 6.5 reveals the impact of 1999 locality pay for GS employees working in the New York–Northern New Jersey–Long Island, and NY-NJ-CT-PA area, where the cost of living and prevailing rates are relatively high.

FEDERAL BLUE-COLLAR PAY

Prior to 1968, there was no comprehensive policy for setting the pay of trade and craft employees. In some local areas, federal agencies paid different rates for the same occupations. This situation was corrected in 1968 when the U.S. Civil Service Commission implemented a Coordinated Federal Wage System (CFWS). This system provided for a common set of policies and operating procedures covering "grade structures, occupational standards, survey coverage, labor organization participation, and other matters." In 1972, Congress enacted the principal features of the CFWS into law (Title 5, U.S. Code).

Under the 1972 law, OPM sets uniform national job-grading standards and criteria to be followed by agencies as they define wage areas, design wage surveys, and set up wage schedules. OPM is advised by an 11-member Federal Prevailing Rate Advisory Committee, consisting of five members representing the agencies, five representing the unions, and a full-time chairperson appointed by the director of OPM. Although agencies do not formally negotiate blue-collar wages, the Federal Wage System (FWS) does allow for considerable union influence in all phases of the process. Local wage surveys are done by "lead agencies," that is, those with large numbers of blue-collar jobs in the area, frequently the Department of Defense. Each lead agency has an agency wage committee made up of two management members, two union members, and a chairperson appointed by the lead agency. The committee advises the lead agency on designing local surveys, interpreting survey findings, and establishing local wage schedules. Finally, the unions as well as management are represented on local wage survey committees that oversee the conduct of the local surveys. Although the president currently has no power to limit wage rate adjustments under the FWS, the Congress has imposed appropriations limitations that have restricted blue-collar wage adjustments to those granted to white-collar employees under the General Schedule.

Figure 6.4 1999 Federal Locality Rates of Pay: Senior Executive Service

1999 LOCALITY RATES OF PAY FOR MEMBERS OF THE SENIOR EXECUTIVE SERVICE

EFFECTIVE JANUARY 1999

SALARY TABLE 1999-ES (LOC)

SENIOR EXECUTIVE SERVICE (SES)

LOCALITY PAY AREA	ES-1	ES-2	ES-3	ES-4	ES-5	ES-6
Atlanta, GA	$109,123	$114,244	$119,470	$125,871	$125,900 *	$125,900 *
Boston-Worcester-Lawrence, MA-NH-ME-CT	111,834	117,082	122,438	125,900 *	125,900 *	125,900 *
Chicago-Gary-Kenosha, IL-IN-WI	112,510	117,789	123,178	125,900 *	125,900 *	125,900 *
Cincinnati-Hamilton, OH-KY-IN	110,780	116,000	121,307	125,900 *	125,900 *	125,900 *
Cleveland-Akron, OH	109,379	114,511	119,750	125,900 *	125,900 *	125,900 *
Columbus, OH	109,932	115,090	120,355	125,900 *	125,900 *	125,900 *
Dallas-Fort Worth, TX	109,942	115,100	120,366	125,900 *	125,900 *	125,900 *
Dayton-Springfield, OH	109,123	114,244	119,470	125,871	125,900 *	125,900 *
Denver-Boulder-Greeley, CO	111,671	116,910	122,259	125,900 *	125,900 *	125,900 *
Detroit-Ann Arbor-Flint, MI	112,663	117,949	123,346	125,900 *	125,900 *	125,900 *
Hartford, CT	112,377	117,649	123,032	125,900 *	125,900 *	125,900 *
Houston-Galveston-Brazoria, TX	115,517	120,937	125,900 *	125,900 *	125,900 *	125,900 *
Huntsville, AL	108,755	113,858	119,067	125,446	125,871	125,871
Indianapolis, IN	108,520	113,612	118,810	125,174	125,599	125,599
Kansas City, MO-KS	108,960	114,072	119,291	125,682	125,900 *	125,900 *
Los Angeles-Riverside-Orange County, CA	113,696	119,031	124,477	125,900 *	125,900 *	125,900 *
Miami-Fort Lauderdale, FL	111,006	116,214	121,531	125,900 *	125,900 *	125,900 *
Milwaukee-Racine,WI	109,195	114,319	119,549	125,900 *	125,900 *	125,900 *
Minneapolis-St. Paul, MN-WI	110,402	115,582	120,870	125,900 *	125,900 *	125,900 *
New York-N. New Jersey-Long Island, NY-NJ-CT-PA	113,093	118,399	123,816	125,900 *	125,900 *	125,900 *
Orlando, FL	108,305	113,387	118,574	124,927	125,350	125,350
Philadelphia-Wilmington-Atlantic City, PA-NJ-DE-MD	110,791	115,989	121,296	125,900 *	125,900 *	125,900 *
Pittsburgh, PA	109,134	114,254	119,482	125,882	125,900 *	125,900 *
Portland-Salem, OR-WA	110,279	115,454	120,736	125,900 *	125,900 *	125,900 *
Richmond-Petersburg, VA	109,062	114,179	119,403	125,800	125,900 *	125,900 *
Sacramento-Yolo, CA	110,760	115,957	121,262	125,900 *	125,900 *	125,900 *
St. Louis, MO-IL	108,612	113,708	118,910	125,281	125,705	125,705
San Diego, CA	111,118	116,332	121,654	125,900 *	125,900 *	125,900 *
San Francisco-Oakland-San Jose, CA	115,660	121,087	125,900 *	125,900 *	125,900 *	125,900 *
Seattle-Tacoma-Bremerton, WA	110,443	115,625	120,915	125,900 *	125,900 *	125,900 *
Washington-Baltimore, DC-MD-VA-WV	110,351	115,529	120,814	125,900 *	125,900 *	125,900 *
Rest of U.S.	108,305	113,387	118,574	124,927	125,350	125,350

* Rate limited to the rate for level III of the Executive Schedule (5 U.S.C. 5304(g)(2)).

Figure 6.5 Federal Locality Pay Area: New York–Northern New Jersey–Long Island, NY-NJ-CT-PA

SALARY TABLE 1999-NY

INCORPORATING THE 3.10% GENERAL SCHEDULE INCREASE AND A LOCALITY PAYMENT OF 10.55% FOR THE LOCALITY PAY AREA OF NEW YORK-NORTHERN NEW JERSEY-LONG ISLAND, NY-NJ-CT-PA

(Net Increase: 3.84%)

Effective January 1999

Annual Rates by Grade and Step

	1	2	3	4	5	6	7	8	9	10
GS-1	$14,772	$15,264	$15,756	$16,244	$16,737	$17,026	$17,509	$17,999	$18,019	$18,482
2	16,608	17,003	17,553	18,019	18,221	18,757	19,293	19,829	20,366	20,902
3	18,121	18,725	19,329	19,932	20,536	21,139	21,743	22,347	22,950	23,554
4	20,342	21,020	21,698	22,375	23,053	23,731	24,408	25,086	25,764	26,441
5	22,760	23,518	24,277	25,035	25,794	26,552	27,310	28,069	28,827	29,585
6	25,369	26,215	27,060	27,906	28,752	29,598	30,443	31,289	32,135	32,980
7	28,191	29,131	30,071	31,010	31,950	32,890	33,829	34,769	35,709	36,648
8	31,222	32,262	33,302	34,342	35,383	36,423	37,463	38,503	39,544	40,584
9	34,486	35,636	36,786	37,935	39,085	40,235	41,384	42,534	43,684	44,834
10	37,977	39,243	40,509	41,775	43,040	44,306	45,572	46,838	48,104	49,369
11	41,726	43,117	44,507	45,898	47,289	48,680	50,070	51,461	52,852	54,242
12	50,008	51,675	53,343	55,010	56,677	58,344	60,011	61,678	63,345	65,012
13	59,468	61,450	63,432	65,415	67,397	69,379	71,361	73,343	75,325	77,308
14	70,273	72,616	74,958	77,301	79,644	81,986	84,329	86,671	89,014	91,356
15	82,662	85,416	88,171	90,926	93,681	96,436	99,191	101,946	104,701	107,456

PAY PRACTICES IN STATE AND LOCAL GOVERNMENTS

State and local governments' payroll costs now amount to well over 50 percent of all expenditures. Although practices vary widely, some states and localities have long histories of progressive pay policies. Their governing bodies review pay rates annually or biennially and authorize adjustments considered necessary to make the rates more competitive. In Georgia, for example, pay schedules are now set up so that each of the 26 pay grades has a minimum salary and a "market midpoint." The midpoint is the average salary paid in business, industry, and government for similar skills, working conditions, and responsibilities, and it is set after a prevailing rate study of comparable jobs in the outside labor market. Research on pay in states and local governments suggests that:

- States and local governments pay more for lower-paying jobs than the private sector, but private employers pay more for white-collar jobs, especially at the higher levels of responsibility.
- State and local governments' pay for professional and administrative positions is significantly lower than that offered by private industry, while the pattern is mixed for technical, clerical, and blue-collar workers.

Although some studies have indicated that the *average* pay of state and local employees is higher than the *average* annual earnings of private workers, controlling for occupational category produces a different picture. The workforces of state and local governments, like that of the federal government, are increasingly professionalized. While under 10 percent of private workers are highly paid professionals, this group makes up over 30 percent of state, and about 40 percent of local government, employees. When this difference is taken into account, although the average wage is much higher in the public sector, the evidence suggests that state pay is comparable to that of the private sector and local governments' pay is somewhat lower. The reasons for state and local success in achieving comparability on the lower levels while falling behind in the white-collar occupations (particularly at the more senior and higher grades) appear to be essentially similar to those operating on the federal level to compress pay scales: the political advantages associated with increasing the pay of large numbers of relatively low-level workers and granting minimal raises to highly graded professional employees (Miller, 1996).

For many states, cities, counties, and school districts, a major factor to be considered over the past 30 years has been collective bargaining. Where collective bargaining takes place on the state and local level, unlike the federal situation, pay and benefits are negotiated. Initially, the spread of collective bargaining in the public sector during the 1960s substantially improved the pay of workers in some occupations such as police, firefighters, teachers, and nurses. State and local employers, feeling threatened by the possibility of employee unionization and collective bargaining, often moved unilaterally to upgrade pay as well as other aspects of compensation. There is, nonetheless, no evidence to suggest that collective bargaining has allowed state and local workers to "loot the treasury." In fact, after a relatively brief "catch-up" period during the 1960s, state and local pay raises for most occupations have at best kept pace with inflation. Actually, since the mid-1970s, there has been little if any change in the pay gaps between equivalent public- and private-sector jobs. Most recently, many employee organizations have been forced to concentrate on protecting jobs and fighting proposed cuts in wages and benefits.

Pressures for reforms on the state and local levels parallel developments in the federal service. Traditional systems of classification and pay are criticized as inflexible and not in tune with management's needs:

> Employers are focusing on pay for performance, incentive pay, knowledge-based pay, and multiple pay systems. They are reviewing pay administration to identify ways to eliminate salary grades, reduce the number of salary ranges, and broaden job descriptions. They are also giving line managers greater authority to make pay decisions and to streamline the pay process. (Matzer, 1988, p. x)

Two areas of particular importance on the state and local levels have been pay for performance, which was discussed in Chapter 5, and comparable worth. Although the comparable worth movement has had little effect on federal pay administration, 20 states and almost 1,000 localities had implemented some form of "pay equity adjustment" designed to address gender-based pay differentials by the early 1990s (Cook, 1991, pp. 102–104).

THE COMPARABLE WORTH DEBATE

Starting in the 1970s, the issue of pay equity for women began to receive widespread attention. Historically, women have been concentrated in lower-paying public- as well as private-sector jobs, creating a wide gap between their earnings and those of men. Since passage of the Equal Pay Act in 1963, it has been illegal in the United States to pay women less than men for the same work. However, the principle of equal pay for equal work does not address issues related to the value placed on jobs traditionally occupied by women. About 80 percent of women in the workforce are concentrated in 20 of the Labor Department's 427 job categories. In 1997, women working full time earned about 75 cents for every dollar earned by men. Women's groups, with strong support from some unions, legislators, and public officials, maintain that occupational segregation characterizes the labor market, with women shunted into low-paying, dead-end jobs. Since segments of the labor market dominated by women are undervalued, when governments conduct prevailing rate surveys, they simply replicate a systemwide pattern of discrimination against women. Advocates of comparable worth argue, therefore, that public employers should implement *equal pay for work of equal value,* an approach they believe should better deal with the traditionally low wages paid for work in occupations dominated by women (Vertz, 1987).

As a way of dealing with gender-based pay disparities, comparable worth is based on the idea that every job has a value or worth to the employer that can be measured using a "worth point" system based on skills, effort, responsibility, and working conditions. It is argued that using such an approach would allow employers to compare different kinds of jobs (e.g., secretary and garbage collector) and to pay them according to their "point value." As a method, therefore, comparable worth relies heavily on objective job evaluations to produce a hierarchy of positions that accurately reflects their relative worth to the organization.

Where job evaluations using point factor systems have been done in the public sector, they often reveal that jobs predominantly occupied by women receive higher point totals than would be suggested by their pay relative to jobs dominated by men. Advocates of comparable worth conclude, therefore, that women are the victims of the subjective position classification methods that are prevalent in the public sector. In short, a key component of the comparable worth argument is that gender-based wage differences are at least in part the result of arbitrary and inaccurate job evaluation methods.

The most hotly debated aspect of comparable worth is the idea that market factors (prevailing rates) should be disregarded in establishing relative worth and pay in organizations. All other things being equal, pay policies based on comparable worth concepts would substitute *administratively* determined rates for those generated by forces of economic markets. Advocates of this approach contend that it is necessary because prevailing rates perpetuate patterns of social and economic discrimination against women.

Critics of comparable worth, on the other hand, argue that although a goal of fairness and pay equity for women is commendable, administratively imposed pay scales would be very costly and highly inefficient. In practical terms, public employers would be placed in the position of having to substantially raise the pay of many employees, whereas lowering the pay of others would be impossible for political and labor market supply reasons. There is considerable debate over how much this would cost the taxpayers, but upward pay adjustments throughout the public sector would inevitably be expensive. In addition, the costs to employers associated with job evaluations and pay administration would increase greatly.

From the standpoint of classical economics, a more fundamental and long-term problem would be politically imposed distortions of the labor market. In other words, comparable worth would force employers to overpay for skills in ample supply and to underpay for scarce and essential human resources. Such economic inefficiencies, critics argue, are not justified by the prospect of eliminating whatever part of the pay gap between men and women is caused by discrimination. Opponents of comparative worth stress their view—a widely accepted one in the United States—that the public money-value of a job cannot in practice be based on the abstract concept of inherent worth, but only on labor prices that "clear" an open market. Systemic and intentional discrimination against women as well as racial and ethnic minorities should be removed through legal and administrative means; if this happens, the market should function even more efficiently *and* be allowed to do so.

Proponents and opponents of comparative worth also disagree on the fundamental question of whether women are *segregated* or *concentrated* in certain occupations. The term *segregation* is designed to describe a situation in which women, for a variety of socioeconomic, cultural, and political reasons, are forced or channeled into low-paying jobs. From this perspective, comparable worth is a necessary intervention if women as a group are to escape wage discrimination against occupations where they predominate.

Opponents of comparable worth, such as the business community in general, dispute that there is occupational segregation of women. They assert that the true condition is one of occupational concentration, which results from the free choice of women to plan their lives differently from men. According to this explanation, many women look forward not to an uninterrupted work career, but to one in which they will leave the workforce for substantial periods of time for family reasons such as child rearing. With such plans, they voluntarily choose not to invest in the education, training, and career development required to qualify for higher-paying jobs. It is these choices, not discrimination, that account for most of the pay gap between women and men (Lieberman, 1986).

Following this line of reasoning, since discrimination is not a major factor, if a majority of women in the workforce prepared for and sought the same careers as men, occupational concentration would end. In fact, if comparable worth were implemented on a large scale, concentration might very well increase, since women would have less of an incentive to qualify for other, now male-dominated and better-paying, occupations. Needless to say, advocates of comparable worth strongly disagree, primarily because they see discrimination as playing a central role in creating and maintaining the wage gap between male- and female-dominated occupations.

The theory of comparable worth has not received a warm reception in the courts. The Department of Justice has argued that the comparable worth argument does not establish a cause for action under federal law, and the EEOC has consistently turned aside complaints based on comparable worth arguments. In *County of Washington v Gunther* (1981), the Supreme Court did rule that the employer was intentionally discriminating against women because they were being paid less than the job evaluation system indicated their position was worth. The Court did not, however, endorse comparable worth. Subsequent decisions by federal appeals courts have allayed public employers' fears that not having done a job evaluation study might leave them open to successful charges of intentional discrimination. Currently, plaintiffs seeking remedies under Title VII of the 1964 Civil Rights Act are required to prove that the employer deliberately discriminated against them. The courts also have a long and continuing tradition of allowing employers to defend themselves against wage discrimination charges by showing that they are paying prevailing rates.

In December of 1983, a U.S. district court in the state of Washington ruled that in setting pay the state government had been guilty of sex discrimination under Title VII of the Civil Rights Act of 1964. Washington had been the first state to recognize sex discrimination and to conduct a study of gender-based pay disparities. In a study completed in 1974, the state's two civil service boards concluded that men and women were being paid differently.

In 1974, the state initiated a comparable worth study and, in 1976, funds were appropriated to implement pay adjustments. However, the newly elected governor blocked this appropriation in 1977, and in 1981 the American Federation of State, County and Municipal Employees and the Washington Federation of State Employees filed sex discrimination charges with the EEOC. The Commission failed to act, and the case was taken to federal district court. In its 1983 decision, the court found intentional discrimination because there was a difference of about 20 percent in pay for mostly male and mostly female job classifications (*AFSCME et al. v Washington et al.*, 1983). The state was ordered to pay thousands of women employees the salaries they were entitled to under a comparable worth plan adopted by the state but only partially implemented. In a major setback for supporters of comparable worth, a three-judge panel of the Ninth Circuit reversed on appeal in 1985 (*AFSCME v Washington,* 1985). Now Supreme Court Justice Kennedy wrote for the unanimous panel.

In terms anticipating the Supreme Court's reasoning in *Wards Cove* (1989), the appeals court concluded that *intentional discrimination* had not been established, and that "discriminatory intent could not be inferred from statistical evidence, even when joined with the defendant's study showing that the jobs in question were of comparable value." Paying market rates could not be interpreted as intent to discriminate. Clearly, the appeals court's reasoning presents serious difficulties to those seeking to pursue pay equity or comparable worth through the courts. Subsequent rulings by the Supreme Court, such as *Wards Cove,* offered even less encouragement.

In light of the federal courts' stance, efforts to advance the cause of comparable worth have focused on legislation, executive initiatives, and negotiated contracts. It is unlikely that the comparable worth debate will "go away" any time in the near future. It encompasses key policy issues that divide employers, elective officials, political parties, women's organizations, and even the unions. The political influence of women on all levels of government continues to grow, and the pressure on public employers to close or eliminate the wage gap between men and women may be expected to continue.

CONCLUSION

Position classification is frequently a key feature of Civil Service Reform II initiatives because it is at the heart of conventional merit systems. Traditional classification systems are designed and administered by central personnel agencies, and they tend to emphasize the regulatory orientation of Civil Service Reform I, often at the expense of flexibility and responsiveness to management's concerns in areas such as recruitment, selection, work systems design, and pay. While radical reforms, such as replacing position-based systems with rank-in-the-person approaches have not been widely tried, devolution of classification authority to the agency level, simplification of the classification process, and broadbanding of classification structures are now common features of reform agendas on all levels of government. The trend toward policies that allow public managers the flexibility needed to tailor classification systems and processes to the specific problems and challenges they confront promises to continue.

Although public employees' pay continues in most instances to be closely tied to pay grades determined through job evaluation procedures, past concerns about maintaining internal equity are losing ground to those related to competing successfully in a variety of labor markets. The federal government appears to be in the process of fragmenting into a wide variety of pay plans, many of which are intended to address the needs of individual agencies to attract and retain certain categories of workers, most importantly skilled professionals and occupations that are in high demand. The locality pay reforms of the GS are in response to the federal government's need to adjust its pay to local labor markets across the nation. Although most states and localities have less need for locality adjustments, changes to classification schemes, such as broadbanding, may allow the flexibility needed to attract highly qualified job candidates and to reward outstanding performance, since the pay ranges within classes available to management are expanded. Incremental changes to existing pay systems are likely to continue over the near future, but there are some more drastic options being discussed. One of these is skill-based pay (SBP), an approach that would pay employees in accordance with the type and extent of their organizationally relevant skills:

> They are paid for skills they are capable of using and for the jobs they are performing at a particular point in time. This is a radical departure from traditional job-based pay that compensates employees for the jobs they hold. Traditional pay relied on paying people for the jobs they do rather than the skills they possess. SBP systems help an organization facilitate the skill-acquisition process by motivating employees to learn needed organizational skills. (Shareef, 1994, p. 61)

According to Shareef (1994), in the SBP format, pay is keyed to one or more measures of skill, including:

- *Depth of Skill,* or the individual's expertise in a particular area of specialization, such as a physical science, law, or engineering.
- *Breadth of Skill,* which involves rewarding employees for having knowledge and skills in areas of organizational activity related to their jobs, so that they are more flexible and more able to self-manage.
- *Vertical Skills,* or the ability to self-manage in such areas as "scheduling work, leading group problem-solving meetings, training, consulting, and coordinating other groups." (Shareef, 1994, p. 62)

Although SBP is virtually unknown in the U.S. public sector, research on its use in business organizations suggests that it has had positive effects on workforce flexibility, job satisfaction, and productivity, especially when used in conjunction with gainsharing and TQM (pp. 71–72).

Since these results are closely aligned with the goals of current reform efforts in the public sector, SBP, as TQM did several years ago, may attract considerable attention from policy makers in the near future.

DISCUSSION QUESTIONS

1. Should public employers try to match private-sector pay for senior executives on the highest levels of responsibility?
2. Will delegations of authority in the pay and classification areas lead to favoritism and systematic violations of the merit principle by managers?
3. Should public employers be required to negotiate pay rates with employee unions?
4. Would a rank-in-the-person system work well where you are employed?
5. Should white- and blue-collar pay be based solely on prevailing rates, or should other factors be considered?
6. How do you know if your pay is competitive with what others in similar jobs are getting from other employers in your area?

REFERENCES

AFSCME v Washington (1985). 770 F. 2d 1401.

AFSCME et al. v State of Washington et al. (1983). No.C82-465T, United States District Court for the Western District of Washington.

Cook, Alice (1991). "Pay Equity: Theory and Implementation," in Carolyn Ban and Norma M. Riccucci (eds.), *Public Personnel Management: Current Concerns—Future Challenges* (New York: Longman), pp. 100–113.

County of Washington v Gunther (1981). 452 U.S. 161.

Federal Register (1997). *Science and Technology Reinvention Laboratory Personnel Demonstration Project at the Naval Sea Systems Command Warfare Centers* (Washington, DC: Federal Register Online), Vol. 62, No. 37, pp. 8585–8607.

Levine, Charles H., and Kleeman, Rosslyn S. (1986). *The Quiet Crisis in the Civil Service: The Federal Personnel System at the Crossroads* (Washington, DC: National Academy of Public Administration), December.

Lieberman, Myron (1986). "The Conversion of Interests to Principles: The Case of Comparable Worth." *Journal of Collective Negotiations,* Vol. 15, No. 2, pp. 145–152.

Matzer, John H., Jr., ed. (1988). *Pay and Benefits: New Ideas for Local Government* (Washington, DC: International City/County Management Association).

Miller, Michael A. (1996). "The Public-Private Pay Debate: What Do the Data Show?" *Monthly Labor Review,* Vol. 119, No. 5, pp. 1–14 (http://web.lexis-nexis.com/univers).

National Academy of Public Administration (1991). *Modernizing Federal Classification: An Opportunity for Excellence* (Washington, DC: NAPA), July.

Nigro, Lloyd G., and Clayton, Ross (1984). "An Experiment in Federal Personnel Management: The Naval Laboratories Demonstration Project," in G. Ronald Gilbert (ed.), *Making and Managing Policy* (New York: Marcel Dekker), pp. 153–172.

Sayre, Wallace (1991). "The Triumph of Technique Over Purpose," in Frank J. Thompson (ed.), *Classics in Public Personnel Policy,* 2nd ed. (Pacific Grove, CA: Brooks/Cole), pp. 154–158.

Shafritz, Jay (1973). *Position Classification: A Behavioral Analysis for the Public Sector* (New York: Frederick A. Praeger).

Shareef, Reginald (1994). "Skill-Based Pay in the Public Sector." *Review of Public Personnel Administration,* Vol. 14, No. 3 (Summer), pp. 60–74.

Shoop, Tom (1990). "Wage Wars." *Government Executive* (June), pp. 40–42.

U.S. Department of State (1998). *Foreign Service Officer Career Paths* (Washington, DC: http://www.state.gov/www/careers/ rfsstages.html).

U.S. General Accounting Office (1990a). *Federal Pay: Comparisons with the Private Sector by Job and Locality* (Washington, DC), May.

——— (1990b). *Recruitment and Retention: Inadequate Federal Pay Cited as Primary Problem by Agency Officials* (Washington, DC), September.

U.S. Merit Systems Protection Board (1991). *The Title 38 Personnel System in the Department of Veterans Affairs: An Alternative Approach* (Washington, DC), April.

U.S. Office of Personnel Management (1981). *A Federal Position Classification System for the 1980s: Report of the Classification Task Force* (Washington, DC).

——— (1997a). *The Classifier's Handbook* (Washington, DC: Workforce Compensation and Performance Service, Classification Programs Division), December.

——— (1997b). *Pay Structure of the Federal Civil Service as of March 31, 1997* (Washington, DC: Office of Workforce Information), September.

———— (1998). *Navy Demonstration Project—"China Lake"*
(http://www.opm.gov/omsoe/demonstr/fact/navy.htm).

Vertz, Laura (1987). "Pay Inequalities Between Women and Men in
State and Local Government: An Examination of the Political
Context of the Comparable Worth Controversy." *Women &
Politics,* Vol. 7, No. 2 (Summer), pp. 43–57.

SUGGESTED READINGS

Edge, Jerry J., and Ghorpade, Jai (1997). *Understanding Skill-Based
Pay: An Approach to Designing & Implementing an Effective
Program* (Scottsdale, AZ: American Compensation Association).

Houser, Robert (1996). *Pay, Equity, & Discrimination* (Boulder, CO:
Westview Press).

Paul, Ellen F. (1988). *Equity and Gender: The Comparable Worth
Debate* (New Brunswick, NJ: Transaction Publishers).

Risher, Howard W. (1997). *New Strategies for Public Pay: Rethinking
Government Compensation Programs* (San Francisco: Jossey-Bass
Publishers).

Siegel, Gilbert B. (1992). *Public Employee Compensation and Its Role in
Public Sector Strategic Management* (New York: Quorum Books).

Silvestre, J.J., and Eyraud, F., eds. (1995). *Pay Determination in the
Public Sector: An International Comparison Between France, Great
Britain & Italy* (Washington, DC: International Labour Office).

Sorensen, Elaine (1994). *Comparable Worth: Is It a Worthy Policy?*
(Princeton, NJ: Princeton University Press).

State of Georgia Job Description

Job Title: Accountant 3, Professional
Job Code: 40804
Last Update: 3/15/98
Salary Plan: Statewide Salary Plan
(SWD)
Pay Grade: 15F

Salary Minimum: $31,302.00/yr
Market Midpoint: $42,012.00/yr
Salary Maximum: $54,822.00/yr

Additional Job Statistics...

Job Summary, Qualifications, Responsibilities, and Standards

General Summary:
Under general supervision and according to Generally Accepted Accounting Principles (GAAP), performs advanced professional accounting duties that require independent judgement and initiative. Duties include analyzing, recording, and interpreting financial transactions, preparing specialized and standard accounting reports and providing information to auditors and other third parties. Performs periodic operational analyses of accounting procedures and systems to recommend methods for the improvement of efficiency and operational effectiveness. May supervise accounting staff, have input into policies and procedures and/or develop and maintain budget and financial records for a section or unit.

Minimum Qualifications:
Completion of a bachelor's degree with a major in a business curricu- lum which included the successful completion of the introductory accounting sequence and the intermediate accounting sequence (note: the introductory accounting sequence is normally completed in ten (10) quarter or six (6) semester hours; the intermediate accounting sequence is normally completed in fifteen (15) quarter or six (6) semester hours.) and three years of professional experience as a staff accountant. Note: graduate coursework in accounting may substitute for experience on a year-for-year basis for a maximum of one year of the required experience.

Preferred Qualifications:
No preferred qualifications information is available.

Job Responsibilities & Performance Standards:

1. Applies generally accepted accounting principles in recording financial activity in accounting systems and varied subsystems.
    1. Correctly applies various accounting theories according to Generally Accepted Accounting Principles (GAAP), Governmental Accounting Standards, applicable state and federal guidelines and agency fiscal policies and procedures.
    2. Carefully reviews documentation, entries and reports for accuracy and completeness.
    3. Accurately and completely records financial transactions according to generally accepted accounting principles (GAAP).
    4. Reviews and analyzes general ledger accounts accurately for fiscal integrity as well as compliance with applicable principles, standards, guidelines, policies and procedures.
    5. Corrects general ledger accounts based on timely recognition of problems and accurate identification of required adjustments.
    6. Coordinates work with colleagues to provide accurate and meaningful financial information in a timely manner.

2. Prepares specialized or non-standard financial and/or accounting reports as well as standard, statutory, regulatory and GAAP financial and/or accounting reports.
    1. Performs adequate research and analysis of collected data for the preparation of reports.
    2. Collaborates with end-user, or designated representative, before preparing the requested report to ensure that the expected results are understood.
    3. Confers with other professionals or separate authorities to obtains advice, information or resources required to create the format or input of the reports as needed.
    4. Develops format and reports to meet specified needs while assuring conformity with appropriate measurement focus or basis of accounting.

continued page 204

5. Ensures accuracy of reports by verifying output and making corrections as appropriate.
6. Submits completed reports within established time frames.

3. Analyzes and reconciles accounting data and transactions that require knowledge of complex rules and regulations and use of advanced research and/or problem-solving skills.
1. Performs work in a timely manner utilizing appropriate theory and judgement and ensuring its conformity with specified principles, measurement focus, policies and regulations.
2. Analyses complex reconciliation documents and other information to arrive at logical and accurate conclusions.
3. Determines appropriate corrective action to take when faced with discrepancies.
4. Adequately analyzes the effects of transactions on reports.

4. Performs operational analyses of accounting systems, subsystems and procedures to ensure accuracy of data, to ensure compliance with Generally Accepted Accounting Principles and to identify improvements in the methods for recording, maintaining and reporting financial transactions.
1. Applies appropriate accounting theory and principles in the evaluation process.
2. Identifies discrepancies between existing procedures and those that are generally accepted or that will result in greater efficiency or operational effectiveness.
3. Formulates specific recommendations based upon analysis of systems, subsystems and procedures.
4. Submits for consideration a timely report of findings that includes advantages to be realized should the recommendations be adopted.

5. Responds to inquiries for solution of difficult accounting problems or for information or interpretation from third parties such as banks, auditors, vendors and governmental entities. Notifies appropriate personnel of pending audit actions.
1. Accurately and concisely explains accounting systems, subsystems, procedures and practices.
2. Accurately determines data required for audits.
3. Follows departmental policies and procedures in providing information. Reviews unusual requests with supervisor prior to releasing information.
4. Formulates a complete and accurate response in the requested format. Submits response in a timely manner.
5. Notifies appropriate personnel of pending audit actions in a timely manner.
6. Maintains availability and effectively communicates with third parties.

6. Develops goals and objectives for assigned responsibility area.
1. Develops appropriate goals and objectives for the assigned area that are consistent with agency goals and objectives.
2. Plans and implements methodologies for attainment of goals and objectives.

7. Assists in the development and/or revision of policies and procedures. Administers policies and procedures for assigned area(s).
1. Identifies need to develop or revise policies and procedures. Initiates appropriate actions to address needs in a timely manner.
2. Appropriately researches policies and procedures for applicability and consistency and for compliance with rules, regulations, guidelines, standards or related policies and procedures.
3. Carefully monitors newly developed and/or revised policies and procedures for effectiveness and viability.

8. Develops, monitors and maintains budget and/or financial records for a department or unit.
1. Ensures budgets are developed on time according to specified guidelines.
2. Develops fiscal impact projections for future growth and needs of the department or unit.
3. Maintains financial records according to established guidelines.
4. Monitors expenditures to ensure conformity with budget category limits. Identifies potential cost variances requiring reallocation of resources or identification of additional resources.

9. Creates and maintains a high performance environment characterized by positive leadership and a strong team orientation.
1. Defines goals and/or required results at beginning of performance period and gains acceptance of ideas by creating a shared vision.
2. Communicates regularly with staff on progress toward defined goals and/or required results; providing specific feedback and initiating corrective action when defined goals and/or results are not met.

continued page 205

3. Confers regularly with staff to review employee relations climate, specific problem areas and actions necessary for improvement.
4. Evaluates employees at scheduled intervals obtains and considers all relevant information in evaluations and supports staff by giving praise and constructive criticism.
5. Recognizes contributions and celebrates accomplishments.
6. Motivates staff to improve quantity and quality of work performed and provides training and development opportunities as appropriate.

10. Guides and advises accounting subordinates in procedural processes in areas of responsibilities. Informs subordinates of procedural changes and assists in problem resolution.
1. Defines job tasks, sets priorities and regulates workloads for subordinates on section needs and incumbent capabilities.
2. Monitors compliance with policies/procedures by spot-checking work at defined intervals.
3. Promptly advises subordinates or variances and proposed corrective actions.
4. Provides appropriate training for subordinate staff when procedural changes are made or upon identification or areas with high numbers of variances.
5. Assists subordinate staff with resolution of problems by providing methodologies that are appropriate and which conform to Generally Accepted Accounting Principles.

11. Maintains knowledge of current trends and developments in the field. Applies relevant new knowledge to performance of responsibilities.
1. Participates in professional continuing educational programs when available.
2. Attends regular meetings of available and applicable professional organizations.
3. Reads and evaluates professional literature on a continual basis.
4. Incorporates knowledge of pertinent new trends and developments into section procedures and makes recommendations for any related organizational changes.

NOTE:
Job description information is extracted daily from the official Phoenix HRMS Job Code database. Problems in conversion may cause formatting errors in some job descriptions.

The information presented, while not an exact or exhaustive listing, describes the work, performance standards, and qualifications typically required of positions or employees in this job. A specific position description or employee performance plan may differ as long as it is consistent with the core Responsibilities, Standards and Qualifications of that job.

TITLE: Agricultural/Biological Science
Technician
SERIES: GS-0404

DESCRIPTION:
This work includes research, development, control and/or testing in laboratories. The technicians assist professional and other technical personnel in any of the biological, medical, or agricultural sciences.
Duties include: preparing human, animal, insect, plant soil, and/or food material for tests; setting up and adjusting equipment, instruments, and apparatus; conducting highly specialized standard or experimental tests; tabulating and recording data.

CONTACT:
Research, Education, and Economics

REQUIREMENTS:
GS-4: Successful completion of two years of post-high school education in an accredited technical school, college or university with courses related to the occupation.
GS-5: Successful completion of the requirements for a bachelor's degree with courses related to the occupation.
GS-6: One-half year of graduate education directly related to the work of the position.
GS-7: One full year of graduate education directly related to the work of the position.
GS-8: One and one-half years of graduate education directly related to the work of the position.
GS-9: Two full years of graduate education directly related to the work of the position.
One year of full-time undergraduate study is defined as 30 semester hours or 45 quarter hours in a college or university or at least 20 hours of classroom instruction per week for approximately 36 weeks in a technical school. A year of full-time graduate education is considered to be the number of credit hours which the school attended has determined to represent one year of full-time study.

Chapter SEVEN

Collective Bargaining in the Public Sector

A significant contributor to the social and political turbulence of the 1960s was the rapid spread of unionism and collective bargaining in the public sector. Collective bargaining is a bilateral decision-making process in which authorized representatives of management and labor: (1) meet and in good faith negotiate wages, hours, and working conditions; (2) produce a mutually binding written contract of specified duration; and (3) agree to share responsibility for administering the provisions of that contract. Millions of public employees joined labor unions, and many were prepared to be militant in their dealings with public employers. During this period, public employee strikes were not uncommon, and employers were often hard-pressed to respond effectively. In many jurisdictions, public employee associations, once satisfied to consult with management and to lobby legislative bodies for improvements in pay and benefits, were transformed almost overnight into labor organizations with contractual "demands" that they brought to the bargaining table. Strikes, slowdowns, and political action by organized employees trying to extract pay raises, improved benefits, better working conditions, and the right to participate in the making of personnel policies became hallmarks of public-sector labor relations, especially in the eyes of a public that suffered the consequences.

Writing in 1972, Arnold M. Zack, a well-known labor arbitrator and mediator, observed that the public sector labor movement of the 1960s had several causes, which includes the following:

- While the number of public employees had grown dramatically during the postwar years, their wages and salaries had fallen well below those of their private-sector counterparts.

- Public employees became generally unhappy with their exclusion from the rights afforded private (nonagricultural) workers under the National Labor Relations Act of 1935.

- A new generation of younger and more militant public employees was not content to accept the "second-class" pay and benefits that traditional public personnel systems had generated.

- Private-sector unions, experiencing stagnant or even declining memberships, targeted the public sector as an untapped source of new members and revenues.

- State and local government workers interpreted President Kennedy's 1962 executive order granting federal employees limited bargaining rights as a signal to challenge long-standing blanket legal prohibitions on these levels of government.

- The civil rights movement, antiwar protests, and other forms of civil disobedience "convinced militant public employees that protest against 'the establishment' and its laws was fruitful and could be a valued vehicle for bringing about desired change." (Zack, 1972, pp. 101–102)

White-collar workers and professionals who a few years earlier would have considered union membership and bargaining to be things that only blue-collar craft and industrial workers did, eagerly joined unions, many of them AFL-CIO affiliated. Some joined large independents, such as the Teamsters. In short order, the "rules of the workplace," previously under the more or less benevolent unilateral control of the public employer, became issues to be resolved through formal negotiations between management and organized labor in many states and thousands of cities and counties. Even the federal executive branch accepted a very restricted form of collective negotiations under President Kennedy's Executive Order 10988.

Across the country, long-established private-sector labor–management practices and concepts invaded the public sector, often to the extreme discomfort of public administrators who saw them as threats to their authority and to the merit principle. Expertise in labor relations had not been needed, and most personnel shops were caught unprepared to help management negotiate or administer a traditional labor relations program. Employee organizations often suffered from a similar lack of experience and skill. Numerous strikes and other disruptions were the direct result of incompetence and ignorance of the traditions and values underpinning the collective bargaining process. Zack observed that "the demonstrated success of initial illegal strikes such as the New York transit strike and some early teachers' strikes became powerful proof that the *power* to strike was of far greater relevance than the *right* to strike" (p. 102).

In some states, the unions' efforts to organize public employees and to secure legislation permitting or requiring collective bargaining were beaten back, but their numerous and sometimes startling successes during the 1960s had fundamentally transformed public personnel administration by the early 1970s. Labor–management relations and collective bargaining were firmly established as objects of public personnel policy, and they became administrative responsibilities as well as areas of technical expertise. On the management side, the need for labor relations training programs in government and for pooling of efforts by governments was soon recognized, and state leagues of municipalities and other existing organizations of public employers became active in this area. New organizations such as the Labor Management Relations Service of the United States Conference of Mayors were established in order to provide information, training, consulting, and other labor relations services. Such labor organizations as the AFL-CIO also expanded their consulting and training programs to include the public sector.

The tidal wave of unionization and collective bargaining that engulfed the public sector between 1962 and 1972 was dramatically slowed by the 1973 recession (the deepest economic decline since the Great Depression of the 1930s), and the subsequent decade of widespread "fiscal stress" was marked by an abrupt end to the phenomenal growth and continuous successes of the public employee unions. Although most of the unions did not suffer great losses in membership, their ranks did not expand at anything resembling the previous rate, and they generally were unable to win large salary increases and other concessions at the bargaining table.

In addition to better-prepared management organizations and negotiators, the unions faced growing public hostility and stiffening resistance to tax increases. Public opinion had turned against the unions to a point that pollster Louis Harris, in effect, advised politicians to run against the unions. Finding it increasingly difficult to get collective bargaining legislation passed, organized labor sought a federal law requiring *all* states and local governments to establish collective bargaining programs. This strategy collapsed in 1976 when the Supreme Court ruled in *National League of Cities et al. v Usery* that Congress was not authorized by the commerce clause of the U.S. Constitution to extend provisions of the Fair Labor Standards Act of

1938 to state and local governments. This decision was widely interpreted to mean that the Court would strike down any federal act requiring collective bargaining. The Court's stance, in combination with the lack of political support, ended any realistic expectation that the Congress would act to advance the unions' interests.

The recession ended but was quickly followed by the "taxpayers revolt," and successful initiatives such as California's Proposition 13 limited local government tax revenues. In the 1980s, yet another recession and decreasing federal aid to states and localities combined to make life difficult for the unions and their members. The 1981 Professional Air Traffic Controllers (PATCO) strike and its disastrous outcome for the union (the strikers were fired and the union decertified) further undermined organized labor's public image, and this encouraged public managers around the country to follow President Reagan's lead by assuming tough stances in their dealings with employee unions. Public employee unions and their leaders were placed in the position of having to fight hard simply to preserve existing jobs, and to prevent severe cuts in pay and benefits. By the end of the 1980s, instead of demanding large pay increases and other improvements, union negotiators were concentrating on keeping pace with inflation, opposing layoffs, resisting contracting-out or privatization, and mobilizing opposition to budget cuts affecting their memberships.

Despite the unions' present difficulties, there is no indication that the existence of collective bargaining in the public sector is threatened. In fact, for many governments, it has become routine and accepted as a way of handling much of the personnel function. By 1985, over 40 states had enacted legislation dealing with public-sector labor relations. During any given year, large numbers of public employees are involved in negotiations leading to contracts. In 1994, for example, about 2.8 million state and local government employees were covered by collective bargaining agreements. Contracts negotiated during 1994 covered a total of 1.2 million workers; of these, about 70 percent worked for local governments and 30 percent for the states (Muhl, 1995). Over 1 million federal employees currently are covered by contracts negotiated under provisions of Title VII of the CSRA, which placed federal labor relations on a statutory foundation (Parker, Schurman, and Montgomery, 1984).

The public sector, therefore, is already highly organized and this, in combination with the relative lack of growth in the public workforce, means that union membership should at best grow slowly during the foreseeable future. There were some legislative successes for organized labor during the 1980s, however. Two large industrial states, Illinois and Ohio, passed comprehensive collective bargaining statutes. Historically, such legislation has promoted strong growth in bargaining. Over half the states now require local employers to bargain with at least some categories of workers, particularly police and fire (Zax and Ichniowski, 1990). Thus, while the era of explosive union growth and spectacular advances at the bargaining table and on the picket lines ended some time ago, collective bargaining is now accepted as a routine feature of human resources management in a very large number of jurisdictions. On the other hand, in some states, for example, Georgia, legislators have successfully resisted efforts to pass laws that would legalize collective bargaining by state and local employees and provide the required administrative infrastructure.

PUBLIC EMPLOYEE ORGANIZATIONS

There are several types of employee organizations active in the U.S. public sector. Some function at just one level of government, others at two or more. Some are organized along craft lines (e.g., electricians) and others by occupation (e.g., social workers). Others are analogous to private-sector industrial unions, such as the United Auto Workers (UAW) and the United Steelworkers of America (USWA), and include many different kinds of nonsupervisory jobs and skills. There are AFL-CIO–affiliated unions such as the American Federation of State, County, and Municipal Employees (AFSCME), and some public employees are in bargaining units represented by the International Brotherhood of Teamsters. There are also independent associations of state and local government employees as well as professional associations such as the National Education Association (NEA) that bargain collectively. In combination, the following five types include most public employees covered by negotiated contracts.

Mixed unions are those with members both in government and in the private sector. Most of their members work for private businesses, but in recent years some have substantially increased their membership in public agencies. *All-public or mostly public unions* are those with all or most of their members in government. Some of these unions are affiliated with the larger labor movement; the others are independent. They do not include police and fire organizations, which form a separate category (see below). *Professional associations* are organizations that draw their memberships from particular professions such as teachers and nurses. They are not affiliated with such national labor organizations as AFSCME. *Independent associations of state and local government employees* have members doing many different kinds of work and function on a statewide or local basis. Most of these associations were created between 1920 and 1950 to represent the interests of employees in the legislative process, and to provide benefits for their memberships, such as low-cost life and health insurance policies. The classification police and firefighter organization overlaps some of the preceding ones, but the purpose of this category is to allow a full description of the kinds of organizations, large and small, that represent police and firefighters, both of whom have been very active in collective bargaining. It should be noted that many public employees covered by negotiated contracts are not members of the unions that negotiated them. Unlike practice in the private sector, negotiated requirements that workers join the union (the union shop) are rare in government (Masters and Atkin, 1989).

THE MIXED UNIONS

This category includes a wide variety of unions that as a group cross-cut all levels of government in the United States. Those with the strongest representation in state and local government are the Service Employees International Union (SEIU), the International Brotherhood of Teamsters, the Amalgamated Transit Union (ATU), the Communication Workers of America (CWA), and the Laborer's International Union (LIU). In the federal government, the largest organization in this category is the Metal Trades Council, which is made up of several national craft unions.

ALL-PUBLIC OR MOSTLY PUBLIC UNIONS

The largest organization of this type is the American Federation of State, County, and Municipal Employees, AFL-CIO. It currently has about 1.3 million members, most of whom work for state and local governments. It includes workers of all kinds, except teachers. AFSCME started in 1936 as a small union dedicated to advancing the cause of merit in state and local governments. During the mid-1960s it changed its orientation under new leadership and aggressively recruited new members, enthusiastically endorsed collective bargaining, and achieved many successes at the bargaining table.

BULLETIN

*From The SEIU
Mission Statement*

"We are the Service Employees International Union, an organization of more than one million members united by the belief in the dignity and work of workers and the services they provide and dedicated to improving the lives of workers and their families and creating a more just and humane society. We are the public workers, health-care workers, building service workers, office workers, professional workers, and industrial workers. We seek a stronger union to build power for ourselves and to protect the people we serve."

Source: (http://www.floridaseiu.org/about.html), 1998.

Another large, predominantly public union is the American Federation of Teachers (AFT). An AFL-CIO affiliate, the AFT reached one million members in 1998, most of whom work for elementary and secondary schools in very large cities. In recent years AFT has also enrolled many members in colleges and universities, where it now represents more faculty and staff than the National Education Association (NEA). The success of the AFT's largest affiliate, the United Federation of Teachers (UFT), in winning the 1961 collective bargaining election in New York City, gave a great nationwide impetus to bargaining in the public schools. The election was the first to be held in a large metropolitan school district, and the UFT succeeded in negotiating a comprehensive contract that was unprecedented in comparison with the then existing AFT local and NEA affiliate agreements.

Other large, mostly public unions may be found in the federal service. With the exception of the postal service employee unions, they all have members in many kinds of positions in a number of federal agencies. Still by far the largest in terms of members and employees represented is the American Federation of Government Employees (AFGE), AFL-CIO. It currently represents close to 600,000 federal employees. The National Federation of Federal Employees (NFFE) is a smaller independent organization representing over 100,000 workers. Like the AFGE, it has suffered major membership losses over the past 15 years. The National Treasury Employees Union (NTEU), another independent union, started in the Internal Revenue Service, expanded to the Treasury Department, and has recently extended its jurisdiction to include workers in other federal agencies. In contrast to the AFGE and NFFE, the NTEU has managed to grow steadily, and it currently represents about 150,000 workers.

The Postal Reorganization Act of 1970 granted the U.S. Postal Service's workers collective bargaining rights that are far more extensive than those available to other federal employees. Most importantly, they have the right to negotiate compensation. Labor relations in the Postal Service are under the jurisdiction of the National Labor Relations Board,

---

BULLETIN

The AFSCME Membership

"AFSCME represents public employees and health care workers throughout the United States, Panama, and Puerto Rico. They include employees of state, county, and municipal governments, school districts, public and private hospitals, universities, and non-profit agencies who work in a cross-section of jobs ranging from blue collar to clerical, professional and paraprofessional. White collar employees account for one-third of the membership, while health and hospital workers constitute the largest sector with more than 325,000 members. About 325,000 AFSCME members are clerical and secretarial employees, making AFSCME the largest union of office workers. One hundred thousand members are corrections officers, making AFSCME the largest union in that profession."

Source: (http://www.afscme.org/about/member.htm), 1998.

the regulatory body that oversees collective bargaining in the private sector under terms of the National Labor Relations Act. Around 700,000 postal workers are covered by negotiated contracts.

Both the American Postal Workers Union (APWU) and the National Association of Letter Carriers (NALC), both AFL-CIO, have memberships exceeding 200,000, and they represent a total of well over 650,000 Postal Service employees. The APWU was created in 1971 as the result of a merger between the AFL-CIO Postal Clerks, the independent National Postal Union, and three smaller AFL-CIO postal unions. The NALC was established in the late nineteenth century and was one of the first affiliates of the AFL-CIO. The NALC and APWU are very strong unions, both at the bargaining table and in lobbying the Congress.

PROFESSIONAL ASSOCIATIONS

By far the largest organization of this kind is the National Education Association or NEA, which has 2.3 million members. The NEA was established to advance the teaching profession, and to provide a variety of services to its members. It did not see itself as a labor organization. Until the 1960s, its leadership steadfastly rejected the idea that teachers needed to bargain collectively with their employers. However, pressures from the membership and the strong competition from the AFT after its 1961 successes in New York forced the NEA to officially adopt collective bargaining in 1962. It now represents workers on all levels of education, and it is as active in the bargaining arena as the AFT. The NEA has been a major force in organizing and representing the faculties of colleges and universities throughout the United States.

There are over 1.5 million nurses working in the United States. Of these, 180,000 are members of the American Nurses Association (ANA), the first professional association to adopt collective bargaining. In 1946, it approved an Economic Security Program "committed to the use of collective bargaining as one of the most effective means of assuring nurses' rights to participate in the implementation of standards of nursing employment and practice" (Gideon, 1979). Of the ANA's 53 constituent associations, 25 act as collective bargaining agents. The ANA's membership is open to all registered nurses, including those working for public employers on all levels of government.

INDEPENDENT ASSOCIATIONS OF STATE AND LOCAL GOVERNMENT EMPLOYEES

The state associations were created for a variety of reasons. In some cases, the purpose was to provide unified general representation for government employees. In others, the motive was to support a particular cause or employee benefit. For example, several were organized to promote or protect a merit system, while others were created to support better retirement systems and insurance benefits. Most of them limit their memberships to state workers, but the number of state associations also admitting local employees has grown recently.

Most of the state associations are federated with the Assembly of Government Employees (AGE), which was established in 1952. The AGE strongly supports merit systems and, like most of its member associations, it did not welcome collective bargaining with open arms. It believed that unions such as AFSCME wanted to completely replace civil service laws and regulations with negotiated agreements. After collective bargaining statutes had been passed in a number of important states, the AGE faced the choice of adapting to the new public policy or of recommending that its members not compete with the "unions" in collective bargaining elections. It chose to accommodate and compete, and many of the state associations have now been engaging in bargaining for some time. An example is the Washington Public Employees Association, which represents about 5,000 state workers, many of them in units that have contracts including a union shop.

The local associations were formed for basically the same kinds of reasons that motivated state employees. Their total membership has been estimated at about 300,000 nationally. Like their state counterparts, they did not originally support collective bargaining, but some now serve as bargaining agents. An increasing number of state and local associations, to build their bargaining power and resources, are affiliating with AFSCME and other AFL-CIO organizations. This pattern is illustrated by the California State Employees Association (CSEA). Established during the early 1930s, the CSEA is now a local of the SEIU that represents over 100,000 workers.

POLICE AND FIREFIGHTERS

Police officers are members of several different kinds of organizations. A few are members of AFSCME or of one of the mixed unions that admit police (e.g., the Teamsters and SEIU). There are also many local police associations not affiliated with any national organization.

BULLETIN

The Police Benevolent Association of NY State Troopers

"The PBA of the New York State Troopers was incorporated in 1944. Over the next two decades, the organization worked to improve the Troopers' difficult working conditions— such as reducing the average workday from 12 hours to eight. With the passage of the historic Taylor Law in 1964 . . . the PBA's role was strengthened. The organization became recognized as the official bargaining unit of the Troopers . . . ."

Source: (http://www.nystpaba.org/pba_ cont.htm), 1998.

There are three national organizations of police personnel: The Fraternal Order of Police (FOP), the International Union of Police Associations (IUPA), and the National Association of Police Officers (NAPO). The members of FOP, which was established in 1915, are regularly appointed or full-time law-enforcement personnel of all ranks who work for the state, local, and federal governments. The FOP does not consider itself a union, but some of its lodges engage in collective bargaining and have taken militant stands. It currently has over 270,000 members in more than 2,000 lodges. IUPA and NAPO were formed after the dissolution of the International Conference of Police Associations in 1978. The Conference's members (state and local police associations) split over the issue of affiliation with the AFL-CIO. One segment formed the IUPA and became a charter member of the AFL-CIO in 1979. By 1997, IUPA had 80,000 members. Those opposed to affiliation created the NAPO as an independent "police only" association.

The International Association of Fire Fighters (IAFF), to which the majority of nation's professional firefighters belong, currently has about 209,000 members (there are over 300,000 fire protection personnel in the United States, many of them in volunteer fire departments). Most IAFF members are employed by local governments, but there are some in the states, U.S. federal service, and Canadian governments. The IAFF was established shortly after World War I, and it has the longest continuous experience with local-level labor management relations of any of the public employee unions. It has vigorously pursued bargaining agreements in most cities of any size.

ELEMENTS OF A COLLECTIVE BARGAINING SYSTEM

Collective bargaining stands in stark contrast to the traditional merit system because it makes the terms of the employment relationship a matter of bilateral negotiations between representatives of two organizations: the public employer and the labor union. Collective bargaining usually takes place within a highly formalized system of rules and procedures. In the private sector, the National Labor Relations Act of 1935 (NLRA) and its amendments provide the basis for procedures and policies set forth by the National Labor Relations Board (NLRB). Title VII of the Civil Service Reform Act establishes a system of labor relations for the federal service in which the Federal Labor Relations Authority (FLRA) "is responsible for issuing policy decisions and adjudicating labor-management disputes" (U.S. General Accounting Office, 1991).

In state and local governments, collective bargaining systems are based on statutes or ordinances except in a few cases where they have been set up by executive orders. In New York State, for example, the Public Employees Fair Employment Act (Taylor Law) became effective in 1967. It was the state's first comprehensive labor relations law, and it was among the earliest passed in the nation. The Taylor Law:

- gives public employees the right to organize and to be represented by employee organizations of their own choice,
- requires public employers to negotiate and enter into agreements with public employee organizations regarding terms and conditions of employment, and
- creates impasse resolution processes to deal with collective bargaining disputes.

In some states where it has been approved by the courts, bargaining takes place on a de facto basis. Here, public management has for some reason decided to bargain with union representatives, and the courts have ruled valid the agreements entered into under these arrangements. In Ohio, for example, the state's supreme court ruled in 1975 that public employers did have the power to negotiate and engage in collective bargaining with their employees (Portaro, 1986). Enabling legislation obligating employers to bargain collectively was not passed in Ohio until 1983. In states such as Virginia, the courts have decided that public employees may not bargain collectively if enabling legislation does not exist (D'Alba, 1979).

THE LABOR RELATIONS AGENCY

The collective bargaining programs of state and local governments are usually administered by an agency created expressly for that purpose. New York State's Public Employment Relations Board (PERB), Ohio's State Employment Relations Board (SERB), and New York City's Office of Collective Bargaining (OCB) are examples. When collective bargaining is provided for by a local ordinance, the administering agency typically is a board or commission. Members of state boards or commissions are appointed by the governor, in most cases with confirmation of the state senate. On the national level, the three members of the FLRA are appointed by the president with Senate confirmation.

BARGAINING AGENTS AND UNITS

Within the traditional framework of collective bargaining, management representatives negotiate with the *exclusive bargaining agent* for a particular *bargaining unit.* All eligible workers within the unit are covered by the negotiated contract, even if they are not members of the union that has won the right to act as the exclusive agent. Although there are variations in procedure, the norm is for exclusive agents to be selected by a majority of those voting in a representation election. The labor relations agency sets the procedures for elections, oversees the process, and certifies the winner. Once certified, the bargaining agent has the exclusive right to represent the unit until such time that it is defeated in another election *or* it is decertified by the labor relations agency because it violated the law governing collective bargaining in its jurisdiction. PATCO, for example, was decertified by the FLRA after it called for and orchestrated an illegal strike by controllers.

Since they are the "building blocks" of collective bargaining, the size, membership, and number of bargaining units can have an effect on all of the following:

- The efficiency of day-to-day governmental operations.
- The quality of the relationship between management and the union.
- The quality of the relationships between employee groups within the bargaining unit.
- The scope of bargaining and the priorities given to particular issues by management and union negotiators.
- The outcomes of representation elections. (Hayford, Durkee, and Hickman, 1979)

The criteria and procedures used to establish bargaining units, in other words, are very important to both management and labor. These broad policy issues initially are dealt with on a political level through legislation and executive orders. Historically, one of the principal functions of labor relations agencies has been deciding how actual bargaining units will be constituted when management and labor disagree in their interpretations of the criteria set forth in law or executive orders.

Determining Bargaining Units

Three different ways of determining bargaining units have been used in the U.S. public sector: (1) case-by-case determinations made by the labor relations agency, (2) specification in the enabling legislation, and (3) determination by the administrative agency through its rule-making procedures.

The case-by-case approach is the most commonly used on the local level, and it is the method used in the federal service. In general terms, the labor relations agency will try to authorize units that group employees so that there is a "community of interest" within each unit based on position classifications, the kind of work or occupation involved, or geographical location. However, these considerations must be balanced against the need for administrative efficiency and an orderly structure of bargaining units.

For public management, the existence of large numbers of fragmented units means that many contracts must be negotiated yearly. Besides increasing the workload, a multiplicity of units improves the unions' chance to "whipsaw" by using a favorable agreement in one unit (e.g., police) to press for the same or better terms in another (e.g., fire). Although management tends to prefer a few large units to a scattering of small ones, neither management nor the unions invariably support larger or smaller units. Each side will develop its strategy in light of the situation it faces. If management is confronted by a powerful union or unions, it may try to divide that power by seeking several small units. Similarly, unions may want larger units if they believe this would increase their bargaining strength.

The case-by-case approach does carry the risk of fragmentation because the administrative agency must deal with requests to establish units as they occur, and it may not be able to wait until units can be rationally constituted. In order to avoid this problem, the legislatures of a number of states specified units for certain state workers in their legal authorizations. In Hawaii, the legislation requires that there be over a dozen units, including units for nonsupervisory blue-collar positions, registered nurses, firefighters, police, and professional and scientific employees. In Massachusetts, the legislature did not specify units, leaving this task to its Labor Relations Commission (MLRC). The Commission rejected a case-by-case approach and decided to use its rule-making powers to create a system of broad units based on occupations.

As Hayford, Durkee, and Hickman (1979) point out, the legislative and rule-making approaches to setting up bargaining units can avoid fragmentation and "greatly reduce the amount of time required to erect a comprehensive unit structure that will not require extensive future alteration." However, a legislature may not be able to develop a successful unit framework, especially if there is intense competition among unions, and management and labor cannot agree on the general outlines of a framework before the legislature acts. "In the absence of such firm policy guidance, the legislative body, which typically lacks expertise in such matters, would probably base its decision on factors (primarily political in nature) other than those normally relied on in unit determination" (p. 95). The rule-making approach does not eliminate political considerations; instead, it shifts the task of dealing with them to the administrative agency.

Status of Supervisors

One bargaining-unit determination issue that is unique to the public sector is the status of supervisory personnel. In the private sector, with the exception of a few skilled craft unions, supervisors from the foreman level up are considered to be "management" and they are excluded from bargaining units. This arrangement is firmly imbedded in a larger tradition of drawing a sharp line between management and labor. The NLRA excludes supervisors from bargaining rights, and most employers argue that their supervisors must be a part of the management team. For many public employers, however, the line between supervisors and nonsupervisors is blurred and controversial.

Actually, three questions are involved in making this distinction. First, it may be hard to determine whether a position is *really* supervisory in nature. Merit systems covering entire workforces have not stressed this distinction. The definition of a supervisory position set forth in the collective bargaining statute may be detailed, but there are frequent disagreements over whether the supervision exercised justifies excluding a particular position from a nonsupervisory bargaining unit. In reality, many public employees occupy positions in so-called supervisory classes that actually involve little or no supervisory activity. Since the size of a unit is important to a union's bargaining position, unions will seek to have ambiguous cases classified as nonsupervisory. Management, on the other hand, may try to reduce union strength by convincing the labor relations agency to define these kinds of jobs as supervisory in order to exclude them from the bargaining unit.

Most collective bargaining statutes do not specify which *individual* positions are to be considered supervisory. This determination is left to the administrative agency that decides bargaining units, and some of these agencies will closely examine the actual duties of positions with supervisory titles and exclude only those involving clearly supervisory duties and powers. Nonetheless, disagree-

BULLETIN

Collective Bargaining in California

"Since passage of collective bargaining (the Ralph C. Dills Act), the Department of Personnel Administration (DPA), as the Governor's representative on labor relations, has negotiated wages, hours, and other working conditions covering represented employees. Approximately 135,000 employees have been placed in one of 21 different bargaining units by the Public Employment Relations Board (PERB), the governing body which oversees the administration of the Act....DPA meets and confers with organizations representing supervisors regarding wages, hours, and working conditions. Although DPA obtains input from these organizations, it does not negotiate labor contracts for supervisors nor reach formal agreements. DPA sets salaries for all managerial, supervisory, and confidential employees, and for all other civil service positions that have been excluded from the collective bargaining process."

Source: (http://www.dpa.ca.gov/lr/ bargain/bargain.htm), 1998.

ment between management, the unions, and the administrative agency over which positions are supervisory is commonplace in the public sector.

The second issue has to do with the desirability of units that contain both supervisors and nonsupervisors. In government, the workforce is predominantly white- rather than blue-collar, and there are numerous levels of supervision. From the beginning, employee associations contained both supervisory and nonsupervisory personnel. Supervisors often were primarily responsible for creating these associations, and it was not unusual for them to hold leadership positions in them. Most of the mixed, predominantly public, and all public employee unions admit lower-level supervisors. Against this historical pattern, when collective bargaining programs were established, union leaders resisted legislation prohibiting "mixed" bargaining units. Nevertheless, most state statutes contain such a prohibition and use the definition of supervisors set forth by the National Labor Relations Act.

The reason for the private-sector precedent of not mixing supervisors and nonsupervisors is the potential for conflict of interest. In these terms, the groups have opposed, not common, interests. Supervisors represent management; the union represents the interests of workers. Since bargaining unit are supposed to be composed of persons having a "community of interest," having them both in the same unit does not make sense. Either the supervisors will permeate the unit with a management point of view, thereby undermining the collective bargaining rights of the workers, or the supervisors will "defect," weakening management's position.

Union leaders who favor mixed units argue that the conflict of interest argument does not hold for the public sector. One of their key points is that supervisors in government do not have the kind of authority and discretion typical of their counterparts in business and industrial settings. Another perspective stresses the idea that, in some occupations and services, supervisors and nonsupervisors share a community of interest that outweighs differences between management and labor. Representatives of nurses, teachers, and police and fire services employees have strongly advanced this point of view. In some local governments, almost all levels of supervision in certain departments have been included in the same bargaining unit as nonsupervisory employees. Cases frequently cited are in police and fire departments. When this happens—and it occurs largely because the unions have been politically effective—there may be only a few executives left to define and represent management's basic interests.

The third question or issue is whether supervisors should be allowed to form their own units and to bargain collectively with the employer. In the private sector, under the Taft-Hartley Amendment to the NLRA, organizations of supervisors do not have bargaining rights. For the most part, government has followed this model, but some states such as New York, Hawaii, and New Jersey do grant bargaining rights to all or some supervisory personnel.

The rationale for not allowing bargaining with units of supervisors is that they are a part of the management team and should represent management's interests in the administration of personnel policies. In other words, if supervisors bargained, it would be very difficult to define managerial roles and responsibilities clearly. Also, if supervisors had bargaining rights, they might see themselves as "labor" and, for example, sympathize with strikes by rank-and-file workers. When strikes or other job actions take place, management often relies on supervisors to perform essential work, and supervisors who have strong feelings of solidarity with organized labor may be unwilling to undermine the workers' position.

For largely practical reasons, many supervisors in both sectors disagree with the idea that consultation with top management is the best way to determine supervisory pay and benefits. It is a fairly common practice for supervisors' compensation to be informally linked to the provisions of negotiated agreements. However, top management is not required to do this, leaving supervisors in a very dependent position. In the public sector, it is not unusual to hear supervisors express the belief that they are disadvantaged in comparison to those who have bargaining rights and the organizational resources needed to pressure management. It is clear that many public employers have given inadequate attention to the pay and other needs of their supervisory personnel. While there may be compelling reasons for not authorizing supervisors' bargaining units, this does not erase an important need to develop alternative organizational mechanisms for representing their interests.

EMPLOYEE RIGHTS

It is the norm for employee rights to be stated in the legal authorization for collective bargaining. The most basic right is to form, join, and participate in employee organizations for the purpose of conferring and bargaining collectively with management. This includes the worker's right to be represented by the majority union in grievances over the terms and conditions of employment. The right of workers *not* to join unions or associations may or may not be stated. If it is, this means that management will not agree to contracts that require those in bargaining units to join the union or to pay dues.

Under such *open shop* arrangements, exclusive bargaining agents are often faced with situations in which they are negotiating contracts for units having more nonmembers than members. Having large numbers of "free riders" in units weakens unions' financial positions, and their bargaining power may be affected because they cannot depend on strong, unified, support from those in the unit. Management, for obvious reasons, prefers to negotiate in an *open shop* environment. The unions, on the other hand, much prefer statutory language that does not say employees have a right not to join unions. If this is the case, it usually means in practice that *union* or *agency* shop agreements may be negotiated.

Under the union shop, which is commonplace in the private sectors of states that do not have so-called "right-to-work" laws, workers must join the union within a specified time period after being hired. If they do not, management is obliged to fire them. Union *membership* is not mandatory under an agency shop, but the equivalent of the union dues must be paid for purposes of representation. This payment is in return for services provided by the exclusive bargaining agent, which is required to represent the interests of all persons in the bargaining unit, whether or not they are members of the union. Most states and the federal government require open shops. Where this is not the case (e.g., Pennsylvania and Hawaii), unions have succeeded in negotiating union or agency shops for some units.

MANAGEMENT RIGHTS AND SCOPE OF BARGAINING

A key to the relative balance of power between management and the unions is the range of personnel policies and practices that are negotiable. In general, unions prefer a wide range, while management usually seeks to narrow the scope of bargaining. In the private sector, the NLRA defines the scope of bargaining to include wages, hours, and working conditions. The NLRB, in turn, has identified three types of issues: (1) those that are nonnegotiable, (2) mandatory issues that must be negotiated, and (3) those that may be negotiated if management agrees to do so. With regard to mandatory issues, it is up to the NLRB and often the courts to decide what the language of the NLRA means in specific circumstances.

In the public sector, overriding laws and court rulings may effectively remove certain issues from the bargaining table; for example, if the enabling state legislation requires the open shop, management and the union are not free to negotiate another arrangement. Employee relations boards and commissions in the public sector are empowered to interpret legislative intent in this area, subject to judicial review. Although they are not bound by its precedents, these agencies have in practice generally followed the NLRB's threefold classification.

As a general rule, the scope of bargaining in government is likely to be narrower than it is in the private sector. Provisions of civil service laws, state education codes, special legislation covering the pay of blue-collar workers, and other statutes (federal, state, and local) make many issues essentially nonnegotiable. Although there are some exceptions, the legal authorizations covering state and local employees typically limit the range of negotiations by providing that subjects already covered by preexisting laws (particularly civil service statutes) may not be negotiated (Williams, 1994). The federal CSRA restricts the scope of bargaining to "conditions of employment," a term the legislation defines as "personnel policies, practices, and matter, whether established by rule, regulation, or otherwise, affecting working conditions, except that such term does not include policies, practices, and matters . . . [that] are specifically provided for by Federal statute." Since the pay and benefits of federal workers covered by the CSRA are set by law, they are not negotiable.

In addition to limits set by other laws, a "management rights" clause often is included in collective bargaining statutes. It is designed to specify managerial powers that may not be bargained away or shared with labor organizations. Traditionally enumerated rights give management control over agency missions, administrative structures, and operating technologies. Other rights include directing the work of employees and the ability to hire, evaluate, promote, assign, and transfer them in light of agency requirements. The CSRA's language on management rights is typical:

> [N]othing in this chapter shall affect the authority of any management official of any agency—(1) to determine the mission, budget, organization, number of employees, and internal security practices of the agency; and (2) in accordance with applicable laws—(A) to hire, assign, direct, layoff, and retain employees in the agency, or to suspend, remove, reduce in grade or pay, or take other disciplinary action against such employees; (B) to assign work, to make determinations with respect to contracting out, and to determine the personnel by which agency operations shall be conducted . . . .

Management rights clauses usually are replicated in contracts, but determining what they mean in specific cases is often a responsibility of the labor relations agency. These interpretations are important because they set the scope of bargaining. Rulings of labor relations agencies and courts concerning which issues are mandatory or permissive vary from state to state. Student–teacher ratios are negotiable in some states, but in others they are not. In an area of great importance to the unions, contracting-out or privatization, there are wide variations.

In their interpretations of management rights, the courts have been "more concerned with preserving those rights that [they] believe management must possess to carry out its public duties and responsibilities under enabling statutes than with providing a safety valve for employees . . . but they do provide some flexibility for employee organizations by making the impact of management actions on wages, hours, and working conditions negotiable" (Gershenfeld and Gershenfeld, 1983, p. 349). In other words, *impact bargaining* expands the arena of mandatory negotiations to include the *effects* of management decisions on those in a bargaining unit. In personnel matters, impact bargaining means that management keeps its power to make program decisions, such as whether to carry out a reduction-in-force or to implement a pay-for-performance system. However, since these kinds of actions will almost certainly have an impact on working conditions, management is obliged to negotiate with the union over procedural issues and ways of dealing with the consequences for employees. In such negotiations, the union may want management to agree to give laid-off workers first consideration when positions become available. In the federal service, the unions may negotiate aspects of pay-for-performance systems that have an impact on working conditions, with the major exceptions of position classifications and "matters specifically provided for by Federal statute." Of course, management is not compelled to grant union demands regarding impact issues, but it cannot simply say they are nonnegotiable.

Unfair Labor Practices

In their dealings with each other, management and labor are constrained by rules defining "unfair labor practices." These rules are designed to prevent "union busting" by management, to make sure that unions do not engage in coercive behavior, and to ensure that both parties negotiate in good faith. Such practices by the *employer* commonly are defined to include the following:

- Interfering, restraining, or coercing employees who are trying to exercise their collective bargaining rights under law. Threatening to fire or transfer workers who participate in union activities is an unfair labor practice.

- Dominating, obstructing, or assisting in the formation, existence, or administration of any employee organization. Employers who try to create "company unions" or to put "their people" into union leadership positions are engaging in an unfair labor practice.

- Encouraging or discouraging membership in any employee organization through discriminatory personnel practices. Not hiring, promoting, or offering training opportunities to union members is an unfair labor practice.
- Discouraging or discriminating against any employee because he or she has joined a union or filed a grievance under the collective bargaining agreement is an unfair labor practice.
- Refusing to negotiate in good faith, lying or distorting information, deliberately provoking conflict, and other steps taken to undermine negotiations are unfair labor practices.

Unfair labor practices by *employee organizations* include the following kinds of behaviors:

- Interfering with, restraining, or coercing employees in the exercise of their bargaining rights. For example, one union may try to coerce workers to vote for it as the exclusive bargaining agent.
- Obstructing an employer's efforts to select its labor relations team, including negotiators and representatives in the grievance process. Unions have been known to use political pressure and threats to undermine management's capacity to function effectively.
- Refusing to negotiate in good faith with the employer in order to provoke an impasse or strike.

A good faith effort by both sides to negotiate, to resolve differences, and to reach an agreement obviously is the foundation of a successful collective bargaining relationship. The parties are entitled to file unfair labor practices charges with the labor relations agency. The agency is authorized to investigate such charges and, if it finds that they are justified, it will order the violator to stop the practice and to take whatever remedial actions are necessary. In the case of dismissals for union activity, management usually will be ordered to reinstate fired employees with back pay. These kinds of orders may be appealed to the courts for a final decision.

Effective labor relations depend in large measure on each side's fully understanding "the rules of the game." Over the years, labor relations agencies and the courts will issue rulings that management and labor are expected to understand and to follow. During the early stages of the expansion of collective bargaining in the public sector, it was not unusual for inexperienced managers and union members to make threatening statements and to behave in ways that provoked charges of unfair labor practices. A derogatory statement about a union and its leadership made in the presence of union members is often enough to bring a complaint against management. Unless management negotiators are aware of which overt acts the labor relations agency considers to be evidence of a lack of good faith bargaining, such as routinely putting off meetings with the union bargaining team or simply refusing to meet with it at all, they run a great risk of being found guilty of an unfair labor practice. The penalties can be substantial. In this, as well as other regards, collective bargaining adds a new dimension to public personnel administration.

CONTRACT NEGOTIATIONS

In the public sector, most negotiated agreements cover one or two years. This means that both sides are almost constantly preparing to negotiate the next contract in addition to administering the provisions of the one in force. In contrast to the corporate or business environment, where it is fairly easy to identify the membership of the "management team" responsible for making preparations, conducting negotiations, and committing the organization to contractual obligations, it is often difficult to say who is "in charge" in government. Thus, when collective bargaining began to spread in government, clearly defining who should have the responsibility for labor relations and the authority to enter into contractual relationships with unions became an important issue. In one writer's words at the time:

> [O]ne of the most difficult problems is to find management and, having found it, to clothe it with the authority it needs to play the part. In a public service setting, managerial authority tends to be divided between a legislature and an executive, between politicians and bureaucrats, between independent commissions and operating departments. Because badly dispersed, it tends to lack substance and definition and almost, at times, to disappear in a forest of checks and balances. (Love, 1966, p. 28)

In addition to the intentional dispersal and sharing of power within the formal institutions of government, there are powerful external interest groups that seek influence in the collective bargaining process. There are many potentially conflicting roles and points of view that make up the management side of the relationship. While elected executives may recommend or request budgetary appropriations, it is up to the legislative body to make those appropriations. Even when legislators delegate to executives the authority to set pay scales, they do not give up their control over fiscal and budgetary matters, and they may simply refuse to make needed funds available.

If tax increases will be required to pay for negotiated pay scales, organized interests of many kinds are likely to become very active. Personnel departments, the courts, and other levels of government may be drawn in by contractual provisions concerning issues such as position classifications, appeals processes, and seniority systems. On the union side, important players include national or state labor organizations, factions within the union itself, and community and special-interest groups with a stake in the outcome of negotiations. Thus, in addition to the bilateral bargaining that takes place across the table, both sides are conducting a process of "multilateral bargaining" with constituencies and authorities that must be recognized and accommodated in any negotiated contract.

The fragmentation of authority and power within public employers led to much confusion and lack of coordination on the management side during the early years of collective bargaining. It was not unusual to see city councils reject or attempt to change contracts negotiated in good faith by a management team. Lack of coordination between personnel departments, budget offices, and line managers frequently produced contracts that were inadequately "costed-out" and at cross-purposes with efforts to improve productivity. Recognizing this weakness, unions often went around management negotiators and, in effect, tried to negotiate with legislators. On the other side of the coin, union leaders would sometimes find that management was covertly mobilizing legislators, courts, and taxpayer groups in an effort to achieve a dominant position.

One consequence of over 30 years of unionization and collective bargaining has been a trend toward the centralization of public management structures and control systems (Kearney, 1983). Public executives have been expected to take the lead in labor relations, and this has resulted in a significant decline in legislative influence over personnel matters in jurisdictions where collective bargaining is well established. Administratively, the pattern has been for executives to establish a direct line of authority over the unit having responsibility for labor relations.

In state and local governments, the labor relations function often is assigned to the director of personnel or to a separate office of labor relations. In either case, specialists in labor relations will be responsible for the program. Many small jurisdictions use part-time consultants to represent management at the bargaining table. In the federal government, all bargaining takes place on the agency level (OPM serves as a management adviser on labor relations). In most cases, the federal agency's labor relations program is handled by a specialized unit of the personnel office or department. A few agencies have a completely separate office of labor relations, a model typical of the private sector. When there is one office responsible for labor relations and another for personnel, experience has shown the need for close coordination between the two. Those negotiating agreements must be thoroughly familiar with personnel laws and regulations, and they should be aware of any personnel problems or issues that relate to the agency's dealings with organized employees. Likewise, the personnel department must be in a position to understand and respond to the implications of proposed contractual agreements. When the functions are combined in one office, but they are handled by different staffs, similar coordination is needed. Whatever the structure, those responsible for labor relations should be in constant contact with line officials in order to assure that management's needs and perspectives are represented in the negotiating process.

STRIKES AND IMPASSE RESOLUTION

At one time, strikes by public employee organizations were probably the single most feared aspect of collective bargaining, at least from management's point of view. Strikes by private-sector workers are legal, and unions see that right as absolutely essential in order to maintain an economic balance of power between management and labor. In contrast, strikes by public employees are illegal in most states and within the federal government. There are two reasons or rationales advanced for denying the right to strike: (1) that many public services are essential and the public has no comparable alternatives, and (2) that strikes by public employees are essentially political weapons that give unions an unfair advantage.

Statutory penalties include dismissal of striking workers, criminal prosecution of union leaders, fines against union treasuries, and decertification of unions calling strikes. Many strikes or work stoppages, nonetheless, have taken place in government, most against local employers and school districts. Although most have been relatively short in duration, some have been protracted, unpleasant, media spectaculars. In many instances, legal penalties could not be enforced, and settlements provided for amnesty. In cases where legal penalties have been imposed, such as the PATCO strike in which over 10,000 experienced controllers were fired outright and not rehired, it may take years for the agency to return to normal operation (U.S. General Accounting Office, 1986).

Its experience with strikes, while unpleasant, has taught public management that they are survivable if contingency plans have been prepared. One measure of confidence on the employer side is legislation in a number of states that permits strikes by *nonessential* workers. Most of these laws were passed in the late 1970s after the period of explosive growth in unionism. The number and duration of work stoppages has declined over the past 15 years. An overall maturation of the relationship between management and labor has been a contributing factor, along with fiscal stress and public opposition to strikes. In the current environment, both sides have many incentives to avoid strikes and job actions such as "slowdowns" and "sickouts."

One of the features of legally authorized collective bargaining programs is that they almost always set up procedures for resolving bargaining deadlocks or impasses. By 1985, over 40 states had passed some kind of law dealing with impasses. Where they exist, the labor relations agencies are responsible for seeing to it that these laws are followed and for arranging the services of *mediators, fact finders,* and *arbitrators* to help resolve impasses. Traditionally, each side shares equally in the costs associated with such third-party interventions.

Mediation usually is the first step. Mediators focus on getting the negotiation process back on track and facilitating communication between the parties. If mediation fails, the next step may be fact finding. Often "the facts" are in dispute; for example, a jurisdiction's ability to pay may be in question. Fact finding is a semijudicial process in which both sides present their version of the facts with documentation such as cost-of-living data and information on prevailing rates of pay. Expert witnesses are likely to be called in to support each side. The fact finder (or fact-finding panel) studies the evidence and issues a report containing a recommended settlement. If these are not accepted by one or both of the parties, in some states they may agree to go to binding arbitration under which an agreement is imposed. In others, a limited strike is a legal option. In about 20 states, the law requires that police and firefighters submit to binding arbitration if they cannot resolve an impasse at the bargaining table.

In both the fact-finding and arbitration processes, management is required to carefully prepare its case. Personnel departments usually have much of the responsibility for collecting, organizing, and displaying information that supports the employer's position. Although most public-sector labor leaders would prefer the strike option, fact finding and arbitration do compensate somewhat by requiring employers to present a rational justification of the positions they have taken at the bargaining table.

APPROVAL OF AGREEMENTS

Public management seldom has the luxury of being able to finalize a contractual agreement with a union. In many municipalities, agreements must be approved by the local governing body, such as the county board of supervisors or city council. In most school districts, approval by the school board is required before a contract may go into effect. In some state governments, the legislature must ratify the agreement; in most, this is not the case. Agreements take effect in the federal service when they are approved by agency heads. With the exception of public authorities having their own sources of revenue, the legislative body must vote funds to finance contracts and so may exercise a veto power.

On the union side, contracts may be submitted to the membership for a ratification vote, but procedures vary. In the federal service, such votes are not required. Ideally, both agency leadership and the union membership have been kept fully informed about the status of negotiations, have in some manner consulted with their negotiators, and will not be surprised by the content of a proposed contract. Management officials presenting an agreement to those legally empowered to give it final approval should be prepared to fully explain its terms and likely consequences on such matters as budgets and tax rates. Union leaders are responsible for explaining a contract's terms and, if a ratification vote is required, recommending its approval or rejection.

CONTRACT ADMINISTRATION

Once a contract is signed and ratified, the labor relations program enters the contract administration phase. Although negotiations and related impasses attract the most public attention, effective day-to-day administration of agreements is the foundation of a successful labor relations program. Contract administration is a bilateral process in which management and labor share responsibility for implementation of an agreement's provisions. Needless to say, disputes over how to interpret some of those provisions are likely to occur, but the emphasis is (or should be) on building a cooperative relationship.

In a study of the federal labor relations program conducted during the early 1990s, the GAO concluded that a cooperative or joint problem-solving orientation often was sadly lacking (U.S. General Accounting Office, 1991). It also noted that "labor-management cooperative programs in the private sector reflect the growing view that an 'us versus them' approach is outdated and unworkable." In fact, labor–management cooperation has become an important stated goal of federal personnel policy. In 1993, President Clinton issued Executive Order 12871 calling for a change in federal labor–management relations "so that managers, employees, and employees' elected union representatives serve as partners . . . ." It established a National Partnership Council to advise the president on labor–management relations, to support and promote labor–management partnerships, and to recommend statutory changes needed to support a cooperative and reform-oriented approach to federal labor relations. Agency heads are now required to establish labor–management partnerships by forming committees or councils to support the reform agenda set forth in the National Performance Review (NPR). Agency heads are to:

- Involve employees and their union representatives as full partners with management representatives to identify problems and craft solutions to better serve the agency's customers and mission,
- Provide training for appropriate agency employees in consensual methods of dispute resolution, and
- Evaluate progress and improvements in organizational performance resulting from labor–management partnerships.

Although the objectives of E.O. 12871 have not been achieved for a variety of reasons, replacing the traditionally adversarial culture of federal labor relations with one that encourages mutual respect, partnership, and goal-oriented cooperation is still a stated objective of the Clinton administration (Reeves, 1997).

On the state and local levels, joint labor–management committees (LMCs) are increasingly popular. LMCs are not a substitute for bargaining, but they provide a mechanism for cooperative efforts to solve a wide variety of problems, such as workplace safety, quality control, and communication. Joint LMCs are created by contract to deal with a single issue such as health care. There is joint representation on the committee of both labor and management but with the final decision reserved to management. Cities such as Phoenix and San Diego have negotiated agreements establishing LMCs, as have the states of Ohio and Massachusetts (Dawson, 1990).

Supervisors are considered key figures in the administration of a public personnel program, since they have the most direct contact with rank-and-file workers. Perhaps the single most positive impact of collective bargaining on personnel administration has been its focus on the administration of contracts by supervisors. Grievance arbitration clauses are now very common in the public sector (see below), and supervisors are expected to understand a contract's provisions and to be able to prevent disputes and resolve conflicts before they result in formal grievances that may undermine cooperation. While some grievances are unavoidable, many are provoked by supervisory ignorance and a confrontational approach.

For supervisors unused to life under a negotiated contract, the presence of union stewards may come as a somewhat unpleasant shock. Elected by the union membership, stewards are the supervisors' counterparts in the process of contract administration. In this role, they are often more diligent than management and the personnel office in detecting supervisory deficiencies, particularly as they relate to contractual requirements.

Located in the workplace where supervision operates, stewards can have intimate knowledge of work activities and of problems affecting both management and the worker. They are sometimes overzealous and so antagonistic toward management that supervisors may have some cause for considering them "troublemakers," but the capable, conscientious steward is a "troubleshooter" who can be a valuable problem solver for both the union and management. Studies of the steward's function have revealed that in large measure it has been a positive factor in improving supervisory skill and assuring equitable treatment of employees in personnel polices and practices (Sulzner, 1979, p. 36). For supervisors and stewards alike, adequate training in labor relations is crucial to a smoothly functioning collective bargaining relationship.

One very important aspect of contract administration is the process through which disputes over interpretations of a contract and its manner of administration are resolved. Typically, authorizing legislation will require that all contracts contain a mechanism for resolving grievances. The standard mechanism is a negotiated grievance procedure. These procedures are designed to have "finality" in the sense that disputes that cannot be resolved by the parties are submitted to a third party "neutral" or arbitrator who makes a final and binding decision. Such finality is essential because neither side can afford to be bogged down in interminable conflicts and ambiguities over how to interpret one part or another of the contract. Although one side or the other is going to be disappointed by the arbitrator's decision, at least it provides a clean end to the dispute and makes it easier to avoid future misunderstandings. Appendix 7.A is the text of the grievance and arbitration procedure negotiated between the State of California and the union representing one of its bargaining units.

The definition of a grievance set forth in legislation is very important because it determines what issues employees will be able to grieve under a negotiated process, as opposed to the system established under civil service laws and regulations. The CSRA's language is very broad, and a grievance is defined as "any complaint about employment, or the interpretation and application of the negotiated agreement or any law, rule, or regulation affecting employees' working conditions." Unless the parties agree to exclude them, this means that the negotiated grievance procedure can be used to deal with matters already covered by the statutory appeals process. Not surprisingly, many managers object to broad definitions of grievances because they believe such definitions expose many of management's decisions on personnel matters to reversals by arbitrators who are not particularly concerned with the day-to-day problems of administering complex organizations and programs.

CONCLUSION

From a public management standpoint, two concerns about collective bargaining have been its effect on the merit principle and its long-term impact on managerial authority and discretion. Despite early fears about "negotiating away merit" and an undermining of public management, collective bargaining would appear to have done neither.

In some ways, collective bargaining may have actually strengthened merit and management. Unions historically have been opposed to patronage systems, and where they have established collective bargaining relationships with public employers, they have negotiated contracts that do more to prevent spoils appointments than many weakly administered merit systems. In such states as California, New York, and Michigan, merit system coverage coexists with collective bargaining (Elling, 1986; Douglas, 1992). With regard to management's capacity to function effectively, there is at best evidence to support the proposition that collective bargaining has encouraged at least some agencies to use human as well as material resources more efficiently and to develop better supervisory skills. At worst, it seems that provisions of negotiated contracts are no more serious impediments than traditional civil service rules and procedures.

In most jurisdictions with merit systems and collective bargaining (dual systems), an accommodation of sorts has been reached between the two. Collective bargaining has partly replaced the unilateral civil service system in such areas as compensation and grievances. However, civil service boards and departments have not been limited to recruitment and examination functions, as some originally feared would be the outcome if the unions' agenda became reality. They generally retain broad policy authority over promotions, transfers, reductions in force, performance standards and evaluation, position classifications, and other aspects of the in-service personnel program. In all or many of these areas, procedures used to implement civil service laws and policies are likely to be governed by contract provisions and, accordingly, the powers of civil service agencies have been meaningfully diminished. In one writer's judgment:

> [W]here collective bargaining laws have been implemented [by states], civil service merit systems have become tired institutions,

are in a period of decline, and may be at the twilight of their existence . . . . [F]or state employees, LRS [labor relations systems],
more than CSMS [civil service merit systems], have become the
primary forces in human resource policy formulation and implementation. Living with dual personnel systems is an option widely
followed yet not recommended. The task ahead is the enactment of
statutory revocation provisions for state civil service merit systems
that conflict with labor relations systems and the preservation of
merit principles within the context of collective bargaining.
(Douglas, 1992, p. 169)

In a number of states such as Wisconsin, the authorizing legislation for state employees requires that negotiated contracts take precedence over civil service rules where conflicts exist (Williams, 1994).
Some states, for example, California, have arrangements whereby contractual agreements on certain subjects (e.g., wages, hours, discipline,
and layoffs) have precedence. In others, contracts prevail only on a
few topics, such as union security provisions. In most local governments, contracts do not automatically supersede civil service; negotiated terms that conflict with existing law may take effect only if the
governing body changes the law.

The most profound impact of collective bargaining in the public sector clearly has been a transformation of the relationship
between employer and employee. Traditional civil service merit systems are based on the proposition that the "rules of the workplace"
set the terms of the relationship between the employer and the *individual worker*. Under collective bargaining, management is required
to negotiate those rules with *another organization*, the labor union
or employee association. Beyond bilateral negotiations, these two
organizations coimplement and coadminister the rules as they
apply to members of bargaining units. For many employees, this
means that they may not individually negotiate terms of employment and, if management dealt with them on this level, it would
be guilty of an unfair labor prac-
tice. For management, it means an
extensive sharing of power over,
and responsibility for, the personnel program, with the leadership
of an employee organization created to serve the interests of the
worker.

BULLETIN

The State of California Supersession Rule

"The following enumerated Government Code
Sections and existing rules, regulations, standards, practices and policies which implement
the enumerated Government Code Sections are
hereby incorporated into this Agreement.
However, if any other provision of this
Agreement alters or is in conflict with any of
the Government Code Sections . . . the
Agreement shall be controlling and supersede
said Government Code Sections or parts
thereof and any rule, regulation, standard, practice, or policy implementing such provisions.
The Government Code Sections listed . . . are
cited in Section 3517.6 of the Ralph C. Dills Act."

DISCUSSION QUESTIONS

1. Do management and labor have fundamentally different interests?
2. Should public employees be allowed to bargain collectively with their employers?
3. Should public employees be allowed to strike like their private-sector counterparts?
4. Should employees in a bargaining unit be required to pay a representation fee to the union, even if they are not members?
5. Can collective bargaining and the merit principle really coexist in practice?
6. Do unionization and collective bargaining make it hard for managers to motivate workers and to effectively manage performance?
7. Should supervisors be allowed to bargain collectively with public employers?
8. Is privatization or contracting-out a strategy for "breaking" public employee unions?

REFERENCES

D'Alba, Joel A. (1979). "The Nature of the Duty to Bargain in Good Faith," in Public Employment Relations Service, *Portrait of a Process: Collective Negotiations in Public Employment* (Fort Washington, PA: Labor Relations Press).

Dawson, Irving O. (1990). "Trends and Developments in Public Sector Unions," in Steven Hays and Richard C. Kearney (eds.), *Public Personnel Administration: Problems and Prospects,* 2nd ed. (Englewood Cliffs, NJ: Prentice-Hall), pp. 153–157.

Douglas, Joel M. (1992). "State Civil Service and Collective Bargaining: Systems in Conflict." *Public Administration Review,* Vol. 52, No. 1 (January–February).

Elling, Richard C. (1986). "Civil Service, Collective Bargaining and Personnel-Related Impediments to Effective State Management: A Comparative Assessment." *Review of Public Personnel Administration,* Vol. 6, No. 3 (Summer).

Gershenfeld, Walter J., and Gershenfeld, Gladys (1983). "The Scope of Collective Bargaining," in Jack Rabin, Thomas Vocino, Bartley W. Hildreth, and Gerald J. Miller (eds.), *Handbook of Public Personnel Administration and Labor Relations* (New York: Marcel Dekker).

Gideon, Jacquelyn (1979). "The American Nurses Association: A Professional Model for Collective Bargaining." *Journal of Health and Human Resources Administration*, Vol. 2. No. 1 (August).

Hayford, Stephen L., Durkee, William A, and Hickman, Charles W. (1979). "Bargaining Unit Determination Procedures in the Public Sector: A Comparative Evaluation." *Employee Relations Law Journal* (Summer).

Kearney, Richard C. (1983). "Monetary Impact of Collective Bargaining," in Rabin et al., *Handbook of Public Personnel Administration and Labor Relations*.

Love, Douglas (1966). "Proposals for Collective Bargaining in the Public Service of Canada: A Further Commentary," in Gerald C. Somer (ed.), *Collective Bargaining in the Public Service: Proceedings of the 1966 Annual Spring Meeting, Industrial Relations Association*, Milwaukee, Wisconsin, May 6–7.

Masters, Marick F., and Atkin, Robert (1989). "Bargaining Representation and Union Membership in the Federal Sector: A Free Rider's Paradise." *Public Personnel Management*, Vol. 18, No. 3 (Fall), pp. 311–323.

Muhl, Charles J. (1995). "Collective Bargaining in State and Local Government, 1994." *Monthly Labor Review*, Vol. 118, No. 6 (June).

Parker, Donald F., Schurman, Susan J., and Montgomery, D. Ruth (1984). "Labor-Management Relations Under CSRA: Provisions and Effects," in Patricia W. Ingraham and Carolyn Ban (eds.), *Legislating Bureaucratic Change: The Civil Service Reform Act of 1978* (Albany: State University of New York Press), pp. 161–181.

Portaro, Ron M. (1986). "Public-Sector Impasse Legislation: Is It Working?" *Employee Relations Law Journal*, Vol. 12, No. 1 (Summer).

Reeves, T. Zane (1997). "Labor-Management Partnerships in the Public Sector," in Carolyn Ban and Norma M. Riccucci (eds.), *Public Personnel Management: Current Concerns, Future Challenges* (New York: Longman), pp. 173–186.

Sulzner, George T. (1979). *Impact of Labor-Management Relations upon Selected Federal Personnel Policies and Practices* (Washington, DC: U.S. Office of Personnel Management).

U.S. General Accounting Office (1986). *FAA Staffing: The Air Traffic Control Workforce Opposes Rehiring Fired Controllers* (Washington, DC), October.

——— (1991). *Federal Labor Relations: A System in Need of Reform* (Washington, DC), July.

Williams, Richard C. (1994). "Resolution of the Civil Service–Collective Bargaining Dilemma." *American Review of Public Administration,* Vol. 24, No. 2 (June), pp. 149–160.

Zack, Arnold M. (1972). "Impasses, Strikes, and Resolutions," in Sam Zagoria (ed.), *Public Workers and Public Unions* (Englewood Cliffs, NJ: Prentice-Hall), pp. 101–121.

Zax, Jeffrey S. and Ichniowski, Casey (1990). "Bargaining Laws and Unionization in the Local Public Sector." *Industrial and Labor Relations Review,* Vol. 43, No. 4 (April), pp. 447–462.

SUGGESTED READINGS

Colosi, Thomas R., and Berkeley, Arthur E. (1992). *Collective Bargaining: How It Works & Why: A Manual of Theory & Practice* (New York: American Arbitration Association).

Coulson, Robert (1993). *Police Under Pressure: Resolving Disputes* (Westport, CT: Greenwood Publishing Group, Inc.).

Fernbach, Dan, and Henkel, Jane R. (1994). *A Survey of Selected States Regarding Collective Bargaining Laws for State Employees & Experience Under Those Laws* (Upland, CA: DIANE Publishing Company).

Florio, James, and Abramson, Jerry (1997). *Working Together for Public Service: Report of the U.S. Secretary of Labor's Task Force on Excellence in State and Local Government Through Labor-Management Cooperation* (Upland, CA: DIANE Publishing Company).

Horowitz, Morris A. (1994). *Collective Bargaining in the Public Sector* (New York: Lexington Books).

Kearney, Richard C., ed. (1993). "Public Sector Labor Relations: Symposium." *Review of Public Personnel Administration,* Vol. 13, No. 3 (Summer).

Kerschner, Charles T., Kuppich, Julia, and Weeres, Joseph G. (1997). *United Mind Workers: Unions & Teaching in the Knowledge Society* (San Francisco: Jossey-Bass Publishers).

Mangum, Garth L. (1992). *Labor Struggle in the Post Office: From Selective Lobbying to Collective Bargaining* (Armonk, NY: M.E. Sharpe, Inc.).

Piskulich, John P. (1992). *Collective Bargaining in State & Local Government* (Westport, CT: Greenwood Publishing Group, Inc.).

Rabin, Jack (1994). *Handbook of Public Sector Labor Relations* (New York: Marcel Dekker, Inc.).

Rhoades, Gary (1998). *Managed Professionals: Unionized Faculty & Restructuring Academic Labor* (Albany: State University of New York Press).

Riccucci, Norma (1990). *Women, Minorities and Unions in the Public Sector* (Westport, CT: Greenwood Publishing Group, Inc.).

APPENDIX 7.A   ARTICLE 5: GRIEVANCE AND ARBITRATION PROCEDURE

Contract Negotiated Between the State of California and Bargaining Unit 19: Health and Social Services/ Professional (AFSCME) (Effective Through June 30, 1999)

ARTICLE 5

GRIEVANCE AND ARBITRATION PROCEDURE

1. PURPOSE

   a. This grievance procedure shall be used to process and resolve grievances arising under this Agreement and employment-related complaints.
   b. The purpose of this procedure is:
      1. To resolve grievances informally at the lowest possible level;
      2. To provide an orderly procedure for reviewing and resolving grievances promptly.

1. DEFINITIONS

   a. A grievance is a dispute of one or more employees, or a dispute between the State and AFSCME, involving the interpretation, application, or enforcement of the express terms of this Agreement.
   b. A complaint is a dispute of one or more employees involving the application or interpretation of a written rule or policy not covered by this Agreement and not under the jurisdiction of the SPB. Complaints shall only be processed as far as the department head or designee.
   c. As used in this procedure, the term "immediate supervisor" means the individual identified by the department head.
   d. As used in this procedure, the term "party" means AFSCME, an employee, or the State.
   e. An "AFSCME Representative" refers to an employee designated as an AFSCME steward or a paid staff representative.

5.3 TIME LIMITS

Each party involved in a grievance shall act quickly so that the grievance may be resolved promptly. Every effort should be made to complete action within the time limits contained in the grievance procedure. However, with the mutual consent of the parties, the time limitation for any step may be extended.

5.4 WAIVER OF STEPS

The parties may mutually agree to waive any step of the grievance procedure.

5.5 NOTIFICATION

During the term of this Agreement, the State agrees to send one copy of any third or fourth level grievance response to a designated AFSCME office of any grievance which is submitted by any representative other than AFSCME.

5.6 PRESENTATION

At any step of the grievance procedure, the State representative may determine it desirable to hold a grievance conference. If a grievance conference is scheduled, the grievant or an AFSCME steward, or both, may attend without loss of compensation.

5.7 INFORMAL DISCUSSION

An employee grievance initially shall be discussed with the employee's immediate supervisor. Within seven (7) calendar days, the immediate supervisor shall give his/her decision or response.

8. FORMAL GRIEVANCE - STEP 1

   a. If an informal grievance is not resolved to the satisfaction of the grievant, a formal grievance may be filed no later than:
      1. Fourteen (14) calendar days after the event or circumstances occasioning the grievance, or
      2. Within seven (7) calendar days after receipt of the decision rendered in the informal grievance procedure.
   b. However, if the informal grievance procedure is not initiated within the period specified in Item (1) above, the period in which to bring the grievance shall not be extended by Item (2) above.
   c. A formal grievance shall be initiated in writing on a form provided by the State and shall be filed with a designated supervisor or manager identified by each department head as first level of appeal.
   d. Within fourteen (14) calendar days after receipt of the formal grievance, the person designated by the department head as the first level of appeal shall respond in writing to the grievance.
   e. No contract interpretation or grievance settlement made at this stage of the grievance procedure shall be considered presidential.

9. FORMAL GRIEVANCE - STEP 2

   a. If the grievant is not satisfied with the decision rendered pursuant to Step 1, the grievant may appeal the decision within fourteen (14) calendar days after receipt to a designated supervisor or manager identified by each department head as the second level of appeal. If the department head or designee is the first level of appeal, the grievant may bypass Step 2.

continued page 244

b. Within twenty-one (21) calendar days after receipt of the appealed grievance, the person designated by the department head as the second level of appeal shall respond in writing to the grievance.

c. No contract interpretation or grievance settlement made at this stage of the grievance procedure shall be considered precedential.

10. FORMAL GRIEVANCE - STEP 3

a. If the grievant is not satisfied with the decision rendered pursuant to Step 2, the grievant may appeal the decision within fourteen (14) calendar days after receipt by a designated supervisor or manager identified by each department head as the third level of appeal. If the department head or designee is the second level of appeal, the grievant may bypass Step 3.

b. Within twenty-one (21) calendar days after receipt of the appealed grievance, the person designated by the department head as the third level of appeal shall respond in writing to the grievance.

11. FORMAL GRIEVANCE - STEP 4

a. If the grievant is not satisfied with the decision rendered at Step 3, the grievant may appeal the decision within fourteen (14) calendar days after receipt by the Director of the Department of Personnel Administration or designee.

b. Within thirty (30) calendar days after receipt of the appealed grievance, the Director of the Department of Personnel Administration or designee shall respond in writing to the grievance.

12. FORMAL GRIEVANCE - STEP 5

a. If the grievance is not resolved at Step 4 within thirty (30) calendar days after receipt of the fourth level response, AFSCME shall have the right to submit the grievance to arbitration.

b. Within seven (7) calendar days after the notice requesting arbitration has been served on the State or at a date mutually agreed to by the parties, the parties shall meet to select an impartial arbitrator. If no agreement is reached at this meeting, the parties shall, immediately and jointly, request the American Arbitration Association, State Conciliation and Mediation Service or the Federal Mediation and Conciliation Service to submit to them a panel of ten (10) arbitrators from which the State and AFSCME shall alternately strike names until one name remains and this person shall be the arbitrator.

c. The parties agree to make reasonable efforts to schedule the arbitration hearing within ninety (90) days of the appeal to arbitration. This time frame shall be waived by mutual agreement.

d. The arbitration hearing shall be conducted in accordance with the Voluntary Labor Arbitration Rules of the American Arbitration Association. The cost of the arbitration shall be borne equally between the parties.

e. An arbitrator may, upon request of AFSCME and the State, issue his/her decision, opinion, or award orally upon submission of the arbitration. Either party may request that the arbitrator put his/her decision, opinion, or award in writing and that a copy be provided.

f. The arbitrator shall not have the power to add to, subtract from, or modify this Agreement. Only grievances as defined in "Definitions" of this Article shall be subject to arbitration. In all arbitration cases, the award of the arbitrator shall be final and binding upon the parties.

g. Arbitration awards for actions which affect classes of employees which involve State funds are to be prospectively enforced from the date of filing of the grievance. Any claims for failure by the State to maintain the status quo will not be covered by this provision. Class is defined as all employees similarly situated as to the claims being made.

5.13 GRIEVANCE RESPONSES

At each step of the grievance procedure, the State's response shall be attached to the original grievance with all its attachments and delivered to the grievant's regular work station, mail box or home address in an envelope marked "confidential". A copy of the response shall go to the representative indicated on the grievance form at the same time.

5.14 FAILURE TO RESPOND

If the State fails to respond to a grievance within the time limits specified for that step, the grievant shall have the right to appeal to the next step.

Chapter**EIGHT**

Workplace Violence

Workplace violence (WPV) is a problem that public employers can ill afford to ignore. On an almost daily basis, the media report dramatic and often bloody episodes of violence in government sites as well as in corporate buildings and offices. Establishing policies and programs designed to prevent workplace violence and to respond effectively when it takes place is a responsibility usually assigned to human resources offices or management teams that include human resources specialists. In addition to an overview of the challenges posed by WPV, we summarize the findings of a recent survey of U.S. local governments' policies and programs in this area (Nigro and Waugh, 1998a; Nigro and Waugh, 1998b).

WPV has received increasing attention from human resources specialists in the public and private sectors as they confront disturbing information about the risks it poses to workers on all levels of their organizations. During the 1990s, for example, managers and policy makers in the United States have learned that:

- During the average year, about 15 percent of all violent crimes occur in the workplace.
- Homicide accounts for about one in six fatal work injuries.
- Department of Justice statistics for 1995 revealed that over one million violent crimes took place in the workplace.
- Federal, state, and local workers were about 30 percent of the victims of WPV, although they were about 18 percent of the U.S. workforce. (Nigro and Waugh, 1996; U.S. Department of Justice, 1994; U.S. Department of Labor, 1996a)

Agencies such as the National Institute of Occupational Safety and Health (NIOSH), the Occupational Safety and Health Administration (OSHA), the Centers for Disease Control and Prevention (CDC), and the Federal Protective Service (FPS) have urged employers in all sectors to recognize the risks posed by WPV and to take steps designed to prevent it, as well as to deal with its consequences if it should happen (U.S. Department of Labor, 1996b; Lewis, 1995; U.S. Department of Health and Human Services, 1993; U.S. Department of Justice, 1994; U.S. General Services Administration, 1996).

Until the 1990s, most public employers had been slow to adopt policies and related programs specifically addressing WPV risks, prevention, and responses. Unfortunately, most of the exceptions to this pattern were reactions to tragic and widely reported events, such as a series of multiple murders in and around facilities of the U.S. Postal Service (Baxter and Margavio, 1996). The term "going postal" is now used to describe employees who, for whatever reason, become violent, sometimes killing their supervisors, coworkers, and others in the workplace. It should be noted that associating workplace homicide with the Postal Service is somewhat unfair, since it employs well over 800,000 people, and its homicide rate has not exceeded the national rate for all employers. Over the past 10 years, public employers have begun to recognize WPV as a meaningful safety and liability issue, one that now requires more than a passive or reactive approach to prevention and mitigation (Nigro and Waugh, 1996).

The available information suggests that WPV, particularly homicide, is a workplace hazard to be taken seriously (Kelleher, 1996). There is, however, a broadening recognition among employers that WPV involves far more than murder by workers, clients-customers, and intruders, including domestic and international terrorists (Yohay and Peppe, 1996). Public employers often apply definitions of workplace violence that go beyond criminal assault and homicide, sometimes called Occupational Violent Crime or OVC. Books, professional articles, and government reports on the threat posed by WPV are now easy to find, as is the growing body of prescriptions about how to prevent and respond to it. While the bombing of the Murrah Federal Building in Oklahoma City was a focusing event for those concerned about protecting government facilities from attacks by terrorists, most acts of WPV in the United States have nothing to do with the actions of terrorists. The National Institute for Occupational Safety and Health (NIOSH) has noted that:

> Defining workplace violence has generated considerable discussion. Some would include in the definition any language or actions that make one person uncomfortable in the workplace; others would

include any bodily injury inflicted by one person on another. Thus the spectrum of workplace violence ranges from offensive language to homicide, and a reasonable definition of workplace violence is as follows: *violent acts, including physical assaults and threats of assault, directed toward persons at work or on duty.* (National Institute for Occupational Safety and Health, 1996, p. 1)

A Florida city, for example, uses the following definition of WPV: "Violence in the workplace shall be defined as making threats, exhibiting threatening behavior and/or engaging in violent acts on City property by an employee, contractor/vendor, spouse or ex-spouse, family member, friend, or any member of the general public" (City of Coconut Creek, 1996).

Many public employers have yet to make serious efforts to identify risk factors, to develop strategies for preventing violence, or to implement response plans. There is, however, a growing recognition among human resources specialists that this problem needs to be addressed in a systematic manner. In fact, a rapidly growing proportion of public employers now has WPV policies and related programs in place. In today's climate, human resources specialists are being asked to do more than simply call the police if violence by psychologically disturbed employees, clients, or intruders is threatened or takes place. WPV, in other words, is now understood to be as much an organizational concern as it is a law enforcement problem.

WPV has many causes. Contemporary thinking requires that human resources specialists be able to help managers understand the potential for violence resulting from adverse actions, interpersonal conflict between workers and their supervisors, authoritarian and abusive management styles, and citizen unhappiness with public policies and organizational performance. Violence by substance abusers is also a real concern. Sexual violence and violence rooted in racism or cultural clashes may be newer concerns, but they now are generally familiar issues for human resources management offices. Recent high-profile cases involving family violence have raised awareness of the problems caused by spousal abuse and other forms of violence by family members or other intimates, as well. Finally, as the Oklahoma City bombing and attempted bombings of other public facilities illustrate, political violence also has become a highly visible threat to some public employers, particularly the federal government. Greater attention is being paid to the vulnerability of public employees to violence by individuals or groups opposed to government in general or to specific policies or actions.

Although they are relatively infrequent, incidents of politically motivated violence have probably fueled public employers' efforts to deal with WPV. There are also worries about exposure to street crime.

Government facilities are often located in deteriorating downtown business districts. These locations may expose public employees to higher levels of street crime as they go to and from work, and intruders are always a concern. Highly publicized shooting incidents in postal facilities, attempted bombings of law enforcement and regulatory agencies, and media reports of attacks on employees in the workplace have gained the attention of employers. The inconvenience of heightened building security has become a price that most public employees routinely are willing to pay in order to *feel* somewhat safer. The U.S. Office of Personnel Management points out that concentrating on dramatic episodes may draw attention away from significant risk factors:

> Planners of workplace violence programs face the dual challenge of reducing employees' anxiety about very rare risk factors while focusing their attention on more likely sources of danger. Undue anxiety about the "office gunman" can stand in the way of identifying more significant, but less dramatic, risk factors such as poorly lighted parking lots or gaps in employee training programs. This anxiety can also make it more difficult to cope with one of the most common workplace violence problems—the employee whose language or behavior frightens coworkers. (U.S. Office of Personnel Management, 1998)

ELEMENTS OF A WORKPLACE VIOLENCE PROGRAM

The U.S. Office of Personnel Management recently made available to all federal agencies via the Internet a publication entitled *Dealing with Workplace Violence: A Guide for Agency Planners*. The purposes of the *Guide* are (1) to set forth a process for developing an effective workplace violence program, (2) to provide "basic technical information in several areas of expertise that may be involved in workplace violence programs," and (3) to offer guidance for planners and managers "based on the collective expertise and experience of Federal Government law enforcement officers, security specialists, criminal investigators, attorneys, employee relations specialists, Employee Assistance Counselors, forensic psychologists, and union officials" (U.S. Office of Personnel Management, 1998, p. 1). A central theme of the *Guide* is that preparation and investments in deterrence are critical: "A little preparation and investment in prevention *now* could save a life." It provides a useful overview of the four main elements of a workplace violence program.

PROGRAM DEVELOPMENT

A planning group should be established to (1) evaluate the agency's existing capacity to handle potentially violent situations, (2) identify internal training needs or sources of outside expertise, (3) develop a procedure for employees to report incidents, and (4) create plans for responding to violent incidents. The planning group should include representatives from key sectors of the organization, such as line management, security, human resources, EEO, legal office, risk management, and union representatives.

DEVELOPMENT OF A WRITTEN POLICY STATEMENT

Policy statements should emphasize that everybody is responsible for maintaining workplace safety and that top management is committed to dealing with reported incidents in an effective and timely manner. A well-crafted policy will encourage employees to report violence, intimidation, harassment, and other forms of workplace violence, and it should specify how and to whom such reports should be made. It is also very important that the policy clearly express management's promise to take steps designed to stop and prevent workplace violence and to actively support supervisors in their efforts to prevent and to respond to threats as well as to cases of actual violence.

PREVENTING WORKPLACE VIOLENCE

The central purpose of any workplace violence program is prevention through a variety of methods, including adequate security for facilities and areas surrounding government buildings and offices. It is also important that supervisors be aware of what is known about behavioral "indicators" of an increased risk of violence by a particular employee. All employees should receive appropriate training on how to report and respond to threats and violent acts, and supervisors need to understand how their management styles and uses of personnel procedures such as performance appraisals can "keep difficult situations from turning into major problems." In other words, supervisors should receive

---

BULLETIN

Indicators of Potentially Violent Individuals Identified by the Federal Bureau of Investigation

- Direct or veiled threats of harm;
- Intimidating, belligerent, bullying, or other inappropriate and aggressive behavior;
- Frequent conflicts with supervisors and coworkers;
- Bringing a weapon to the workplace, brandishing a weapon in the workplace, making inappropriate references to guns, or fascination with weapons;
- Statements showing fascination with incidents of workplace violence and approval of violence as way of resolving conflicts;
- Indications of desperation and threats of suicide related to personal problems;
- Drug and/or alcohol abuse; and
- Extreme changes in normal patterns of behavior.

Source: U.S. Office of Personnel Management, *Dealing with Workplace Violence: A Guide for Agency Planners* (Washington, DC), pp. 15–16.

training in effective general supervision as well as how to prevent and to deal with violence itself. Other ways of preventing violence are (1) using reasonable and legal preemployment screening techniques, such as background checks and drug testing, to minimize the likelihood that those predisposed to violence will be hired; and (2) supplementing traditional employee appeals procedures with alternative dispute resolution(ADR) procedures, which involve using a neutral third party to mediate and resolve disagreements and conflicts between members of the organization.

DEALING WITH WORKPLACE VIOLENCE

One recommended approach is to create incident response teams staffed by representatives of the organizational functions needed to prevent as well as respond to threats and acts of violence by employees, clients, and intruders. Typically, a response team would include representatives from security, human resources, employee assistance, and risk management. In addition to working closely with agency management, the team should build the working relationships with external law enforcement and emergency management organizations that are needed to mount a comprehensive and coordinated prevention and response effort. The training of incident response teams often is focused on practicing appropriate responses to a variety of scenarios, such as the two case studies in Appendix 8.A.

LOCAL GOVERNMENT RESPONSE TO WORKPLACE VIOLENCE:
SURVEY FINDINGS

Although the federal government has developed a broad-gauged and comprehensive approach to WPV over the past decade, as illustrated by OPM's *Guide*, the responses of the states and localities have been varied, ranging from doing nothing to implementing programs that mirror the federal approach. For example, a recent survey revealed that about one-third of cities and counties with populations over 100,000 had WPV policies and programs in place by 1998 (Nigro and Waugh, 1998a). The respondents' view of the level of risk or threat currently faced by their local governments was that it was probably exaggerated by the media and overstated in the professional literature. One of them expressed the opinion that WPV "is a very minor cause of work related injury and death. Media attention has created an issue [but] driver safety and other standard safety practices . . . would do more to reduce injury and death in the workplace, which should be the *real* issue." Well over half of the 315 respondents did believe,

Table 8.1 Perceived Sources of WPV in Local Governments (N = 309)

	Level of Perceived Threat			
Source	% High	% Medium	% Low	% MD
Clients	9.7	46.0	40.8	3.6
Coworkers	2.9	30.7	63.1	3.2
Strangers	3.6	27.5	65.4	3.6
Former employees	5.2	35.3	55.7	3.9
Inmates/prisoners	15.2	26.9	49.8	8.1
Relatives/family	4.5	38.5	52.8	4.2
Domestic terrorists	0.6	9.7	84.5	5.2
International terrorists	0.3	2.9	90.9	5.8

MD = Missing data

Source: Lloyd G. Nigro and William L. Waugh, Jr. "Workplace Violence Policies of U.S. Local Governments," *Public Administration Quarterly*, Vol. 22, No. 3 (Fall 1998), pp. 349–364.

nonetheless, that the danger posed by WPV in their jurisdictions had increased over the last 10 years and is worse for public employees in general. As we noted above, public employees are in fact more likely to be victims of WPV.

As the OPM states in its *Guide* for federal agencies, while homicides and acts of political terrorism receive the greatest attention, WPV comes in a wide variety of forms that are much more common. Local government personnel directors, seem to understand this point, as shown in Table 8.1. The potential sources of WPV identified by 40 percent or more as being "high" or "medium" in intensity are by far the most frequently addressed in professional journals and books, as well as by the mass media. The very low level of threat assigned to domestic and international terrorists is noteworthy, especially since the survey was conducted after the bombing of the Murrah Building in Oklahoma City.

Very few of the respondents actually had been assaulted or injured, but quite a few reported that they had been threatened or felt in immediate danger at some time during their careers. Many of them knew about threats and attacks against others in the workplace, as shown in Table 8.2.

As of 1998, most U.S. cities and counties did not have a WPV policy, and the typical reasons given for this state of affairs were (1) that WPV was not seen by policy makers as a problem for the jurisdiction; and (2) in any case, existing personnel rules and regulations were deemed sufficient to handle any rare episodes of violence. WPV,

Table 8.2 The Respondents' WPV-Related Experiences

Experience	% Responding "Yes"
Felt in personal danger (N = 305)	24.6
Had been threatened (N = 305)	32.1
Had been assaulted (N = 304)	2.6
Had been injured (N = 304)	1.3
Had known a coworker who was attacked (N = 305)	25.6
Had known of someone attacked in their agency or building (N = 304)	55.6
Had a family member attacked or threatened at work (N = 304)	12.8

Source: Nigro and Waugh, "Workplace Violence Policies."

Table 8.3 Major Actors in Developing Local Government WPV Policies

Actor	Combined %	City %	County %
Director of HR	79.3	83.6	75.0
Appointed CEO	29.3	34.5	23.3
Legal counsel	28.4	30.9	25.0
Elected CEO	16.4	23.6	10.0
Other elected	12.1	9.1	15.0
Other appointed	9.5	12.7	6.7
Employee groups	7.8	7.3	8.3
Employee unions	6.9	5.5	8.3
Community groups	1.7	1.8	1.7
Other actors*	32.8	25.5	38.3

*Most frequently cited "others" were: risk manager, security/safety manager, employee assistance program manager, and police department personnel. Of the balance, most were offices or personnel directly related to human resources or personnel management.

Source: Nigro and Waugh, "Workplace Violence Policies."

in other words, was simply not seen as a serious threat or to be one that could not be handled by the existing human resources program. The national trend, nonetheless, is for more and more localities to adopt WPV policies and programs. Most existing policies and programs were implemented after 1989, and many of the respondents to the survey indicated that they were working on policies that should be in place by the end of the 1990s.

Table 8.4 Types of Violence Addressed by Local Government's WPV Policies (N = 117)

Type of Violence	Overall %	City %	County %
Coworker conflict	79.1	84.6	74.1
Worker-manager conflict	78.2	86.5	70.7
Employee-intimates violence	71.8	69.2	74.1
Discipline-related violence	73.6	78.8	70.0
Family–personal problems conflicts	70.0	76.9	63.8
Violence by intruders	72.7	73.1	72.4
Drug-alcohol abuse related	65.5	65.4	65.5
By employees against clients	62.7	65.4	60.3
Related to dismissals	67.3	73.1	62.1
Violence against women	64.5	65.4	63.8
Related to RIFs	50.0	55.8	44.8
By prisoners or other	45.4	47.1	43.1
Institutionalized persons	30.9	25.0	36.2
By terrorists against employees	27.3	28.8	25.9
Other sources of WPV	10.9	3.8	17.2

Source: Nigro and Waugh, "Workplace Violence Policies."

Directors of Personnel and Human Resources Offices have taken the lead in developing and implementing WPV policies and programs. City and county managers have also taken a leadership role in this area, particularly in cities. Similarly, members of legal counsel were frequently identified as important contributors. As Table 8.3 shows, the typical coalition behind a WPV policy included the director of human resources, the appointed CEO, the legal counsel, and one or more specialists in security, liability, and employee services.

What do local governments' WPV policies cover? Some address only a few kinds of situations and forms of violence, while others are wide-ranging in their coverage. Table 8.4 summarizes the survey's findings in this regard. The typical policy covers violence arising from interpersonal conflicts involving workers and their families, acts related to drug and alcohol abuse, violence precipitated by adverse actions, and assaults and homicides by intruders. It is less likely to cover attacks by clients against employees, violence stemming from reductions in force, or violence by persons being held against their will by the employer (prisoners and persons institutionalized for medical or psychiatric reasons). Preventing and responding to attacks by terrorists of all kinds is covered in only about 27 percent of the cases. At least with regard to the threat posed by terrorists, coverage in those cities and counties with WPV policies seems to be a reflection of a general tendency to believe that terrorists, domestic as well as international, are not much of a threat to local governments. The relatively high coverage in the area of violence by employees against clients (in comparison to clients against employees) is probably a reflection of problems associated with institutional settings, such as hospitals and correctional facilities, where ill-trained or inadequately supervised staff may physically attack inmates.

With regard to programs intended to implement WPV policies, there are at least five potential areas of administrative activity: (1) improving the physical security of buildings and other facilities, (2) collecting, analyzing and disseminating information related to WPV, (3) establishing effective procedures for reporting and dealing with WPV, (4) employee support and training investments, and (5) building cooperative relationships with external agencies and departments outside human resources.

SECURITY STUDIES AND TARGET HARDENING

While about 60 percent of the programs included studies to identify potential hazards in the work site, actual "target-hardening" activities were reported by fewer than half of the cities and counties that responded to the survey. Target hardening, as the term suggests, refers to steps such as the installation of better lighting, locks, closed-circuit cameras, metal detectors, and protective barriers, and the hiring of professional security guards. Concern about security arrangements was a recurring theme in many of the written comments made by the respondents. Of 303 who replied to a question asking if their jurisdiction had good security for its facilities, 159 said "no." One, in response to a question about what more needed to be done, said in part, "Utilize security on all city premises . . . [and] make offices more conducive to a safe environment; add bullet proof glass at centers; add cipher locks on doors; and have an appointment system for customer-oriented jobs." A second called for "greater security in parking lots and better street lighting in all areas." Another reported that, "we are moving from less reliable contract guards to a combination of cameras, electronic alarms, identification badges, access control, and roving police officers."

INFORMATION

Dissemination of WPV-related information was found to be a fairly common feature of local governments' programs. Over half of the cities and counties with programs reported that they provided infor-

Table 8.5 WPV Program Components: Employee Support and Training (N = 113)	
Component	**Percentage Including**
Employee Assistance Program	90.3
Counseling and debriefing for victims and witnesses	76.1
Worker safety and/or health teams	38.9
Mandatory training of employees to deal with WPV and threats	42.5
Conflict management and resolution training for supervisors	69.0

Source: Lloyd G. Nigro and William L. Waugh, Jr., "Local Government Responses to Workplace Violence," *Review of Public Personnel Administration,* Vol. 18, No. 4 (Fall 1998), pp. 5–17.

mation on WPV and the jurisdiction's prevention and response plans and activities. Management information systems for purposes of trend analysis and program evaluation are much less common, with around 20 percent having such systems. Information systems focused on accurately documenting cases of WPV have been established by about 40 percent of the local governments with programs.

PROCEDURES

There is a high level of attention to administrative procedures by local governments with WPV policies. Many of the respondents' comments addressed this area. One wrote: "I think we need to put together a specific policy on workplace violence which spells out what people should do in a variety of situations." Other ideas included "establishing a planning committee to create procedures to follow, investigation, reporting, and aftermath," doing "more thorough background checks," and "developing a multiagency task force to develop a prevention and action plan." In one local government, "A workplace violence response team may be activated by HR, which includes law enforcement, legal, safety, EAP, and appropriate department heads." Also, with regard to "zero tolerance" as a management stance, another human resources director urged that WPV programs be administered in ways designed to "continue assurances in the workplace that even the slightest act of hostile behavior will be dealt with in an aggressive manner."

EMPLOYEE SUPPORT AND TRAINING

Local governments appear to be quite active in the general area covered by Table 8.5, and many of the comments were in this category. Employee/victims' assistance programs and conflict management training, for example, are widespread features of WPV programs. Topics addressed through written comments included the need for employee "wellness" and assistance programs, the desirability of training in a variety of areas such as domestic violence and conflict resolution, and the importance of creating a psychologically supportive work environment: "Treat employees, citizens, and other contacts with dignity and respect."

COOPERATIVE RELATIONSHIPS

About a third of the local governments with WPV programs had made some effort to coordinate and/or liaison with external agencies. Very few had gone so far as to merge WPV with comprehensive multijurisdictional emergency management and disaster response agencies. Observers often point out the need to establish inter-agency coordination and cooperation as integral elements of a general effort to prevent as well as to deal with episodes of WPV. One of the respondents noted this by saying that there was a need to "continue building interagency partnerships and . . . to [establish] proactive relationships with law enforcement. . . ."

CONCLUSION

Given growing concern in professional circles as well as media attention, the pace of change in this area is likely to accelerate, and the percentage of local governments with broadly framed policies and programs will almost certainly increase

---

BULLETIN

From the Federal Protective Service: Guidance on How to Act in Threatening Situations

For an angry or hostile customer or coworker
- Stay calm. Listen attentively.
- Maintain eye contact.
- Be courteous. Be patient.
- Keep the situation in your control.

For a person shouting, swearing, and threatening
- Signal a coworker, or supervisor, that you need help. (Use a duress alarm system or prearranged code words.)
- Do not make any calls yourself.
- Have someone call the FPS, contract guard, or local police.

For somone threatening you with a gun, knife, or other weapon
- Stay calm. Quietly signal for help.
- Maintain eye contact.
- Stall for time.
- Keep talking—but follow instructions from the person who has the weapon.
- Don't risk harm to yourself or others.
- Never try to grab a weapon.
- Watch for a safe chance to escape to a safe area.

The FPS is a unit of the U.S. General Services Administration.

significantly over the next five to ten years. On the local level, city and county offices of human resources will play a major role in both the formulation and implementation of WPV policy. Workplace violence has been added to the long list of controversial issues, complex problems, and difficult challenges confronting local government administrators, particularly those professionals who specialize in human resources policy and management. Human resources agencies will inevitably find themselves on the "front lines" of an effort to respond effectively to the threats posed by WPV.

Clearly, many of the causes of WPV originate in the larger society, and public employers can do little to control or eliminate them. The National Institute for Occupational Safety and Health (NIOSH) points out that, "We cannot wait to address workplace violence as a social issue alone but must take immediate action to address it as a serious occupational safety issue" (National Institute for Occupational Safety and Health, 1996, p. 2). In addition to developing effective ways of anticipating and preventing WPV, human resources offices should take steps designed to prepare their organizations to respond in a planned and coordinated manner if it does happen. In NIOSH's words:

> [N]o definitive strategy will ever be appropriate for all workplaces [but] we must begin to change the way work is done in certain settings to minimize or remove the risk of workplace violence. We must also change the way we think about workplace violence by shifting the emphasis from reactionary approaches to prevention, and by embracing workplace violence as an occupational safety and health issue. (p. 2)

DISCUSSION QUESTIONS

1. What are the three most important steps public employers could take to prevent WPV?
2. Why are public employees relatively more at risk from WPV than private-sector workers?
3. In your experience, are most supervisors sensitive to the possibility that their treatment of subordinates may result in violence?
4. Are the buildings and facilities where you work secure?
5. Does your employer have a WPV policy? If not, why? If so, what does it say?
6. Why should alternative dispute resolution (ADR) programs be a part of a WPV prevention strategy?

REFERENCES

Baxter, Vern, and Margavio, Anthony (1996). "Assaultive Violence in the U.S. Post Office." *Work and Occupations,* Vol. 23 (August), pp. 277–296.

City of Coconut Creek (1996). *Administrative Order on Violence in the Workplace,* City of Coconut Creek, Florida (September).

Kelleher, Michael D. (1996). *New Arenas for Violence: Homicide in the American Workplace* (Westport, CT: Praeger).

Lewis, Janice S. (1995). "Workplace Violence: Information Sources." *RQ: Reference Quarterly,* Vol. 34 (Spring), pp. 287–295.

National Institute for Occupational Safety and Health (1996). *Violence in the Workplace: Risk Factors and Prevention Strategies,* Publication No. 96-10 (Washington, DC: U.S. Department of Health and Human Services).

Nigro, Lloyd G., and Waugh, William L., Jr. (1996). "Violence in the American Workplace: Challenges to the Public Employer." *Public Administration Review,* Vol. 56, No. 4 (July–August), pp. 326–333.

———— (1998a). "Workplace Violence Policies of U.S. Local Governments." *Public Administration Quarterly,* Vol. 22, No. 3 (Fall), pp. 349–364.

———— (1998b). "Local Government Responses to Workplace Violence." *Review of Public Personnel Administration,* Vol. 18, No. 4 (Fall), pp. 5–17.

U.S. Department of Health and Human Services (1993). *Alert: Request for Assistance in Preventing Homicide in the Workplace* (Washington, DC: Centers for Disease Control and Prevention), September.

U.S. Department of Justice (1994). *Crime Data Brief: Violence and Theft in the Workplace,* NCJ-148199 (Washington, DC: Bureau of Justice Statistics), July.

U.S. Department of Labor (1996a). *Fatal Work Injuries and Work Hazards: Job-Related Homicides Profiled,* Fact Sheet CFOI 96-2 (Washington, DC: Bureau of Labor Statistics, Office of Safety, Health, and Working Conditions), August.

———— (1996b). *Guidelines for Workplace Violence Prevention Programs for Night Retail Establishments* (Washington, DC: Occupational Safety and Health Administration), June.

U.S. General Services Administration (1996). *What You Should Know About Coping with Threats and Violence in the Federal Workplace.* (Washington, DC: U.S. Protective Service) (http://www.gsa.gov/pbs/fps/fps1.html).

U.S. Office of Personnel Management (1998). *Dealing with Workplace Violence: A Guide for Agency Planners* (http://www.opm.gov/workplac/index. htm), April.

Yohay, Stephen C., and Peppe, Melissa L. (1996). "Workplace Violence: Employer Responsibilities and Liabilities." *Occupational Hazards,* Vol. 58 (July), pp. 21–26.

SUGGESTED READINGS

Braverman, Mark (1999). *Preventing Workplace Violence: A Guide for Employers and Practitioners* (Thousand Oaks, CA: Sage Publications, Inc.).

Dickinson, Philip D. (1997). *Workplace Violence & Employer Liability* (Brentwood, TN: M. Lee Smith Publishers and Printers).

Heskett, Sandra L. (1996). *Workplace Violence: Before, During & After* (Worburn, MA: Butterworth-Heinemann).

Minor, Marianne, and Henry, Carol, eds. (1994). *Preventing Workplace Violence: Positive Management Strategies* (Menlo Park, CA: Crisp Publications, Inc.).

Southerland, Mittie D., Collins, Pamela, and Scarborough, Kathryn E. (1997). (Cincinnati, OH: Anderson Publishing Co.).

CASE STUDY

Case Study 1 –
A Shooting

The Incident

The report comes in: Two employees have been killed in the workplace and two have been wounded. A witness has called 911 and the police and ambulances have arrived. The perpetrator (an agency employee) has been taken into custody, the victims are being sent to the hospital, and the police are interviewing witnesses and gathering evidence.

Response

In this situation, the agency's crisis response plan called for the immediate involvement of:

(1) A top management representative,

(2) A security officer,

(3) An employee relations specialist,

(4) An Employee Assistance Program counselor, and

(5) An official from the public affairs office.

Top management representative. The manager, an Assistant Director of a field office with 800 employees, coordinated the response effort because she was the senior person on duty at the time. In addition to acting as coordinator, she remained available to police throughout the afternoon to make sure there were no impediments to the investigation.

She immediately called the families of the wounded and assigned two other senior managers to notify the families of the deceased. She also arranged for a friend of each of the deceased coworkers to accompany each of the managers. She took care of numerous administrative details, such as authorizing expenditures for additional resources, signing forms, and making decisions about such matters as granting leave to coworkers. (In this case, the police evacuated the building, and employees were told by the Assistant Director that they could go home for the rest of the day, but that they were expected to return to duty the following day.) To ensure a coordinated response effort, she made sure that agency personnel involved in the crisis had cell phones for internal communication while conducting their duties in various offices around the building.

Security staff. The security staff assisted the police with numerous activities such as evacuating the building.

Employee Relations Specialist. The employee relations specialist contacted the agency's Office of the General Counsel (OGC) and Office of Inspector General (OIG) and alerted them to the situation so that they could immediately begin to monitor any criminal proceedings. He made a detailed written record of the incident, but he did not take statements from witnesses because it could have impeded the criminal investigation and possible subsequent prosecution of the case. He also helped the supervisor draft a letter of proposed indefinite suspension pending the outcome of the potential criminal matter. He worked closely

continued page 262

with the OGC, OIG, and prosecutor's office to obtain relevant information as soon as it was available so the agency could proceed with administrative action when appropriate.

Employee Assistance Program (EAP) counselor. The agency had only one EAP counselor on duty at the time. However, in prior planning for an emergency, the agency had contracted with a local company to provide additional counselors on an "as needed" basis. The one EAP counselor on duty called the contractor and four additional counselors were at the agency within an hour. The counselors remained available near the scene of the incident to reassure and comfort the employees. Since they were not agency employees, they wore readily visible identification badges.

After the Office of Inspector General received permission from the prosecutor's office, the agency EAP counselor arranged for a series of Critical Incident Stress Debriefings (CISD) to take place two days later (see page 136 for a discussion of CISD). She also arranged for two contract EAP counselors to be at the workplace for the next week to walk around the offices inquiring how the employees were doing and to consult with supervisors about how to help the employees recover.

Public Affairs Officer. The Public Affairs Officer handled all aspects of press coverage. She maintained liaison with the media, provided an area for reporters to work, and maintained a schedule of frequent briefings. She worked closely with the agency's Office of Congressional Relations, who handled calls from congressional offices about the incident.

Questions for the Agency Planning Group

1. How would your agency have obtained the services of additional EAP counselors?

2. How would employees be given information about this incident?

3. Who would clean up the crime scene?

4. Would you relocate employees who worked in the area of the crime scene?

5. What approach would your agency take regarding granting excused absence on the day of the incident and requests for leave in the days/weeks following the incident?

6. How would you advise management to deal with work normally assigned to the victims/perpetrator?

7. What support would your agency provide to supervisors to get the affected work group(s) back to functioning?

continued page 263

CASE STUDY

Case Study 4 – Stalking

The Incident

A supervisor called the Employee Relations office to request a meeting of the workplace violence team for assistance in handling a situation he's just learned about. He was counseling one of his employees about her frequent unscheduled absences, when she told him a chilling story of what she's been going through for the past year. She broke up with her boyfriend a year ago and he's been stalking her ever since. He calls her several times a week (she hangs up immediately). He shows up wherever she goes on the weekends and just stares at her from a distance. He often parks his car down the block from her home and just sits there. He's made it known he has a gun.

Response

This agency's plan calls for the initial involvement of security, the Employee Assistance Program (EAP), and employee relations in cases involving stalking. The security officer, the EAP counselor, and employee relations specialist met first with the supervisor and then with the employee and supervisor together. At the meeting with the employee, after learning as much of the background as possible, they gave her some initial suggestions.

♦ Contact her local police and file a report. Ask them to assess her security at home and make recommendations for improvements.

♦ Log all future contacts with the stalker and clearly record the date, time, and nature of the contact.

♦ Let voice mail screen incoming phone calls.

♦ Contact her own phone company to report the situation.

♦ Give permission to let her coworkers know what was going on (she would not agree to do this).

♦ Vary her routines, e.g., go to different shops, take different routes, run errands at different times, report to work on a variable schedule.

The team then worked out the following plan:

1. The **Employee Relations** specialist acted as coordinator of the response effort. He made a written report of the situation and kept it updated. He kept the team members, the supervisor, and the employee apprised of what the others were doing to resolve the situation. He also looked into the feasibility of relocating the employee to another worksite.

2. The **Security** officer immediately reported the situation to the local police. With the employee's consent, she also called the police where the employee lived to learn what steps they could take to help the employee. She offered to coordinate and exchange information with them. The security officer arranged for increased surveillance of the building and circulated photos of the stalker to all building guards with instructions to detain him if he showed up at the building. She brought a tape recorder to the employee's desk and showed her the best way to tape any future voice mail messages from the stalker. She also contacted the agency's phone company to arrange for its involvement in the case.

continued page 264

3. The **Employee Assistance Program** counselor provided support and counseling for both the employee and the supervisor throughout the time this was going on. He suggested local organizations that could help the employee. He also tried to convince her to tell coworkers about the situation.

4. The **Union** arranged to sponsor a session on stalking in order to raise the consciousness of agency employees about the problem in general.

After a week, when the employee finally agreed to tell coworkers what was going on, the EAP counselor and security officer jointly held a meeting with the whole work group to discuss any fears or concerns they had and give advice on how they could help with the situation.

Resolution

In this case, the employee's coworkers were supportive and wanted to help out. They volunteered to watch out for the stalker and to follow other security measures recommended by the security specialist. The stalker ended up in jail because he tried to break into the employee's home while armed with a gun. The security officer believes that the local police were able to be more responsive in this situation because they had been working together with agency security on the case.

Questions for the Agency Planning Group

1. Do you agree with the agency's approach in this case?

2. What would you do in a similar situation if your agency doesn't have security guards?

3. What would you do if coworkers were too afraid of the stalker to work in the same office with the employee?

4. What would you do if/when the stalker gets out of jail on bail or out on probation?

5. Would your Office of Inspector General have gotten involved in this case, e.g., coordinated agency efforts with local law enforcement agencies?

Chapter NINE

Drugs, Alcohol, and Tobacco: Substance Abuse in the Workplace

When the authors of the Pendleton Act included a section stating "[t]hat no person habitually using intoxicating beverages to excess shall be appointed to, or retained in, any office, appointment, or employment to which the provisions of this act are applicable," they were addressing a fact of American life: a very long and well-documented history of using and abusing alcohol and other intoxicating substances. Public employers have not been insulated from the problems caused by substance abuse. In 1829, Postmaster General Amos Kendall was moved to issue rules of conduct for federal employees, including one warning that "[g]ambling, drunkenness, and irregular and immoral habits will subject any clerk to instant removal."

The failed experiment with prohibition and today's faltering "war against drugs" illustrate how difficult it has been to control, much less eliminate, the widespread use of illegal drugs and the abuse of alcohol by Americans. During the past decade, smoking has been added to the list of threats to workers' health that employers are being asked to address. Like other problems, they are not left at the front door when public employees come to work. Left unattended, they threaten to undermine productivity, to compromise workplace safety, and to lower public confidence in government.

For the entire U.S. workforce, available research indicates that there are about 10 million illegal drug users, and about 500 million workdays are lost to alcoholism every year. One study found "substance abuse to be the number one health problem in the country, resulting in more deaths, illnesses, and disabilities than any other preventable health condition" (Rhodes, 1998, p. 136). The public sector's share of the costs associated with substance abuse in all of its forms is probably about 20 percent, since there is no evidence to suggest that the situation faced by public employers is significantly better or worse than that confronted by their private counterparts.

Public attention, and that of policy makers, has been focused on illegal drugs such as cocaine, marijuana, and heroin. Alcohol abuse, nonetheless, is still the single most pervasive problem confronted on a day-to-day basis by employers (French et al., 1995). One expert who has studied substance abuse in the workplace for many years estimated that around 8 percent of workers abuse alcohol, "twice the level of any other single drug" (Bornstein, 1989, p. 46).   In other words, while there are important social, political, and organizational reasons for the current policy emphasis on illegal drugs, the abuse of alcohol (a legal drug in most jurisdictions) has not declined and it continues to be a significant problem for public employers. According to one estimate, "The cost to the United States of this one addiction is calculated at up to $43 billion annually. This includes the costs of job absenteeism, health and welfare services, property damage, accidents, and medical expenses" (Rhodes, 1998, p. 136).

Other facts related to drug use in the workplace include:

- The overall rate of positive tests for drugs is down somewhat in recent years. In 1997, about 5.4 percent were positive, which is much lower than the over 18 percent rate in 1987.
- Of the positive tests in 1997, 59 percent were for marijuana, 18 percent involved cocaine, 8 percent were opiates-related, and other drugs like PCP made up the balance.
- Abuse of prescription drugs appears to be increasing. These include painkillers, antianxiety drugs, and stimulants. (Bahls, 1998)

BULLETIN

The Costs of Drug Use

"Consider the numbers. The U.S. Department of Labor estimates that drug use in the workplace costs employers $75 billion to $100 billion annually in lost time, accidents, health care and workers' compensation costs. Sixty-five percent of all accidents on the job are directly related to drugs or alcohol. Substance abusers are absent three times more often and use 16 times as many health care benefits as nonabusers."

Source: Jane Easter Bahls, *HRMagazine,* Vol. 43, No. 2 (February, 1998), p. 81.

Another addictive behavior that has received great attention recently is smoking and, more broadly, the use of all tobacco products. The health risks posed to users of tobacco products are well documented, and there is growing concern about the effects of second-hand smoke on others in the workplace. In response, a rapidly growing proportion of public as well as private employers has banned smoking entirely or limited it to certain areas. Some employers have gone so far as to hire only nonsmokers and to require all employees to quit if local laws and labor contracts permit such policies (Pulliam, 1993/1994). Currently, about 80 percent of U.S. workers are covered by corporate smoking policies, and that percentage is even higher in the public sector. One measure of the significance of smoking as an organizational problem is an Environmental Protection Agency (EPA) estimate that the annual cost of treating conditions related to second-hand smoke would be reduced by $2.7 billion if strict smoking bans were imposed. The EPA has also estimated that the savings from banning smoking in all public buildings produce a net benefit of up to $72 billion, and a "smoke-free society" should prevent between 7,000 and 13,000 deaths annually. Absenteeism increases with tobacco use, as it does with drug and alcohol abuse. Absenteeism rates for smokers run 50 percent higher than those of nonsmokers, and former smokers are more likely to take days off than those who have never smoked (Anonymous, 1997).

RESPONSES TO THE THREATS POSED BY DRUGS, ALCOHOL, AND SMOKING

In the current environment, testing for illegal drugs and alcohol has become a first line of defense for many public as well as private employers. From the employer's standpoint, the goals of a testing program are (1) to avoid hiring persons who are using illegal drugs, (2) to discourage all employees from using illegal drugs, (3) to prevent accidents related to drug and alcohol abuse by employees in safety-sensitive jobs, and (4) to obtain physical evidence if there is a reasonable suspicion that an employee is using illegal drugs or is under the influence of alcohol while at work. Most periodic testing focuses on illegal drugs, as opposed to alcohol. Drug tests take a variety of forms, including:

- Preemployment testing of job applicants. Applicants are informed that a positive test will automatically result in disqualification.
- Random testing of current employees, which is unannounced and not related to any suspicions about a specific person.

- Reasonable-cause testing, which is unannounced and based on events or behaviors that cause a supervisor to suspect an employee is under the influence of drugs or alcohol.
- Tests routinely administered to employees after they are involved in on-the-job accidents. (Sorohan, 1994)

In 1996, the American Management Association surveyed its membership (primarily large companies) and found that over 80 percent tested their employees for drugs. Of these, over 75 percent tested some or all new hires, almost 34 percent tested employees on a regular or random basis, and over 70 percent tested workers who were involved in accidents or suspected by supervisors of drug use (Bahls, 1998). Federal employers are required to periodically test workers in jobs where substance abuse poses a direct threat to public safety or national security, and agencies may test some or all job applicants, but testing of current employees is limited to cases where compelling reasons may be shown. The federal and state governments also require testing of persons working for private businesses in certain industries, such as transportation and nuclear power, if they occupy jobs that involve public safety (Sorohan, 1994).

Some public employers, most notably police departments, national security agencies, and the armed forces, have been routinely testing job applicants for many years. Mandatory drug tests based on "reasonable suspicion" are widely used, and random testing of police and corrections personnel have been upheld by most state and federal courts (Hickey and Reid, 1995). While preemployment testing is not particularly controversial, mandatory testing of some or all current employees has raised serious issues. In government, there has been considerable political pressure to ensure a "drug-free workplace" by testing all applicants for civil service positions and requiring large numbers of workers to submit to periodic testing as a condition of continued employment. In addition to the obvious question of whether this is an effective strategy for controlling substance abuse, it has raised serious legal issues.

For example, the Reagan administration issued an executive order (E.O. 12564) in 1986 requiring federal agencies to set up rather sweeping mandatory drug testing programs. Public employee organizations and others immediately challenged the constitutionality of mandatory drug testing, especially where there is no concrete reason to suspect that an employee is using illegal drugs. In large measure, they were successful, and the federal drug testing program was eventually limited to employees in safety-sensitive and national security jobs, reasonable suspicion cases, preemployment testing, and regular testing of employees undergoing or recently having completed drug rehabilitation programs and returned to work. One measure of the intensity of the issue was the number of federal court decisions on drug testing between 1987 and 1990: out of a total of 136 cases, 69 dealt with the public sector (Thompson, Riccucci, and Ban, 1991, p. 516). In general terms, the courts have taken steps to limit employers' drug testing programs by requiring that mandatory testing be limited to job applicants, for-cause or reasonable-suspicion tests of individuals, and random testing of workers in safety-related positions.

KEY SUPREME COURT DECISIONS ON DRUG TESTING

In 1989, the U.S. Supreme Court handed down two important decisions on drug and alcohol testing in the work-place. Its ruling in *Samuel K. Skinner, Secretary of Transportation et al. v Railway Labor Executives' Association et al.* reaffirmed a tradition of balancing public against individual interests in Fourth Amendment cases. This case dealt with the Federal Railroad Administration's (FRA) regulations requiring blood and urine tests of workers involved in train accidents. The FRA is a unit of the U.S. Department of Transportation (DOT). The railroad industry's effort to curb workers' use of alcohol and drugs were not yielding satisfactory results and, therefore, the FRA decided that government intervention was necessary. In the process of reviewing the industry's accident investigation reports, the FRA had identified a long list of serious incidents in which alcohol or drug use was a contributing factor. The resulting regulations allowed a railroad to require that all employees involved in a train accident submit to both blood and urine tests.

The Railway Labor Executives' Association and certain of its member organizations sued in federal district court, requesting that the FRA regulations be enjoined on statutory and constitutional grounds. The labor organizations based their case largely on the Fourth Amendment's provision that "the right of the people to be secure in their persons, houses, papers, and effects, against unreasonable searches and seizures, shall not be violated." The district court said that the railroad employees did "have a valid interest in the integrity of their own bodies" that deserved protection under the Fourth Amendment. However, it ruled that their interest was outweighed by the "public and governmental interest in the . . . protection of . . . railway safety, safety

---

BULLETIN

The Fourth Amendment

The right of the people to be secure in their persons, houses, papers, and effects, against unreasonable searches and seizures, shall not be violated, and no Warrants shall issue, but upon probable cause, supported by Oath or affirmation, and particularly describing the place to be searched and the persons or things to be seized.

for employees, and safety for the general public. . . ." Accordingly, it upheld the FRA regulations.

A divided panel of the Ninth Circuit Court of Appeals overruled the district court, saying that there had to be "reasonable suspicion" that the performance of an employee involved in an accident had been impaired by alcohol or drugs. Hearing the case on appeal, the Supreme Court upheld the FRA regulations. In essence, it agreed with the district court's reasoning that an overriding public interest in safety made testing of railroad employees constitutionally acceptable (*Skinner v Railway Labor Executives*, 1989).

The other case decided on March 21, 1989, was *International Treasury Employee Union et al. v Von Raab, Commissioner, United States Customs Service*. The issue here was the U.S. Customs Service's rules requiring testing of employees who were seeking transfers or promotions to positions: (1) in drug interdiction programs, (2) requiring authorization to carry firearms, or (3) involving the handling of classified materials. For these kinds of jobs, the last stage in the screening process was a requirement that the applicant pass a closely supervised urine test for illegal drugs.

The National Treasury Employees Union (NTEU) challenged the Customs Service's drug testing program in federal district court, arguing that it violated employees' Fourth Amendment rights. The district court agreed, finding that the program was an "overly intrusive policy of searches and seizures without probable cause or reasonable suspicion, in violation of legitimate expectations of privacy." It enjoined the testing program, but the circuit court of appeals vacated the injunction.

The circuit court stated that drug testing was indeed a search within the meaning of the Fourth Amendment, but it held that the Customs Service's program was "reasonable" because of its rational connection to the agency's law enforcement mission and its need to maintain public confidence in its integrity. In terms consistent with its reasoning in *Railway Labor Executives*, the Supreme Court upheld most of the Customs Service's testing program. It did exclude applicants for positions handling "classified material" because of the agency's lack of precision in defining that term and related criteria to be used in determining when drug testing should be used under this rubric.

The Court's reasoning in *NTEU v Von Raab* is instructive, especially for public employers contemplating drug testing programs. Referring to its decision in *Railway Labor Executives*, it stated that when a Fourth Amendment "intrusion" serves special governmental needs, it is always necessary to balance the individual's privacy expectations against the government's interests to establish if it is *impractical* to require a warrant or some level of individualized suspicion. In the opinion of the majority, the Customs Service's effectiveness would have been compromised if it had been "required to seek search warrants in connection with routine, yet sensitive, employment decisions." Further, under certain conditions, the government's need to know about and to prevent substance abuse by employees "is sufficiently compelling to justify the intrusion on privacy entailed by conducting such searches without . . . individualized suspicion"(*NTEU v Von Raab*, 1989).

The Supreme Court's rulings in these cases make it clear that it is not predisposed to agree with those who argue that *all* mandatory blood and urine tests are unconstitutional according to the Fourth Amendment. Employers should understand that such tests are "searches" and they must be "reasonable." There are, however, no universally accepted standards for judging the extent of the government's needs and the degree to which the intrusiveness of its actions are reasonable in relation to the privacy rights of citizens. Rather, the effort to balance public and individual interests requires a case-by-case approach, and this leaves ample room for judicial disagreement and public controversy.

Despite protests by employee organizations and other groups, a majority of the Supreme Court now appears to be inclined to give employers the benefit of the doubt on issues relating to the balancing of interests. However, its own rules require (1) that public employers demonstrate a rational connection between drug testing programs not involving individualized suspicion and the public interest, and (2) that they be able to show that such programs are not unreasonable violations of privacy under existing conditions.

COMPELLING REASONS

The federal courts have consistently invalidated drug testing programs when they have determined that public agencies do not have compelling reasons for them. A good example is the decision in *American Postal Workers Union, AFL-CIO, Boston Metro Area v Frank*.

BULLETIN

California Supreme Court Approves Testing for New Hires Only

"In 1997, the California Supreme Court ruled that state and local employers could require job applicants to take drug tests as a condition of employment, but they cannot require the same of current employees seeking promotion. The case arose from a 1986 City of Glendale policy under which applicants for hiring or promotion had to be screened for drugs and alcohol as a part of the required physical examination. This policy was challenged as a violation of the individual's right to be free from unreasonable searches and the right of privacy. On appeal of the trial court's decision, the Supreme Court 'concluded it was not constitutionally reasonable for the government to conduct suspicionless urinalysis drug testing of current public employees seeking a promotion without regard to the nature or duties of the position at issue.'"

Source: Wayne E. Barlow et al., "Court Okays Drug Tests for New Hires Only," *Workforce*, Vol. 76, No. 3 (March 1997), p. 110.

Starting in late 1986, the Postal Service administered drug tests to all applicants for career employment as part of a study to determine the relationships between the results of preemployment drug tests and job performance. The on-the-job performance of those who got jobs with the Postal Service was evaluated according to such criteria as absenteeism, discipline, injuries, and length of employment (turnover). Only the researchers and one data clerk had access to the drug test results.

The American Postal Workers Union challenged this project, raising three serious issues. First, applicants who might have had false positives had no chance to question the results. Department of Health and Human Services drug testing program certification standards required that employees have this opportunity. Second, the union's negotiated agreement with the Postal Service required the Service to offer assistance to workers with substance abuse problems. Under the federal guidelines, these workers should have been referred to an employee assistance program (EAP), and the health insurance plan included coverage for treatment of drug abuse. The research design precluded making such offers to those who tested positive. A study by the GAO had indicated that EAPs are relatively effective in helping victims of substance abuse, with over 50 percent of those testing positive completing rehabilitation and still working in so-called testing designated positions. Third, and finally, the union asserted that the anonymity of the test results increased the chance that workers using illegal drugs would end up operating machinery dangerous to themselves and coworkers (*NTEU v Frank,* 1989).

The federal judge deciding this case noted that Supreme Court rulings had "tipped the balance" in favor of the government on questions relating to the constitutionality of urinalysis drug testing for public employees occupying safety-related positions. In this case, however, the Postal Service's effort to study the relationships between drug use and productivity had gone too far and was unconstitutional.

Drug Test Accuracy and Interpretation

Critics of drug testing charge that perfect accuracy is never achieved by the available methods, and a certain percentage of false positives should be expected. This means that it is inevitable that some innocent employees and job applicants will be accused of using illegal drugs or abusing prescription drugs. At a minimum, therefore, a drug testing program should provide for retesting and appeals procedures.

The federal effort to limit the damage potentially caused by false positives has several components. In addition to a final review and interpretation by an experienced physician, tests must be conducted by Department of Health and Human Services certified laboratories, and positive tests are subjected to a second, more rigorous analysis. Like the federal government, most state and local governments require that a second confirmatory test be given before someone who initially tests positive may be discharged or denied employment.

Test accuracy depends on the quality of the laboratories doing the tests. A GAO study of drug testing procedures in the workplace revealed that:

■ There was no effective nationwide regulation of the many laboratories doing employee drug testing.

■ In some states, drug testing was controlled through statutes and regulations that deal with testing of employees.

■ In other states, control was exercised through general medical or chemical laboratory statutes and regulations that did not include specific drug testing standards.

■ Almost half the states had no laws or regulations applying to state or local employee drug testing. (U.S. General Accounting Office, 1988)

The American Management Association recommends that employers follow the National Institute of Drug Abuse's (NIDA) guidelines for drug testing and employ only NIDA-certified laboratories. The federal government requires laboratories to meet NIDA's *Mandatory Guidelines for Federal Workplace Drug Testing Programs.* These guidelines apply to all laboratories doing drug testing for federal employers. It is clearly in the best interest of all concerned that broadly accepted standards regulating laboratory staffing policies and technical operations be in force. In an area as sensitive as mandatory drug testing, sloppy testing procedures and doubts about accuracy may lead to legal challenges and a loss of confidence in the fairness and objectivity of drug testing programs.

In light of considerable political pressure on public employers to test more rather than fewer workers, critics of drug testing argue that it is already being overused. One line of reasoning in support of this conclusion is that "fishing expeditions" should not be substituted for testing based on "reasonable suspicion." Instead of random or universal testing of employees in safety or security-sensitive positions, employers should be required to show that there is a reasonable probability that someone is using illegal drugs before testing may be authorized. Reasonable suspicion, according to this argument, should be based on a person's *behavior,* not the *position* he or she holds. Public employee organizations have consistently favored suspicion-based testing, provided the employee has the right to appeal any management decision to require that he or she be tested. In the absence of overriding legislation, management and unions often negotiate the details of an employer's drug testing program.

A second line of criticism focuses on cost. Random or universal drug testing can be very expensive and, in terms of the number of genuine positives or "hits" obtained, highly inefficient. A report issued in 1992 by the U.S. House's Civil Service Subcommittee found that drug use among federal workers and applicants was so rare (well under 1 percent) that each positive test cost the taxpayers $77,000. A GAO report issued in 1991 had revealed that, in less than a year, some 40 federal agencies had conducted over 31,000 tests, yielding a grand total of 169 positives (U.S. General Accounting Office, 1991). Given the testing costs, the potential for heavy expenses associated with legal challenges by individuals and employee organizations, the potential for widespread employee dissatisfaction, and the possibility that recruitment efforts will be negatively affected, large-scale testing programs should be approached cautiously. As Thompson, Riccucci, and Ban (1991) put it, "one lesson of federal drug testing seems clear: employers who are considering the initiation or expansion of drug testing should view the federal program as a flashing red light. Stop; proceed with caution if at all" (p. 523).

Another trend is a search for less intrusive indicators of substance abuse and reliable ways of determining if performance is impaired. The traditional drug tests rely on urine and blood samples, but hair sampling is effective in some cases, and nonmedical performance testing may be an option. Urine and blood tests are highly intrusive, and there is potential for tampering. Laboratory analysis of hair samples can be used to determine if someone has used drugs during the 90-day period preceding the test, but urine or blood tests are still needed for accident investigations. Nonintrusive impairment tests, on the other hand, establish a performance "baseline" for each employee in areas such as perception, problem solving, and

BULLETIN

The Air Force Civilian Drug Testing Program

"[The] Program identifies specific positions, by title and grade, that are subject to random drug testing, reasonable suspicion drug testing, and drug testing due to direct involvement in an accident that resulted in injury or damage to property. . . .Upon assignment to a Testing Designated Position, an employee is provided with a notice being subject to drug testing. . . . Employees are randomly selected for testing using procedures similar to those in effect for military employees. If positive results are received from the laboratory, and the installation's Medical Review Officer concurs with the findings, then disciplinary and adverse action must be taken against the employee. . . .The first step is to refer the employee to the Employee Assistance Program for substance abuse counseling and treatment."

Source: (http://www.afpc.af.mil/permiss/per_data/592.htm), July 1, 1996.

hand-eye coordination. This baseline is then used to test the employee at regular intervals:

> [W]orkers pass or fail based on their past performance. According to manufacturers, the tests take between 30 seconds and three minutes to perform and are easy to learn and administer. . . .For example, the computer screen might display two randomly generated patterns of dots; the test-taker would indicate if the patterns are the same or different by pressing a button on the keypad. A failing score might be 20 percent or more below a person's baseline. Companies also would look for scores that suddenly improve dramatically, because certain drugs can temporarily heighten performance. (Sorohan, 1994, p. 117)

EDUCATION, INTERVENTION, AND REHABILITATION PROGRAMS

Until recently, most employers assumed that they had no formal responsibility to help their employees to avoid or to deal with problems arising from substance abuse. If alcoholism or drug addiction was undermining job performance and creating personal problems, workers should expect to be left to their own devices. No matter the causes, continued substandard performance was grounds for dismissal, demotion, or other adverse action. This way of handling employees with alcohol and drug abuse problems has now been replaced with an approach based on the idea that organizational commitments to education, intervention, and rehabilitation yield far better results for all concerned than the traditional punishment-centered model (Spencer, 1979).

Employers are recognizing the value of education and training programs designed to prevent and to help detect substance abuse. Often, employee awareness and training programs are combined with drug testing and counseling. In addition to providing information about the risks associated with using illegal drugs, alcohol, and tobacco, these programs are designed to give employees facts about the symptoms of substance abuse and guidance about what to do if they believe a coworker is under the influence of drugs or alcohol. Particular emphasis is placed on equipping supervisors with the information they need to recognize substance abuse by workers and how to go about applying the agency's policy and procedures with regard to testing, discipline, and referral to resources such as employee assistance programs (McPheters, 1995). Training of this kind may take a variety of forms—ranging from day-long sessions including presentations by experts, group discussions, and exercises to one-hour videotapes about substance abuse. Some employers may require that all workers undergo training every year, while others make it a part of the orientation for new employees. Often, basic supervisory training includes a substance abuse component.

EMPLOYEE ASSISTANCE PROGRAMS

It is now widely understood that people are unlikely to escape the grip of an addiction to alcohol or drugs without professional help and support. Nicotine is currently considered to be an addictive substance, as well. In other words, it is unrealistic to expect that most employees will simply "kick the habit" and improve their job performance after they are told that their job or career is at risk. From a purely practical point of view, therefore, employers unwilling to invest in intervention and rehabilitation programs may pay a high price in the long run. The costs of lowered productivity, excessive use of sick leave and health insurance, and high rates of absenteeism and turnover are very likely to greatly exceed those associated with programs designed to rehabilitate workers who test positive for drugs or alcohol, and even greater benefits are likely to flow from making educational and counseling resources available to all employees. Aside from the productivity or "bottom-line" arguments in favor of such programs, social attitudes and values have changed, and employers are expected to try to help their workers prevent and overcome psychological as well as physical illnesses.

In the private sector, employee assistance programs (EAPs) have been for some time the keystone of employers' efforts to intervene and assist workers with serious personal problems. In this context, EAPs are workplace-centered programs established to help employees with a variety of personal problems, including substance abuse. These programs usually have three phases: (1) identification of individuals with problems, (2) motivating these people to recognize the problem and to seek assistance, and (3) directly or indirectly providing counseling, medical treatment, and other forms of support intended to rehabilitate.

EAPs come in at least three basic forms: internal programs, external or contracted programs, and consortia arrangements. Internal programs are staffed and operated on-site by the employer. Because they follow the employers policies and procedures, internal EAPs are easier to tailor to specific needs and unusual problems, and management can hold them directly accountable. Critics of internal programs question whether they can assure employee privacy and confidentiality, since the EAP's staff is part of the management hierarchy and its files are the employer's property.

External EAPs use contractors to provide services to employees and they are located off the job site. They typically offer a broader range of services than internal EAPs, and employees tend to be more comfortable with the level of confidentiality they offer. In general, external EAPs are a part of the benefits package, usually under group health insurance policies. In the United States, most EAPs are external. In some cases, several employers will form a consortium to buy external EAP services, which allows the participants to save on costs and broaden the range of services available to their employees. Most EAPs are broad-gauged in the sense that they are designed to help workers cope with a variety of personal and family problems, not only substance abuse. Often, substance abuse is a symptom of personal and relationship problems, and employees often are more willing to use an EAP to deal with them than they are to directly confront their substance abuse issues (Wirt, 1998).

Once a rarity in the public sector, EAPs now function in many jurisdictions and agencies. In the federal service, they are required by OPM regulations under Executive Order 12564. All covered agencies must offer EAPs with high-level direction, emphasizing education, referral to rehabilitation, and coordination with available community resources. EAP services are available to federal employees who voluntarily seek their help, and to those the employer determines are abusing alcohol and/or drugs.

The policies of public employers vary with respect to the rehabilitation of workers who test positive for drugs. OPM's regulations have given federal agencies considerable discretion and, for example, the GAO found in the late 1980s that well over half of those testing positive in three agencies entered EAPs and remained in jobs targeted for testing (U.S. General Accounting Office, 1989). Given the choice between immediate termination and treatment, most local employers "have chosen to permit each employee at least one positive drug test without punitive action, provided that the employee receives appropriate help (Carey, 1988, p. 183).

THE ROLE OF ARBITRATORS UNDER NEGOTIATED AGREEMENTS

If an employer bargains collectively with one or more employee organizations, arbitrators may play an important role in setting the disciplinary processes used to deal with employees under substance abuse policies. Through their decisions, arbitrators often establish important elements of these policies. For example, negotiated contracts usually state that management may discipline an employee for "just cause" only, and the agreement may provide for specific adverse actions or dismissal of any employee who possesses or consumes alcohol or illegal drugs on the employer's property. If the employee grieves such a dismissal under terms of the contract, and the issue is not resolved at an earlier step of the grievance process, an arbitrator will be called in to hold a hearing and to investigate the factual basis of management's case. The arbitrator may uphold, cancel, or modify the employer's disciplinary action. Typically, the contract specifies that such decisions are final and binding.

Labor arbitrators are increasingly likely to accept the proposition that alcohol and drug abuse are *illnesses* that require treatment as opposed to punishment, and they will expect employers to try to provide such assistance. In practical terms, this approach may produce a decision that says the employer *does not* have just cause for dismissal if the employee can be shown to be a sick person who is unable to change his or her habits without the employer's positive support and treatment.

A study of arbitrators' decisions in discharge cases involving drug and alcohol abuse over a seven-year period during the 1980s (Elkiss and Yaney, 1991) revealed the following pattern:

- Arbitrators were reluctant to give management broad powers to discharge workers who violate the employer's rules due to "chemical dependency." They tended to treat such dependency as a medical condition requiring treatment, as opposed to punishment. If employees were "cured," they should be returned to their jobs.

- It was not unusual for them to reduce the severity of the proposed disciplinary action if management did not offer the worker an opportunity to enter a rehabilitation program (either through an EAP or insurance coverage).

- Often, in conjunction with enrollment in an EAP, they made reinstatement of the employee concerned contingent upon attending counseling sessions, group therapy and support such as Alcoholics Anonymous, or similar treatment for a specified period of time after initial rehabilitation. Another frequently imposed condition of reinstatement was that the employee agree to submit to periodic drug testing in the future.

SMOKING IN THE WORKPLACE

A couple of examples should suffice to show the strength of the movement to ban smoking in the American workplace. In his first official appearance before the U.S. Senate's Committee on Labor and Human Resources in 1998, the head of the Occupational Safety and Health Administration, Charles Jeffress, recommended that the Congress pass legislation banning smoking in the workplace. Jeffress noted that OSHA's rule-making process could take up to eight years to produce an indoor air quality standard in the absence of such legislation (Finnegan, 1998). The urgency suggested by his call for congressional action is reflected in the rate at which employers are moving toward smoking bans. In 1986, only about 2 percent of U.S. employers had imposed a total ban on smoking; by 1991, however, around 34 percent had prohibited smoking in their buildings. One such employer is the U.S. Postal Service, which banned all smoking within the Service's facilities and left the option of designated outside smoking areas up to the local managers in 1993 (Pulliam, 1993/1994).

Although some employers have gone so far as to make nonsmoker status a job requirement, and a few even make smoking off the job grounds for dismissal, this is not the norm. In some states, refusing to hire smokers or taking adverse action against employees who smoke may be illegal. Virginia and Arizona have passed laws making it illegal to discriminate against state employees or job applicants who smoke. Other states, such as Colorado and North Dakota, have enacted general legislation that prohibit adverse actions against employees for engaging in *any* legal behavior off the job site and during nonworking hours (Pulliam, 1993/94).

For the most part, public employers' efforts to deal with smoking have focused on two approaches. First, they have concentrated on establishing and enforcing no-smoking policies within and near their buildings and other facilities and, given the possible air pollution risks, on setting up so-called designated smoking areas that are outdoors and effectively separated from spaces used by nonsmokers. Second, they have tried to create environments that encourage employees who smoke to quit and to provide access to smoking cessation programs and individual counseling through EAPs. (Appendix 9.A is President Clinton's 1997 executive order on smoking in federal workplaces.) It may also be possible to offer financial incentives—such as lower health and life insurance premiums—to non-smokers. No-smoking policies consistently enforced, broad employee support of the policy, material incentives, and employers'

BULLETIN

Employers Responding to Smoking

"Although most employers are not yet cordoning smokers from their pool of job candidates, many are acting on their concerns about smoking as a work-site safety hazard, health benefits cost inflater and detriment to productivity. A joint survey by the Society for Human Resources Management and the Bureau of National Affairs shows that in 1991, 85 percent of 833 organizations prohibited or restricted smoking in their facilities, up from 54 percent in 1987 and 36 percent in 1986."

Source: Rudy M. Yandrick, "More Employers Prohibit Smoking." *HRMagazine,* Vol. 39, No. 7 (1994), p. 68.

willingness to provide resources needed to help employees quit smoking appear to be quite effective over the long run (Yandrick, 1994).

CONCLUSION

Public employers have made significant strides in their efforts to respond positively and effectively to substance abuse. Clearly, alcoholism and drug addiction are deeply rooted in American society, and it would be naive to assume that legal proscriptions and personnel policies will come even close to eradicating them in the foreseeable future. The available evidence, however, suggests that they do have an important role to play. Preemployment testing has shown a rather consistent trend toward fewer positive tests over the past 15 years. Targeted-random and reasonable-suspicion testing programs may be deterrents although studies of the effectiveness of substance abuse programs are inconclusive. Educational and employee support and counseling programs do appear to be having beneficial results (Sorohan, 1994).

Drug testing, especially targeted testing of employees in safety-sensitive positions, is becoming a feature of the employment relationship on all levels of government as the courts work out the constitutional ground rules that employers must follow. It is now more and more the case that public employers understand that dealing with substance abuse involves more than testing and discipline of those who violate substance abuse policies. EAPs have become widespread elements of substance abuse prevention and response programs. For better or worse, demonstrating a commitment to making a "drug-free workplace" continues to be a popular theme among elected officials seeking to provide symbolic evidence that the nation's leadership is indeed serious about prosecuting the "war on drugs" on all fronts. The more recent effort to deal with the health problems, costs, and exposure lawsuits associated with smoking and secondhand smoke on the organizational

BULLETIN

Bans Help Employees Quit

"When your peers don't smoke, you're not as likely to smoke, says Daniel R. Longo, a health policy researcher at the University of Missouri-Columbia School of Medicine. . . .Five years after hospitals banned smoking—the first nationwide industry to go smoke free—researchers found that 51 percent of smokers employed in hospitals had quit the habit. This figure compares to a quit rate of less than 38 percent in the general population. . . .The rate of cessation for smokers subjected to workplace smoking bans tops those reported among smokers using other common techniques, like nicotine patches, counseling sessions, or support groups.

Source: Elaine McShulkis, "Workplace Bans Help Employees Quit," *HRMagazine,* Vol. 41, No. 8 (1996), pp. 20–22.

level may be expected to continue to gain momentum. Antismoking policies that affect the general public and commercial interests, particularly local ordinances prohibiting smoking in public places such as restaurants and bars, will generate controversy, but a general consensus that smoking in the workplace should be eliminated or at least limited to outside locations and regularly scheduled breaks seems to be emerging.

The current state of affairs now requires that public employers have rational and enforceable substance abuse policies that will withstand judicial scrutiny, are consistent with state laws and local ordinances, and include programs designed to help employees overcome dependence on drugs, alcohol, and tobacco. Such policies should:

- Clearly explain the reasons for the policy, including the fact that substance abuse is not a problem restricted to certain categories of workers or social groups.
- State the employer's position on the use and possession of alcohol, drugs, and tobacco products on and off the job site.
- Specify the conditions under which preemployment, random, and suspicion-based drug tests will be administered.
- State the criteria used to select laboratories and the procedures to be used in order to minimize the risk of false positives and to interpret test results.
- Specify the disciplinary and other actions that management will take if it determined that an employee has violated the policy or policies in question.
- Set forth the employer's position on intervention and rehabilitation, and describe the treatment opportunities available to workers.
- Provide an accessible and clearly defined appeals process under civil service regulations and identify any grievance procedures that may exist for employees covered by negotiated contracts.

DISCUSSION QUESTIONS

1. Do you believe employers should be able to require that workers not use alcohol or tobacco products when they are not at work?
2. Is it a good idea to randomly test employees in certain positions for drugs and alcohol, or should the standard be that reasonable suspicion must exist before an individual is required to undergo testing?

3. Should employees be expected to report coworkers whom they suspect of using illegal drugs or being under the influence of alcohol to their supervisors?

4. Does drug testing really act as a deterrent to substance abuse or just encourage more sophisticated efforts to avoid detection?

5. Should employees who test positive for illegal drugs be fired or required to participate in rehabilitation programs through EAPs or other resources?

6. Should public employers' group health and life insurance programs offer lower rates to nonsmokers?

REFERENCES

AFL-CIO v Frank (1989). C.A. No. 87-1264—M(D.C. Mass., Nov. 21).

Anonymous (1997). "The Hazards of Second-Hand Smoke." *Business and Health: What Cigarettes Do to Americans Supplement* (August), pp. 10–13.

Bahls, Jane Easter (1998). "Drugs in the Workplace." *HRMagazine,* Vol. 43, No. 2 (February), pp. 80–87.

Bornstein, Tim (1989). "Getting to the Bottom of the Issue: How Arbitrators View Alcohol Abuse," *Arbitration Journal,* Vol. 44, No. 4 (December), pp. 46–50.

Cary, Paul L. (1988). "Drugs and Drug Testing in the Workplace," in John Matzer ed., *Personnel Practices for the '90s* (Washington, DC: International City Management Association), pp. 183–193.

Elkiss, Helen, and Yaney, Joseph (1991). "Recent Trends in Arbitration of Substance Abuse Grievances." Proceedings of the 1991 Spring Meeting (Industrial Relations Research Association), pp. 556, 560.

Finnegan, Lisa (1998). "Jeffress to Congress: Ban Workplace Smoking." *Occupational Hazards,* Vol. 60, No. 4 (April), p. 12.

French, Michael T., Zarkin, Gary A., Hartwell, Tyler D., and Bray, Jeremy W. (1995). "Prevalence and Consequences of Smoking, Alcohol Abuse, and Illicit Drug Use at Five Work Sites," *Public Health Reports,* Vol. 110, No. 5 (September), pp. 593–599.

Hickey, Thomas J., and Reid, Sue Titus (1995). "Testing Police and Corrections Officers for Drug Use After Skinner and Von Raab." *Public Administration Quarterly,* Vol. 19, No. 1 (Spring), pp. 26–41.

McPheters, Wallace E. (1995). "Training That Targets Drug Deterrence." *Security Management,* Vol. 39, No. 6 (June), pp. 44–47.

McShulskis, Elaine (1996). "Workplace Bans Help Employees Quit." *HRMagazine,* Vol. 41, No. 8 (August), pp. 20–22.

NTEU v Von Raab (1989). 489 U.S. 656 (1989).

Pulliam, Lynne L. (1993/1994). "Smoking in the Workplace: Developing a Policy that Works for Your Company." *Employee Relations Law Journal,* Vol. 19, No. 3 (Winter), pp. 279–286.

Rhodes, Don (1998). "Drugs in the Workplace," *Occupational Health and Safety,* Vol. 67, No. 10 (October), pp. 136–138.

Skinner v Railway Labor Executives (1989). 489 U.S. 602 (1989).

Sorohan, Erica Gordon (1994). "Making Decisions About Drug Testing." *Training & Development,* Vol. 48, No. 5 (May), pp. 111–117.

Spencer, Janet M. (1979). "The Developing Notion of Employer Responsibility for the Alcoholic, Drug Addictive or Mentally Ill Employee: An Examination Under Federal and State Employment Statutes and Arbitration Decisions." *St. John's Law Review,* Vol. 53, No. 4 (Summer), pp. 659–720.

Thompson, Frank J., Riccucci, Norma M., and Ban, Carolyn (1991). "Drug Testing in the Federal Workplace: An Instrumental and Symbolic Assessment." *Public Administration Review,* Vol. 51, No. 6 (November–December), pp. 515–525.

U.S. General Accounting Office (1988). *Drug Testing: Regulation of Drug Testing Laboratories* (Washington, DC), September.

——— (1989). *Actions by Agencies When Employees Test Positive for Illegal Drugs* (Washington, DC).

——— (1991). *Employee Drug Testing, Status of Federal Agencies' Programs* (Washington, DC), May.

——— (1992). *Employee Drug Testing: Estimated Cost to Test All Executive Branch Employees and New Hires* (Washington, DC), June.

Wirt, Gary L. (1998). "The ABCs of EAPs." *HR Focus,* Vol. 75, No. 11 (November), p. S12.

SUGGESTED READINGS

Bacharach, Samuel B., Bamberger, Peter, and Sonnenstuhl, William J. (1994). *Member Assistance Programs in the Workplace: The Role of Labor in the Prevention & Treatment of Substance Abuse* (Ithaca, NY: Cornell University Press).

Brown, Elizabeth D., O'Farrell, Timothy J., Maisto, Stephen A., Boies-Hickman, Karen, and Suchinski, Richard, eds. (1997). *Accreditation Guide for Substance Abuse Programs* (Thousand Oaks, CA: Sage Publications, Inc.).

DIANE Publishing (1995). *Workplaces Without Alcohol & Other Drugs: What Works* (Upland, CA: DIANE Publishing Company).

———— (1997). *Management of Alcohol & Drug-Related Issues in the Workplace* (Upland, CA: DIANE Publishing Company).

———— (1995a). *Alcohol, Drugs & Disability* (New York: Gordon Press Publishers).

Gordon Press (1995b). *Alcohol, Tobacco & Other Drugs: Prevention in the Workplace: A Resource Guide* (New York: Gordon Press Publishers).

Hoffman, John P., Brittingham, Angela, and Larison, Cindy (1998). *Drug Use Among U.S. Workers: Prevalence & Trends by Occupation & Industry Categories* (Upland, CA: DIANE Publishing Company).

Hutchison, William S. Jr., and Emener, William G., eds. (1997). *Employee Assistance Programs: A Basic Text* (Springfield, IL: Charles C. Thomas Publisher, Limited).

Roman, Paul M., and MacDonald, Scott, eds. (1994). *Research Advances in Alcohol and Drug Problems: Drug Testing in the Workplace* (New York: Plenum Publishing Corporation).

Executive Orders

PROTECTING FEDERAL EMPLOYEES AND THE PUBLIC FROM EXPOSURE TO TOBACCO SMOKE IN THE FEDERAL WORKPLACE

THE WHITE HOUSE

Office of the Press Secretary

For Immediate Release   August 9, 1997

EXECUTIVE ORDER

- - - - - -

PROTECTING FEDERAL EMPLOYEES AND THE PUBLIC FROM
EXPOSURE TO **TOBACCO SMOKE** IN THE FEDERAL **WORKPLACE**

By the authority vested in me as President by the Constitution
and the laws of the United States of America and in order to protect
Federal Government employees and members of the public from exposure
to **tobacco smoke** in the Federal **workplace**, it is hereby ordered as
follows:

Section 1. Policy. It is the policy of the executive branch to
establish a **smoke**-free environment for Federal employees and members
of the public visiting or using Federal facilities. The **smoking** of
tobacco products is thus prohibited in all interior space owned,
rented, or leased by the executive branch of the Federal Government,
and in any outdoor areas under executive branch control in front of
air intake ducts.

Sec. 2. Exceptions. The general policy established by this order
is subject to the following exceptions:

(a) The order does not apply in designated **smoking** areas that
are enclosed and exhausted directly to the outside and away from
air intake ducts, and are maintained under negative pressure
(with respect to surrounding spaces) sufficient to contain **tobacco**
smoke within the designated area. Agency officials shall not
require workers to enter such areas during business hours while
smoking is ongoing.

(b) The order does not extend to any residential accommodation
for persons voluntarily or involuntarily residing, on a temporary
or long-term basis, in a building owned, leased, or rented by the
Federal Government.

(c) The order does not extend to those portions of federally owned
buildings leased, rented, or otherwise provided in their entirety to
nonfederal parties.

continued page 286

(d) The order does not extend to places of employment in the private sector or in other nonfederal governmental units that serve as the permanent or intermittent duty station of one or more Federal employees.

(e) The head of any agency may establish limited and narrow exceptions that are necessary to accomplish agency missions. Such exception shall be in writing, approved by the agency head, and to the fullest extent possible provide protection of nonsmokers from exposure to environmental **tobacco smoke**. Authority to establish such exceptions may not be delegated.

Sec. 3. Other Locations. The heads of agencies shall evaluate the need to restrict **smoking** at doorways and in courtyards under executive branch control in order to protect workers and visitors from environmental **tobacco smoke,** and may restrict **smoking** in these areas in light of this evaluation.

Sec. 4. **Smoking** Cessation Programs. The heads of agencies are encouraged to use existing authority to establish programs designed to help employees stop **smoking**.

Sec. 5. Responsibility for Implementation. The heads of agencies are responsible for implementing and ensuring compliance with the provisions of this order. "Agency" as used in this order means an Executive agency, as defined in 5 U.S.C. 105, and includes any employing unit or authority of the Federal Government, other than those of the legislative and judicial branches. Independent agencies are encouraged to comply with the provisions of this order.

Sec. 6. Phase-In of Implementation. Implementation of the policy set forth in this order shall be achieved no later than 1 year after the date of this order. This 1 year phase-in period is designed to establish a fixed but reasonable time for implementing this policy. Agency heads are directed during this period to inform all employees and visitors to executive branch facilities about the requirements of this order, inform their employees of the health risks of exposure to environmental **tobacco smoke,** and undertake related activities as necessary.

Sec. 7. Consistency with Other Laws. The provisions of this order shall be implemented consistent with applicable law, including the Federal Service Labor-Management Relations Act (5 U.S.C. 7101 et seq.) and the National Labor Relations Act (29 U.S.C. 151 et seq.) Provisions of existing collective bargaining agreements shall be honored and agencies shall consult with employee labor representatives about ·the imple-mentation of this order. Nothing herein shall be construed to impair or alter the powers and duties of Federal agencies established under law. Nothing herein shall be construed to replace any agency policy currently in effect, if such policy is legally established, in writing, and consistent with the terms of this order. Agencies shall review their current policy to confirm that agency policy comports with this order, and policy found not in compliance shall be revised to comply with the terms of this order.

Sec. 8. Cause of Action. This order does not create any right to administrative or judicial review, or any other right or benefit, substantive or procedural, enforceable by a party against the United States, its agencies or instrumentalities, its officers or employees, or any other person or affect in any way the liability of the executive branch under the Federal Tort Claims Act.

Sec. 9. Construction. Nothing in this order shall limit an agency head from establishing more protective policies on **smoking** in the Federal **workplace** for employees and members of the public visiting or using Federal facilities.

WILLIAM J. CLINTON
The White House,
August 9,1997.

Chapter TEN

Sexual Harassment

Sexual harassment in the workplace is a form of illegal discrimination that public employers must actively seek to prevent and, if it happens, to address in a manner that punishes the perpetrator and makes whole the victim. Sexual harassment has become a major public issue and concern. During the past decade, a sitting president, a Supreme Court nominee, and several members of Congress have been accused of sexually harassing their employees. There is no reason to believe that sexual harassment of women by men in the workplace is a new phenomenon. It should also be noted that cases of sexual harassment of men by women are not unheard of, and gays may be victimized by both sexes. What has happened in the United States is a reversal of a historical pattern of tolerance by employers. Sexual harassment is now widely seen to be an unacceptable and costly behavior that public management must address through formal policies that are enforced, disciplinary procedures, training programs, and other ways of eliminating it from the workplace.

The reasons for the spotlight now shining on this previously dark corner of the workplace are not hard to find. First, women are not only rapidly becoming fully half of the civilian labor force, they are moving into traditionally "male" job categories, including managerial positions. Thus, in addition to the public attention drawn to sexual harassment by the complaints of a growing number of women who are no longer willing to tolerate it in any form, cases of blatant harassment by workers who resent the desegregation of all-male enclaves such as police and fire departments have received particular attention. Second, attitudes are changing. Traditional definitions of sex roles and power relations between men and women in society are breaking down, and behaviors once considered at worst impolite or unfortunate are now simply not acceptable in many settings. Third, in conjunction with shifting social values, the political climate has changed significantly. In response to their growing political influence, women's issues now get far more attention than they did a few years ago, and this reality is reflected in legislation, court rulings, rules promulgated by agencies such as the Equal Employment Opportunity Commission (EEOC), and personnel policies on all levels of government.

The federal government, as a case in point, has been tracking its employees' attitudes about sexual harassment for almost 15 years. A survey conducted by the Merit Systems Protection Board (MSPB) in 1994 revealed that "more people of both sexes have come to view more behaviors as sexual harassment" (U.S. Merit Systems Protection Board, 1995, p. 5). The MSPB tracked employees' answers to the question "Is it sexual harassment?" for six behaviors by supervisors and coworkers in 1980, 1987, and 1994. Its findings are summarized in Table 10.1.

SEXUAL HARASSMENT AND THE LAW

Title VII of the Civil Rights Act of 1964 prohibits employment discrimination on the basis of race, color, religion, national origin, *and sex*. The EEOC is responsible for enforcement in this area and it (along with the federal courts) has interpreted Title VII to mean that sexual harassment is a form of sex discrimination. There are other types of sex discrimination, such as refusing to hire or promote qualified women and, of course, paying women less than men for the same kind of work (Lee and Greenlaw, 1996). Sexual harassment is illegal, and violators (including the employer) may be prosecuted and held liable for damages. For the public employer, therefore, sexual harassment charges made by workers or clients are serious legal matters.

What behaviors or practices constitute sexual harassment? The EEOC has issued the following guidelines:

> Harassment on the basis of sex is a violation of Sec. 703 of Title VII. Unwelcome sexual advances, requests for sexual favors, and other verbal or physical conduct of a sexual nature constitute sexual harassment when (1) submission to such conduct is made either explicitly or implicitly a term or condition of an individual's employment, (2) submission to or rejection of such conduct by an individual is used as the basis for employment decisions affecting such individual, or (3) such conduct has the purpose or effect of substantially interfering with an individual's work performance or creating an intimidating, hostile, or offensive working environment. (Equal Employment Opportunity Commission, 1980)

Table 10.1 Federal Employees' Definition of Sexual Harassment

Uninvited Behavior by a Supervisor	Percentage of Women Who Consider It Harassment		
	1980	1987	1994
Pressure for sexual favors	91	99	99
Deliberate touching, cornering	91	95	98
Suggestive letters, calls, materials	93	95	94
Pressure for dates	77	87	91
Suggestive looks, gestures	72	81	91
Sexual teasing, jokes, remarks	62	72	83
Uninvited Behavior by a Coworker	**Percentage of Women Who Consider It Harassment**		
	1980	1987	1994
Pressure for sexual favors	81	98	98
Deliberate touching, cornering	84	92	96
Suggestive letters, calls, materials	87	84	92
Pressure for dates	65	76	85
Suggestive looks, gestures	64	76	88
Sexual teasing, jokes, remarks	54	64	77

Percentages of men who defined these behaviors by supervisors and coworkers as sexual harassment were lower for all 3 surveys, but the gap narrows considerably by 1994. The 1994 data are based on responses from 8,000 federal employees.

Source: U.S. Merit Systems Protection Board, *Sexual Harassment in the Federal Workplace* (Washington, DC: U.S. Government Printing Office, 1995).

Terms such as "verbal or physical conduct of a sexual nature" require clarification through specific policies. Following the EEOC guidelines, the City of Atlanta amended its code of ordinances in 1996 by adding a Sexual Harassment Policy (see Appendix 10.A for the full text) that includes a long list of examples of sexual harassment:

Examples of sexual harassment include, but are not limited to: unwanted sexual advances; demands for sexual favors in exchange for favorable treatment or continued employment; repeated sexual jokes, flirtations, advances or propositions; verbal abuse of a sexual nature; graphic verbal commentary about an individual's body, sexual prowess or sexual deficiencies; leering, whistling, touching, pinching, assault, coerced sexual acts or suggestive, insulting, obscene comments or gestures; display in the workplace of sexually suggestive objects or pictures; ostracizing an employee in conformity with sexual conduct; sexual conduct that reasonably causes mental and emotional detriment to the victim; retaliation against an individual for reporting or complaining about sexually harassing conduct. This behavior is unacceptable in the workplace and is unacceptable in other work-related settings such as business trips and business-related social events. (City of Atlanta, 1996, Section 114-601)

Concrete examples such as these make it easier for workers, supervisors, and managers to apply the EEOC's general terminology to specific events in the workplace.

Items (1) and (2) of the EEOC guidelines are straightforward and evoke little controversy; they prohibit making submission to unwelcome sexual behavior by a superior a condition of employment or using responses to such behavior as grounds for personnel actions (e.g., firing or denying pay raises to employees who refuse to submit). This is often called quid pro quo harassment. Most, but not all, federal circuit courts apply the following criteria to determine if a plaintiff has been subjected to quid pro quo harassment:

- The employee must be a member of a protected class.
- There must be proof that the employee was subjected to unwelcome sexual demands.
- It must be established that the harassment was based on sex.
- It must be shown that the employee was expected to comply in order to avoid a job-related penalty or to receive a job benefit.
- Employer liability under Title VII must be determined; the plaintiff's superior has to have acted as an "agent" of the employer. (Lee and Greenlaw, 1996, pp. 16–17)

Item (3) in the EEOC guidelines relating to the creation of a hostile or offensive environment is far broader in its application, and it does not require that the plaintiff prove that she (or he) was denied a tangible benefit such as a job or promotion. What has to be established is that the defendant's behavior toward the plaintiff created a hostile or offensive working environment. Not surprisingly, most sexual harassment charges in government are based on the hostile environment effect.

The EEOC's inclusion of category (3) violations was a "radical departure from the case law on the subject," but the Supreme Court agreed in *Meritor Savings Bank v Mechelle Vinson et al.* (1986). This decision provided much-needed guidance for employers, and it established that hostile and abusive work environments are serious matters and that employers should follow the EEOC's guidelines carefully if they expect to prevail in the court

The first point the Court made in *Meritor v Vinson* was that Title VII is violated if serious and continuing unwelcome sexual behavior creates a "hostile or abusive work environment," even if the plaintiff was not denied any material benefits. In this case, a female bank employee charged her male supervisor with four years of sexual harassment, including fondling, psychologically coerced sexual relations, and rape. After her dismissal for taking "excessive sick leave" in 1978, Vinson brought action against the supervisor and the bank in district court.

In response to Vinson's charges, her supervisor denied allegations of sexual activity and asserted that Vinson's charges were in response to a "business-related dispute." In its defense, the bank claimed that it was unaware of any sexual harassment and, if it had taken place, it was without its consent or approval. The district court ruled against Vinson, stating that if she and her supervisor had "engaged in an intimate or sexual relationship during the time of [her] employment with [the bank] that relationship was a voluntary one having nothing to do with her continued employment or her advancement or promotions at that [bank]."

The court of appeals for the District of Columbia reversed the district court's decision. Previously, the appeals court had ruled that violations of Title VII could be based on either of two kinds of sexual harassment, (1) "harassment that involves the conditioning of concrete employment benefits on sexual favors, and (2) harassment that, while not affecting economic benefits, creates a hostile or offensive working environment." Since the district court had not considered whether a violation of the second kind had occurred, the appeals court remanded the case, noting that employers are "absolutely" liable for sexual harassment practiced by their supervisory personnel.

Hearing the case on appeal, the Supreme Court agreed with the court of appeals, stating that "unwelcome sexual advances that create an offensive or hostile working environment violate Title VII." As to the supervisor's and the bank's contention that there was no violation because Vinson had suffered no loss of a tangible benefit, the Court disagreed. Congress, the Court said, intended to "strike at the entire spectrum of disparate treatment of women" in terms of employment. The EEOC guidelines, while not binding on the courts, "do constitute a body of experience and informed judgment to which courts and litigants may properly resort for guidance." Accordingly, the case was sent back to district court for further proceedings consistent with the Supreme Court's opinion.

The second point in *Meritor v Vinson* focused on employer liability. Meritor Bank had argued that it should not be held liable because it had a written policy against discrimination and Vinson had not used an existing grievance procedure. The Court disagreed with both claims: The policy was vague and did not specifically address sexual harassment, and the grievance procedure discouraged complaints.

The Court, however, did not fully resolve the issue of employer liability. Writing for the majority, Chief Justice Rehnquist "noted that while employers are absolutely liable for acts of their supervisors when economic benefits are involved, some limits might be placed on employer liability when hostile work environments were the issue" (Morlacci, 1987–88, pp. 513–515).

Since 1986, the Supreme Court has handed down several important rulings that do much to clarify its position on employer liability. In *Harris v Forklift Systems, Inc.* (1993), it unanimously reasserted the principle it set forth in *Meritor* that Title VII does not require the victim of sexual harassment to show psychological damage before the behavior in question can be considered illegal. The Court stated in its decision that a hostile environment can undermine employees' performance, encourage resignations that otherwise would not have taken place (constructive discharge), and destroy careers. It noted that it was taking a "middle path" and leaving the determination of whether specific instances of offensive conduct were illegal to a case-by-case approach. Although the Court did not specifically describe the behaviors that create an illegal hostile environment, it stated that all relevant factors need to be considered, including answers to the following:

- How often had the conduct in question occurred?
- How serious was the behavior?
- Were physical threats involved or was the behavior limited to verbal statements and comments?
- Did the behavior unreasonably interfere with the victim's job performance?
- Did the victim actually perceive the work environment to be abusive and hostile?

In 1998, the Court issued several anxiously awaited rulings, including *Oncale v Sundowner Offshore Services Inc., Faragher v City of Boca Raton,* and *Burlington Industries, Inc. v Ellerth.* In these rulings, the Court sought to clarify the law regarding (1) whether a claim of same-sex sexual harassment may be brought under Title VII, (2) what legal standard should be used to determine if employers are liable for sexual harassment by supervisors, and (3) if a claim of quid pro quo harassment can proceed "without showing that the employee submitted to sexual advances or was harmed for refusing such advances" (Muhl, 1998, p. 61).

In *Oncale,* a unanimous Court ruled that Title VII applies to sexual harassment between members of the same sex. While working on an oil rig, Joseph Oncale charged that male coworkers subjected him to sex-related harassment by two supervisors in front of other members of the crew. Although these events were reported to Sundowner's management, no remedial steps were taken. In its decision, the Court stated:

> There is no justification in Title VII's language or the Court's precedents for a categorical rule barring a claim of discrimination "because of . . . sex" merely because the plaintiff and the defendant (or the person charged with acting on behalf of the defendant) are of the same sex. Recognizing liability for same-sex harassment will not transform Title VII into a general civility code for the American workplace, since Title VII is directed at discrimination because of sex, not merely conduct tinged with offensive sexual connotations. . . .

In *Faragher v City of Boca Raton*, the issue was employer liability for the harassing behavior of supervisors. Here, the Court ruled that employers are "subject to vicarious—or strict—liability for sexual harassment caused by a supervisor" (Muhl, 1998, p. 61). Beth Ann Faragher, a lifeguard, brought an action against her immediate supervisors and the City, charging that the two supervisors had created a sexually hostile environment at work by repeatedly subjecting her and other female lifeguards to "uninvited and offensive touching," "lewd remarks," and comments that described women in "offensive terms." A district court held the City liable because it concluded that the harassment had created a hostile environment pervasive enough to "support an inference that the City had knowledge or constructive knowledge of it." The district court, therefore, held under traditional *agency* principles, that the supervisors were acting as the City's agents. The Court of Appeals, however, reversed the district court's decision, arguing that constructive knowledge could not be imputed to the City and it could not be held liable for negligence. The Supreme Court, in turn, reversed and remanded, holding that an "employer is vicariously liable for actionable discrimination by a supervisor, but subject to an affirmative defense looking to the reasonableness of the employer's conduct as well as that of the plaintiff victim." In *Meritor*, the Court had indicated that questions of employer liability should be evaluated under principles of agency law, which says that employers can be held liable for the actions of employees if they are within the scope of a supervisor's job-related duties. In *Faragher*, it clarified its position by indicating that supervisors are always "assisted in sexual misconduct by the supervisory relationship." Employers, however, are not *automatically* liable whenever a supervisor engages in sexual harassment. The City of Boca Raton was held liable under this standard because (1) its supervisors created a hostile work environment and they had almost unlimited authority over their subordinates, and (2) it did not disseminate its sexual harassment policy among beach employees and made no effort to monitor the behavior of supervisors in that setting. Boca Raton, in other words, could not mount an affirmative defense, since it had not exercised reasonable care to prevent the supervisors' illegal conduct.

The Court used its reasoning in *Faragher* to decide *Burlington Industries, Inc. v Ellerth*. In this case, the central issue was whether an employee who does not submit to a supervisor's sexual demands or suffer any material job-related consequences may sue for quid pro quo sexual harassment. It held that employees may be entitled to damages, even if they do not submit to sexual demands by a supervisor and suffer no adverse consequences as a result. While employers are subject to vicarious liability under these conditions, the Court noted that they may "raise an affirmative defense to liability or damages, subject to proof by a preponderance of the evidence. . . ."

> The defense comprises two necessary elements: (a) that the employer exercised reasonable care to prevent and correct promptly any sexually harassing behavior, and (b) that the plaintiff employee unreasonably failed to take advantage of any preventive or corrective opportunities provided by the employer. . . .No affirmative defense is available, however, when the supervisor's harassment culminates in a tangible employment action.

Explaining that the labels *quid pro quo* and *hostile work environment* are not controlling for determining employer liability, the Court concluded that Ellerth should have an opportunity to prove on the trial court level that she had a claim that would result in vicarious liability.

SEXUAL HARASSMENT POLICIES

Public employers are legally required to do everything reasonably possible to prevent sexual harassment in the workplace. A fundamental part of such an effort is a broadly disseminated written policy statement by management that incorporates the EEOC guidelines,

BULLETIN

From the dissent by Justice Thomas, with whom Justice Scalia joined, to the Court's decision in Burlington Industries v Ellerth:

"When a supervisor inflicts an adverse employment consequence upon an employee who has rebuffed his advances, the supervisor exercises the specific authority granted to him by his company. His acts, therefore are the company's acts and are properly chargeable to it. . . .If a supervisor creates a hostile work environment, however, he does not act for the employer. As the Court concedes, a supervisor's creation of a hostile work environment is neither within the scope of his employment, nor part of his apparent authority. Indeed, a hostile work environment is antithetical to the interest of the employer. In such circumstances, an employer should be liable only if it has been negligent. That is, liability should attach only if the employer either knew, or in the exercise of reasonable care should have known, about the hostile work environment and failed to take remedial action."

establishes an administrative procedure for initiating and dealing fairly with complaints, and describes clearly the penalties for violations. A member of top management should be ultimately responsible for implementing and monitoring the program. The potential liability of executives, supervisors, and others should be explained, including a provision of the Civil Rights Act of 1991 under which victims of sexual harassment may receive up to $300,000 in compensatory and punitive damages.

For purposes of clarity, sexual harassment policies should provide descriptions of unacceptable behaviors such as that included in the City of Atlanta's policy. Enforcement procedures should assure "that swift and proportional remedies will be applied when indicated," and managers and supervisors "must be trained to respond to problems quickly and effectively." It is important that training designed to familiarize all employees with the elements of an agency's sexual harassment policy be required of all employees. Identifying and stopping problems before they become sexual harassment complaints should be a key goal of the policy and related procedures. It is also important to make sure "that the complaint processing system is understood by all trainees and [to] stress that it is constructed to balance the rights of both complainants and respondents" (Spann, 1990, pp. 59–60).

Policies prohibiting sexual harassment are now the norm for public- as well as private-sector employers. In the federal government, all of the 22 major departments and agencies have policies that are regularly updated. In its 1994 survey, the MSPB found that more than "80 percent of the respondents counted establishing and publicizing sexual harassment policies among the most effective actions an organization can take to reduce or prevent sexual harassment" (U.S. Merit Systems Protection Board, 1995, pp. 40–41). In fact, two-thirds or more of the respondents rated universal training of employees, publicizing penalties and complaint channels, protecting victims from reprisals, training of all managers and supervisors, and enforcement of strong penalties as essential to preventing sexual harassment (p. 41). Although a "sizable minority" of federal employees did not see agency sexual harassment policies as particularly effective, the MSPB concluded that they are "almost as important for what they represent as for what they actually say or do."

> The policies are evidence that agency leaders are on record as intending to deal appropriately with sexual harassment. That stated commitment from the top can be critical in backing up managers and supervisors at levels who are trying to foster a workplace environment in which sexual harassment is not tolerated. (p. 41)

By the late 1990s, most states had implemented statewide or agency-level sexual harassment policies, with Michigan's 1979 policy being the first. While the states have clearly recognized the need to have a policy prohibiting sexual harassment "on the books," as late as 1996 few if any had comprehensive programs that fully met the standards set by the courts (Bowman and Zigmond, 1996). Likewise, the vast majority of cities with populations over 100,000 have instituted sexual harassment policies, and most of them have some kind of formal training program in place. Typically, the central human resources office has responsibility for conducting this training. A 1989 survey of large cities revealed that they were taking "affirmative steps to protect themselves from potential liability suits and damaging publicity" (Kirk-Westerman et al., 1989, p. 104).

CONCLUSION

By all accounts, sexual harassment is probably one of the most underreported forms of discrimination in the workplace, but this situation appears to be changing rapidly. Growing public awareness and media attention have created an environment in which those who believe they are victims of sexual harassment are more likely to take advantage of the remedies available to them. The number of sexual harassment complaints on all levels of government has increased, and this trend may be expected to continue. In addition to having sexual harassment policies and related administrative procedures in place that meet current legal standards, public employers should be taking affirmative steps to prevent and to deal with sexual harassment. The MSPB made four general recommendations to federal agencies that appear to be equally applicable on the state and local levels:

- Agency management should forcefully publicize penalties and encourage assertive responses by employees who are victims of sexual harassment.
- Managers and supervisors must respond according to the seriousness of the offense, not the rank of the offender, and they should be firm and consistent in using progressive discipline to deal with those who are proven to be guilty of harassment
- Public employers should consider it their responsibility to determine the extent and seriousness of sexual harassment in their organizations so that they can take appropriate and effective steps in response.
- The effectiveness of sexual harassment training for workers, managers, and supervisors should be systematically evaluated in order to assure that it is addressing existing

problems, meeting legal standards, and encouraging victims to report sexual harassment and to make formal complaints without fear of retaliation. (U.S. Merit Systems Protection Board, 1995, pp. 53–56)

At this time, public employers are expected to understand that sexual harassment is illegal discrimination with regard to the terms and conditions of employment. They should know that employers have the duty to maintain a working environment free of sexual harassment. This duty goes beyond simply having a sexual harassment policy, because it requires them to take positive steps to eliminate it and to remedy its effects (Webster, 1994, 142).

DISCUSSION QUESTIONS

1. Do you think that the EEOC and the courts should use a "reasonable woman" standard as they seek to determine if a hostile environment has been created by a male supervisor?
2. Is growing concern about sexual harassment complaints undermining normal relationships between men and women in the workplace?
3. Does your employer or university have a sexual harassment policy? If so, do you know what it says? Do you think it effectively prevents sexual harassment by supervisors, coworkers, or teachers?
4. What are the steps *you* would take to solve the problem of sexual harassment in the work place?
5. Do you agree with the Supreme Court's reasoning about employer liability in *Faragher*?
6. How would you deal with a supervisor who made "sexually suggestive and insulting" comments to you on several occasions?

REFERENCES

Bowman, James S., and Zigmond, Christopher J. (1996). "Sexual Harassment Policies in State Government: Peering into the Fishbowl of Public Employment." *Spectrum: The Journal of State Government,* Vol. 69, No. 3 (Summer), pp. 24–36.

Burlington Industries, Inc. v Ellerth (1998). No. 97-569, 123 F. 3d 490.

City of Atlanta (1996). "Sexual Harassment Policy." Code of Ordinances, Chapter 114, Article VI, Division 5, Sections 114-600 through 114-608 (July).

Equal Employment Opportunity Commission (1980). "Discrimination Because of Sex Under Title VII of the Civil Rights Act of 1964: Adoption of Final Interpretive Guidelines." *Federal Register,* Vol. 45 (November), pp. 74676–74677.

Faragher v City of Boca Raton (1998). No. 97-282, 111 F. 3d 1530.

Harris v Forklift Systems (1993). 510 U.S. 17

Kirk-Westerman, Connie, Billeaux, David M., and England, Robert E. (1989). "Ending Sexual Harassment at City Hall: Policy Initiatives in Large American Cities." *State and Local Government Review* (Fall), pp. 100–105.

Lee, Robert D., and Greenlaw, Paul S. (1996). "The Complexities of Human Behavior: Recent Instances of Alleged Quid Pro Quo Sexual Harassment." *Review of Public Personnel Administration,* Vol. 16, No. 4 (Fall), pp. 15–28.

Meritor Savings Bank v Vinson (1986). 477 U.S. 57, 91 L. Ed. 2d 49; 106 S Ct 2399.

Morlacci, Maria (1987–88). "Sexual Harassment Law and the Impact of *Vinson.*" *Employee Relations Law Journal,* Vol. 13 (Winter), pp. 501–519.

Muhl, Charles J. (1998). "Sexual Harassment." *Monthly Labor Review,* Vol. 121, No. 7 (July), pp. 61–62.

Oncale v Sundowner Offshore Services, Inc. et al. (1998). No. 96-568, 83 F. 3d 118.

Spann, Jeri (1990). "Dealing Effectively with Sexual Harassment: Some Practical Lessons From One City's Experience." *Public Personnel Management,* Vol. 19, No. 1 (Spring), pp. 53–69.

U.S. Merit Systems Protection Board (1995). *Sexual Harassment in the Federal Workplace* (Washington, DC: U.S. Government Printing Office).

Webster, George D. (1994). "EEOC's Proposed Guidelines on Harassment." *Association Management,* Vol. 6, No. 5 (May), pp. 142–143.

SUGGESTED READINGS

Francke, Linda Bird (1997). *Ground Zero: The Gender Wars in the Military* (New York: Simon & Schuster Trade).

Hartell, Lynda J. (1995). *Sexual Harassment: A Selected Annotated Bibliography* (Westport, CT: Greewood Publishing Group, Inc.).

Levy, Anne (1996). *Workplace Sexual Harassment* (Paramus, NJ: Prentice-Hall).

Morewitz, Stephen (1996). *Sexual Harassment & Social Change in American Society* (Bethesda, MD: Austin & Winfield Publishers).

Paludi, Michele A. (1998). *Sexual Harassment, Work, & Education: A Resource Manual for Prevention,* 2nd ed. (Albany: State University of New York Press).

Pellicciotti, Joseph M. (1997). *Title VII Liability for Sexual Harassment in the Workplace,* 3rd ed. (Alexandria, VA: International Personnel Management Association).

Reese, Laura A. (1998). *Implementing Sexual Harassment Policies: Challenges for the Public Sector* (Thousand Oaks, CA: Sage Publications).

Rutter, Peter (1997). *Understanding & Preventing Sexual Harassment: The Complete Guide* (New York: Bantam Books).

A SUBSTITUTE ORDINANCE AS AMENDED
BY EXECUTIVE COMMITTEE

AN ORDINANCE TO AMEND CHAPTER 114,
ARTICLE VI OF THE CITY OF ATLANTA CODE
OF ORDINANCES, SO AS TO CREATE A NEW
DIVISION 5, SECTIONS 114-600 THROUGH 114-
608, TO BE ENTITLED "SEXUAL HARASSMENT
POLICY"; TO REPEAL CONFLICTING ORDI-
NANCES; AND FOR OTHER PURPOSES.

BE AND IT IS HEREBY ORDAINED BY THE COUN-
CIL OF THE CITY OF ATLANTA, GEORGIA, AS FOLLOWS:

Section 1.   That Chapter 114, Article VI of the Code
                           of Ordinances of the City of Atlanta be
                           amended so as to create a new Division 5,
                           Sections 114-600 through 114-608, to be
                           entitled "Sexual Harassment Policy" to
                           read as follows:

Section 114-600   Statement of Policy

The City of Atlanta is proud of its tradition of a collegial work
environment in which all individuals are treated with respect and
dignity. Each individual has the right to work in a professional
atmosphere that promotes equal opportunities and prohibits discriminatory practices, including sexual harassment. Sexual
harassment, whether verbal, physical, or environmental, is unacceptable and will not be tolerated. In the event incidents of sexual harassment do occur, it is the policy of the City of Atlanta to
take prompt remedial action, calculated to end the harassment.
Retaliation for making a complaint of sexual harassment will not
be tolerated.

Section 114-601   Definition of Sexual Harassment

It is illegal and against the policies of the City of Atlanta for any
employee, male or female, to sexually harass another employee.
It is also illegal and against City policy for any employee who
may be deemed a representative of the City of Atlanta to sexually harass a nonemployee. Sexual harassment is defined as

continued page 302

unwelcome sexual advances, requests for sexual favors, and other verbal or physical conduct of a sexual nature when:

- submission to such conduct is made either explicitly or implicitly a term or condition of an individual's employment;

- submission to or rejection of such conduct by an individual is used as the basis for employment decisions affecting such individual;

- such conduct has the purpose or effect of unreasonably interfering with an individual's work performance or creating an intimidating, hostile, or offensive working environment.

Examples of sexual harassment include, but are not limited to: unwanted sexual advances; demands for sexual favors in exchange for favorable treatment or continued employment; repeated sexual jokes, flirtations, advances or propositions; verbal abuse of a sexual nature; graphic, verbal commentary about an individual's body, sexual prowess, or sexual deficiencies; leering, whistling, touching, pinching, assault, coerced sexual acts or suggestive, insulting, obscene comments or gestures; display in the workplace of sexually suggestive objects or pictures; ostracizing an employee in conformity with sexual conduct; sexual conduct that reasonably causes mental and emotional detriment to the victim; retaliation against an individual for reporting or complaining about sexually harassing conduct. This behavior is unacceptable in the workplace and is unacceptable in other work-related settings such as business trips and business-related social events.

Section 114-602   Individuals Covered

A. The provisions of this ordinance are applicable to all City of Atlanta employees. The use of the term "employee" shall include any person holding any position or employment with the City, to include without any limitation, employees of any status or tenure, appointed and elected officials,

continued page 303

members of commissions and boards, agents, representatives, or interns. The City encourages reporting of all incidents of sexual harassment, regardless of who the offender may be, in accordance with the methods set forth in Section 114-603.

B. In order to ensure the integrity of the work environment, managerial and supervisory personnel are required to ensure adherence to and compliance with this policy and, upon being informed of possible harassment, are required to take appropriate, prompt action in response thereto, including informing complainants of their rights under the procedures set forth in this policy.

C. Return to the Workplace Upon a Finding of "Cause":

As the staffing needs of the City dictate, and whenever possible and practical, an employee who has been disciplined upon a finding of "cause" and who returns to the workplace shall not be returned to the same location or assignment that placed him/her in close proximity to the victim, for a period of at least one (1) year from the date of the last act of sexual harassment. As the staffing needs of the City dictate, and whenever possible and practical, a victim's request for a transfer to an assignment or location away from that of the harasser shall be granted for a period of at least one (1) year from the date of the last act of sexual harassment. This provision shall not be mandatory where impractical, inefficient, logistically impossible or contrary to the best interests of the City as a whole, or a department, bureau, office, or agency.

Section 114-603   Complaint and Investigation Procedure

Employees who feel that they have been victims of sexual harassment should file a discrimination complaint. Prompt reporting of complaints is strongly encouraged, as it allows for rapid response and resolution of objectionable behavior or conditions for the complainant and any other affected employees. An individual who believes he or she has been subjected to sexual harassment should report the incident to any of the following: employee's departmental EEO Coordinator or complaint investigator, the City's Affirmative Action Officer, or the employee's supervisor,

continued page 304

bureau/office director, or commissioner. In the case of employees in the departments of police, fire, or corrections, complaints of sexual harassment may also be made at their respective office of professional standards. The aggrieved employee may elect, at his or her option, to use formal or informal procedures as follows:

A. Informal Complaint Procedure:

1. Each Department shall designate the Departmental EEO Coordinator (DEEOC) and at least one man and one woman from the Department to serve as complaint investigators.

2. The complainant will meet with a complaint investigator of his/her choosing to discuss any complaint of sexual harassment. A written statement will be taken. An accurate record of objectionable behavior is necessary to resolve a complaint of sexual harassment.

3. The complaint investigator will immediately attempt to resolve the complaint through discussions with appropriate managers, scheduling of meetings with concerned parties, and other informal efforts as appropriate, taking care to preserve confidentiality to the maximum reasonable extent.

4. Upon completion of the investigation, the complaint investigator will forward a written report of the investigation to the department head, with recommendations for resolution or corrective action as appropriate.

5. If the investigative report indicates that there is "reasonable cause" to believe that sexual harassing conduct has occurred, the department head shall implement disciplinary procedures, as outlined below in Section 114-604 (B) (1) (a) or (b), as may be appropriate.

6. If the informal efforts are unsuccessful, the complaint investigator will inform the complainant of his/her right to file a formal complaint with the Affirmative Action Division, and will provide the complainant with a copy of the formal charge form.

continued page 305

B. Formal Complaint Procedure: If the complainant elects not to pursue the informal procedures or is not satisfied with the results of the informal procedures, a formal complaint may be filed with the Affirmative Action Officer in the Department of Personnel and Human Resources as follows:

1. The complaint will be reduced to a written statement on an appropriate form. An accurate record of objectionable behavior is necessary to resolve a complaint of sexual harassment.

2. The Affirmative Action Officer will review the complaint to assure that the issue is appropriate for the discrimination complaint process. If it is incomplete, the Affirmative Action Officer will seek clarification.

3. The Affirmative Action Officer will notify the appropriate departmental officials of the complaint.

4. An investigation of the formal complaint will be initiated by the Affirmative Action Division within five (5) working days of notification.

5. Upon completion of the investigation, the Affirmative Action Officer will forward a report of the investigation, with recommendations for appropriate resolution or corrective action, to the Commissioner of the Department of Personnel and Human Resources for review and any recommended changes.

6. The Commissioner of the Department of Personnel and Human Resources shall forward the report to the head of the bureau or department in which the harassment is alleged to have taken place.

7. If the investigative report indicates that there is "reasonable cause" to believe that sexually harassing conduct has occurred, the department head shall initiate disciplinary procedures, as outlined below in Section 114-604 as may be appropriate.

continued page 306

8. The finding of "reasonable cause" by the Affirmative Action Officer as approved by the Commissioner of the Department of Personnel and Human Resources on a formal complaint will result in the issuance of a Notice of Proposed Adverse Action, where appropriate.

C. A member of the public who believes that he or she has been subjected to sexual harassment by a City employee should report the incident to the employee's department head or to the Affirmative Action Officer, for investigation by the Affirmative Action Officer in the manner outlined in subparagraph B above. Alternatively, members of the public may make sexual harassment complaints against employees of the departments of police, fire, and corrections at the office of professional standards of the appropriate department.

Section 114-604   Resolving the Complaint

A. Determination of "No Cause": If the investigation reveals that there is no "reasonable cause" to believe that the allegation of sexual harassment is true, the matter shall be deemed resolved for City purposes and the parties shall be free to pursue other available legal remedies.

B. Determination of "Cause":
   1. Discipline of Employees: If the investigation reveals that there is "reasonable cause" to believe that the allegation of sexual harassment is true, the employee determined to have committed the offense of sexual harassment shall be subject to disciplinary action. The complainant shall be informed of the disciplinary action taken.

   2. Penalty: Sexual harassment is considered a sufficient ground for serious adverse personnel action. Failure to comply with any part of this policy will result in disciplinary action, up to and including dismissal. A severe or pervasive violation of this policy may result in an employee's termination for the first offense. Where appropriate, specific disciplinary action will follow the process prescribed by Section 114-526 through 114-556 of this code of ordinances. The employee's appointing authority shall impose discipline within the following ranges:

continued page 307

    a. First Offense: Sexual harassment training and disciplinary action ranging from a ten (10) day suspension to dismissal.

    b. Second Offense: Dismissal.

Section 114-605   Complaints Against Elected Officials

A. Complaints against elected officials can be reported through either the "informal" or "formal" processes in Section 114-603; however, such complaints shall be promptly investigated by an independent investigator specifically selected for this purpose. Such investigator shall be selected by the City Attorney and shall be a member in good standing of the State Bar of Georgia with appropriate skills and experience. Upon completion of the investigation, the findings and recommendations of the investigator shall be transmitted by the City Attorney, to the complainant, the alleged harasser and to the City Council President or the Chair of the Committee on Council or the Committee on the Executive, as appropriate.

B. Upon a determination of cause, the City Council President, or the Chair of the Committee on Council, or the Chair of the Committee on the Executive, as appropriate, shall take remedial action against the harasser. That remedial action may include, but is not limited to, counseling by the City Council President or Committee Chair, or a resolution sponsored by the appropriate Council Committee censuring the offending official.

C. Any further remedies against an elected official for violation of this sexual harassment policy would be those provided to the electors by the Georgia Recall Statute (O.C.G.A. § 21-4-1, et seq.).

Section 114-606   Confidentiality

In an attempt to protect the privacy of all persons involved, confidentiality will be exercised throughout the investigatory process to the greatest extent practicable. Inasmuch as the City of Atlanta is subject to the Open Records Act (O.C.G.A. §50-18-70, et seq.) and the Open Meetings Acts (O.C.G.A. § 50-14-1, et seq.), absolute confidentiality cannot be assured.

continued page 308

Section 114-607   Retaliation

No City employee, official, or officer shall discriminate or retaliate against an individual who makes a report of sexual harassment. Retaliation is a very serious violation of this policy and should be reported immediately. Any individual found to have retaliated against an individual for reporting sexual harassment, or against anyone participating in the investigation of a complaint, will be subject to the disciplinary actions as provided by Section 114-604.

Section 114-608   Sexual Harassment Prevention Training

A. Supervisory and Management Employees

1. Each supervisory and management employee shall receive an initial training course of at least four hours and a one-hour annual update training session.

2. The training course for supervisory and management employees shall include instruction on what sexual harassment is, how to prevent it, what the repercussions are, and the complaint process.

3. Training for supervisory and management employees shall include sensitivity training.

4. Training shall be conducted by the Affirmative Action Officer or his/her designee, who shall be assisted by at least one person of the opposite gender.

B. Other Employees

1. Each nonsupervisory, nonmanagement employee shall receive an initial training course of at least three hours and a one-hour annual update training session, separate and apart from supervisory and management employees.

2. The training course for nonsupervisory and nonmanagement employees shall include instruction on what sexual harassment is, how to respond to it, what the repercussions are, and the complaint process.

continued page 309

3. Training shall be conducted by the Affirmative Action Officer or his/her designee, who shall be assisted by at least one person of the opposite gender.

Section 114-609   False Allegations

If an investigation results in a finding that the complainant willfully made a false complaint of sexual harrassment, that complainant shall be subject to disciplinary action as provided by Section 114-604.

Section 2.   All ordinances or parts of ordinances in conflict herewith are hereby repealed.

Mayor's Task Force on Sexual Harassment Draft, February 21, 1996; Rubens; Law 3.21.96

A true copy

Olivia P. Wood

Municipal Clerk, CMC

ADOPTED as amended   July 01, 1996
APPROVED by the Mayor   July 08, 1996

Chapter ELEVEN

Responding to the New American Workforce

As we noted in Chapter 1, the characteristics of the civilian labor force (CLF) in the United States have changed greatly over the past 50 years. Personnel systems are being asked to respond to these changes as public employers struggle to attract, retain, and effectively manage needed human resources. Here, we will focus on several challenges that public employers should expect to confront during the early part of the twenty-first century as the American workforce continues its transformation.

THE NEW AMERICAN FAMILY

A very significant change in the CLF is the rapidly growing percentage of female workers, many with young children at home. Between 1971 and 1991, the number of working women grew from 31.5 to 57 million. In 1994, women were 46 percent of the CLF, up from 38 percent in 1970. The Bureau of Labor Statistics (BLS) expects that these trends will continue, "with the female participation rate reaching as high as 66.1 percent and the male participation rate falling as low as 72.9 percent by the year 2005" (U.S. General Accounting Office, 1992, p. 23). In addition to contributing to the growing diversity of the American workplace, the movement of women out of the home and traditional roles and into the workplace in many occupations and on many levels presents a whole new set of challenges to the employer.

Primary among these challenges is how to respond to a new set of family-related issues in ways that effectively meet the needs of both employees and employers. For example, in terms of the substantial increase in the number of working mothers over the past 30 years, less than 20 percent of married women with children under the age of six worked in 1960; by 1990, 60 percent were in the labor market. By the mid-1990s, 42 percent of all wage and salaried female workers had children under the age of 18 at home (Galinski, Bond, and Friedman, 1993, p. 42). Many working women are the sole source of family income. In the words of the Commission on Family and Medical Leave, "Approximately 23 percent of all workers with families have no spouse in the household to share wage-earning or care-giving responsibilities—and women now account for around 80 percent of that group" (Commission on Family and Medical Leave, 1996, p. 5). In addition to there being more single-parent families, the number of "dual-career" couples in the CLF has also expanded significantly. In 1990, about 70 percent of the nation's working men had wives who worked for wages or salaries. This figure had been around 32 percent in 1960. Children are not the only issue, since up to 15 percent of working adults are giving assistance to an older relative, and another 5 to 10 percent are helping a person under the age of 65 or with a disability (p. 10). Many of these workers are also raising young children. These new realities increasingly require public employers to come up with creative supportive conditions under which their employees are able to both meet their family responsibilities and be productive workers.

The traditional "Ozzie and Harriet" family of the 1950s, in which the husband worked and the wife stayed home to raise the children, now represents a relatively small segment of American society—well below 20 percent of all family units (Bureau of National Affairs, 1989; U.S. Bureau of the Census, 1992). Many public employers, however, continue to use human resources policies that assume the workforce of the 1990s is homogeneous, that traditional families prevail, and that organizational practices and norms based on industrial models represent the only way to structure relationships between employers and employees. It has only been during the past 20 years or so that serious consideration has been given to questions about the "fit" between policies such as those governing benefits and working hours and the needs of certain groups of today's workers. It is now better understood that growing numbers of public employees "face the challenge of trying to manage personal responsibilities, such as child care and elder care, from the office or worksite" (U.S. General Accounting Office, 1992b, p. 11). It is, in other words, increasingly difficult for many workers to keep family concerns isolated from their working lives. In 1992, the GAO observed that public as well as private employers were notoriously unresponsive to the new realities of family life in the United States:

> Employees trying to balance family and work responsibilities have often found traditional employment policies unaccommodating. For example, workplace stress is heightened for parents when an inflexible work schedule conflicts with school hours or day care arrangements. In the absence of backup child care, parents must often miss work when a child is sick at home or regular day care arrangements break down. (p. 11)

From the employers' standpoint, these kinds of problems have important organizational as well as social and economic implications. Today's workers are more likely to want a balance between their on- and off-the-job responsibilities, and the available research suggests that responsiveness to these concerns can be an important factor in recruitment, retention, and productivity (Friedman, 1991). The inability of traditional employment practices to deal successfully with the challenges presented by the "new family" has focused attention on a search for new approaches. In practice, there are some signs that public employers are beginning to respond, albeit slowly in some respects. For example, between 1985 and 1994, the proportion of state and local employees eligible for child care benefits subsidized in some manner by their employers grew from 2 to 9 percent (Bureau of Labor Statistics, 1998, p. 5). Social values and demographic trends are largely beyond the direct control of public employers, but personnel policies that reflect and adapt to new realities and exploit new opportunities are certainly possible, and examples may be found in many jurisdictions. These include (1) creative approaches to the content and administration of benefits plans, (2) flexible working arrangements, (3) family leave, and (4) child and elder care programs.

MORE FLEXIBLE AND COST-CONSCIOUS EMPLOYEE BENEFIT PLANS

For public employers, the costs associated with employee benefits range from 20 to 40 percent of the total compensation package, and "it is necessary to treat benefits with the same strategic pay considerations to which wage and salary decisions are subjected" (Daley, 1998, pp. 5–6). At one time, the benefits received by public employees came in "one-size-fits-all" plans set up by their employers. The components of these plans generally could be expected to include paid time off for certain purposes, health and life insurance, and a retirement or pension plan. However, the contemporary emphasis is on developing flexible combinations of benefits that allow public employers to attract and retain needed human resources:

Table 11.1 State and Local Employee Benefits 1994

Type	Percent Eligible*
Paid time off	
Holidays	73
Vacations	66
Personal leave	38
Funeral leave	62
Jury duty	94
Military service	75
Sick leave	94
Family leave	4
Unpaid time off	
Family leave	93
Insurance	
Long-term disability	30
Medical care	87
Dental	62
Life insurance	87
Retirement	
All	96
Defined benefit	91
Defined contribution	9

*These percentages include full- and part-time employees. Part-time employees generally are far less likely to be eligible for certain benefits, such as paid sick leave (40%) and health care insurance (30%).

Source: Bureau of Labor Statistics, *Employee Benefits in State and Local Governments. 1994* (Washington, DC: U.S. Department of Labor, 1998).

> Creative benefit-packaging includes traditional insurance programs (health, dental, life, vision and disability) and such innovations as flex-time, family-leave options, bonus programs, stock options, office equipment and support, personal access to company-owned technology, general education and training programs, employee assistance programs, child care, food services, transportation, recreation, and domestic partner benefits. (Fredericksen and Soden, 1998, p. 25)

In 1994, the BLS survey of benefits received by state and local public employees revealed the pattern of coverages shown in Table 11.1.

Over the past decade, rapidly increasing costs and changing employee needs have combined to build employer interest in so-called "cafeteria benefit plans" where employees have some choices with regard to alternative health care and retirement plans, as well as combinations of other optional benefits, such as disability and life insurance, flexible spending accounts, and child care. An example of current trends is provided by the results of a survey of its members conducted by the International City/County Management Association in 1995 (Moulder and Hall, 1995). The survey found that:

- Almost half of the localities surveyed paid their employees for unused sick leave, and over 13 percent allowed conversion of unused sick leave into paid vacation leave.
- Thirty percent offered flexible working hours and over 10 percent made job sharing available.
- Close to 90 percent made telecommuting an option for some of their employees, while over 10 percent made it available to everybody.
- About one-third have moved to a cafeteria selection of benefits in some areas, although a smaller proportion offers a choice of health care plans. (Streib, 1996)

One area in which there was relatively little activity was on-site and subsidized child care, but it noted that growing private-sector interest in meeting the child care needs of employees might signal a general move in that direction by employers in both sectors in the relatively near future. Nonetheless, it did find a number of jurisdictions that had on-site child care and several that offered subsidies. A few made both available to all of their employees.

Another very visible development in benefits is a dramatic trend away from a reliance on traditional fee-for-service or indemnity plans in favor of health maintenance organizations (HMOs) and preferred provider organizations (PPOs). By 1994, 30 percent of local governments offered HMOs to their workers, and another 30 percent had PPO plans in operation. In 1990, fully 61 percent of localities relied on indemnity plans. By 1994, this figure was down to 38 percent (Bureau of Labor Statistics, 1998;

BULLETIN

Child Care Benefits of
Selected Cities and Counties

City/County	On-Site	Subsidized
Birmingham, AL	No	Yes
Broward Co., FL	No	Yes
Cobb Co., GA	Yes	No
Dallas, TX	Yes	No
Fairfax, VA	Yes	Yes
Honolulu, HI	Yes	No
Los Angeles Co.	Yes	No
City of Los Angeles	Yes	No
Minneapolis, MN	No	Yes
Wichita, KS	No	Yes

Source: Evelina Moulder and Gwen Hall, *Special Data Issue: Employee Benefits in Local Government* (Washington, DC: ICMA, 1995), p. 6. These data are for 1994 and cover localities that make one or both of these benefits available to all employees.

Streib, 1996). Larger jurisdictions are more likely to offer employees a choice between plans, usually between an indemnity plan and either an HMO or a PPO.

In general terms, the combination of a need to address the rising costs of benefits and to be more responsive to employee needs has driven public employers to consider and, in many cases, implement innovative and more flexible benefits packages. The steep climb in health care costs to employers has moderated over the past few years, a trend that appears to reflect the increasing use of HMOs and PPOs, both of which are designed to contain and "ultimately to reduce costs, thereby increasing the financial viability of the organization" (Perry and Cayer, 1997, p. 10). Of the three types of plans, HMOs do generate the highest levels of *employee* complaints, but public *employers*, at least those on the local level, appear to be most satisfied with HMOs when employee complaints, number of services offered, and previous cost increases are all taken into account:

> As is true in the health care services generally, it is likely that traditional indemnity plans will continue to lose their appeal in municipal government. Given that human resources managers associate them with lower levels of satisfaction and view them as more costly, they are likely to view them less favorably as options for their employees. (Perry and Cayer, 1997, p. 17)

With regard to retirement benefits, as the data in Table 11.1 suggest, there has been some movement in the public sector toward making *defined contribution* plans available as alternatives to long-standing *defined benefit* plans. Defined contribution plans typically involve a savings arrangement under which tax-deferred employee contributions are matched in some proportion by the employer. In the private sector, most employers offer at least one defined contribution plan. Well over half of these plans make at least five different investment options available to participating employees. Defined benefit plans, under which retirees receive a fixed benefit based on a formula that includes years of service and salary, are still offered by the vast majority of employers in both sectors (Anonymous, 1996).

FLEXIBLE WORK PROGRAMS

Until recently, most public personnel systems had standardized work schedules and job designs for all employees. No effort was made to adjust to the personal and family-related needs of workers. Everybody was on a "9-to-5" schedule, five days a week. Over the past 20 years, however, public as well as private employers have come to recognize that flexible work programs may significantly enhance their capability to recruit, retain, and motivate a high-quality workforce. These programs are designed to create a better "fit" between organizational requirements and employees' needs and preferences. Specific examples include part-time work and job sharing, alternative schedules, and telecommuting. These and other flexibilities may be highly attractive to potential as well as current employees. For example, one study of federal agencies and private corporations revealed that flexible scheduling was highly valued by almost 40 percent of the public employees (Fredericksen and Soden, 1998, p. 32). Many public employers, including the federal government, have instituted a variety of flexible work programs, and private corporations are now investing heavily in this approach. Over two-thirds of businesses offered flexible work schedules in 1996, and almost the same percentage makes part-time employment available. Other popular options include job sharing (36 percent), compressed work schedules (22 percent), and telecommuting/working at home (20 percent) (McShulskis, 1997).

Alternative work schedules (AWS) are now found on all levels of government. The various forms of AWS are modifications of the traditional "9-to-5" five-days-a-week schedule. Two basic forms are widely used. One form, called *flexitime* in the federal government, divides the work day into core time and flexible time. Under flexitime, the worker must be on the job during core time, but flexible time allows for variations in starting and stopping. Currently, there are five types of flexible work schedules used by the federal government: flexitour, gliding schedule, variable day schedule, variable week schedule, and maxiflex. The second form of AWS is *compressed time,* which involves an 80-hour biweekly basic work requirement scheduled for less than 10 workdays. Compressed schedules offer a variety of options for workers who want to free up a day or two for personal and family use. Detailed descriptions of the flexitime compressed time options may be found in Appendix 11.A.

Most evaluations of flextime are based on private-sector studies, but these findings are very likely to apply to government as well as nonprofit employers. These studies

---

BULLETIN

The STATE OF GEORGIA
Flexible Benefits Program

The options available through the program are:

Legal insurance	Dental insurance
Long-term care	Flexible spending accounts for health care and dependent care
Health care: Indemnity and HMO	Life insurance
Dependent life	Accidental death and dismemberment
Short-term disability	Long-term disability

Source: Georgia Merit System (http://gms.state.ga.us// flex/options.htm), July 1998.

indicate that flexible scheduling does have positive effects on productivity, morale, absenteeism, and use of overtime (Ezra and Deckman, 1996, p. 175). With regard to family life, a recent study of federal employees showed that:

- Parents using flexitime were more likely to be satisfied with their child care.
- Parents using flexible schedules "were more likely to be satisfied with their work/family balance than parents who did not." (p. 177)

As a trendsetter in the use of AWS, the federal government's experience may offer useful guidance to states and localities. The first flexible work schedules were established by the Bureau of Indian Affairs and the Social Security Administration during the early 1970s. Both agencies began their AWS experiments in an effort to deal with "tardiness, lost productivity, low morale, and, in the case of the SSA, an extensive amount of leave without pay (LWOP)." For both, the results were positive. However, AWS programs were not technically legal until 1979, when the Federal Employee's Flexible and Compressed Work Schedules Act of 1978 became effective.

This legislation created a three-year experimental program intended to evaluate the effects of AWS. OPM had lead responsibility for setting up, managing, and evaluating the program. The Congress required OPM to evaluate the AWS program in six areas: (1) efficiency of government operations, (2) impact on mass transit and traffic, (3) energy consumption, (4) service to the public, (5) opportunities for full- and part-time employment, and (6) responses of individuals and families. Highly favorable results led to passage of the Federal Employees Flexible and Compressed Work Schedules Act of 1982, which established AWS as an ongoing program and imposed a three-year "sunset" provision. Subsequently, strongly positive evaluations by OPM, the GAO, the Congress, and others set the stage for passage of Public Law 99-196, which made AWS a permanent program in 1985 (U.S. General Accounting Office, 1985).

FLEXIBLE WORKPLACES

Flexible workplace and *flexiplace* are terms describing several forms of paid employment and employer-employee relationships in which the work site is shifted away from the traditional primary office. These situations include work done at home or at satellite offices and telecommuting, or teleworking, in which sophisticated communication and computer systems are used to carry out work assignments from remote locations.

The idea of designating an employee's home as the official work site is not new to the public sector. In 1957, the U.S. Comptroller General authorized federal agencies to pay employees for work done at home if the agencies were able to verify and evaluate performance, if the work involved could really be done at home, and if it made sense from an agency perspective to use the home as a work site. Such arrangements were used informally to handle situations, but no organized federal flexiplace effort existed until 1990 when a pilot program covering 500 federal employees in 13 agencies was launched. The guidelines for the pilot noted that flexiplace offered several potential benefits to public employers:

> . . . attract[ing] and retain[ing] employees in critical occupations and positions, such as technical and scientific researchers or computer programmers; targeting new labor markets such as severely handicapped individuals; reducing space and associated costs; or enabling agencies to better conduct the organization's work by allowing increased flexibility in the location of the work site. (President's Council on Management Improvement, 1990, p. 3)

The pilot yielded encouraging results, and the GAO stated in 1992 that there were "some early indications that the federal flexiplace initiatives can improve productivity and lower costs." OPM also reported that monthly focus group meetings for participants showed favorable results, and "90% of employees and 70% of supervisors said they consider flexiplace a desirable work arrangement" (U.S. Office of Personnel Management, 1991). By 1997, when the GAO investigated agency policies and views on flexiplace and reported its findings, it noted a significant general growth in the program (from around 4,000 to 9,000 participants) as well as President Clinton's goal of achieving 60,000 federal telecommuters by the end of FY 1998 (U.S. General Accounting Office, 1997).

Overall, the GAO found that federal agencies saw many benefits, including increased productivity and job satisfaction, decreased need for office space, and lessened environmental impacts (p. 12). There were also some reasons found for not using telecommuting, such as isolation, inadequate work space at home, and lack of self-discipline. Agencies felt that "the best flexitime participants are disciplined self-starters who need little supervision" (p. 13). In practice, this means that most telecommuters are professionals. The major source of resistance to telecommuting on the agency level is management opposition, with other barriers being budget constraints, the nature of the work involved, and the need to protect the security of sensitive data.

By 1998, OPM (U.S. Office of Personnel Management, 1998c) was prepared to issue a general rationale for telecommuting for agency use that included the following claims:

- It improves the quality of work life and job performance and productivity by reducing office overcrowding and providing a distraction-free environment for reading, thinking, and writing.
- Morale is improved and stress reduced because telecommuting gives employees more options to balance work and family demands.
- It increases customer access to public services by creating more locations where they are available.
- It may allow an agency to continue to provide services when the regular office is closed by disasters or emergencies.
- Telecommuting enhances agencies' ability to recruit and promote diversity by expanding the geographic recruitment pool.
- It extends employment opportunities to those with disabilities and health problems who are able to work at home.
- Traffic congestion, energy consumption, and air pollution can be reduced if significant numbers of workers telecommute.

For these reasons, telecommuting and other flexiplace arrangements are likely to become increasingly popular with public employers. Appendix 11.B is an OPM document designed to answer questions about telecommuting that might be asked by employees and their supervisors.

PART-TIME WORK

These programs respond to the situations of employees who want (or must) spend more time with their families than the normal 40-hour week allows. The BLS defines part-time employment as working less than 35 hours a week.

The Federal Employees Part-Time Career Employment Act was passed in 1978 in an effort to expand part-time opportunities in the federal service. According to the Act, "many individuals in our society possess great productive potential which goes unused because they cannot meet the requirements of a standard workweek." The Congress determined that making part-time employment available should have a number of benefits, including:

- Helping older workers make the transition into retirement.
- Opening employment opportunities for persons with disabilities and others who might need a shorter work week.

- Making it easier for parents to meet family responsibilities if both have to work.
- Supporting students' efforts to finance their education or vocational training part-time.
- Reducing costly turnover and absenteeism caused by demands on some workers' time that make it difficult to work a full 40-hour week.
- Expanding agencies' recruitment pools by adding qualified persons who otherwise could not be attracted to public employment. (Public Law 95-437)

The Congress acted in 1978 to correct what it saw to be serious weaknesses in the national government's approach to part-time employment. It urged federal agencies to "make a substantial good faith effort to set goals which would represent meaningful progress and to move toward them." In 1986, however, the GAO concluded that not much progress had been made. In 1991, the Merit Systems Protection Board observed that a few agencies like the Department of Veterans Affairs and OPM had established formal programs, but most part- time positions in the federal civil service had probably been created in response to requests from full-time employees, rather than as a part of a planned program or policy (U.S. Merit Systems Protection Board, 1991, pp. 40–42). The MSPB noted at the time that opportunities to expand the number of part-time jobs did exist throughout the federal service and that nothing prevented federal agencies from hiring several part-time employees to fill what were previously full-time positions, and it concluded that the lack of progress was the result of "bureaucratic inertia." Since then, however, some progress has been made. As of July 1998, there were over 175,000 part-time federal employees, which represented about 6.3 percent of the civilian workforce (U.S. Office of Personnel Management, 1998a, p. 12).

Job sharing is a form of part-time work in which two or more employees share the responsibilities of one full-time position by

---

BULLETIN

Federal Telecenters

"Telecenter sites were selected based on GSA's observation that 16,000 federal employees commuted at least 75 miles each way on congested roads in the Washington, D.C., metropolitan area. In the spring of 1993, GSA began working in partnership with state and local governments in the Washington area, and by December 1994, the Washington area had four telecenters—one each in Hagerstown, Maryland; Charles County, Maryland; Winchester, Virginia; and Fredericksburg, Virginia. These telecenters had a total of 80 workstations, 143 participants, and a 55 percent utilization rate. Twenty organizations in 10 executive branch departments and agencies used these 4 centers."

Source: U.S. General Accounting Office, *Federal Workforce: Agencies' Policies and Views on Flexiplace in the Federal Government* (Washington, DC: GAO/GGD-97-116, 1997), p. 24.

splitting workdays or weeks. In addition to sharing a job on the basis of time, workers may also divide job tasks "depending on their skills and expertise." A job's salary and benefits typically are split among the job sharers. Job sharing is a more complicated form of part-time work because it involves using two or more persons to fill one full-time slot, so "there must be at least two employees in the same agency and post of duty who are personally and professionally compatible, and who want to share one job" (U.S. Merit Systems Protection Board, 1991, p. 43). For these reasons, job sharing is not currently widely used in the federal government or elsewhere.

In 1990, under authority of the Part-Time Career Employment Act, the Congress required OPM to set up a formal job sharing program. OPM is expected to function as a "clearinghouse" through which persons looking for job sharing opportunities are matched with positions that may be filled under such an arrangement. In response, OPM implemented a pilot-automated registration project called the "OPM Connection." Covering the cities of Boston, Chicago, Los Angeles, and Washington, D.C., the project was intended to match employees looking for job sharing partners, allowing these "teams" to apply for full-time vacancies announced by agencies. Federal agencies are also able to get from OPM the names of workers interested in part-time and shared job opportunities. As of early 1991, about 800 employees were sharing jobs, but a significant expansion of this approach to part-time employment was considered to be unlikely, primarily because of the inevitable coordination and scheduling complexities. In the long term, however, public employers stand to benefit if they have well-crafted part-time employment programs. It is likely that a growing percentage of the workforce will be looking for part-time arrangements.

FAMILY LEAVE POLICIES

On the national level, the political debate over family leave rights for American workers has been intense. On two occasions, the Congress passed legislation requiring businesses with 50 or more employees

BULLETIN

State of Georgia Personnel Board Rule # 30

"In accordance with the provisions of this rule, an appointing authority may adopt a policy to permit eligible employees to donate or receive leave from other employees of the same department. A leave donation policy shall specify criteria to be utilized in authorizing solicitations for donated leave and designate staff authorized to administer leave donations. Such policy shall be accessible for review by employees. Leave donations shall be from employee to employee and shall be strictly voluntary. The identity of donors shall be confidential and shall not be provided to the recipient or to any other individual unless necessary to administer the donation or required by law."

Source: State Personnel Board, Rule #30, Section 30.100, General Provisions (Atlanta, GA).

to grant them 10 workweeks of unpaid leave during any 24-month period for births, adoptions, and family illnesses. The legislation would also have allowed federal employees up to 18 weeks of unpaid leave for the same reasons. President Bush vetoed both bills, arguing that they would undermine productivity and were an unjustified governmental intrusion into the normal operation of the labor market. The introduction to the vetoed Family and Medical Leave Act of 1989, clearly defined its rationale:

> H.R. 770 addresses a profound change in the composition of the workforce that has had a dramatic effect on families. Sixty percent of all mothers are currently in the labor force, which is three times what it was thirty years ago. In the great majority of families today, all of the adult members work. The role of the family as primary nurturer and care-giver has been fundamentally affected by a new economic reality. Families are struggling [to] find a way to carry out the traditional role of bearing and caring for children and providing the emotional and physical support to their members during times of greatest need. When families fail to carry out these critical functions, the social costs are enormous. (Family and Medical Leave Act of 1989, p. 2)

The Family and Medical Leave Act of 1993 (FMLA) was signed into law by President Clinton. This legislation requires all businesses with 50 or more employees and all public agencies (state, local, federal, and educational) to provide up to 12 weeks of unpaid, job-protected leave for the following reasons:

- Care of a newborn, newly adopted or foster child.
- Care of a child, spouse, or parent with a serious health condition.
- A serious health condition of the employee, including maternity-related disability.

Employers must maintain health insurance coverage for workers on leave and place them in the same job or an equivalent when they return. Under the FMLA, employees are covered if they have worked for the employer for one year or a total of at least 1,250 hours (Commission on Family and Medical Leave, 1996, p. 15). In the private sector, the law covers about 11 percent of all work sites or about 60 percent of all workers.

Although public employers may choose to offer more generous family leave benefits, the FMLA sets a minimum standard that virtually all must follow. Roughly 12 million state and local employees are covered, with about 33 percent being eligible for more than the required 12 weeks. In 1994, the average benefit for state and local employees was 6 months (Kim, 1998, p. 45). Paid family leave is seldom available, but public employers are experimenting with approaches that allow their workers to share or donate annual leave and to use sick leave to care for family members. For example, in 1994, the federal government enacted the Federal Employees Family Friendly Leave Act, which allows employees to use up to 13 days of sick leave to care for family members or to arrange for or attend the funeral of a family member. Federal employees may also use sick leave for purposes related to the adoption of a child. In testimony before the House Subcommittee on Compensation and Employee Benefits, Committee on Post Office and Civil Service, a representative of the GAO made the following points in support of this legislation:

> Our work has shown that the practice of giving employees paid time off to care for ill family members is becoming quite common among leading nonfederal employers. In our report comparing federal and nonfederal work/family programs, we found that most of the nonfederal organizations we visited permitted employees to use all or a portion of their paid sick leave to care for family members who are ill. Other approaches to this issue [that] some employers used included providing separate "family emergency" leave allowances and combining vacation and sick time into one account to give employees the flexibility to take time off for any reason. (U.S. General Accounting Office, 1994, p. 3)

Another way of supporting employees is to make *leave sharing programs* available. They are designed to help employees who have used up their paid leave and are faced with the prospect of having to ask for unpaid leave or, even worse, resigning their positions in order to care for family members. The Federal Employees Leave Sharing Act of 1988, as amended, authorizes federal agencies to allow donations of annual leave (paid vacation days) by employees to coworkers who have exhausted their annual leave and face a family medical emergency that requires extended absence from work resulting in loss of income. Under the federal plan, agencies establish leave banks, and employees are allowed to contribute a specified amount of annual leave to the bank every year. Members of the bank with medical emergencies can then withdraw leave from the bank if they use up their own leave (U.S. Office of Personnel Management, 1998b, pp. 1–2). According to the GAO, the leave sharing program is "quite successful and is widely supported by federal agencies and employees alike" (U.S. General Accounting Office, 1994, p. 1). Appendix 11.C is OPM's fact sheet for federal employees on leave policies.

CHILD CARE PROGRAMS

For single-parent families and those in which both parents work, child care is an important issue. Families often have difficulty arranging affordable child care, and those having the most problems are likely to experience frequent work disruptions and high levels of absenteeism (Weisberg and Buckler, 1994, pp. 101–113).

By the mid-1990s, two-thirds of all preschool children, or nearly 15 million, had mothers in the workforce. Over three-fourths of all school-age children have mothers who work. American workers face a chronic shortage of affordable, quality child care services. By the late 1980s, Americans were spending close to $24 billion on such assistance (Peters, 1997, p. 281). In 1997, about 29 million U.S. families included children under the age of 14; in close to 15 million of these families, both parents were employed, and about 5 million were headed by women who worked. Since the availability of affordable child care has a significant impact on workers' productivity, public as well as private employers have a vested interest in doing whatever they can to help meet this need. In addition to the flexible work programs described above, public employers have several options to choose from, including (1) assistance in the form of information about child care resources and referral services; (2) financial assistance for day care, such as vouchers, subsidies, and tax shelters (flexible spending accounts); and, (3) day care facilities on or near the job site.

Using their employee assistance programs (EAPs), or through a contractor, public agencies can provide information and support to workers needing child care. These services can range from simply making lists of providers available to actively helping employees locate and select an appropriate child care facility. New York State's program contracts with local child care providers who go to the work site to help workers seeking information and referrals. In the federal service, basic agency-level information and referral services are often provided by agencies.

Day care can be a very expensive proposition, especially for workers on the lower end of the pay scale. Parents may expect to pay several thousand dollars per year or more for each child they have in full-time day care. In general, public

BULLETIN

Child Care in France

"In the U.K. as in the U.S., the work-family conflict has been addressed by a combination of partially paid parental leave and the decision of many mothers with young children to work part-time. Public financed child care is virtually nonexistent. But France spends more than $40 billion a year on various forms of child care. There, a 10-week paid maternity leave is followed by one of two statutory options: a four-day workweek or a one- to three-year unpaid parental leave, with a guarantee of the same or similar job at the end." Other benefits include: (1) government payments to cover Social Security contributions for a baby-sitter, (2) payments and tax breaks to help pay for child care, and (3) pre-primary schooling at no cost. "In the U.S., just one-third of eligible children are in preschool programs, and only moms on welfare receive subsidies."

Source: Ann Crittenden, "Work-Family Solutions: Why French Women Are Ahead," *Working Woman,* Vol. 20, No. 9 (September, 1995), p. 12.

employers do not offer their workers direct financial assistance, but some, like the federal government do subsidize child care by providing space rent-free, negotiating discounts with private providers, and covering initial membership fees and costs associated with joining child care networks.

Since 1985, federal agencies have been authorized to spend public funds for space and services for child care facilities. Users must be a group composed of at least 50 percent federal employees, and federal employees are to be given priority access. Many civilian agencies have established on-site child care centers on their own or in conjunction with other agencies (U.S. General Accounting Office, 1992a, pp. 85–86). In a tragic example, there was a child care center in the Murrah Federal Building when it was bombed, and many of the victims were young children. Agency subsidies make costs to parents somewhat lower than those charged by non-federal child care facilities.

Somewhat different approaches to child care are used by the states of New York and California. In New York, the state provides free space in state buildings, and the centers charge sliding fees based on employees' income. In many states and localities, employee organizations and management have negotiated contracts addressing child care for employees. In California, a contract negotiated by the state and employee organizations included the following provisions:

- It shall be State policy to encourage the development of child care services for dependent children.
- The State agrees to establish programs and provide financial assistance, within budgetary constraints, for the development of child care centers.
- The State agrees to establish a State Labor–Management Child Committee, the functions of which include encouraging State employees to form nonprofit corporations to

BULLETIN

The Benefit of the '90s

Elder care programs are likely to become increasingly relevant to American workers and their families. A variety of studies show that over 70 percent of care givers are women and almost 65 percent of these are employed outside the home. Annually, care givers spend around $2 billion of their own money on food, medicines, and care giver support services. On average, the care giver devotes 18 hours per week to this often stressful and demanding role.

Source: Jo Horne Schmidt, "Who's Taking Care of Mom and Dad?" *Journal of the American Society of CLU & ChFC*, Vol. 51, No. 1 (November, 1997), pp. 82–87.

provide child care services, and to make recommendations to the Department of Personnel Administration about which providers should receive child care funds.

■ The State may provide the use of its facilities for child care centers, which may include a rental/lease agreement. (California Department of Personnel Administration, 1998)

Although progress has been made, it is clear that establishing adequate, safe, and affordable child care facilities for employees will continue to be a major challenge to public employers. Meeting this challenge, of course, will require public policies that make the needed resources available to workers and employers. Employers' attitudes will also need to change, in many cases, and it is likely that they will as the connections between "family-friendly" personnel practices and organizational success in the labor market become clearer.

ELDER CARE PROGRAMS

In the United States, the number of persons over age 55 is rapidly increasing. In 1997, about 34 million American were 65 or older, and that percentage is expected to more than double by the year 2030. There are now about 4 million over the age of 84 and this number is projected to grow to 6 million by 2010.

Although most of the elderly are capable of taking care of themselves, it is clear that a steadily growing group of workers will be providing care for older parents, relatives, or friends. In all likelihood, this group will be composed largely of middle-aged working women (U.S. Department of Labor, 1998). Many public employers, such as the federal government, fit the description of those projected to be hit hardest by elder care problems. They already have relatively high proportions of female and middle-aged workers, and the projected trend is for steady increases (West, 1998, pp. 94–96). For a large part of the public workforce, child care responsibilities will be followed or even accompanied by a potentially even longer-term commitment to elder care.

The effects on productivity and turnover are likely to rival those connected with child care problems. In the words of the Commission on Family and Medical Leave (1996):

> To care for elders' many and changing needs, employed primary care givers often put in long hours providing informal care on top of their work hours. They often rearrange their work schedules, work fewer hours than they wish to, or take time off without pay. (p. 11)

In addition, other problems found to be associated with caring for elderly relatives are (1) work interruptions to deal with emergencies and phone calls, (2) increased employee stress that leads to taking time off and resignations, (3) reluctance to relocate or travel, and (4) lowered morale (Schmidt, 1997, p. 2).

Indifference to the needs of workers providing or contemplating elder care will surely be a competitive disadvantage in the labor market of the future. For the most part, public sector responses to elder care needs parallel those of the private sector. Both sectors emphasize educational programs and resources referral networks. The former are designed to help prepare employees for elder care responsibilities, and the latter are intended to assist in finding the services that elderly dependents may require. Overall, about one-third of all private employers offer some elder care benefits. Of these, about 80 percent have resource and referral programs, and around 20 percent make long-term care insurance and counseling available to employees (Walter, 1996; U.S. Department of Labor, 1998).

Other options that may become necessary as the number of working care givers continues to grow include providing on-site elder care centers, subsidizing employee use of elder care centers, and employee assistance programs (EAPs) designed to provide a variety of psychological and "respite" support services. One study of workers in a variety of public service agencies found that they ranked improved leave policies for care of dependent elders as the most important benefit an employer could offer. Other benefits that these workers valued were, in order of importance: (1) home visitors, (2) elder care referral services, (3) adult care facilities, (4) financial assistance, (5) leaves of absence, (6) educational seminars, (7) flexible spending accounts, and (8) job sharing and part-time work opportunities (Kossek, De Marr, Blackman, and Kollar, 1993; U.S. Department of Labor, 1998). One interesting innovation is the intergenerational center, where child and elder care facilities and programs are combined. There are more than 200 such centers in operation across the country (Gubernick, 1996).

BULLETIN

Adult Day Care

"Although there is no legislation authorizing Federal agencies to use space for adult day care centers, Easter Seals and the Employee Activities Association (EEA) located at the Social Security Administration (SSA) and the Health Care Financing Administration (HCFA) in Baltimore, Maryland, are sponsoring Break-a-Way, a conveniently located, affordable senior adult day program for elderly relatives of employees. . . .The EEA is a non-profit employee group that provides services (e.g., fitness centers and child care centers) to employees at SSA and HCFA. . . .The center opened in 1997 and serves up to 50 people a day. . . .There is transportation from home and back for persons who live within a 3-mile radius of the center."

Source: U.S. Department of Labor, Women's Bureau, *Facts on Working Women—Work and Elder Care: Facts for Caregivers and Their Employers* (Washington, DC, U.S. Department of Labor), May, 1998.

CONCLUSION

Building family-friendly workplaces promises to be an ongoing challenge for public employers, and specialists in human resources may expect to play a major role in the effort to develop innovative and effective ways of addressing it. At one level, creating family-friendly workplaces starts with breaking down a set of outdated stereotypes and assumptions about the social and economic conditions and needs of American workers. It also requires a willingness on the part of management to see flexible benefits, family leave, child and elder care, and other responses as rational *investments* in the human resources needed to achieve high levels of organizational productivity, quality products and services, and employee commitment. Equally obvious is the reality that responding effectively to many of the human resources challenges flowing from the changing demographics of the American population and its workforce will require a comprehensive reform of the institutions and policies that govern the workplace (Johnston, 1987, p. xxv). While public personnel agencies are certainly in a position to exercise leadership on the organizational level, problems such as those afflicting the U.S. health care, social insurance, and welfare systems are public policy issues that must be acted on by the nation's political leadership.

DISCUSSION QUESTIONS

1. What *is* your employer doing to provide a family-friendly work environment?
2. What *should* your employer be doing to be more responsive to the family-related needs of employees?
3. What are the most important benefits employers should offer?
4. Should public employers be required to offer subsidized child/elder care to employees?
5. Does providing family-friendly benefits, flexible schedules, and child care services create conditions under which employees *without children* are treated less generously than those who are eligible because they have children?

REFERENCES

Anonymous (1996). "More Choice, Flexibility Seen in U.S. Benefits Plans." *National Underwriter—Property & Casualty Risk & Benefits Management,* Vol. 100, No. 16 (April 15), p. 29.

Bureau of Labor Statistics (1998). *Reports on Employee Benefits in State and Local Governments, 1994* (Washington, DC: http://stats.bls.gov/ebs).

Bureau of National Affairs, Inc. (1989). *101 Key Statistics on Work and Family for the 1990s* (Washington, DC).

California Department of Personnel Administration (1998). State Labor Contract with Bargaining Unit 1, Professional Administrative, Financial and Staff Services (Local 1000 SEIU), Article 20, 1992–1995.

Commission on Family and Medical Leave (1996). *A Workable Balance: Report to Congress on Family and Medical Leave Policies* (Washington, DC: U.S. Department of Labor).

Daley, Dennis M. (1998). "An Overview of Benefits for the Public Sector." *Review of Public Personnel Administration,* Vol. 18, No. 3 (Summer), pp. 3–22.

Ezra, Marni, and Deckman, Melissa (1996). "Balancing Work and Family Responsibilities: Flextime and Child Care in the Federal Government." *Public Administration Review,* Vol. 56, No. 2 (March/April), pp. 174–179.

Family and Medical Leave Act of 1989 (1989). 101st Congress, H.R. 770, April 13.

Family and Medical Leave Act of 1993 (1993). PL. 103-3 Stat. 7 (February 5).

Fredericksen, Patricia J., and Soden, Dennis L. (1998). "Employee Attitudes Toward Benefit Packaging." *Review of Public Personnel Administration,* Vol. 18, No. 3 (Summer), pp. 23–41.

Friedman, Dana E. (1991). *Linking Work-Family Issues to the Bottom Line* (New York: Conference Board).

Galinski, Ellen; Bond, James T.; and Friedman, Dana E. (1993). *The Changing Workforce: Highlights of the National Study* (New York: Family and Work Institute).

Gubernick, Lisa (1996). "Granny Care and Kiddie Care." *Forbes,* Vol. 158, No. 15 (December 30), pp. 74–75.

Johnston, William B. (1987). *Workforce 2000: Work and Workers for the 21st Century* (Indianapolis, IN: Hudson Institute).

Kim, Soonlee (1998). "Administering Family Leave Benefits and New Challenges for Public Personnel Management." *Review of Public Personnel Administration,* Vol. 18, No. 3 (Summer), pp. 42–57.

Kossek, Ellen Ernst, DeMarr, Beverly J., Blackman, Kirsten, and Kollar, Mark (1993). "Assessing Employees' Emerging Elder Care Needs and Reactions to Dependent Care Benefits." *Public Personnel Management,* Vol. 22, No. 4 (Winter), pp. 617–638.

McShulskis, Elaine (1997). "Work and Family Benefits are Increasingly Popular." *HRMagazine,* Vol. 42, No. 7 (July), pp. 26–29.

Moulder, Evelina, and Hall, Gwen (1995). *Special Data Issue: Employee Benefits in Local Government* (Washington, DC: International City/County Management Association).

Perry, Ronald W., and Cayer, N. Joseph (1997). "Factors Affecting Municipal Satisfaction with Health Care Plans." *Review of Public Personnel Administration,* Vol. 17, No. 2 (Spring), pp. 5–19.

Peters, H. Elizabeth (1997). "The Role of Child Care and Parental Leave Policies in Supporting Family and Work Activities," in Francine D. Blau and Ronald G. Ehrenberg (eds.), *Gender and Family Issues in the Workplace* (New York: Russell Sage Foundation), pp. 280–283.

President's Council on Management Improvement, Human Resources Committee (1990). *Guidelines for Pilot Flexible Workplace Arrangements* (Washington, DC), January.

Public Law 95-437 (1978). 92 Stat. 1055, October 10.

Schmidt, Jo Horne (1997). "Who's Taking Care of Mom and Dad?" *Journal of the American Society of CLU&ChFC,* Vol. 51, No. 1 (November), pp. 82–87.

Streib, Gregory (1996). "Municipal Health Benefits: A First Step Toward a Useful Knowledge Base." *American Review of Public Administration,* Vol. 26, No. 3 (September), pp. 345–360.

U.S. Bureau of the Census (1992). *Statistical Abstract of the United States; 1992,* 112th ed. (Washington, DC), Table 620.

U.S. Department of Labor (1998). *Work and Elder Care: Facts for Caregivers and Their Employers* (Washington, DC: Women's Bureau, No. 98-1), May.

U.S. General Accounting Office (1985). *Alternative Work Schedules for Federal Employees* (Washington, DC), July.

——— (1992a). *The Changing Workforce: Demographic Issues Facing the Federal Government* (Washington, DC), March.

——— (1992b). *The Changing Workforce: Comparison of Federal and Nonfederal Work/Family Programs and Approaches* (Washington, DC), April.

——— (1994). *Federal Employment: H.R. 4361, Federal Employees Family Friendly Leave Act,* Statement of Timothy P. Bowling, Associate Director, Federal Human Resource Management Issues, General Government Division (Washington, DC: GAO/T-GGD-94-152), May 18.

——— (1997). *Federal Workforce: Agencies' Policies and Views on Flexitime in the Federal Government* (Washington, DC), July.

U.S. Merit Systems Protection Board (1991). *Balancing Work Responsibilities and Family Needs: The Federal Civil Service Response* (Washington, DC), November.

U.S. Office of Personnel Management (1991). "If It's Wednesday, It Must Be Home." *Federal Staffing Digest,* Vol. 3, No. 3 (December), p. 7.

—— (1998a). *The Fact Book: Federal Civilian Workforce Statistics* (Washington, DC).

—— (1998b). *Family Friendly Leave Policies* (Washington, DC: http://www.opm.gov/oca/leave/html/fflafact.htm), June.

—— (1998c). *Reasons for Telecommuting* (Washington, DC: http://www.opm.gov/wrkfam/telecomm/reasons.htm).

Walter, Kate (1996). "Elder Care Obligations Challenge the Next Generation." *HRMagazine,* Vol. 41, No. 7 (July), pp. 98–103.

Weisberg, Anne C., and Buckler, Carol A. (1994). *Everything a Working Mother Needs to Know* (New York: Doubleday).

West, Jonathan P. (1998). "Managing an Aging Workforce," in Stephen E. Condrey (ed.), *Handbook of Human Resource Management in Government* (San Francisco: Jossey-Bass Publishers), pp. 93–115.

SUGGESTED READINGS

Dwyer, Jeffrey W., and Coward, Raymond T. (1992). *Gender, Family, and Elder Care* (Thousand Oaks, CA: Sage Publications, Inc.).

Estess, Patricia S. (1996). *Work Concepts for the Future: Managing Alternative Work Arrangements* (Menlo Park, CA: Crisp Publications, Inc.).

Kugelmass, Joel (1995). *Telecommuting: A Manager's Guide to Flexible Work Arrangements* (San Francisco: Jossey-Bass Publishers).

McCaffery, Robert M. (1993). *Employee Benefits Basics* (Scottsdale, AZ: American Compensation Association).

McDaniel, Charlotte (1994). *Health Care Benefits Problem Solver for Human Resource Professionals and Managers* (New York: John Wiley & Sons, Inc.).

Neal, Margaret B., Chapman, Nancy J., Ingersoll-Dayton, Berit, and Emlen, Arthur C. (1993). *Balancing Work and Caregiving for Children, Adults, and Elders* (Newbury Park, CA: Sage).

Niles, Jack (1998). *Managing Telework: Strategies for Managing the Virtual Workforce* (New York: John Wiley & Sons, Inc.).

Reynolds, John D. (1993). *Flexible Benefits Handbook* (Boston: Warren, Gorham & Lamont, Inc.).

UNITED STATES
OFFICE OF PERSONNEL MANAGEMENT

HANDBOOK ON

ALTERNATIVE WORK

SCHEDULES

December 1996

Prepared by:
U.S. Office of Personnel Management
Human Resources System Service
Office of Compensation Policy
Compensation Administration Division
Washington, DC 20415

continued page 334

Appendix A • Comparison of Flexible and Compressed Work Schedules

Flexible Work Schedules

a. Basic Work Requirement

The **basic work requirement** for a full-time **employee** is 80 hours in a **biweekly pay period. Agencies** may also establish daily or weekly work requirements. The **agency** head determines the number of hours a part-time **employee** must work in a specific period. **Agencies** may permit **employees** to complete their **basic work requirement** in less than 10 workdays.

b. Tour of Duty

The **tour of duty** defines the limits within which an **employee** must complete his or her **basic work requirement.**

c. Credit Hours

Hours may be worked in excess of the **basic work requirement** at the option of the **employee** in order to vary the length of the workday or workweek. Not all **FWS** programs provide for **credit hours.**

d. Overtime Work

Overtime work consists of hours of work that are officially ordered in advance and in excess of 8 hours in a day or 40 hours in a week, but does not include hours that are worked voluntarily, including credit hours, or hours that an employee is "suffered or permitted" to work which are not officially ordered in advance. (See 5 CFR 551.401(a)(2).)

Compressed Work Schedules

a. Basic Work Requirement

A full-time **employee** must work 80 hours in **biweekly pay period** and must be scheduled to work on fewer than 10 workdays. A part-time **employee** has a fixed schedule of fewer than 80 hours in a **biweekly pay period** and must be scheduled to work on fewer than 10 workdays.

b. Tour of Duty

The **tour of duty** is defined by the fixed **compressed work schedule** established by the **agency.**

c. Credit Hours

The law provides **credit hours** only for **flexible work schedules.** There is no legal authority for **credit hours** under a **CWS** program. See 5 U.S.C. 6121(4).

d. Overtime Work

For a full-time **employee,** overtime work consists of all hours of work in excess of the established **compressed work schedule.** For a part-time **employee,** overtime work must be hours in excess of the **compressed work schedule** for the day (more than at least 8 hours) or for the week (more than at least 40 hours).

continued page 335

Flexible Work Schedules

e. Compensatory Time Off

An **agency** may, at the request of an **employee,** approve compensatory time off in lieu of overtime pay for non-SES **employees.** (See 5 U.S.C. 6123(a)(1).) Mandatory compensatory time off is limited to FLSA-exempt **employees** (who are not **prevailing rate employees**) whose rate of basic pay is greater than the rate for GS-10, step 10. (See 5 CFR 550.114(c).)

f. Night Pay

For GS and other **employees** covered by 5 U.S.C. 5545(a), **agencies** must pay night pay for those hours that must be worked between 6 p.m. and 6 a.m. to complete an 8-hour daily **tour of duty. Agencies** must also pay night pay for all designated **core hours** worked between 6 p.m. and 6 a.m. and for any regularly scheduled overtime work between those hours.

g. Pay for Holiday Work

Holiday premium pay for nonovertime work is limited to a maximum of 8 hours in a day for full-time or part-time **employees.** A part-time **employee** scheduled to work on a day designated as an "in lieu of" holiday for full-time **employees** is not entitled to holiday premium pay for work performed on that day.

Compressed Work Schedules

e. Compensatory Time Off

Compensatory time off may be approved in lieu of overtime pay only for irregular or occasional overtime work by an **"employee"** as defined in 5 U.S.C. 5541(2) or by a **prevailing rate employee** as defined in 5 U.S.C. 5342(a)(2), but may not be approved for an SES member. Mandatory compensatory time off is limited to FLSA exempt **employees** (who are not **prevailing rate employees**) whose rate of basic pay is greater than the rate for GS-10, step 10.

f. Night Pay

The regular rules governing entitlement to night pay, at 5 CFR 550.121 and 122, apply. (See 5 CFR 532.505 for **prevailing rate employees.**)

g. Pay for Holiday Work

Holiday premium pay for nonovertime work is limited to the number of hours normally scheduled for that day. A part-time **employee** scheduled to work on a day designated as an "in lieu of" holiday for full-time **employees** is not entitled to holiday premium pay for work performed on that day.

continued page 336

Flexible Work Schedules	Compressed Work Schedules
h. <u>Pay for Sunday Work</u>	h. <u>Pay for Sunday Work</u>
A full-time **employee** who performs regularly scheduled nonovertime work during a period of duty, part of which is performed on Sunday, is entitled to Sunday premium pay (25 percent of the rate of basic pay) for the entire period of work up to 8 hours. (See 5 CFR 550.171.) A part-time **employee** is not entitled to Sunday premium pay for Sunday work. (See 5 U.S.C 5546 (a), 46 Comp. Gen. 337 (1966), and 5 CFR 610.111 (d).)	A full-time **employee** who performs regularly scheduled nonovertime work during a period of duty, part of which is performed on Sunday, is entitled to Sunday premium pay (25 percent of the rate of basic pay) for the entire scheduled period of duty that day. (See 5 U.S.C. 6128(c) and 5 CFR 610.111(d).) A part-time **employee** is not entitled to premium pay for Sunday work.
i. <u>Holidays</u>	i. <u>Holidays</u>
A full-time **employee** prevented from working on a holiday (or an "in lieu of" holiday) is entitled to pay for 8 hours for that day. A part-time **employee** prevented from working on a holiday is entitled to pay for the number of hours he or she would have worked but for the holiday, not to exceed 8 hours. When a holiday falls on a nonworkday of a part-time **employee,** there is no entitlement to pay for an "in lieu of" holiday. (See 5 U.S.C. 6124.)	A full-time **employee** prevented from working on a holiday (or an "in lieu of" holiday) is entitled to pay for the number of hours of the **compressed work schedule** for the **employee** on that day. A part-time **employee** prevented from working on a holiday is entitled to pay for the number of hours of the **compressed work schedule** on that day. When a holiday falls on a nonworkday of a part-time **employee,** there is no entitlement to pay or an "in lieu of" holiday. (See 5 CFR 610.406 and Comptroller General opinion B-217080, June 3, 1985.)
j. <u>Excused Absence</u>	j. <u>Excused Absence</u>
The amount of excused absence to be granted an **employee** covered by an FWS program should be based on his or her typical schedule.	All **compressed work schedules** are fixed schedules. The regular **agency** practices applicable to administration of excused absence apply.

continued page 337

Flexible Work Schedules	Compressed Work Schedules
k. Temporary Duty	k. Temporary Duty
The **agency** may allow an **employee** covered by an **FWS** program to continue the existing schedule, modify that schedule, or require him or her to follow the schedule used at the temporary work site.	(Same as **Flexible Work Schedules**)
l. Travel	l. Travel
Time spent in a travel status is considered to be hours of work only as provided in 5 CFR 550.112(g) or 5 U.S.C. 5544 (**prevailing rate employees**) for FLSA exempt **employees,** and as provided in 5 CFR 550.112(g) or 5 U.S.C. 5544 <u>and</u> 551.422 for nonexempt **employees.** **Agencies** may find it advisable to establish procedures to revert **employees** to standard fixed schedules when traveling.	(Same as **Flexible Work Schedules**)
m. Application of Flexible Work Schedules in Unorganized Units	m. Application of Flexible Work Schedules in Unorganized Units
Agencies may unilaterally install **FWS** programs in unorganized units. There is no requirement for a vote of affected **employees.**	In an unorganized unit, a majority of affected **employees** must vote to be included in a **CWS** program. (See 5 U.S.C. 6127(b).)
n. Determining Hardships under Flexible Work Schedules	n. Determining Hardships under Flexible Work Schedules
Since **FWS** programs generally provide employees the flexibility to continue to work traditional schedules, the **agency** is not required to consider exclusion of an **employee** from the **FWS** program for personal hardship.	An **employee** for whom a **CWS** program would impose a personal hardship may request to be excluded from the program. The request must be submitted to the **agency** in writing. The **agency** must determine whether a personal hardship exists. If so, the **employee** must be excepted from the **CWS** program or reassigned to the first position that meets the criteria in 5 U.S.C. 6127(b)(2)(B).

continued page 338

Appendix B • Models of Flexible Work Schedules

FLEXITOUR	GLIDING SCHEDULE	VARIABLE DAY SCHEDULE	VARIABLE WEEK SCHEDULE	MAXIFLEX
<u>Basic Work Requirement</u> A full-time **employee** must work 8 hours a day, 40 hours a week, and 80 hours a **biweekly pay period.** The **agency head** determines the number of hours a part-time **employee** must work in a day, in a week, or in a **biweekly pay period.**	<u>Basic Work Requirement</u> (See **Flexitour.**)	<u>Basic Work Requirement</u> A full-time employee must work 40 hours a week. The **agency head** determines the number of hours a part-time **employee** must work in a week.	<u>Basic Work Requirement</u> A full-time **employee** must work 80 hours in a **biweekly pay period.** The **agency** head determines the number of hours a part-time **employee** must work in a **biweekly pay period.**	<u>Basic Work Requirement</u> (See **Variable Week Schedule.**)
<u>Tour of Duty</u> **Agencies** establish **flexible hours** surrounding **core hours,** which include a standard meal period.	<u>Tour of Duty</u> **Agencies** establish flexible and **core hours. Gliding schedules** provide for **flexible time bands** at the start and end of the workday and may also allow for **flexible hours** at midday (during the lunch break). **Employees** must work during **core hours.**	<u>Tour of Duty</u> (See **Gliding Schedule.**)	<u>Tour of Duty</u> (See **Gliding Schedule.**)	<u>Tour of Duty</u> (See **Gliding Schedule.**) However, **agencies** may choose not to establish **core hours** on each workday, thus providing maximum flexibility for **employees.**

continued page 339

	FLEXITOUR	GLIDING SCHEDULE	VARIABLE DAY SCHEDULE	VARIABLE WEEK SCHEDULE	MAXIFLEX
Core Hours	A **employee** must account for missed **core hours** (if permitted) with leave, **credit hours,** or compensatory time off.	(See **Flexitour.**)	(See **Flexitour.**)	(See **Flexitour.**)	See **Flexitour.** Employees may work fewer than 10 days biweekly because of the absence of **core hours** on one of the normal workdays (e.g., "Flexible 5/4-9").
Overtime Work	Overtime work is work in excess of 8 hours in a day or 40 hours in a workweek, ordered in advance by management. See 5 U.S.C. 6121(6).	(See **Flexitour.**)	(See **Flexitour.**)	(See **Flexitour.**)	(See **Flexitour.**)
Flexibility	**Employees** select arrival and departure times subject to **agency** approval. (This results in a fixed schedule until the next selection period, as determined by the **agency.**) At the request of an **employee,** the **agency** may approve an adjusted arrival and departure time.	**Employees** may vary arrival and departure times on a daily basis during the established **flexible hours.**	(See **Gliding Schedule.**) An **employee** may also vary the length of the workday. An **agency** may limit the number of hours an **employee** may work on a daily basis.	(See **Variable Day Schedule.**) An **employee** may also vary the length of the workweek.	(See **Variable Week Schedule.**)

continued page 340

Appendix C • Models of Compressed Work Schedules

FOUR-DAY WORKWEEK	THREE-DAY WORKWEEK	5/4-9 COMPRESSED PLAN
Basic Work Requirement A full-time **employee** must work 10 hours a day, 40 hours a week, and 80 hours a **biweekly pay period**. The **agency** head determines the number of hours a part-time **employee** must work in a 4-day workweek and the number of hours in a **biweekly pay period**.	Basic Work Requirement A full-time **employee** must work 13 hours and 20 minutes a day, 40 hours a week, and 80 hours a **biweekly pay period**. The **agency** head determines the number of hours a part-time **employee** must work in a 3-day workweek and the number of hours in a **biweekly pay period**.	Basic Work Requirement A full-time employee must work eight 9-hour days and one 8-hour day for a total of 80 hours in a **biweekly pay period**. The **agency** head determines the number of hours a part-time **employee** must work in a 9-day **biweekly pay period**.
Tour of Duty The **"tour of duty"** is established by the **agency** and is limited to four 10-hour days.	Tour of Duty The **"tour of duty"** is established by the **agency** and is limited to three 13-hour and 20-minute days in a week and 80 hours in a biweekly **pay period**.	Tour of Duty The **"tour of duty"** is established by the **agency** and is less than 10 workdays in a **biweekly pay period**.
Overtime Work Overtime work is work ordered or approved in advance by management and is in excess of the **compressed work schedule's basic work requirement.**	Overtime Work (See **Four-Day Workweek**.)	Overtime Work (See **Four-Day Workweek.**)

continued page 341

Appendix D • Flexifinder

Midday Flex Times — Workday Ending Times

Workday Starting Time	30 Min	35 Min	40 Min	45 Min	50 Min	55 Min	1 Hour	1 Hr. 05	1 Hr. 10	1 Hr. 15	1 Hr. 20	1 Hr. 25	1 Hr. 30	1 Hr. 35	1 Hr. 40	1 Hr. 45	1 Hr. 50	1 Hr. 55	2 Hrs.
6:30	3:00	3:05	3:10	3:15	3:20	3:25	3:30	3:35	3:40	3:45	3:50	3:55	4:00	4:05	4:10	4:15	4:20	4:25	4:30
6:35	3:05	3:10	3:15	3:20	3:25	3:30	3:35	3:40	3:45	3:50	3:55	4:00	4:05	4:10	4:15	4:20	4:25	4:30	4:35
6:40	3:10	3:15	3:20	3:25	3:30	3:35	3:40	3:45	3:50	3:55	4:00	4:05	4:10	4:15	4:20	4:25	4:30	4:35	4:40
6:45	3:15	3:20	3:25	3:30	3:35	3:40	3:45	3:50	3:55	4:00	4:05	4:10	4:15	4:20	4:25	4:30	4:35	4:40	4:45
6:50	3:20	3:25	3:30	3:35	3:40	3:45	3:50	3:55	4:00	4:05	4:10	4:15	4:20	4:25	4:30	4:35	4:40	4:45	4:50
6:55	3:25	3:30	3:35	3:40	3:45	3:50	3:55	4:00	4:05	4:10	4:15	4:20	4:25	4:30	4:35	4:40	4:45	4:50	4:55
7:00	3:30	3:35	3:40	3:45	3:50	3:55	4:00	4:05	4:10	4:15	4:20	4:25	4:30	4:35	4:40	4:45	4:50	4:55	5:00
7:05	3:35	3:40	3:45	3:50	3:55	4:00	4:05	4:10	4:15	4:20	4:25	4:30	4:35	4:40	4:45	4:50	4:55	5:00	5:05
7:10	3:40	3:45	3:50	3:55	4:00	4:05	4:10	4:15	4:20	4:25	4:30	4:35	4:40	4:45	4:50	4:55	5:00	5:05	5:10
7:15	3:45	3:50	3:55	4:00	4:05	4:10	4:15	4:20	4:25	4:30	4:35	4:40	4:45	4:50	4:55	5:00	5:05	5:10	5:15
7:20	3:50	3:55	4:00	4:05	4:10	4:15	4:20	4:25	4:30	4:35	4:40	4:45	4:50	4:55	5:00	5:05	5:10	5:15	5:20
7:25	3:55	4:00	4:05	4:10	4:15	4:20	4:25	4:30	4:35	4:40	4:45	4:50	4:55	5:00	5:05	5:10	5:15	5:20	5:25
7:30	4:00	4:05	4:10	4:15	4:20	4:25	4:30	4:35	4:40	4:45	4:50	4:55	5:00	5:05	5:10	5:15	5:20	5:25	5:30
7:35	4:05	4:10	4:15	4:20	4:25	4:30	4:35	4:40	4:45	4:50	4:55	5:00	5:05	5:10	5:15	5:20	5:25	5:30	5:35
7:40	4:10	4:15	4:20	4:25	4:30	4:35	4:40	4:45	4:50	4:55	5:00	5:05	5:10	5:15	5:20	5:25	5:30	5:35	5:40
7:45	4:15	4:20	4:25	4:30	4:35	4:40	4:45	4:50	4:55	5:00	5:05	5:10	5:15	5:20	5:25	5:30	5:35	5:40	5:45
7:50	4:20	4:25	4:30	4:35	4:40	4:45	4:50	4:55	5:00	5:05	5:10	5:15	5:20	5:25	5:30	5:35	5:40	5:45	5:50
7:55	4:25	4:30	4:35	4:40	4:45	4:50	4:55	5:00	5:05	5:10	5:15	5:20	5:25	5:30	5:35	5:40	5:45	5:50	5:55
8:00	4:30	4:35	4:40	4:45	4:50	4:55	5:00	5:05	5:10	5:15	5:20	5:25	5:30	5:35	5:40	5:45	5:50	5:55	6:00
8:05	4:35	4:40	4:45	4:50	4:55	5:00	5:05	5:10	5:15	5:20	5:25	5:30	5:35	5:40	5:45	5:50	5:55	6:00	6:05
8:10	4:40	4:45	4:50	4:55	5:00	5:05	5:10	5:15	5:20	5:25	5:30	5:35	5:40	5:45	5:50	5:55	6:00	6:05	6:10
8:15	4:45	4:50	4:55	5:00	5:05	5:10	5:15	5:20	5:25	5:30	5:35	5:40	5:45	5:50	5:55	6:00	6:05	6:10	6:15
8:20	4:50	4:55	5:00	5:05	5:10	5:15	5:20	5:25	5:30	5:35	5:40	5:45	5:50	5:55	6:00	6:05	6:10	6:15	6:20
8:25	4:55	5:00	5:05	5:10	5:15	5:20	5:25	5:30	5:35	5:40	5:45	5:50	5:55	6:00	6:05	6:10	6:15	6:20	6:25
8:30	5:00	5:05	5:10	5:15	5:20	5:25	5:30	5:35	5:40	5:45	5:50	5:55	6:00	6:05	6:10	6:15	6:20	6:25	6:30
8:35	5:05	5:10	5:15	5:20	5:25	5:30	5:35	5:40	5:45	5:50	5:55	6:00	6:05	6:10	6:15	6:20	6:25	6:30	6:35
8:40	5:10	5:15	5:20	5:25	5:30	5:35	5:40	5:45	5:50	5:55	6:00	6:05	6:10	6:15	6:20	6:25	6:30	6:35	6:40
8:45	5:15	5:20	5:25	5:30	5:35	5:40	5:45	5:50	5:55	6:00	6:05	6:10	6:15	6:20	6:25	6:30	6:35	6:40	6:45
8:50	5:20	5:25	5:30	5:35	5:40	5:45	5:50	5:55	6:00	6:05	6:10	6:15	6:20	6:25	6:30	6:35	6:40	6:45	6:50
8:55	5:25	5:30	5:35	5:40	5:45	5:50	5:55	6:00	6:05	6:10	6:15	6:20	6:25	6:30	6:35	6:40	6:45	6:50	6:55
9:00	5:30	5:35	5:40	5:45	5:50	5:55	6:00	6:05	6:10	6:15	6:20	6:25	6:30	6:35	6:40	6:45	6:50	6:55	7:00
9:05	5:35	5:40	5:45	5:50	5:55	6:00	6:05	6:10	6:15	6:20	6:25	6:30	6:35	6:40	6:45	6:50	6:55	7:00	
9:10	5:40	5:45	5:50	5:55	6:00	6:05	6:10	6:15	6:20	6:25	6:30	6:35	6:40	6:45	6:50	6:55	7:00		
9:15	5:45	5:50	5:55	6:00	6:05	6:10	6:15	6:20	6:25	6:30	6:35	6:40	6:45	6:50	6:55	7:00			
9:20	5:50	5:55	6:00	6:05	6:10	6:15	6:20	6:25	6:30	6:35	6:40	6:45	6:50	6:55	7:00				
9:25	5:55	6:00	6:05	6:10	6:15	6:20	6:25	6:30	6:35	6:40	6:45	6:50	6:55	7:00					
9:30	6:00	6:05	6:10	6:15	6:20	6:25	6:30	6:35	6:40	6:45	6:50	6:55	7:00						

To find the time an **employee's** workday ends, find the time he/she began the workday along the left-hand column of the grid; then along the top of the grid find the amount of time he/she spent in the midday flex band (for lunch and/or personal time). The point at which the **Workday Starting Time** row intersects the **Midday Flex** column is the Ending Time for an 8-hour day.

U. S. Office of Personnel Management

Telecommuting

Answers to Frequently Asked Questions

Question - Who is responsible for approving an employee's request to telecommute?

Answer - Each Federal agency sets up its own approval process, but generally the immediate supervisor must agree to a specific employee's request.

Question - What role do unions play?

Answer - Agencies are strongly encouraged to develop their telecommuting programs in partnership with their unions and other stakeholders. Telecommuting affects conditions of employment and agencies must consult and negotiate with unions, as appropriate, regarding telecommuting programs.

Question - Does an employee have a right to telecommute? Could an employee be forced to work at home?

Answer - No, to both questions. Subject to any applicable union agreement, management decides whether the employee can work off-site, depending on the nature of the position and the characteristics of the employee. Management has the right to end an employee's use of the telecommuting option if, for example, the employee's performance declines or if the arrangement no longer meets the organization's needs.

Question - Can telecommuting help an employee with child or other dependent care needs?

Answer - Telecommuting can provide valuable assistance with dependent care. Time saved commuting to work can be spent with family members. For example, a parent may need less after school care for a school age child, or an adult child may have time to take an aging parent to the doctor. However, employees should not be caring for children when they are working at home.

Question - Won't the employee's work suffer without direct, onsite supervision?

Answer - The opposite is more often the case, partly because the employee working at home has fewer interruptions and distractions and partly because the individual has a strong incentive to demonstrate the value of working at home.

Question - How can the supervisor monitor work performance when the employee is not physically present?

Answer - Managers can measure what the employee produces by examining the product or results of the employee's efforts. It is also helpful to use project schedules, key milestones, regular status reports, and team reviews. Supervisors may call employees who are working at home.

Question - Can telecommuters follow an alternative work schedule?

Answer - Yes. In fact, telecommuting work schedules should be sufficiently flexible to permit periodic work schedule adjustments. Initial telecommuting schedules may require trial and error adjustments to determine the optimal schedule to meet the needs of the employee and the organization.

Question - What about the impact on the office when some employees are working at an alternative worksite?

Answer - Certain guidelines must be established to minimize adverse impact on other staff members before employees begin to work at alternative worksites. The overall interests of the office must take precedence over working at alternative sites. A supervisor may require an employee to work at the main worksite on a day scheduled for an alternative worksite if the needs of the office so require.
Telecommuting should not put a burden on staff remaining in the office. An equitable distribution of work load should be maintained, and methods should be instituted to ensure that main office employees are not saddled with the telecommuter's responsibilities.

continued page 344

Question - What equipment will the employee need at the home based worksite and who will provide it?

Answer - The needed equipment and who will provide it will vary by situation. Generally speaking, organizations are not required to provide equipment at home based worksites. Each agency must establish its own policies on the provision and installation of equipment.

Question - Do all telecommuters work with high-tech equipment?

Answer - No. While technology can be very helpful to most telecommuters, a simple telephone may suffice for many.

Question - Who is responsible for maintaining and servicing Government or privately owned equipment used at the alternative worksite?

Answer - Generally, the Government will be responsible for the service and maintenance of Government-owned equipment. Telecommuters using their own equipment are responsible for its service and maintenance.

Question - Who pays for any increase in home utility expenses incurred by employees as a result of telecommuting?

Answer - Work-at-home arrangements may increase an employee's home utility costs. Balanced against these increases are potential savings to the employee resulting from reduced commuting, child care (during the period the employee would otherwise be commuting to and from work), meals, and clothing expenses. Potential cost and savings to the employee and the Government cannot be viewed in isolation from each other. An agency may not use appropriated funds to pay for items of personal expenses unless there is specific statutory authority.

Question - Are business phone calls made from the home reimbursable?

Answer - An employee may be reimbursed for business related long distance phone calls over the employee's personal phone. GSA regulations (41 CFR 101.7) provide for reimbursement on SF 1164 for telephone calls approved by the supervisor. Agencies may also provide employees with Government telephone credit cards.

Question - Who is liable for work related injuries and/or damages at the alternative worksite?

Answer - The Federal Government. Government employees suffering from work related injuries and/or damages at the alternative worksite are covered under the Military Personnel and Civilian Employees Claims Act, the Federal Tort Claims Act, or the Federal Employees Compensation Act (workers' compensation).

U. S. Office of Personnel Management
Compensation Administration

FAMILY-FRIENDLY LEAVE POLICIES FOR FEDERAL EMPLOYEES

Do you need time off from work for personal, family, or medical needs?

Are you confused about your options?

The following may help to put things into perspective. See your agency's personnel office for additional information on each of these leave policies.

ANNUAL LEAVE

Annual leave is designed to give you vacation periods for rest and relaxation and to provide time off for your personal business or family needs. Your annual leave must be scheduled and approved in advance.

SICK LEAVE

Sick leave may be used when you--

- Receive medical, dental, or optical examination or treatment;
- Are incapacitated by physical or mental illness, injury, pregnancy, or childbirth;
- Would, because of exposure to a communicable disease, jeopardize the health of others by your presence on the job; or
- Must be absent from work for adoption-related activities.

In addition, you may use a limited amount* of sick leave to--

- Provide care for a family member as the result of physical or mental illness, injury, pregnancy, childbirth, or medical, dental, or optical examination or treatment; or
- Make arrangements necessitated by the death of a family member or attend the funeral of a family member.

* If you are a full-time employee, you may use up to 40 hours (5 days) of your sick leave each leave year for family care and bereavement purposes. An additional 64 hours (8 days) may be used as long as you maintain a balance of at least 80 hours of sick leave in your sick leave account.

Part-time employees and employees with uncommon tours of duty are also covered, and the amount of sick leave they may use for these purposes is pro-rated.

FAMILY AND MEDICAL LEAVE

Under the Family and Medical Leave Act of 1993 (FMLA), covered employees are entitled to a total of 12 administrative workweeks of unpaid leave (leave without pay) during any 12-month period for--

- The birth of a son or daughter and care of the newborn;
- The placement of a son or daughter with you for adoption or foster care;
- The care of your spouse, son, daughter, or parent with a serious health condition; and
- Your own serious health condition that makes you unable to perform the duties of your position.

Upon return from FMLA leave, you must be returned to the same or equivalent position. While on FMLA leave, you are entitled to maintain health benefits coverage. If you are on leave without pay under the FMLA, you are responsible for paying the employee share of the health benefits premium.

You may choose to substitute annual leave for unpaid leave under the FMLA. You may also substitute sick leave in those situations in which the use of sick leave is permitted.

LEAVE FOR BONE-MARROW OR ORGAN DONATION

As a Federal employee, you are entitled to use 7 days of paid leave each calendar year (in addition to annual or sick leave) to serve as a bone-marrow or organ donor.

continued page 346

LEAVE SHARING

If you have a medical emergency and have exhausted your own leave, the leave transfer program allows other Federal employees to donate annual leave to you.

There may also be a leave bank program where you work. These bank programs allow members (those who contribute a specific amount) to apply for leave from the leave bank in the event of a medical emergency.

Federal leave policies can work together to help you manage your work and family responsibilities. Here are some examples of how employees may use leave when facing a personal, medical, or family emergency.

- Laura is a single mother with two children who has worked for the Government for 2 1/2 years. Laura has 201 hours of sick leave and 80 hours of annual leave. Laura's children have problems with recurring ear infections and strep throat and must occasionally be kept home from school and afternoon day care. Laura may use up to 13 days of sick leave a year to care for her children when they are ill (as long as her sick leave balance does not drop below 80 hours). By doing so, Laura may be able to conserve her annual leave for a possible family vacation or to care for her children when her child care provider is unavailable.
- Michael has worked for the Federal Government for only 5 months. He had 40 hours of sick leave and 36 hours of annual leave before he underwent an emergency appendectomy last week. He has been absent for 5 days, and his doctor wants him to use at least 6 weeks to recuperate. Fortunately, Michael is a member of his agency's leave bank program. He may apply to the bank for donated leave to help support him until he can return to work. Other employees may also wish to donate leave to Michael through the leave transfer program. He may also request advanced sick and/or annual leave if the donated leave is not sufficient.
- Carol is expecting a baby in 4 months. Carol has 260 hours of sick leave and 200 hours of annual leave. She wants to spend as much time as possible with her new baby. Carol's doctor anticipates that she will need 6 weeks to recuperate after the baby's birth. Carol has requested 240 hours of sick leave. She has also requested 4 weeks of annual leave and 3 months of leave without pay (LWOP). Her supervisor approves the sick and annual leave and informs her of her entitlement to unpaid leave under the FMLA. Carol decides to invoke her FMLA entitlement and use 4 weeks of leave without pay under the FMLA following her approved annual leave. In addition, she and her supervisor work out a leave schedule that permits Carol to use FMLA leave without pay on an intermittent basis 2 days a week for 3 months following her return to work.
- Jeff and his wife plan to travel abroad soon to adopt a child. Jeff has a sick leave balance of 280 hours and an annual leave balance of 160 hours. Jeff may use sick leave for absences related to the adoption, including travel time. His agency may advance him up to 30 days of sick leave if requested. Jeff may also request annual leave to spend time with his new son or daughter after the adoption. In addition, he may invoke his entitlement to leave without pay under the FMLA.
- Tom fell off his roof while cleaning the gutters and broke his hip. The doctor says Tom will need to be absent from work for at least 16 weeks. Tom has 240 hours of sick leave and 137 hours of annual leave. His installation is understaffed, and Tom is worried that when his sick leave is gone, his supervisor will refuse to grant him annual leave. He is most concerned about the possibility of losing his job and with it his medical benefits. Tom may use his sick leave and then invoke his entitlement to unpaid leave under the FMLA. He may then substitute his annual leave for part of the FMLA leave without pay. While he is on FMLA leave, his reemployment rights and medical benefits are protected. In addition, Tom may apply for and use donated leave from his agency's leave transfer program.
- Ruth and her husband have both worked for the Government for 10 years. Their daughter was recently diagnosed with a terminal illness. Ruth and her husband want to care for their daughter at home for as long as possible. They have sufficient sick leave in their accounts for each to use 13 days to care for their daughter. Ruth has also requested 160 hours of annual leave. Ruth's supervisor was sympathetic, but based on work-related needs, he felt he could approve only 80 hours of annual leave. Ruth notified her supervisor of her intent to invoke her entitlement to leave without pay under the FMLA. Ruth used her 80 hours of approved annual leave and then substituted her remaining annual leave for FMLA leave without pay. Her husband may also invoke his entitlement to leave under the FMLA. When their annual leave is exhausted, Ruth and her husband may each apply for and receive donated leave from their agencies' leave transfer programs. In this way, they will be able to care for their daughter at home until hospitalization is necessary.
- Emilio's sister needs a kidney transplant, and Emilio has decided to donate his kidney to her. Emilio may use 7 days of paid leave to be a bone marrow or organ donor. This includes the time required for testing to see if he is a compatible donor, plus the time required to undergo the transplant procedure and recuperate. Emilio may get additional time off from work by requesting annual and/or sick leave, advanced leave, and donated leave through his agency's leave transfer program (if he exhausts his own available paid leave).

Chapter TWELVE

The Future of Public Personnel

The 1990s were years of significant change for public personnel on all levels of government in the United States. Civil service reform, reinvention, reengineering, privatization, and related ideas became popular agendas with public managers as well as elected officials. The diagnoses and recommendations of the Winter and Volcker Commissions, and the NPR, have had a major impact on policy makers' thinking about the central responsibilities of public personnel offices and, very significantly, about the goals of the human resources function. Public personnel enters the twenty-first century stressing policies and practices oriented to meeting managerial needs, increasing organizational performance, and assuring responsiveness to executive leadership. The human resources management and development functions will still have the goal of attracting, developing, and retaining the people and skills public agencies need to sustain effectiveness and efficiency, but it is now clear that the ways they go about meeting these challenges are changing. Overviews of three ongoing trends that promise to change fundamentally the landscape of public personnel in the United States in the relatively near term are set forth here.

EXTENDING THE BOUNDARIES OF CIVIL SERVICE REFORM

There are few signs that the civil service reforms discussed in the preceding chapters will be reversed, although hard evidence in support of claims that their goals are being achieved on any level of government is hard to find. It is, nonetheless, fairly apparent that the era of building personnel systems on foundations consisting of merit systems designed to regulate and restrict public managers' discretion is effectively over. In one form or another, *reducing bureaucratic structures and procedures, decentralizing authority and accountability, contracting-out or privatization, and supporting management* promise to be major values driving the public personnel systems of the new century. The criteria used to judge the performance of personnel systems will stress organizational performance and program outcomes, not adherence to civil service rules and procedures. According to Richard Kearney and Steven Hays:

> Evaluated simply in terms of the rapid and unprecedented diffusion of its components, reinventing government is a resounding success. Efforts to debureaucratize and decentralize, privatize, and managerialize public management have had a marked impact on public management, and they show no sign of abating in the foreseeable future. (Kearney and Hays, 1998, p. 44)

The State of Georgia's Civil Service Reform Act may offer a preview of things to come. On January 10, 1996, Georgia's Governor Zell Miller delivered a State of the State Address in which he announced his plan to "revise" a merit system that had been established in 1943 to "create a professional workforce that was free of political cronyism" (State of Georgia, 1996, p. 6). The result was Act 816, reform legislation that went beyond anything attempted by other states or the federal government in that it made *all* state hires after July 1, 1996, "at will" positions not subject to the rules and regulations of the State Personnel Board. These unclassified positions are not covered by the state merit system. In the words of *Governing*, a magazine directed at state and local government administrators: "While other states have been reforming their civil service laws, Georgia went to the edge. . ." (*Governing*, 1999, p. 39). By the end of the first decade of the twenty-first century, most of Georgia's state employees will be in the unclassified service, occupying positions that at least in theory do not afford any "property rights." They will be working in a personnel system that has been so extensively decentralized that it is actually *several* departmental systems operating within very broadly defined and highly flexible state policies and procedures. The logic underpinning the Georgia approach to reform was set forth by Governor Miller:

> Folks, the truth of the matter is that a solution in 1943 is a problem in 1996. The problem is governmental paralysis, because, despite its name, our present Merit System is not about merit. It offers no reward to good workers. It only provides cover for bad workers. (State of Georgia, 1996, pp. 6–7)

While at this moment no other states have gone so far as to put their classified civil services on the road to oblivion, political pressures for extending reforms in this direction are still strong (Selden, 1999). The Georgia model may spread across the country during the early part of the new century if current attitudes and trends persist. If this is indeed the case, the core value of merit systems, neutral competence, could itself be discarded along with "old" administrative solutions. In an environment of political hostility toward bureaucrats, scarce resources, and eroding job security, the wholesale elimination of the classified civil service might make it even more difficult to attract and retain the highly qualified professionals governments need to carry out their mandates efficiently and effectively. Careful, objective evaluations of civil service reforms such as Georgia's are needed. All too often, however, evaluation is at best an afterthought.

INTEGRATING HUMAN RESOURCES MANAGEMENT (HRM) AND DEVELOPMENT (HRD)

Although many of the human resources management tasks assigned to personnel or HR departments will not change, the ways in which they are carried out will be changed by new technologies and organizational arrangements that require enhanced as well as new skills. A growing proportion of government jobs will require highly trained and extensively educated professionals who must *continuously* upgrade their abilities in order to keep pace with the intellectual and technical demands of their positions.

Training is a "big business" in the United States; private-sector employers spent at least $37 billion on training of all kinds during 1995, and 70 percent of their employees had received some kind of training during the previous year (U.S. Bureau of Labor Statistics, 1999a). Table 12.1 shows the kinds of formal training received by persons working in establishments with 50 or more employees.

Public employers have a long history of failing to make sustained investments in the training and development of their workforces. Often, they have been reluctant to spend the money needed to provide anything but the most basic training, and training and development budgets traditionally are among the first to be cut or eliminated during periods of fiscal stress. Training and development programs designed to prepare organizations to meet anticipated (future) needs for new or improved SKAs have been rare and precarious initiatives in the public sector. To a significant extent, the traditional merit system's emphasis on positions has encouraged a static view of the "fit" between organizational needs and workforce

Table 12.1 Percent of Trained Employees Participating in Formal Training Activities by Selected Characteristics

Characteristic	Classes Conducted by Company Personnel	Workshops Conducted by Outside Trainer	Courses Paid for by Employer and Taken at Institutions	Attended Lectures, Conferences, or Seminars on Work Time
All employees	75.7	48.3	17.1	36.3
Men	70.3	50.0	11.2	30.1
Women	80.7	46.7	22.6	42.0
White	74.8	50.4	18.5	41.1
Black	76.0	38.2	7.1	13.6
HS grad or less	80.9	34.0	8.1	19.9
Some college	78.1	49.0	21.5	43.9
BA or higher	66.7	63.9	21.8	45.5

Source: U.S. Bureau of Labor Statistics, *Employer Provided Training* (http://stats.bls.gov/news.release/sept.t10.htm), 1999.

qualifications. It is assumed that those hired have the skills, knowledge, and abilities needed to perform the job in question in a satisfactory manner. The pace of change, however, is such that position descriptions, qualifications, and classification plans are seldom current, and they are even less likely to be coordinated with agencies' shifting mandates, technological developments, and the shifting patterns of supply and demand in the labor market. Position-based systems, to make matters worse, make formal career planning and development systems very difficult to establish because they do not assume that employees will be continuously moving through a *predictable* series of different and increasingly more complex and challenging roles. Under these conditions, there is little incentive for employers to build the training and development infrastructures needed to support *careers,* as opposed to *positions.* OPM's description of the Government Employees Training Act of 1958 reflects the dominant point of view that employers' efforts should be considered *supplementary,* with employees assuming the major responsibility for their training and development:

> The Act recognizes the importance of self-development efforts of Federal employees and declared it to be necessary and desirable in the public interest that self-education, self-improvement, and self-training by such employees be supplemented and extended by government-sponsored programs. (U.S. Office of Personnel Management, 1999a, p. 1)

Public employees often are not encouraged to think in terms of developing the SKAs or getting the experiences that will be needed in the future. Individuals' efforts in this regard are seldom supported in material terms, since employers commonly require that any training they pay for be directly related to a job, not a career plan. Training and development programs, to the extent they exist, are focused on the SKAs employees need to perform well in their current positions. On both the organizational and individual levels, public-sector programs are not future-oriented. Public employers have been notoriously slow to adopt workforce planning systems that would allow them to better anticipate and respond to training and development—as well as staffing—needs.

Neglecting human resources development needs, or giving them low priority, promises to become a highly risky proposition in an environment in which high levels of productivity, performance, and responsiveness are demanded of public agencies. In all likelihood, public employers increasingly will be forced to deal with the reality that sustained investments in training and development are needed and, in the long run, cost-effective. The fiscal and political costs associated with not making such investments and then having to address problems in a crisis mode will be very high. A trend that is likely to accelerate over the next decade as public personnel becomes much less regulatory in perspective and moves away from position-dominated merit systems is a shift toward a human resources development or HRD perspective.

According to the American Society for Training and Development, HRD "is the integrated use of training and development, organization development, and career development to improve individual, group, and organizational effectiveness" (American Society for Training and Development, 1990, p. 3). HRD is an emerging field that focuses on three key areas of practice:

- *Training and Development,* which involves identifying and helping to develop in a planned manner "the key competencies that enable individuals to perform current or future jobs." (p. 4) Training and development concentrates on people in organizational roles or jobs, and it uses a variety of methods, including on- and off-site training, on-the-job-training or OJT, supervisory coaching, and other ways of encouraging learning by individuals.

- *Organization Development,* which concentrates on building effective and productive social-psychological relationships within and between work groups in organizations. Organization development uses a variety of process-oriented interventions on the individual and group levels with the goal of improving the overall performances of organizations.

- *Career Development,* which seeks to coordinate individual career planning and organizational career management processes to "achieve an optimal match of individual and organizational needs." (p. 4)

While these three areas of practice comprise the core of the HRD field, four closely related areas of human resources are (1) organization and job design, (2) human resource planning, (3) performance management systems, and (4) selection and staffing. The ASTD's definition, therefore, is broad enough to encompass the traditional training efforts of many public employers while making it clear that these efforts are only a part of a much larger HRD arena:

> . . . HRD can include almost anything from a single training activity to entire systems for achieving strategic goals within an organization. Often defined by the uses that individuals and organizations make of it, HRD's common denominator is that it results in the learning of skills or behaviors on the part of the individuals and the organizations. (p. 5)

On the federal level, and in many states and localities, the term *training program* is gradually being replaced with *human resources development program.* In the federal government, such programs may be authorized to carry out a wide variety of training and development activities, including:

- Orienting new employees to the federal government, their agencies, their jobs, and conditions of employment.
- Providing the guidance new employees need to achieve satisfactory performance during their probationary period.
- Providing the skills and knowledge employees need to improve job performance.
- Equipping selected employees with the skills and knowledge they will need to handle increased responsibility as a part of the agency's overall strategic plan for meeting future staffing requirements.
- Arranging continuing technical and professional training to prevent knowledge and skills obsolescence.
- Developing the managerial workforce's competencies on the supervisory, middle-management, and executive levels in such areas as interpersonal skills, communication, leadership, financial management, and program evaluation.

- Providing education and training leading to academic degrees if necessary to attract and retain workers with critical skills in occupations where shortages and highly competitive markets are expected.
- Assisting in career transition, training, and retraining of employees who have been displaced by downsizing and restructuring. (U.S. Office of Personnel Management, 1999a, pp. 1–2)

Federal agencies are required by law to have processes for identifying their performance improvement needs, and they must have human resources development programs designed to meet these needs in efficient and effective ways. These processes, according to OPM, might include the following elements:

- Setting performance goals and determining the gaps, if any, between these goals and actual performance.
- Identifying the reasons for performance gaps and deciding if specific training and development initiatives should close or eliminate them.
- Regularly collecting and analyzing information about organizational training needs and using these data to guide decisions about investments in human resources development.
- Involving management and employees on all levels in planning and implementing HRD activities, and integrating training plans and programs with other human resources management functions.

An example of the federal approach to HRD is the Department of Health and Human Services' (HHS) Career Management Framework. This framework is intended to allow HHS to respond effectively to a variety of demographic, technological, and society forces and trends. In HHS's words, "Organizations need to address issues such as training employees for

BULLETIN

Career Management at HHS

"Career management is a planned process enabling individuals to work in jobs and environments which are well-matched to their capabilities, interests, career goals, and lifestyles. Career management enables an organization to meet the human resource requirements of its mission, goals, and work, now and in the future. When efforts to match individual and organizational needs are successful, the individual finds work and the work environment satisfying, and the organization produces products and services which are effective and of high quality."

Source: U.S. Department of Health and Human Services, *An Overview of Career Management in HHS: Career Management Framework* (http://www.hhs.gov/progorg/ohr/oed/ cmc/), March 23, 1999, p. 1.

Table 12.2 The HHS Career Management Path Framework

	Organization	Individual
Characteristics	Customers, culture, workforce, HHS policies, operating systems, future trends, technology, mission, programs, external environment	Education, experience, interests, values, accomplishments, training, skills, barriers to career progress, cultural background, attitudes, goals
Needs	Different mix of skills, different skills levels, different number of employees, increased workforce diversity, retention of employees	Opportunities to learn, grow, and develop; change of pace, environment, improved financial situation; higher status; better match of individual values with organizational culture; accommodations to lifestyle demands; enhanced performance
HR planning strategies	Job structuring and restructuring, recruiting, staffing, formal training and development, informal training and development, outplacement	Remain in current position, change to another position, change to another career, leave organization
Types of shared information	Self-assessment activities, career guides, vacancy announcements, supervisor and mentor advice, formal career counseling, program announcements, training offices, job fairs and showcases, career information newsletter, networking	

*The matching process "comes into play as the organization decides on the strategies it will use to fill a need, and the individual decides on the strategies to use to change the work situation."

jobs which use new technology, using fewer permanent employees to accomplish work, and managing a diverse workforce" (U.S. Department of Health and Human Services, 1999, p. 1).

The HHS career management framework has three elements: an *organizational* path, an *individual* path, and an *information-sharing and matching process*. The organizational path includes an agency's characteristics, its human resources needs, and the strategies it employs to meet those needs. The individual path, on the other hand, is composed of individuals' characteristics, needs, and career-planning strategies. Information-sharing and matching processes are the "means by which the individual and the organization define their respective needs and find complementary solutions" (p. 2). Table 12.2 summarizes the HHS career management framework.

The Department of Health and Human Services offers its employees a wide variety of job- and career-related training programs. Its Training Catalog includes programs on administrative skills, computer skills, leadership and management, personnel management, communication skills, and professional development. The Department of Veterans Affairs has established a Virtual Learning Center that offers close to 400 lessons on its computer network. Appendix 12.A is a partial list of the lessons available to the Department's employees.

The U.S. Department of Agriculture's (USDA) Graduate School is an example of another approach to training and career development. The USDA Graduate School "is a continuing education institution offering career-related courses primarily to U.S. federal, state, and local government employees" (U.S. Department of Agriculture, 1999, p. 1). Its mission is to help government organizations improve their performance through "education, training, and related services." On the individual level, it seeks to support individuals' efforts to "improve their job performance and pursue lifelong learning." Although it is affiliated with the USDA, the Graduate School does not receive government funding. It is a nonprofit "entrepreneurial government entity that supports itself through tuition fees." More than 1,200 part-time faculty drawn from academia, government, and the private sector teach a wide variety of applied (practical) courses for students at the Graduate School. In addition to personnel management, the School's curriculum includes courses on administrative and business skills, communication skills, financial management, and management development. In the personnel management area alone, six major categories included a total of well over 50 different courses offered by the School during 1999:

- General personnel management
- Equal employment opportunity
- Labor and employee relations
- Position classification
- Staffing and placement
- Training and career development

Other elements of the federal career development strategy are OPM's Management Development Centers (MDCs) and its Federal Executive Institute. The central goals of the Management Development Centers are to provide career-oriented training and development in "essential executive leadership skills" and to encourage the emergence of a sense of "corporate community among the government's leaders" (U.S. Office of Personnel Management, 1999b, p. 1). The Centers' seminars and programs are available to supervisors, managers, and executives who are nominated by their agencies. In addition to U.S. military officers, they also accept participants from state, local, foreign, and Indian tribal governments. In OPM's words:

> The MDCs offer a variety of programs designed by our resident faculty specifically with the needs of career government leaders in mind. Each program provides a focused opportunity for current and future government executives, managers, and supervisors to improve their performance in one or more critical areas of leadership, management and policy implementation. (p. 2)

The MDCs' core curriculum includes three leadership and management development seminars that comprise a foundation for government managers who need to broaden their perspectives and to understand "the breadth and responsibility of their profession as leaders within the Executive branch of government." These three seminars cover the 27 competencies that make up the five executive core qualifications required of the Senior Executive Service (SES). A partial list of these competencies offers some insight into the challenging role of the federal senior executive:

- *Continual Learning,* which involves mastering new information and technologies, self evaluation, and self-development.
- *Service Motivation,* or being able to create and sustain an organizational culture of high performance and commitment to public service.
- *Vision,* in the form of an ability to think and plan in the long term and to act as an agent of organizational change.
- *Accountability,* or developing the knowledge and skills needed to assure the integrity of management systems and program activities.
- *Technology Management,* which means using effective and efficient ways of integrating established and new technologies into the workplace.
- *Partnering,* or establishing networks and alliances, building collaborative relationships with other agencies and stakeholders, and securing strong internal support bases.

In addition to the core curriculum, the MDCs offers several other programs, including Public Policy and Contemporary Government

Issues seminars, Leadership and Management Assessment programs, and a Supervisory and Team Leadership Institute.

Beyond the MDCs, OPM offers senior executives a "capstone" career development resource in the form of the Federal Executive Institute (FEI). Established in 1968, and located in Charlottesville, Virginia, the FEI offers a curriculum designed to help federal administrators acquire the broad perspectives and competencies needed for effective performance in the Senior Executive Service. Federal agencies select those who attend and cover tuition costs. Since its founding, over 15,000 senior executives have attended the FEI (U.S. Office of Personnel Management, 1999c, p. 1). Examples of programs offered by FEI during 1999 are shown in Appendix 12.B.

The emergence of "entrepreneurial," fee- or tuition-supported governmental centers for training and development is a national trend. California's State Training Center (CST) offers a wide range of training courses for *all government employees* (state, local, and federal). The Office of Statewide Continuous Improvement (OSCI), a unit of the California Department of Personnel Administration, makes consulting services available to all governments in the general area of continuous quality improvement (California Department of Personnel Administration, 1999a, 1999b). Specific services include the following:

- Customer service
- Leadership
- Quality planning
- Team building
- Facilitation
- Process improvement
- Surveys
- Teamwork

The OSCI maintains a list of nearly 500 consultants, trainers, and process facilitators who are prepared to help government agencies develop, implement, or expand quality and continuous improvement programs. They also consult in areas such as conflict resolution, strategic planning, and privatization. The OSCI's services are a good example of the trend

BULLETIN

FEI Program Objectives

"Most of the participants in FEI's programs are already highly educated professionals: nearly all have baccalaureate degrees and almost two-thirds have master's degrees or Ph.D.'s. The FEI curriculum builds on and enriches that technical education by helping executives develop an understanding of and appreciation for the political, social, economic, environmental, and cultural conditions in which they work."

Source: U.S. Office of Personnel Management, *Federal Executive Institute: Mission* (http://opm.gov/fei/html/FEI2.HTM), 1999, p. 1.

toward a broadening of public personnel's role to include organization development functions. In California and a growing number of jurisdictions, the personnel department enters into contracts for training and development services with customer departments or governments, or it brokers contracts for such services between third-party providers and its customers.

Growing Pressures to Abandon the Model Employer Ideal

Public employers will continue to experience growing fiscal and political pressures to move away from the idea that government should be a "model employer." Efficiency, cost savings, and flexibility have become increasingly important factors in the choices made by public-policy makers, and this trend has underscored the advantages offered by human resources strategies that stress investing scarce material resources in *essential* public employees. These employees should be treated, on the one hand, as organizational "assets." Other categories of workers who are not essential in the sense that they are relatively easy to attract and replace, on the other hand, should be treated as "costs" to be minimized. In effect, this approach means that governments' human resources practices should mirror those of the private sector, as opposed to setting a high or model standard for the treatment of *all* workers. As the costs (pay, benefits, working facilities, and the HR system itself) associated with attracting, motivating, and retaining highly educated and skilled personnel who are needed to achieve and sustain necessary levels of organizational performance escalate, controlling and lowering labor costs in other areas has become a prime objective for public as well as private employers. Two major ways of trying to achieve this objective have been privatization or contracting-out and expanding use of temporary or part-time workers.

Privatization comes in a variety of forms, including transferring previously public functions to the private sector, voucher systems and tax expenditure subsidies instead of direct governmental provision of services, and contracting-out of services traditionally performed by public employees. In all of its forms, privatization seeks to use competitive markets to allocate resources efficiently and to control costs. In general terms, advocates of privatization argue that "bureaucracy" and "bureaucrats" are inherently inefficient because they are effectively insulated from the disciplining forces of a competitive marketplace.

The effects of privatization on public employees have been widely debated, but there is evidence to suggest that privatization initiatives, particularly moves to contract-out public services, are likely to have three kinds of consequences. First, public employee unions will be placed on the defensive as they seek to defend themselves against charges that collective bargaining is an essentially political process that results in artificially high labor costs. Private contractors often are able to keep labor costs down because they do not deal with unionized workers. Second, to the extent that privatized arrangements are implemented, public employees stand to lose their jobs. Even if their functions have not been privatized, many public employees now work under the threat that they will lose their jobs to contractors if costs are not lowered and program performance levels raised. An organizational climate driven by fear of privatization is likely to have strongly negative consequences for worker morale and commitment. Third, privatization inevitably raises serious questions about how to assure and achieve fair and equitable treatment of the combinations of public and private employees who are now performing once exclusively governmental functions, such as operating prison systems. Current enthusiasms for organizational flexibility, results-oriented management, and market mechanisms threaten to undermine long-standing rights and protections enjoyed by public employees under merit systems (Kettl, 1997). Those working for private contractors also are placed in legal and political environments that present to them new challenges, such as exposure to civil liability for violating the constitutional rights of citizens (Cooper and Newland, 1997; Koenig, 1998).

A related trend is the increasing use of temporary and part-time employees by public as well as private employers. Governments on all levels also may enter into service contracts with private firms that use large numbers of part-time or temporary workers. In 1999, there were 25 million part-time workers in the United States, with about 19 million of these comprising a relatively permanent pool of part-time employees. This is, of course, a very significant segment of the entire labor force of about 130 million. Temporary workers are employees supplied to clients by temporary help firms. Although the client supervises the temporary worker, he or she is on the payroll of the help supply firm (Bureau of Labor Statistics, 1999c, p. 1). The temporary-help-supply services sector has grown much more rapidly than the rest of the economy since 1989, by about 43 percent in comparison to 5 percent. By the mid-1990s, there were over 1 million "temps"—about half in white-collar jobs and the rest in blue-collar and service positions.

In comparison to full-time, permanent, employees, part-time and temporary workers receive fewer benefits. Often, contractors' ability to provide services at lower costs than public agencies can be explained at least in part by their not having to spend a great deal on employee benefits. Many temporary-help-supply firms offer benefits, such as paid holidays, paid vacations, and health insurance. Health

Table 12.3 State and Local Employee Benefits: Full- and Part-Time Workers
(1990, 1992, 1994)

Benefit Program	Full-Time (%)			Part-Time (%)		
	1990	1992	1994	1990	1992	1994
Holidays	74	75	73	34	34	30
Vacations	67	67	66	26	26	22
Personal leave	39	38	38	20	17	18
Sick leave	95	95	94	49	45	42
Medical care	93	90	87	38	43	31
Dental care	62	65	62	25	37	27
Unpaid family leave	51	59	93	28	32	62
All retirement	96	93	96	48	51	58
Child care	9	8	9	5	2	6

Source: *BLS Report on Employee Benefits in State and Local Governments, 1994*
(http://stats.bls.gov/news.release/ebs2.toc.htm), May 4, 1999, pp. 8–10.

insurance is available to around half of all temporary employees, and paid holidays and vacations are available to about three-quarters. However, the Bureau of Labor Statistics notes that:

> [F]ew temporary workers actually receive these benefits, either because they fail to meet the minimum qualification requirements or, as in the case of insurance plans, they elect not to participate. In firms employing most of the temporary workers, less than one-half of the workers—often less than one-tenth—qualified for holiday and vacation benefits. Similarly, most firms reported that less than 10 percent of their temporary workers participated in a company-sponsored health insurance program. These insurance plans typically require the employee to pay part or all of the cost of coverage. (U.S. Bureau of Labor Statistics, 1999c, p. 3)

In the public sector, part-time employees are generally less likely to participate in benefit programs. Table 12.3 highlights data on state and local government benefits for full-time and part-time workers for three years during the 1990s.

BLS data from 1995–97 on benefits offered by private employers to their full- and part-time employees roughly parallel those for states and localities in the sense that full-time workers have a substantial advantage across all categories of benefits. In certain respects, those who work part-time for private establishments do somewhat better. For example, 40 percent receive paid holidays in comparison to 30 percent in state and local governments. Paid vacations are also more common in the private sector. In all of the other benefits areas shown in Table 12.3, however, state and local part-time workers do substantially better than their counterparts (U.S. Bureau of Labor Statistics, 1999b). To the degree that government contracting-out brings more private-sector part-time workers into the labor force engaged in delivering public services, pressures to reduce the benefits of part-timers employed by public agencies may build. Another result may be a steady decline in the number of part-time workers in civil service on all levels as governments seek to exploit the advantages of lower labor costs.

The issues confronting public employers in this area of human resources policy are difficult. Should they follow the lead of the private sector and concentrate on developing competitive pay, benefits, and working conditions for a "core" of highly skilled and essential workers, or do they have an obligation to serve as "model employer" by offering a set of relatively expensive benefits to all of their employees? Is it part of government's role as an employer to set a positive example for the rest of the society in areas such as equal opportunity, pay equity, employee rights and legal protections, meaningful jobs for the disabled, and benefits? How important should these values be in comparison to organizational efficiency, program cost-effectiveness, and management flexibility as choices are made about how to provide or arrange public services?

CONCLUSION

In one very important sense, the more things change, the more they stay the same: In the public sector, human resources policy and administration will continue to be a dynamic arena of competing values and interests. The policies and practices that define public personnel administration at any given point in time are the results of interacting and interrelated choices, choices made on the social, political, organizational, and individual levels. The context of choice is in constant motion politically, socially, and economically; frames of reference change, often at different paces and for different reasons. The outcomes of these choices may be expected to have significant consequences, some anticipated and some largely unanticipated. What solves problems in the short run may create serious problems in the long run and, of course, a problem in one context may not be one in another. The "new public personnel administration," in the final analysis, is more a horizon of emerging challenges and choices than it is a contemporary set of practices and public policies. This horizon is undergoing constant change; it is always "new."

Discussion Questions

1. Do you believe that eliminating the classified civil service and making all public employees "at will" is a good idea? Is it in the public interest?
2. Can the merit principle survive the current wave of civil service reforms? Should it?
3. Should public employers pay for training and education that is not directly related to the requirements of the position or job held by the employee?
4. Should government be a model employer? Under existing conditions, can it be?
5. In addition to the three discussed in this chapter, are there other major trends related to public personnel/human resources that you believe will be important during the early part of the twenty-first century?

References

American Society for Training and Development (1990). *An Introduction to Human Resource Development Careers,* 3rd ed. (Alexandria, VA: American Society for Training and Development), September.

California Department of Personnel Administration (1999a). *California State Training Center* (http://www.dpa.ca.gov/stcosci/stc/stcmain.htm), April 23.

——— (1999b). *Office of Statewide Continuous Improvement* (http://www.dpa.ca.gov/stcosci/osci.htm), April 23.

Cooper, Phillip J., and Newland, Chester A., eds. (1997). *Handbook of Public Law and Administration* (San Francisco: Jossey-Bass Publishers).

Governing (1999). "Grading the States: A 50-State Report Card on Government Performance." *Governing,* Vol. 12, No. 5 (February).

Kearney, Robert C., and Hays, Steven W. (1998). "Reinventing Government, the New Public Management and Civil Service Systems in International Perspective." *Review of Public Personnel Administration,* Vol. 18, No. 4 (Fall), pp. 38–54.

Kettl, Donald F. (1997). "Privatizing: Implications for the Public Work Force," in Carolyn Ban and Norma M. Riccucci (eds.), *Public Personnel Management: Current Concerns, Future Challenges* (White Plains, NY: Longman), pp. 295–309.

Koenig, Heidi (1998). "Richardson v. McKnight: What Does the Future of Qualified Immunity Hold for Nongovernmental

Employees?" *Public Administration Review*, Vol. 58, No. 1 (January–February), p. 8.

Selden, Sally Coleman (1999). "Human Resource Practices in State Governments: Findings from a National Survey." Paper presented at the American society for Public Administration's 60th National Conference, Orlando, Florida (April 10–14).

State of Georgia (1996). "Remarks by Governor Zell Miller." *State of the State Address* (Atlanta, GA: Office of the Governor), January.

U.S. Bureau of Labor Statistics (1999a). *BLS Reports on the Amount of Formal and Informal Training Received by Employees* (ftp://146.4.23/pub/news.release/sept.txt), May 4.

———— (1999b). *Employee Benefits Survey: Table 3. Percent of Employees Participating in Selected Employee Benefits Programs, Various Employment Groups, 1995–97* (http://stats.bls.gov/news.release/ebs3.t03.htm), May 5.

———— (1999c). *New Survey Reports on Wages and Benefits for Temporary Help Services Workers* (http://stats.bls.gov/news.release/occomp.toc.htm), May 5.

U.S. Department of Agriculture (1999). *Graduate School FAQ* (http://grad.usda.gov/org.html), April 23.

U.S. Department of Health and Human Services (1999). *An Overview of Career Management in HHS* (http://www.hhs.gov/progorg/ohr/oed/cmc), April 23.

U.S. Office of Personnel Management (1999a). *Government Overview of Training in the Federal Government with Questions and Answers* (http://www. opm.gov/hrd/lead/faq.htm), April 23.

———— (1999b). *Management Development Centers: About OPMs Management Development Centers* (http://www.opm.gov/mdc/htm), April 23.

———— (1999c). *Federal Executive Institute: Mission* (http://www.opm.gov/fei/html/FEI2.HTM), April 23.

SUGGESTED READINGS

Brinkerhoff, Robert O., and Gill, Stephen J. (1994). *The Learning Alliance: Systems Thinking in Human Resource Development* (San Francisco: Jossey-Bass Publishers).

French, Wendell L., and Bell, Cecil H. (1994). *Organization Development: Behavioral Science Interventions for Organization Improvement*, 5th ed. (Paramus, NJ: Prentice-Hall).

Giley, Jerry W. (1998). *Improving HRD Practice* (Melbourne, FL: Krieger Publishing Co.).

Handler, Joel F. (1996). *Down from Bureaucracy: The Ambiguity of Empowerment and Privatization* (Princeton, NJ: Princeton University Press).

Hitchin, David, and Ross, Walter (1995). *The Strategic Management Process: Integrating the OD Perspective* (Reading, MA: Addison Wesley Longman, Inc.).

James, Adrian, Bottomley, Keith, and Clare, Emma (1997). *Privatizing Prisons: Rhetoric and Reality* (Thousand Oaks, CA: Sage Publications, Inc.).

Massey, Oliver T. (1995). *Evaluating Human Resource Development Programs: A Practical Guide to Public Agencies* (Needham Heights, MA: Allyn & Bacon, Inc.).

Ramnarayan, S., and Venkateswara, Rao T. (1998). *Organization Development: Interventions and Strategies* (Thousand Oaks, CA: Sage Publications, Inc.).

Robbert, Albert A., Gates, Susan M., and Elliott, Marc N. (1997). *Outsourcing of DoD Commercial Activities: Impacts on Civil Service* (Santa Monica, CA: Rand Corporation).

Rothwell, William J., McLean, Gary N., and Sullivan, Roland (1995). *Practicing Organization Development: A Guide for Consultants* (San Francisco: Jossey-Bass Publishers).

Sidak, J. Gregory, and Spulber, Daniel F. (1996). *Protecting Competition from the Postal Monopoly* (Washington, DC: American Enterprise Institute).

Smither, Robert D., Houston, John M., and McIntire, Sandra A. (1996). *Organization Development: Strategies for a Changing Environment* (Reading, MA: Addison-Wesley Educational Publishers, Inc.).

Stewart, F., and McGoldrick, J. (1996). *Human Resource Development: Perspectives, Strategies, and Practice* (London: Pitman).

Swanson, Richard A., and Holton, Elwood F. III, eds. (1996). *Human Resource Development Research Handbook: Linking Research and Practice* (Upland, CA: DIANE Publishing Co.).

Department of Veteran Affairs — Developed By **Veterans Health Administration**

BROWSE LESSONS

As of 9/2/99 there are 369 Intranet lessons in the Virtual Learning Center
As of 9/2/99 there are 1 Internet lessons in the Virtual Learning Center

Select a lesson and click on its link to view.

- **'A Message from Mrs. Miller: Putting Veterans First' (videotape)** [04/07/1999 : VAMC Dayton, OH]

  Employees were introduced to the VISN 10 philosophy and an organizational model for the VISN. A videotape highlighting every employee's role for 'Putting Veterans First' was narrated by the Network Director.

- **'Cool Mist Station' Utilized At Large Public Events** [06/18/1999 : VAMC Dayton, OH]

  Learn how to build a 'Cool Mist Station' that can be utilized at large public events to promote public relations, reduce heat related emergencies, and ultimately register unique veteran patients.

- **"High Performance Development Model Summit," national meeting held in St. Louis February 8-11, 1999** [04/23/1999 : VA Headquarters]

  The High Performance Development Model is a conceptual model for creating a learning organization focused on all-employee development. It is not a standard curriculum or program. It will be most useful through local customization and linkage with Network business and strategic plans.

- **24 Hours, 7 Days, Mental Health Coverage** [02/04/1999 : VAMC New Orleans, LA]

  The Mental Health Service Line at VA Medical Center New Orleans instituted a cost effective plan to provide 24 hour Mental Health coverage seven days a week.

- **A Creative Technique for Promoting Interdisciplinary Patient Education** [03/05/1998 : VAMC Boston, MA]

  A workshop, 'Working Together for Patient Education: An Interdisciplinary Approach' was used as a tool to foster interdisciplinary patient education and to improve patient outcomes. A unique quality of the workshop was the active participation of staff in working towards these goals.

- **A Fun and Creative Technique to Promote Patient Education and Provide Staff Education** [03/03/1999 : VAMC Milwaukee, WI]

  An in-house Health Fair was used as a mechanism to familiarize both veterans and staff with the Patient Education resources available at the Medical Center and to provide one hour of educational credit for staff members.

- **A Headache Education Course** [09/25/1998 : VAMC Little Rock, AR]

  Head pain is one of the most frequent presenting complaints in ambulatory care clinics.

- **A Laboratory in Transition, How We Changed Our Organizational Culture** [03/06/1998 : VAMC Dayton, OH]

  By changing the traditional Organizational structure of our Clinical Laboratory, we were able to prepare for the challenges inherent to downsizing and Managed Care.

- **A Method of Providing Food With Medications 'Ensure With Medication'** [07/22/1999 : VAMC Dayton, OH]

  Nutrition and Food Service determined after review of current practice, sampling of nourishment products and extensive cost analysis that 2 ounces of Ensure would be provided with each medication requiring food. This solution is both beneficial nutritionally and cost effective ($.073 per 2 oz.).

- **A Retrospective Review of No-show Patients in the Women's Health Clinic by Comparing Characteristics Reported in the Literature.** [06/02/1998 : VAMC Gainesville, FL]

continued page 366

■ **365** ■

Patients who fail to keep appointments are costly to the institution and also disrupt their own health care. Definitions used in this review were defined as: No-show-Patients scheduled for an appointment who either do not come or do not cancel. No-show rate - The total number of patients with appointments who didn't show divided by appointments scheduled.

- **A Standardized Method to Evaluate Dyspnea and/or Shortness of Breath.** [09/30/1998 : Health Care System San Diego]

    The modified Borg Scale would provide a common method of communicating the subjective sensation of dyspnea.

- **A Structured Referral Program Between Ambulatory Care and Outpatient Psychiatry** [09/30/1998 : VAMC Columbia, SC]

    Traditionally, psychiatric referrals at our facility came unannounced from Ambulatory Care and had to be seen as 'drop-ins'. This process was very disruptive to the operation of the Mental Health Clinic, and patients frequently became more agitated while waiting to be 'worked-in'. A structured triage system was developed to address problems with these unannounced mental health referrals.

- **AARP AUDIT** [06/21/1999 : VAMC Albany, NY]

    Establishing rigorous data validation processes can result in excellent results of AARP audit of reimbursable claims.

- **Alerts for Consults Sent to Inactive Users** [08/04/1999 : VAMC Dayton, OH]

    By monitoring Consult Services on a monthly basis, we have been able to decrease the number of consults for which staff are not being appropriately notified.

- **Aligning the Behavior of VHA Employees with the Goal of Customer Service Excellence: Barriers and Opportunities** [03/10/1998 : VAMC Boston, MA]

    Preliminary evidence from our study points to the importance of aligning the performance goals of employees throughout VHA to promote service excellence.

- **Ambassador Club** [03/04/1999 : Health Care System North Texas]

    The Ambassador Club is a group of employees who have gone through a selection process and have agreed to serve 2 hours per pay period as Ambassadors of good will to the veteran. Their primary purpose is to make veterans feel welcome and able to find his/her way around this complex medical center.

- **Ambassador Greeter Program** [02/08/1999 : VAMC Battle Creek, MI]

    Greeters form one component of the volunteer Ambassador Program. The goal of volunteer Greeters as well as the entire Ambassador Program is to help make each outpatient's visit to the Medical Center a positive experience. Greeters provide a warm smile and welcome to each person entering the Ambulatory Care area. This program is one more way of improving customer service.

- **Ambulatory Surgery Clinic Process Improvement** [01/19/1999 : Health Care System Eastern Kansas]

    The Surgical Ambulatory Care Process Improvement (PI) Team was chartered with a goal of using a primary care model to improve utilization of resources and enhance efficiency in the outpatient surgical clinic.

- **An Advance Directives Clinic for Outpatients** [09/28/1998 : VAMC Columbia, SC]

    The Columbia SC VAMC participated in a national research project in 1994, examining patient education related to advance directives. The investigator interviewed 150 patients at the hospital: 75 were inpatients and 75 were outpatients. One of the findings was that outpatients were far more comfortable and prepared to discuss advance directives than were inpatients.

- **An Easy Access Clinic-Based Program for Bipolar Disorder** [10/01/1998 : VAMC Providence, RI]

    This clinical program has been shown to reduce costs, increase treatment delivered, and increase patient satisfaction for a highly recidivist population. The results were sufficiently promising that the VA Cooperative Studies Program is now funding a 12-site controlled trial to establish its effectiveness.

- **An Outpatient Cardiac Catheterization Program** [09/18/1998 : VAMC Ann Arbor, MI]

    To reduce health care costs, our hospital has attempted to identify diagnostic procedures that could safely be performed in an outpatient environment. One initiative is the Cardiac Observation Unit (COU) in which outpatients safely undergo invasive cardiac procedures, including diagnostic catheterizations and electrophysiology studies.

continued page 367

- **An Outpatient Model for Comprehensive SCI Annual Evaluations** [01/13/1998 : VAMC Augusta, GA]

  An outpatient model was developed for the provision of annual evaluations for veterans with SCI. The veterans receive a comprehensive evaluation by the SCI multidisciplinary team in two-three days and the VA contracts with a community personal care home for lodging and personal care assistance during their stay.

- **Analysis of Facility Integrations** [03/06/1998 : VAMC Boston, MA]

  While there is no simple formula for integrating VHA facilities, an analysis of 14 integrated systems provides lessons for current and future integrations.

- **Appointment Reminder** [01/05/1999 : VA DOM White City, OR]

  The intent of the initiative was to reduce the number of 'no-shows' to scheduled clinic appointments by making telephone contact with the patient prior to the scheduled visit.

- **Automated appointment reminder system** [02/22/1999 : VAMC Muskogee, OK]

  Mumps Audio Fax was purchased 03-01-1993. Implementation was soon after that date. This system automatically calls the veteran two days before scheduled appointment.

- **Bed Central Process** [06/04/1999 : VAMC Charleston, SC]

  The hospital admission process, at best, can be very frightening for patients. For customers, internal and external, the process can be tedious, frustrating, and inefficient. The Bed Central Office was instituted to streamline, facilitate, and maintain accountability for the admission process.

- **Beepers for Surgical Patients' Families** [11/17/1997 : VAMC Oklahoma City, OK]

  Beepers have been used successfully to maintain contact with families of veterans undergoing surgery resulting in increased patient and staff satisfaction.

- **Bi-Annual Veteran Personal Information Update** [03/23/1999 : VAMC Hampton, VA]

  Patient Information Management System (PIMS) database necessitates routine update of demographic data in order to ensure that information is accurate and current. Form developed allowed veterans to update such information as address, telephone number, health insurance, employer, spouse information, etc. It also served to remind veterans that monies collected from insurance companies would be returned to the medical center for use.

- **Birthday Meal** [12/21/1998 : VAMC Northport, NY]

  Description: Patients who are hospitalized on their birthdays are able to select items from a restaurant style menu, to be served on the special day.

- **Blood Culture Contamination Rate Reduced with the Consolidation of the Central Processing Unit into Microbiology.** [07/23/1999 : VAMC Dayton, OH]

  With the consolidation of the Central Processing Unit into the Microbiology Department we were able to eliminate one supervisory position and obtained the additional benefit of reducing the blood culture contamination rate from an average of 4.3% to 2.8%(or a 1.5-% decrease).

- **Building a Post Acute Care Continuum to Improve Both Efficiency & Patient Care: Bridging Acute to Primary Care.** [02/20/1998 : Health Care System Greater Los Angeles]

  Improved patient care AND improved efficiency have been achieved via the development of a defined Post Acute Care Continuum together with the development of a Post Acute Referral Coordination Process by matching patient care needs with service at the most appropriate level, with efficient patient flow. This was accomplished by Outcomes Management, or the process and structure that applies Quality Tools to enable change in health care delivery to improve patient outcomes.

- **CAMP (Continuous Assessment Management Program)** [01/02/1999 : Health Care System Southern Nevada]

  This project provides update organizational status (as it pertains to JCAHO criteria) while providing ongoing education to responsible staff

- **Card Access System For Training Rooms** [08/17/1999 : VAMC Dayton, OH]

  A wide variety of staff conduct training in the IRM training rooms. We needed to safeguard the pc workstations yet provide easy access to the training rooms during all hours.

continued page 368

- **Care in Patient Focused Orthopedics** [09/18/1998 : VAMC Iowa City, IA]

  The Iowa City VAMC is undergoing reorganization and moving toward patient centered care.

- **Case Management** [01/02/1999 : Health Care System Greater Los Angeles]

  The use of nursing case managers in the acute care setting allows appropriate admission and discharge planning as well as enhanced continuity of patient care.

O P M

Program Guide
Introduction

Management
Development
Center Programs

Leadership Curriculum

Leadership Skills

National Policy

Federal Executive
Institute Programs

Leadership For A
Democratic Society

Center For
Executive Leadership

Custom Seminars
and
Consulting Services

Executive Core
Qualifications
(ECQ's)

Schedule

Registration

Contact Us

Specials

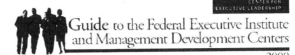

Guide to the Federal Executive Institute and Management Development Centers

2000

Managing the Human Side of Change

Does your organization need to change? Are there technological innovations, management challenges, or changes in mission that will drive fundamental alterations in the ways you do business?

The models for organizational change that have emerged in the past 15 years-total quality management, reengineering, and the learning organization, for example-have focused on systems, processes, technical aspects and organizational culture. They have not, however, addressed the issues of the people involved.

FEI's Managing the Human Side of Change program is designed to help you and your employees deal with the stages and stresses of organizational change.

This program is not just about theory. We'll ask you to identify a specific change that you are involved with. Then test the ideas and approaches presented in relation to your real-life experience by calling on colleagues and faculty to discuss practical application of program materials.

As a participant in the Managing the Human Side of Change program, you will:

- Identify the major needs people have during change
- Develop specific approaches for meeting those needs
- Learn proven and creative methods for managing communication during change
- Learn the three phases people experience during change and how you can help people move through them

Dates

March 23-24, 2000 (Ask for program M011)

Tuition

$1,545 per person includes instruction, meals, and lodging!

Program Leader

Dr. Russ Linden Management consultant -Faculty-University of Virginia -Author, From Vision to Reality & Seamless Government -Ph.D. University of Virginia

Note:

The program begins at 10:30 a.m. Thursday and ends at 4:00 p.m. Friday.

continued page 370

■ **369** ■

- Understand six overall strategies for leading the human side of change

The Managing the Human Side of Change program enables you to help your employees deal with the fears, anxieties, questions, doubts, cynicism, and other attitudes they have regarding change. Whether you're working with individuals, small groups, or larger numbers of employees, the program will help you have a positive impact on your organization.

Two special features make this a program you will not forget:

- A special guest presenter-a psychologist who is an expert on individual and system change-will engage in a dialogue on the psychology of change
- A site visit to a local organization will introduce you to a manager who has successfully led a major change

* REGISTER
NOW

Intro | Management Development Center Programs | Custom Seminars & Consulting Services
Federal Executive Institute Programs | Executive Core Qualifications | Home

TOP OF PAGE

Page updated 18 August 1999

continued page 371

Guide to the Federal Executive Institute and Management Development Centers

2000

360 Degree Leadership

This program is about gaining power and using influence. While people have different forms of power, some are more effective applying that power-that is, influencing others to do what they want them to do.

The 360 Degree Leadership program enables you to:

- Lead Up-Influence the boss and others above you in the agency hierarchy
- Lead Across-Influence co-workers in your organization and associates in others
- Lead Down-Influence subordinates and those below you in the agency hierarchy
- Lead Out-Influence those who do not work for your agency

How are 360 degree leaders different from traditional managers? Managerial influence is bound by organizational roles. It influences down the hierarchy. It is based on "being in charge" and "being the boss." It can't be used to manage up or manage across. Only those below you in the hierarchy must comply.

360 degree leaders can use their influence in all directions. And anyone can gain and apply 360 Degree Leadership influence. If your organization is undergoing dramatic change, using teams, attempting to empower employees, or needs more or better leadership, it is important that you and your colleagues participate in the 360 Degree Leadership program.

Not only will 360 Degree Leadership enable you to communicate your message with more impact and maximize your capacity to get your ideas across, it will also teach you to define the specific areas where you need to apply more

Dates

May 4-5, 2000 (Ask for program M013)

Tuition

$1,545 per person includes instruction, meals, and lodging!

Program Leader

Dr. Warren Blank
President-Leadership Group
-Author, The Seven Natural Laws of Leadership
-Ph.D. University of Cincinnati

Note:

The program begins at 10:15 a.m. Monday and ends at 4:15 p.m. Tuesday.

continued page 372

effective influence skills.

What will you be able to do if you learn and apply the key principles of 360 Degree Leadership?

- Achieve more and better results in your job
- Take a leadership role in any situation
- Acquire more position power
- Enhance your personal power
- Adopt a more effective approach when others have a negative impact

This program provides knowledge, skill development, and application to develop the key skill of leadership influence. 360 Degree Leadership is highly interactive and is based on participant experiences.

You'll learn in small and large group activities and discussions, simulations, segments from popular videos, self-assessment, presentation, and action planning.

Intro | Management Development Center Programs | Custom Seminars & Consulting Services
Federal Executive Institute Programs | Executive Core Qualifications | Home

TOP OF PAGE

Index

THE NEW PUBLIC PERSONNEL ADMINISTRATION
Fifth Edition
Edited by John Beasley
Production supervision by Kim Vander Steen
Designed by Cynthia Crampton Design, Park Ridge, Illinois
Composition by Point West, Inc., Carol Stream, Illinois
Paper, Finch Opaque
Printed and bound by McNaughton & Gunn, Saline, Michigan